The Gospels

THE COMPLETE PORTRAIT
OF THE MESSIAH

Volume 2

Also available from Time to Revive and Laura Kim Martin

reviveDAILY: A Devotional Journey from Genesis to Revelation, Year 1
reviveDAILY: A Devotional Journey from Genesis to Revelation, Year 2

The Gospels

THE COMPLETE PORTRAIT
OF THE MESSIAH

Volume 2

Kyle Lance Martin

Time to Revive and reviveSCHOOL

time to
revive
Richardson, Texas

The Gospels

Published in conjunction with
Iron Stream Media
100 Missionary Ridge
Birmingham, AL 35242
IronStreamMedia.com

Library of Congress Control Number: 2022947980

978-1-63204-098-5 (hardback)
978-1-63204-099-2 (e-book)

2 3 4 5—26 25 24

DEDICATION

Greetings friends and colaborers of the Lord Jesus Christ!

I am writing to you with an excitement that is beyond words. For I would like to dedicate this book to individuals like yourselves whose desire to grow closer to Jesus and go deeper in the Word of God brings such JOY to my heart. And my prayer for each one of you is that the Holy Spirit will reveal more of Himself to you in this in-depth time of studying the Word of God daily. Jesus said, "Blessed are those who hunger and thirst for righteousness, for they will be satisfied" (Matthew 5:6 NASB). So as you embark on this journey of studying each book of the Bible, may you experience a freshness and a fulfillment that can only come from the Spirit of God. You will have days that you won't want to wake up early and read. There will be moments when life throws you a situation that delays your personal devotional time with Him. But please press in and allow the Holy Spirit to strengthen your every step. This will allow you to exercise your faith muscles and walk out what you are learning in this. From my experience, obedience will bring education to life!

It will be quite a strenuous commitment, yet it's a part of an intentional strategy to equip the saints for His return. And your participation with reviveSCHOOL is a unique part of this preparation.

May the Lord receive all the glory, honor, and fame in this pursuit of righteousness.

Praying,
Dr. Kyle Lance Martin

CONTENTS

WEEK 20

WEEK 21

WEEK 22

WEEK 23

WEEK 24

WEEK 29

reviveSCHOOL History and Introduction

In January of 2015, our ministry, Time to Revive, was invited from our home base in Richardson, Texas, to Goshen, Indiana, to help equip the local church to learn how to go out and share the gospel in their community. We called it reviveINDIANA. During this frigid first trip in January, our intention was to help facilitate a week of prayer and outreach as a form of training, which we hoped would lead to an intentional week of outreach later that year. Little did we know that God had other plans.

The week of prayer and outreach started with about 450 people from various churches in the community and, to our surprise, quickly swelled to over 3,000. And by the end of that first week, the Holy Spirit confirmed to a group of us, including local pastors, that the Time to Revive team should stay for 52 straight days! Imagine the phone calls we had to make to our spouses telling them we were going to stay a "little" longer.

Over the course of these seven weeks, the local church witnessed God move in mighty ways, and each person involved could tell you miraculous testimonies of how they witnessed, firsthand, how God was moving. The 52 days culminated on March 4 of that year where an estimated 10,000 people showed up to brave the cold temperatures and go out and share the love of Jesus Christ.

All the while, word of this was spreading throughout the state, and it led to the Time to Revive team being invited to seven different cities in Indiana over the course of the next seven months. We continued to witness the local body of believers in these various communities encouraged and equipped to continue to take out their faith and share with others. The gospel wasn't intended to stay only in the church building. Jesus commissioned each one of us to go and make disciples in our own Jerusalem, Judea, and Samaria and to the ends of the earth. Back in Goshen, the local body continued to go out regularly after those initial 52 days while keeping track of the days since that first amazing week. A couple of years later in 2017, the local believers invited our team to celebrate their 1,000th day of outreach in their community. It was during that time when a local man shared with us a dream he had, which led us to start a two-year Bible study in the community. Similar to the Apostle Paul as he taught 12 disciples in Ephesus to study the Word of God on a daily basis, Time to Revive's desire was to also provide in-depth teaching that would focus on where the Messiah is found in every book of the Bible from Genesis to Revelation. We knew this would deepen their commitment to sharing the gospel as well as deepen their relationship with the Lord and with those whom they were discipling.

But when some became hardened and would not believe, slandering the Way in front of the crowd, he withdrew from them and met separately with the disciples, conducting discussions every day in the lecture hall of Tyrannus. —Acts 19:9

This local Bible study started with 12 men who signed up and committed to study the Word of God in a barn on a county road in Goshen, Indiana. And on January 1, 2018, we launched reviveSCHOOL with 54 men in this initial group. They studied the Scriptures daily, using the online resources, then gathered in the barn to discuss them in person. Each student studied the Bible daily using these resources:

- a Scripture reading plan to stay on track,
- a 29-minute teaching video (by Kyle Lance Martin, Indiana pastors, and TTR teachers),
- a devotion (written by Laura Kim Martin),
- reading guide questions to help facilitate discussion and critical thinking,
- lesson plans to summarize the daily teaching, and
- a painting of each book of the Bible by Mindi Oaten.

Upon the completion of the two-year study in the Word, Time to Revive celebrated over 200 students who had joined reviveSCHOOL with a graduation ceremony in January 2020. Plans were made for these individuals to take the Word and launch reviveSCHOOL groups not only in the United States but also throughout various nations. However, with worldwide travel restrictions due to the COVID-19 pandemic, this travel didn't happen. Thankfully, God had another plan, His plan was "above and beyond" all that Time to Revive could ask or think of (Ephesians 3:20–21).

With all the reviveSCHOOL materials already available online, the Holy Spirit spread the word to pastors and leaders of nations all throughout the world. Believers were hungry for biblically sound teaching and resources to grow closer to the Lord. As exemplified in Acts 19 with Paul and the disciples, and all the people of Asia, the Word of God through reviveSCHOOL truly spread—from a barn in Indiana to the nations.

And this went on for two years, so that all the inhabitants of Asia, both Jews and Greeks, heard the message about the Lord. —Acts 19:10

By God's grace, reviveSCHOOL has become an outlet for individuals to gain fresh insight into the Messiah all throughout the Scriptures, as well as to develop an understanding of the role of Israel from a biblical perspective.

I am humbled and honored that you would select reviveSCHOOL for your learning. When we started with 12 guys in a Bible study, we had no idea that reviveSCHOOL would be as far reaching as it has become. Our team would delight in knowing that you are studying the Word of God and using the resources with reviveSCHOOL. We pray that through these resources you will grow closer to the Lord and that you are inspired to walk out the plans that God has for your life by exposing others to the love of Christ.

To God be the glory!
Dr. Kyle Lance Martin

For further information about how to sign up for this two-year study in the Word of God or if you would like to launch a reviveSCHOOL group in your community, state/province, or country, please go online to www.reviveSCHOOL.org.

How to Use this Bible Study Series

The Complete Portrait of the Messiah Bible study series contains multiple components for each lesson. These components work together to provide an in-depth study of how Jesus is revealed throughout the whole of Scripture. Below is a description of each component and how you can use each one to maximize your study experience.

Teaching Notes & Video Lessons
The teaching notes summarize the main points of each video lesson and include a QR code to access the video teaching. If you have access to the internet via your phone or tablet, you can scan the QR code to watch the video lesson.*

The Daily Word Devotional
Dig deeper into personal application for each lesson through "The Daily Word" devotion. This day-by-day devotion encourages you with thoughts for application and further Scripture readings.

Reading Guide Questions
These questions will guide you into a more detailed exploration of each lesson's content. Examine the concepts of the daily Scripture readings in more detail.

The Bible Art Collection
This Bible study series is augmented by a one-of-a-kind, especially inspired series of original artwork created by artist Mindi Oaten. These 66 acrylic paintings creatively depict the revelation of Christ in each book of the Bible. Viewing each of these original art pieces will inspire and further enrich your understanding of Jesus throughout all of the Scriptures. These can be found at https://www.mindioaten.com/pages/mindi-oaten-art-bible-art-collection or https://www.reviveschool.org/

About the Cover

Matthew
"Messiah the King: Promise Fulfilled"

Artist Notes: Mindi Oaten

As the book of Matthew begins the New Testament, I felt it was important to connect the garden in Genesis, the very beginning, to the arrival of Jesus on earth. The promised *Seed* is now represented as a full-grown tree. The manger on top of this tree represents the birth of the promised Messiah. He was born under the humblest of circumstances, in a stable, but would grow up to reign as *King*. Many Old Testament prophecies pointed to this moment, the arrival of the long-awaited Messiah, the *Deliverer*, who came as the *Atonement* for our sins and to set up the kingdom of God on earth.

The Tree

> *The historical record of Jesus Christ, the Son of David, the Son of Abraham.* —Matthew 1:1

The tree represents the generational line of Jesus recorded in chapter 1. Jesus, the promised *Seed*, was born of the virgin Mary, who was a descendant in the line of David, and traces back to Abraham. Jesus came to save the world and bring God's kingdom to earth where He will reign as eternal *King*. This painting is like part two of Genesis. The seed is now the tree fully grown. Jesus has come!

The Manger

Through the manger, I wanted to symbolize the birth of Jesus, His entrance as Savior on earth, as well as the promised Seed fulfilled. I realize the manger detail is not mentioned in Matthew like it is in Luke 2:7, but it seemed the best way to portray His birth in this painting.

The Crown

> *This took place so that what was spoken through the prophet might be fulfilled:*
>
> > *Tell Daughter Zion,*
> > *"Look, your King is coming to you,*

> *gentle, and mounted on a donkey,*
> *even on a colt,*
> *the foal of a beast of burden."*
> —Matthew 21:4–5

> *They twisted together a crown of thorns, put it on His head, and placed*
> *a reed in His right hand. And they knelt down before Him and mocked*
> *Him: "Hail, King of the Jews!"* —Matthew 27:29

Jesus is Messiah the *King*. Therefore, I painted half the crown as twisted thorns (born to die) and half as a king's crown (eternal kingship). The dual crown shows his purpose as an eternal *King* who was to suffer and die—being the ultimate sacrifice to redeem us back to the Father and eventually reigning over the kingdom of heaven set up on earth.

The Starry Sky and the Star

> *After hearing the king, they went on their way. And there it was—the*
> *star they had seen in the east! It led them until it came and stopped*
> *above the place where the child was. When they saw the star, they were*
> *overjoyed beyond measure.* —Matthew 2:9–10

The background, emphasized by the star of Bethlehem guiding the wise men to the stable and declaring His arrival, represents the sky on the night Jesus was born. While painting the sky, I had an incredible experience of feeling the presence of God and seeing His hand in creation. It was overwhelming.

Flowers—Garden Flowers from Genesis

On the ground, under the tree, are garden flowers that reference back to Genesis. I painted twelve species of flowers to represent the twelve tribes, including Judah, the lineage of Jesus Christ. This speaks to the chosen generational line until the arrival of the Messiah who was Jewish. God chose Jesus to come through His elect people, the Israelites, and He is the fulfilment of Old Testament prophecy that the Messiah would be a descendant of David. In this composition, I included the yellow Star of Bethlehem flowers as they seemed an appropriate witness to the star that guided the wise men.

*In reviveSCHOOL, the theme name for Jesus in Matthew is *King*.

Lesson 1: Matthew 1
King: Jesus' Family Tree

Teaching Notes

Intro

We've just finished our study of the Pentateuch (Genesis, Exodus, Leviticus, Numbers, and Deuteronomy) which was written by Moses, and we're now beginning our study of the Gospels (Matthew, Mark, Luke, and John). We're going to keep doing that—moving from the Old Testament to the New Testament—over a two-year period. The word "gospel" literally means "good news." Throughout the Gospels, we're going to be talking about the good news. All of us have the bad news of sin and death, but praise the Lord, we have the good news of Jesus Christ our Lord. Remember that in the Old Testament, we gave one word for each of the books we studied, such as *Seed* for the Book of Genesis. Through the seed of Abraham, we can see how it ultimately points to the *Seed*, Jesus Christ. The one word for Matthew that talks about Jesus is *King*. In the Book of Mark, Jesus is the *Servant*. In the Book of Luke, the emphasis is on the *Son of Man*, and in John, the emphasis is on the *Son of God*. In Matthew, we'll focus on Jesus as *King*. The word "King" is used 22 times in the Book of Matthew and "kingdom" is used 32 times. The author, Matthew, was one of the 12 disciples. He was also known as Levi and was a former tax collector who left everything behind to follow Yeshua. His audience was mostly Jewish Christians.

In Matthew 1, we'll walk through Jesus' family tree. Several things are unique to the Book of Matthew: the genealogy of Jesus, Joseph's dreams, the visitation of the wise men, the flight to Egypt, Herod's threat to kill all the male children under two years of age, Judas' repentance, Pilate's wife's dream about John the Baptist, the bribery of the soldiers, and the Great Commission. Studying Matthew 1 is like studying the Pentateuch again because it provides historical records from the Old Testament.

Teaching

Matthew 1:1–6a: Verse 1 gives the historical record of Jesus' lineage. The genealogy itself is divided into three sections of 14 generations each for a total of 42 generations. The name of Jesus was common in the first century, and His last name was not "Christ." It is also a common name today in the Hispanic and Latino cultures with a different pronunciation. Matthew first identified Jesus as the Son of David. Second Samuel 7:12 provides the importance of this identification: "When your time comes and you rest with your fathers, I will raise up after you your descendant, who will come from your body, and I will establish his kingdom." When Matthew's readers read Jesus' genealogy, it immediately connected them to the Davidic covenant, passing through David's son Solomon and down to Jesus.

Nelson's Commentary gave three reasons why Jesus' genealogy was so important for Matthew: (1) it verified that Jesus was an Israelite and a Jew, (2) it identified that Jesus was connected to the tribe of Judah, and (3) it showed that He was qualified for certain religious duties.[1] This means that proving someone's genealogy allowed him to walk in his calling. Genesis 12 talks about the *Seed* that will rule forever.

In verse 2, His lineage begins with Abraham, Isaac, Jacob, and Judah. The first 14 generations go from Abraham to David. Within Jesus' lineage, five women are listed, including Tamar (who had sexual relations with her father-in-law), Rahab (a prostitute that protected the Israelite spies), and Ruth (a foreigner and a worshipper of idols). Tom Constable gives several reasons why the women were included: (1) to show that Jesus came for sinners, (2) to show that Jesus came for everyone, regardless of gender or race, (3) to prepare his readers for the role of Mary as a part of Jesus' lineage, (4) to show that there were "irregular marital unions" in Jesus' lineage, and (5) to show how God used Gentiles to show "extraordinary faith in contrast to Jews."[2] This section of genealogy ends with the first mention of a king–King David (v. 6). These show that God can use anybody at any given time, regardless of the mistakes in their lives.

Matthew 1:6b–11: In verse 6b, Matthew recorded that "David fathered Solomon by Uriah's wife." Matthew does not name Bathsheba because he is tying her to a Hittite, he is showing us that God can also use foreigners. The second set of 14 generations go from David to the Babylonian exile when the Israelites were taken away as slaves. This section is full of people whose names are not well-known, which shows again that God can use anyone, redeem them, and use them to point to the Messiah. John 1:14 gives the significance of His coming: "The Word became flesh and took up residence among us." Notice that

---

[1] Earl D. Radmacher, Ronald B. Allen, and H. Wayne House, eds., *Nelson's New Illustrated Bible Commentary* (Nashville: Thomas Nelson, 1999), 1137.

[2] Thomas L. Constable, *Expository Notes of Dr. Thomas Constable: Matthew*, 34, https://planobiblechapel.org/tcon/notes/pdf/matthew.pdf.

Matthew didn't include everyone in the genealogy, but that doesn't impact the background of Jesus or His lineage.

Matthew 1:12–16: The third set of 14 generations go from the end of the Babylonian exile to the Messiah. Matthew began the genealogy in verse 1 with Jesus, and he ended it with Jesus. In verse 16, Matthew tied Jesus' lineage to Joseph. John MacArthur describes how this is important, even though Joseph was not Jesus' biological father: "The genealogy, nonetheless, establishes His claim to the throne of David as Joseph's legal heir."[3]

Matthew 1:17: Verse 17 summarizes the breakdown of the 42 generations of Jesus. After establishing Jesus' family lineage, Matthew moved on to give the details of Jesus' birth. The rest of the Book of Matthew is about the life of Jesus.

Matthew 1:18–25: In the first century, engagement was seen as binding as a legal marriage. In verse 18, Joseph "discovered before they came together that [Mary] was pregnant by the Holy Spirit." Joseph was described as a righteous man who didn't want to disgrace Mary and was going to divorce her secretly (v. 19). However, before Joseph could do these things, an angel appeared to him (v. 20). The angel acknowledged Joseph's lineage (son of David) and explained that God had orchestrated Mary's pregnancy through the Holy Spirit. In verse 21, Joseph was given the name of the child, "Jesus, because He will save His people from their sins."

Closing

We are the beneficiaries of the stubbornness of the Jews, of what they went through in rebellion against God, and it's our job to minister and give back to them in any way we can.

Daily Word

As part of God's plan for the world, Joseph and Mary had a virgin-born son. When you hear the news that someone has had a baby, many times the first question you ask is, "What did the parents name the baby?" After an angel of the Lord appeared to Joseph in a dream, he obediently named their son, Jesus, the Greek form of the Hebrew name Joshua, which means "Yahweh saves." Joseph and Mary may not have realized the magnitude of Jesus' name at the time of His birth, that their newborn son was born to be the Savior of the world. He was, as the prophets foretold, Immanuel—God with us.

---

[3] John MacArthur, *The MacArthur Bible Commentary* (Nashville: Thomas Nelson, 2005), 1120.

Think about the meaning of your own name, and pray through what it means. Ask the Lord to reveal to you how He wants to use you to impact the kingdom of God. Give thanks for Jesus, Yeshua, the great I Am, who was born to save and deliver you from your sins.

She will give birth to a son, and you are to name Him Jesus, because He will save His people from their sins. —Matthew 1:21

Further Scripture: Genesis 32:28; Luke 2:11; 1 John 4:10

Questions

1. How do you see God's promise to Abraham fulfilled in Matthew 1 (Genesis 12:3; Matthew 1:1, 16)?

2. Women were rarely mentioned in ancient genealogies. Who are the four Old Testament women mentioned in Matthew's genealogy (Matthew 1:2–6)? Why do you think these particular women were mentioned? What does this tell you about God's grace and who He chooses to use for His glory (Genesis 38; Joshua 2:4–6; Ruth 1; 2 Samuel 11)?

3. What was Matthew trying to get his readers to understand about Joseph (Matthew 1:16)?

4. What did an angel of the Lord tell Joseph about Jesus (Matthew 1:21; Acts 4:12; 13:23; Hebrews 7:25)? How did Joseph respond to this news?

5. What should have happened to Mary according to the Old Testament law of adultery (Deuteronomy 22:23–24)? Since this did not happen, what does this say about Joseph?

6. What did the Holy Spirit highlight to you in Matthew 1 through the reading or the teaching?

Lesson 2: Matthew 2
King: The Search for Jesus

Teaching Notes

Intro

This is lesson 2 on the Book of Matthew. Studying Scripture shows us how it all fits together. In Matthew 1, we looked at the lineage of Jesus, the family tree of which Jesus is the head. Jesus is connected to the son of Abraham and the son of David, and came after 42 generations in the Old Testament. Looking at the lineage, there are five women included in the list of men. Some of these people messed up, and yet God still used them—Jesus can use anyone to point others to Himself.

reviveSCHOOL was started based on Acts 19 when Paul studied with 12 others who talked about the Word every day. So as we talk about Jesus being the Messiah, share what you're learning, talk with other people about Jesus. The Word must leave the building and go into the lives of others outside of the church.

Teaching

Matthew 2:1–3: Bethlehem means "house of bread." People left their homes, their families, their villages to go experience Jesus at Bethlehem of Judea. The wise men came to Jerusalem, asking people where to find "the King of the Jews" (v. 2a). They had seen "His star in the east and [had] come to worship Him" (v. 2b). The wise men were not kings. They might have been magicians or astrologers, or men who studied the stars. Something prompted them to recognize one star as that of the *King's* star. This is the best verse you're going to find about Jesus as the *King*. Think about this . . . when Jesus was crucified on the cross, the sign that was hung over His head proclaimed that He was "The *King* of the Jews." That title is found at both the beginning and the end of His life, although at the end it was said in mockery. Even at this point, I believe that was a declaration from God. The American Christmas tradition always portrays three wise men, but we don't know how many there were. King Herod became disturbed at the threat of another king and "all Jerusalem with him" (v. 3). Most commentators say the star was not a super nova but was a supernatural reality, like the shekinah glory of God in the Old Testament. God's presence moved the star to show the wise men where to go.

Matthew 2:4–6: In verse 4, Herod brought all the religious leaders together to ask them where the Messiah would be born. This is a time when God used the extraordinary faith of Gentiles (the wise men) to point the way to His Son when the Jews didn't do that. The Jews knew the answer based on Micah 5:2 in the Old Testament—Bethlehem of Judea: "And you, Bethlehem, in the land of Judah, are by no means least among the leaders of Judah: because out of you will come a leader who will shepherd My people Israel" (Matthew 2:6). Imagine these groups (scribes and Pharisees, Jerusalem leaders) coming to Herod to tell him where the *King* would be born.

Micah 5:2 points to two roles the Messiah would fulfill—He would be a leader and a shepherd. MacArthur states that "the Greek word for 'ruler' evokes the image of strong, even stern leadership. 'Shepherd' emphasizes tender care. Christ's rule involves both."[1] Micah 5:2 points to Revelation 12:5: "But she gave birth to a Son—a male who is going to shepherd all nations with an iron scepter—and her child was caught up to God and to His throne." This *King* is a leader and a shepherd. Psalm 78:70–72 describes the dual role of the leader/shepherd: "He chose David His servant and took him from the sheepfolds; He brought him from tending ewes to be shepherd over His people Jacob—over Israel, His inheritance. He shepherded them with a pure heart and guided them with his skillful hands."

Matthew 2:7–9: As a result of his conversation with the religious leaders, Herod met with the wise men and asked the exact time they had seen the star appear (v. 7). In verse 8, Herod sent them to Bethlehem to find the child and asked them to report back so he could go and worship Him as well. Herod used the wise men. After meeting with Herod, the wise men left, saw the star again, and followed it to the exact location where the child was (v. 9). Notice the word "child" there and not "baby." What we've done in the American Christmas culture is portray three wise men showing up at the manger to see the newborn baby. The reality is that the wise men arrived one or two years after the birth of the child.

Matthew 2:10–11: Verse 10 says, "When they saw the star, they were overjoyed beyond measure." Don't miss this. When we can experience something of the Lord, we should stop and enjoy that moment. They were filled with joy because

---

[1] John MacArthur, *The MacArthur Bible Commentary* (Nashville: Thomas Nelson, 2005), 1131–1132.

of the Lord's presence. When you start walking out your calling, you'll be filled with joy because it comes from the Lord. 1 Peter 1:6–8 says,

> You rejoice in this, though now for a short time you have had to struggle in various trials so that the genuineness of your faith—more valuable than gold, which perishes though refined by fire—may result in praise, glory, and honor at the revelation of Jesus Christ. You love Him, though you have not seen Him. And though not seeing Him now, you believe in Him and rejoice with inexpressible and glorious joy.

There's joy even in the struggles. At that moment, the wise men might not have even seen the child yet, but they saw the star, knew they were in the child's presence, and rejoiced with inexpressible and glorious joy.

Verse 11 says they entered the house (not the stable), saw the child, and fell to their knees in worship. The second the wise men saw Jesus, they worshipped Him. Then they presented their gifts. These wise men came prepared to be in the presence of the Lord. They brought three gifts—gold, frankincense (gum from a tree), and myrrh (a sap-like substance). In Isaiah 60:6 is a prophetic picture of these gifts: "Caravans of camels will cover your land—young camels of Midian and Ephah—all of them will come from Sheba. They will carry gold and frankincense and proclaim the praises of the LORD."

The gifts of the Gentile wise men call attention to the gifts we bring to God. Romans 15:25–27 addresses the obligation Christians have to minister to Jews: "Right now I am traveling to Jerusalem to serve the saints, for Macedonia and Achaia were pleased to make a contribution for the poor among the saints in Jerusalem. Yes, they were pleased, and indeed are indebted to them. For if the Gentiles have shared in their spiritual benefits, then they are *obligated to minister to Jews* in material needs."

Matthew 2:12–15: In a dream, the wise men were warned not to return to Herod (v. 12). After the wise men were gone, an angel appeared to Joseph in a dream and told him to take his family to Egypt (v. 13). The angel told Joseph to stay there until he returned to tell Joseph that it was safe to go back Israel. Joseph did not process this, or consider pros and cons, but he left immediately (v. 14). Joseph, out of obedience, spared the *King* of the Jews by taking Him to Egypt. They stayed until Herod's death, so that the prophecy in Hosea 11:1 would be fulfilled: "Out of Egypt I called My Son" (v. 15). I believe Joseph could obey what the angel said because he knew the Word of God and understood the prophetic message that the Messiah would come out of Egypt. Many of us hear from the Lord, but we're not in the Word so we don't know if what we hear aligns with the

Word. We're hesitant about being led by the Spirit. It makes life a lot easier when you know the Word of the Lord.

Matthew 2:16–23: In verse 16, Herod realized he had been outwitted by the wise men and "He gave orders to massacre all the male children in and around Bethlehem who were two years old and under." Because Joseph obeyed the instructions from God, the *King* of the Jews was saved and the prophecy from Hosea was fulfilled. Verse 18 records the fulfillment of these words from Jeremiah 31:15: "A voice was heard in Ramah, weeping, and great mourning, Rachel weeping for her children; and she refused to be consoled, because they were no more." In verses 19–20, the angel suddenly appeared to Joseph and told him to take his family back to Israel. Joseph waited on the Lord, and God spoke. In verse 21, Joseph obeyed. He did what he heard from the Lord. In verses 22–23, Joseph again obeyed, and because he knew the Word of God, he knew where to take his family.

Closing

The wise men saw a star. Joseph heard from the Lord in dreams. How we hear from the Lord and see things from the Lord can be different all the time. It could be through a pastor preaching a sermon or a friend from reviveSCHOOL speaking into your life. Out of obedience, we need to keep walking it out, waiting, and listening to hear from the Lord, because He is the *King* of the Jews.

Daily Word

Joseph, Mary, and Jesus moved from Jesus' birthplace in Bethlehem to Egypt before settling in Nazareth, where Jesus eventually grew up. Each time they moved or altered their travel plans, it was because Joseph had a dream. After each dream, Joseph immediately obeyed and moved his family to where he was told to go—even if it meant leaving in the middle of the night.

As a believer in relationship with Jesus, He will speak to you, and He may even do so in a dream. Dreams may come and go in your life, and sometimes you may think nothing about them. However, next time you have a dream, pause, write it down, and ask the Lord what He's telling you through that dream. If He reveals something to you, then act on it in faith and obedience. Joseph moved in faith. He acted immediately, and, in doing so, he saved his son. The wise men were warned in a dream not to go back to Herod; they immediately took a different route and were saved. Praise the Lord for guiding and directing your steps, even speaking to you through dreams.

> After they were gone, an angel of the Lord suddenly appeared to Joseph in a dream, saying, "Get up! Take the child and His mother, flee to Egypt, and stay there until I tell you. For Herod is about to search for the child to destroy Him." So he got up, took the child and His mother during the night, and escaped to Egypt. —Matthew 2:13–14
>
> Further Scripture: Psalm 119:60; Joel 2:28; Matthew 2:12

Questions

1. The wise men were serious about finding Jesus. They had one thing in mind and that was to find Jesus and worship Him. How serious are you about your worship? Does a hunger for worship or the world influence your life?

2. There are at least four prophecies from the Old Testament concerning Jesus in Matthew 2. Find each one in the chapter and look them up (Matthew 2:6, 15, 18, 23). *Note: The last prophecy in this chapter is not found anywhere in the Old Testament but was believed to have been spoken by the prophets.*

3. What were the three dreams that Joseph had in Matthew 2 (Matthew 2:13, 19, 22)? Why do you believe that Joseph was quick to obey these dreams? Has the Lord ever spoken to you in a dream? Was it something to obey? If so, did you?

4. What do you notice about the comparison of the wise men and the shepherds as both were searching for Jesus (Matthew 2:1, 9–11; Luke 2:15–20)? Which of the two saw Jesus first?

5. It's hard to read a verse like Matthew 2:16. Why do you think God would allow this to happen (Psalm 19:9; Isaiah 55:11; Jeremiah 1:12; Matthew 2:17–18)?

6. What did the Holy Spirit highlight to you in Matthew 2 through the reading or the teaching?

Lesson 3: Matthew 3

King: Baptism by the Holy Spirit and Fire

Teaching Notes

Intro

In the first two chapters, Matthew recorded Jesus' family tree, and the wise men who came looking for the *King* of the Jews. In this chapter, John the Baptist proclaimed that he came to prepare the way for the *King* of the Jews. The one who announced the coming of a *King* was also called a forerunner. John Walvoord says that the forerunner went before the king to announce that the king was coming to visit a town and to make sure that the town was in good condition to receive him. Sometimes, the forerunner would be asked to do minor work to smooth the road for the king to come, preparing for His arrival.[1]

Teaching

Matthew 3:1: The area John was in is located to the west of the Dead Sea (or the Salt Sea). You have to wonder why someone who came to announce the coming of a *King* would be preaching in a wilderness area where no one was, but it shows that this was how God designed it (1 Corinthians 1:26). God put John the Baptist in the wilderness so everyone would know that it wasn't about him but about God.

Matthew 3:2: In verse 2, John gave his message, "Repent, because the kingdom of heaven has come near!" To repent means to radically change your old way of doing things, to radically change your thoughts about how you've been doing things, to turn your back on that sin, and to radically run to the kingdom of heaven. The Jews do not like to say the name "God" because they want to honor and respect Him, so Matthew used the term "kingdom of heaven" instead of "kingdom of God." MacArthur states that Matthew's "kingdom of heaven" points to the "kingdom of Jesus" that resides "in the hearts of His people . . . and

---

[1] John Walvoord, *Matthew: Thy Kingdom Come* (Grand Rapids: Kregel, 1974), 29; quoted in Thomas L. Constable, *Expository Notes of Dr. Thomas Constable: Matthew*, 76, https://planobiblechapel.org/tcon/notes/pdf/matthew.pdf.

requires internal repentance, not just external submission."[2] John the Baptist said to the people that they needed to begin to change their hearts.

Matthew 3:4–6: John had "a camel-hair garment with a leather belt around his waist, and his food was locusts and wild honey." In Leviticus 11:22, these were allowed to be eaten: any kind of locust, katydid, cricket, and grasshopper." In 2 Kings 1:8 is a description of the prophet Elijah, another forerunner of Christ: "A hairy man with a leather belt around his waist." Both Elijah and John the Baptist seem to have the same image before the people. The people flocked to John (v. 5) and were "baptized by him in the Jordan River as they confessed their sins" (v. 6).

John the Baptist, as the forerunner, was to reflect what Jesus would later communicate. *Nelson's Commentary* gives a comparison of John the Baptist and Jesus: (1) they were both agents of God sent by God; (2) they both had a message to proclaim; (3) they will both experience conflict with Israel; (4) they will both be delivered into and die from the hands of Israel; (5) they both die violently and in a shameful way.[3] All of these things are done to the forerunner, then to Jesus.

How was John the Baptist's baptism different from Jesus' baptism? It was a foreshadow of what was to come; it wasn't the complete picture. In the Old Testament, the Israelites had purification rituals, so there's a connection between baptism and the Old Testament. If a Jew was going to come before the presence of the Lord, he had to be cleansed and put on clean clothes first.

Matthew 3:7–12: The Pharisees and Sadducees joined the people who were coming to repent (v. 7). John said to them, "Brood of vipers! Who warned you to flee from the coming wrath?" (v. 8). His language in this and the following verses sound very much like the words of Jesus (Matthew 12:34). John said that if there was true repentance that took place in the lives of these religious leaders, then they should have begun to see tangible fruit (change) in their lives (v. 8). First Thessalonians 1:9 gives a picture of true repentance. If the Pharisees and the Sadducees had repented, they would no longer be focused on themselves or their religious duties but on the Lord.

John then told the Pharisees and the Sadducees to stop thinking that they could depend upon being descendants of Abraham (v. 9). They could not depend upon their religious lineage to receive a special place in God's plan, because God could raise up children to take their place. In verse 10, John the Baptist said that the axe could strike at the very root of the trees because they were not bearing fruit. As the forerunner, part of what John the Baptist had to do was to prepare

---

[2] John MacArthur, *The MacArthur Bible Commentary* (Nashville: Thomas Nelson, 2005), 1124.

[3] Earl Radmacher, Ronald B. Allen, and H. Wayne House, eds., *Nelson's New Illustrated Bible Commentary* (Nashville: Thomas Nelson, 1999), 1142–1143.

the bumpy road, fix the potholes, and get rid of the religious junk so all would be ready for Jesus.

John told the Pharisees and the Sadducees that One was coming for whom he was unworthy to even remove His sandals (v.10), and that One was coming to baptize with the Holy Spirit and with fire. MacArthur explains that three types of baptism were listed here: (1) baptism "with water unto repentance"—John the Baptist's baptism of repentance; (2) baptism "with the Holy Spirit"—which all believers receive; and (3) baptism "with fire"—as a measure of judgment and refinement[4] (Acts 1:5, 8). Just as John the Baptist came as the forerunner of Jesus, we are empowered by the Holy Spirit to be the forerunners of Jesus' coming again—His return. The way we get ready is be baptized by the Holy Spirit *and* by fire.

Leviticus 6:13 says: "Fire must be kept burning on the altar continually; it must not go out." In the presence of God, the fire must not go out. The fire of God inside of you never goes out. The baptism of fire is to burn away the chaff that is inside of you so that you can express the Holy Spirit in your everyday life (v. 12). Why? So, you can be a forerunner for the return of the Messiah. The burning up of the chaff should always point us to Him and to others. I believe that if we never understand that the fire of God that is within us is burning away the chaff in our lives, then we'll never address the issues in our lives, and we become religious again. We become those who say we're going to repent but never bear fruit.

Matthew 3:13–17: In verses 13–14, Jesus came to John the Baptist for baptism. John didn't think he was worthy to even untie Jesus' sandals, nor to baptize Jesus. Jesus responded, "Allow it for now, because this is the way for us to fulfill all righteousness" (v. 15). John did as Jesus asked. Jesus actually was baptized in the water. He got all in—He got all wet. *Nelson's Commentary* says there are four things we should see in Jesus' baptism: (1) it pictures death and resurrection; (2) it prefigures the significance of Christians following Jesus in baptism; (3) it marked Jesus' first public identification with those whose sins He came to bear; and (4) it affirmed Jesus' Messiahship publicly by the testimony directly from heaven.[5]

Closing

Wiersbe points out that God spoke three times from heaven: "at Christ's baptism, at the Transfiguration (Matthew 17:3), and as Jesus approached the cross (John 12:27–30)."[6] Wiersbe continues that in the past, God spoke to His Son,

---

[4] MacArthur, 1125.

[5] Radmacher et al., 1145.

[6] Warren W. Wiersbe, *The Bible Exposition Commentary: Matthew–Galatians* (Nashville: Thomas Nelson, 1989), 17.

but that today, Jesus sits at the right hand of the Father and God speaks through His Son to us.[7] This is an incredible picture. If you want to get in tune with the Lord, it's no longer about religious ritual. It's about coming through the Son, who is sitting next to the Father. It all starts with obedience. Is the Lord asking you to turn to Him? If He is, just do it, because the Father speaks to us today through His Son.

Daily Word

John the Baptist, a forerunner for Christ, preached a message focused on repentance and the coming kingdom of heaven. He foretold of the One who was to come, Jesus, who would baptize His followers with the Holy Spirit and fire. Repentance often leads to an outward change in people's lives, but Jesus brings true inner transformation.

When you become a follower of Christ and repent, you receive fire and the gift of the Holy Spirit. Fire burns up the chaff. The chaff represents areas in your life that do not reflect Christ, such as selfishness, pride, worshipping other gods/idols, or anger. The Holy Spirit works within you, refining you, essentially burning these areas out of your life with a continual fire so you reflect more of the light of Christ. Just as God the Father delights in His beloved Son Jesus, so also Jesus delights in you and loves you. He loves when you seek Him and walk closer with Him. Allow the Holy Spirit to work in your life today. May His power work through you so you may be a bright, shining light and a forerunner for Christ's ultimate return!

I baptize you with water for repentance, but the One who is coming after me is more powerful than I. I am not worthy to remove His sandals. He Himself will baptize you with the Holy Spirit and fire. His winnowing shovel is in His hand, and He will clear His threshing floor and gather His wheat into the barn. But the chaff He will burn up with fire that never goes out. —Matthew 3:11–12

Further Scripture: Ezekiel 36:26; Matthew 3:17; Acts 1:5

---

[7] Wiersbe, 17.

Questions

1. What is the difference between John's baptism and Jesus' baptism (Matthew 3:2, 11)?

2. What truth did John reveal to the Pharisees and Sadducees in Matthew 3:7–10? What does "raising up children for Abraham out of stones" mean in verse 9?

3. In what ways did John the Baptist "prepare the way for the Lord"? In what ways did God use other things/people to prepare you to know Him? How are you being used by God to prepare someone else to receive Christ?

4. What is a "winnowing fan" or "winnowing fork" in Matthew 3:12?

5. What does Matthew 3:17 reveal about God's heart towards His children? If you are a child of God, do you truly believe that God loves you and that He is pleased with you (Psalms 86:15; 149:4; 1 John 3:1)?

6. What did the Holy Spirit highlight to you in Matthew 3 through the reading or the teaching?

Lesson 4: Matthew 4
King: Satan's Temptations

Teaching Notes

Intro

If you're new to reviveSCHOOL, welcome to our study of Matthew. We always have one painting and one word or phrase that points to Jesus in each book of the Bible. Our word for Matthew is *King.* You can see that the story today teaches what we've already studied in this book: (1) Jesus' family tree, (2) the birth of Jesus and the magi who followed the star from the east, (3) John the Baptist preparing the way for Jesus and proclaiming that Jesus would baptize people with the Holy Spirit and with fire, and (4) Jesus being water baptized, which was done before His ministry started. We probably won't get to every verse today, and by now you've probably realized that I'm OK with that. As you study on your own, reading every day, you have the reading guide, small discussion groups, Laura's Daily Word devotions, and you have the Holy Spirit to fill in what does not get covered by my teaching.

Teaching

Matthew 4:1: In verse 1, Jesus was taken into the wilderness "to be tempted by the devil." Sometimes, God is going to take you on paths and to places that you would rather not go. Joseph probably didn't want to go to Egypt, but he knew the Word of God and he knew that he needed to go there to fulfill prophecy. When we put our trust in God, we have the Holy Spirit inside us and we, too, can be led (Romans 8:14). Jesus was led by the Spirit to be tempted by the devil—not God (v. 1). The devil does all the tempting (James 1:13). Temptations are everywhere—Satan is literally crouching at the door. The challenge is to not give in to those temptations (Hebrews 4:15–16). This was one of the testings He went through to connect with us. When we say, "Jesus, I don't want to give in to this temptation," He can say, "Yep. I've been there and I didn't give in either."

Adam met Satan in a beautiful garden, while Jesus met Satan in the desert wilderness. Adam had everything in the garden; Jesus had nothing in the wilderness. Adam lost; Jesus won. Jesus redeemed everything Adam went through (John 12:31). Jesus, because of His victory by not giving in to temptation, will cast out the ruler of this world. Just so you know Colossians 2:15 has the end of the story. Jesus wins!

As we go through the three temptations that Jesus went through, the most important thing to understand is that Jesus didn't give in to anything. How did He not give in? Wiersbe emphasized that Jesus fought the battle as a man by depending upon the Spirit and the Word of God.[1] Jesus fought the daily battle with the help of the Holy Spirit and the Word of God. What I think has happened to the church is that we're hesitant to talk about the Holy Spirit and we only want to talk about the Word of God. However, we don't know if the Holy Spirit is showing us something in the Word of God. That means we have all this knowledge, but if we're not led to do something with it, we might be led to give in to temptation. That's why we have these great men and women who are in the Word of God, but if they're not guided by the Holy Spirit, they'll give in to temptation. Jesus shows us the model. How do we fight temptation? Through the Spirit of God and the Word of God.

Matthew 4:2: Verse 2 begins with, "After He had fasted 40 days and 40 nights." He was in the wilderness for 40 days and nights, eating nothing. After this time, Jesus was hungry. Why? Because Jesus was human. Forty days and 40 years are significant throughout the Old Testament. This is the backdrop that the Jews understood (Genesis 7:4; Numbers 14:33; 32:13; Deuteronomy 9:25; Jonah 3:4).

Matthew 4:3–4: After reading verse 2, we should expect verse 3 to happen because it said He was hungry: "Then the tempter approached Him and said, 'If You are the Son of God, tell these stones to become bread.'" The *first temptation* was *physical appetite* because He hadn't eaten in 40 days. Jesus fought the temptations with the Holy Spirit and the Word of God by quoting Deuteronomy 8:3. The physical appetite was first challenged in Genesis (Genesis 3:1; 1 John 2:16). Jesus was tempted with the lust of the eyes to do something that was temporary. Warren Wiersbe said, "Feeding on and obeying God's Word is more important than consuming physical food. In fact, it is our food."[2] We can't let our physical appetites be a temptation.

Matthew 4:5–7: The *second temptation* was *personal gain*. Satan took Jesus to the southeast corner of the temple complex, 450 feet high above the Kidron Valley.[3] The Jews expect the Messiah to come to the temple mount based on Malachi 3:1.

---

[1] Warren W. Wiersbe, *The Bible Exposition Commentary: Matthew–Galatians* (Colorado Springs: David C. Cook, 2001), 18.

[2] Wiersbe, 18.

[3] Wiersbe, 18.

In verse 6, Satan again misquoted God's Word, this time in Psalm 91:11–12. Jesus responded, "It is also written: Do not test the Lord your God" (v. 7).

Satan promised to give Jesus everything if He threw Himself down. Everything Jesus used to combat Satan came from the Old Testament (the New Testament hadn't been written yet). Yet, because Jesus used the Old Testament Word to combat temptation, we can as well (Genesis 3:4; Matthew 4:7). This time, Satan tempted Jesus with the lust of the flesh (1 John 2:16).

Everything that belongs to the world is part of the lust of the flesh.

Matthew 4:8–10: The *third temptation* was *power*. This time, Satan took Jesus to a high mountain, possibly Jericho, and showed Him the world (v. 8). This time, all Satan wanted from Jesus was His worship, because he wanted to be God (Isaiah 14:12). Satan will do whatever he can to make you worship him. Remember that one third of the angels followed Satan. We encounter these angels as demons in spiritual warfare. Satan is ruler of the air today. Right now, Satan has free reign and he is going to come after us, but John 12:31 says: "Now is the judgment of this world. Now the ruler of this world will be cast out." He is considered the god (little *g*) of this age (2 Corinthians 4:4). Even though Satan has this power right now, ultimately, Jesus will be victorious (Genesis 3:15; Matthew 4:10; 16:21–23; 1 Peter 1:11; 1 John 2:16).

Matthew 4:11–13: When the devil left, the angels immediately came to serve Jesus. He defended His ministry through the power of the Holy Spirit and the Word of God, and then He began to walk out His ministry. Jesus went from Nazareth to Capernaum in the region of Zebulun and Naphtali and began to walk through the prophetic word of Zebulun and Naphtali. Jesus started to overcome the seed of temptations for us.

Matthew 4:23–25: Because He triumphed over these temptations, Jesus was teaching and preaching and "healing every disease and sickness among the people." Because of that triumph, the news began to spread throughout Syria (v. 24). Because Jesus overcame these temptations, the door to ministry exploded—everybody began to flock to Jesus (v. 25).

Closing

I believe Jesus used this time in the wilderness and these temptations to get prepared for His ministry. My prayer is that God will show what you need to live out in Matthew 4.

Daily Word

When Jesus called the first disciples to follow Him, all four men—Simon, Andrew, James, and John—*immediately* left their nets, their boats, and their fathers to follow Jesus. *Immediately* means right away, without delay, instantly. The disciples responded *immediately*, and right away they witnessed Jesus preaching the good news of the kingdom and healing people with diseases and sicknesses.

Today's culture is fast-paced, and many things in life are immediately at your fingertips. People don't like to wait for anything, and technology continues to allow for this instant-gratification lifestyle. However, when it comes to following Jesus and living in obedience, do you act immediately? You may doubt you truly hear from the Lord and don't take the next step of obedience. Today, walk in *immediate* obedience and watch the Lord's faithful hand in your life! Leave a job, turn away from a distraction, repent from sin, ask for forgiveness, go on a mission trip, or give a gift the Lord has put on your heart. Maybe you have never said yes to Jesus and received His love for you in faith. Stop overanalyzing it and follow Christ! Today is the day for an *immediate* yes to Jesus!

Immediately they left their nets and followed Him. —Matthew 4:20

Further Scripture: Matthew 21:2–3; 2 John 1:6; Revelation 14:12

Questions

1. Why do you think the Spirit led Jesus into the wilderness to be tempted by the devil (Matthew 4:1)? In what ways was the devil tempting Jesus (Matthew 4:2–10)?

2. What method did Jesus use for combatting the devil when he was being tempted? How does this encourage you, and how can you apply this to your life? How do you combat temptation (1 Corinthians 10:13; Galatians 5:16; Hebrews 2:18; James 1:13–18)?

3. How was Isaiah 9:1–2 being fulfilled by Jesus' ministry in Matthew 4?

4. What were Jesus' first disciples doing when Jesus approached them (Matthew 4:18–21) and how did Jesus encounter them? How do you approach people to talk about Jesus? What can you learn from Jesus' example of "calling" the first disciples?

5. Practically, how did the news about Jesus spread (Matthew 4:24–25)? What do you imagine the discussion was like when people contemplated bringing their friend/family member to Jesus for healing; faith or skepticism?

6. What did the Holy Spirit highlight to you in Matthew 4 through the reading or the teaching?

Lesson 5: Matthew 5
King: Fulfillment of the Law

Teaching Notes

Intro

In Matthew 4, we looked at a different perspective of how Jesus was getting ready for ministry as He had to deal with the temptations. After Jesus dealt with the temptations, His ministry was off and running. At the end of Matthew 4, Jesus was teaching, preaching, and healing, and people were flocking to Him.

Teaching

Matthew 5:1: This is the beginning of the Sermon on the Mount, which is found in Matthew 5–7. Jesus said, "Don't assume that I came to destroy the Law or the Prophets. I did not come to destroy but to fulfill" (v. 17). Notice that the word "destroy" was used twice in this verse. God is not wiping out everything; through Jesus, He's fulfilling it. In this discussion about the Law and the Prophets, I am not using any oral traditions that the Jews elevated to the status of the Mosaic teachings or of Jeremiah or even the Psalms.

Matthew 5:17: With regard to the Law, *Nelson's Commentary* says this: "As a covenant system with Israel, it ended at the cross when the temple veil was rent and a new priesthood was established; as a set of spiritual and moral principles, it is eternal."[1] I want to consider the Law, temporarily and eternally, and how Jesus fits into this. The Law is *still* applicable today (Galatians 3:19; Ephesians 2:15; 1 Timothy 1:9; Hebrews 7:12). The moral ethics of the Law have not been removed. So part of the Law was temporary. At the same time, part of the Law is eternal. If Jesus had come to destroy the Law, then there would be nothing eternal about it.

Matthew 5:18: There are certain things in the Law that haven't been accomplished yet (Romans 3:31; 8:4). Jesus didn't come to destroy the Law, but to remove the temporary parts of it. Luke 24:25–27 is about the road to Emmaus:

[1] Earl Radmacher, Ronald B. Allen, and H. Wayne House, eds., Nelson's New Illustrated Bible Commentary (Nashville: Thomas Nelson, 1999), 1148.

Jesus' conversation with two of the disciples, after His resurrection. Jesus took all the Laws and the Prophets and told His disciples that these were all about Him. In the New Testament, the writers repeatedly reference the Law and the Prophets (Matthew 7:12; 11:13; Luke 24:44; Acts 13:15).

The word "fulfill" simply means "to fill out, to expand or complete." It does not mean to bring to an end. How does Christ fulfill the Old Testament? According to *Nelson's Commentary*, Jesus fulfilled the Old Testament in these ways. First, "He obeyed it perfectly and he taught its correct meaning."[2] This means that Jesus obeyed and walked it out (Matthew 3:17; 17:5; Galatians 4:4). If Jesus wasn't teaching what the Law accurately said, God would never have said this.

Second, "He will one day fulfill all of the Old Testament types and prophecies."[3] Yesterday, we talked about the belief the Jews hold that the Messiah will one day come back to the temple. That hasn't happened yet. That means that Jesus is still working out the fulfillment of the Old Testament. He's completing the prophecies that haven't taken place yet (Galatians 3:13; Hebrews 9:23; 10:8). This shows that Jesus bore the curse of the Law and established a second. Some of these Old Testament prophecies have already happened . . . the temple is no longer there, and Jesus is the temple. There are other prophetic words that have not yet come to fruition. For example, when Jesus returns, He will split the Mount of Olives in half. That obviously hasn't happened yet.

Third, "He provided a way of salvation that meets all Old Testament requirements and demands"[4] (Romans 3:20–21). None of us can keep up with the works required of us. No one will be justified by work. We can't keep up the pace of praying enough or studying the Scriptures enough or doing all that God calls us to do. But we can find righteousness through Christ. That part, our salvation through Jesus, is done. But other prophecies in the Old Testament are not done *yet*.

Wiersbe uses the acorn theory to explain that many think the Old Testament is no longer relevant and would smash it with a hammer to get rid of it. God, however, chose not to destroy the acorn, but to "plant it in the ground and let it *fulfill itself* by becoming an oak tree."[5] Prophetically speaking, eventually the desert of Israel will become a garden (Isaiah 35:1). Sixty percent of the land mass of Israel is wilderness; but one day, it will become a garden. If we destroy this land, we destroy the prophetic word that Isaiah gave. Jesus said that He came to fulfill that whole process.

---

[2] Radmacher et al., 1148.

[3] Radmacher et al., 1148.

[4] Radmacher et al., 1148.

[5] Warren W. Wiersbe, *The Bible Exposition Commentary: Matthew–Galatians* (Colorado Springs: David C. Cook, 2001), 22.

Here are four academic viewpoints that some hold:

- One view is that "Jesus came to fulfill (keep) the moral law (the Ten Commandments), but that He abolished Israel's civil and ceremonial laws."[6]
- Another view is that "Jesus came to fill out its meaning, to expand its full significance that until then remained obscure."[7]
- A third view is that Jesus came to extend the demands of Old Testament law to new lengths.[8]
- "Probably Jesus meant that He came to establish the Old Testament fully, to add His authoritative approval to it."[9] This seems to be what we've been proving here.

These are different perspectives in how this passage can be interpreted (Ephesians 2:11–13; Hebrews 10:19). The path to God has been opened to us through Jesus. To fulfill the Old Testament, Jesus opened the way for us to God. He also broke down the wall that separated Jews and Gentiles, so part of fulfilling the Law and the Prophets was to actually break down these barriers. He's allowed us to come beyond the wall (Ephesians 2:11–13), and there are no more temples made with hands. Acts 7:48 says, "However, the Most High does not dwell in sanctuaries made with hands, as the prophet says."

Closing

Jesus did many things to fulfill the Law and the Prophets, yet there are things He did destroy. He did tear down walls, He did tear down the veil, He did tear down sanctuaries made by hands—He did away with the buildings. But He didn't tear down the Law and the Prophets because those things pointed to the moment of Christ. How do we personally fulfill the Law? Two ways: to represent and replicate Jesus: We walk according to the Spirit (Romans 8:1–4), and we love others (Romans 13:10).

---

[6] Craig L. Blomberg, *Matthew*, 103–5; quoted in Thomas L. Constable, *Expository Notes of Dr. Thomas Constable: Matthew*, 155–56, https://planobiblechapel.org/tcon/notes/pdf/matthew.pdf.

[7] Richard C. Lenski, 205–7; quoted in Constable, 156.

[8] Wolfgang Trilling, *Das wahre Israel: Studien zur Theologie des Matthäus Evangeliums*, vol. 10 of Studien zum Alten und Neuen Testament (Munich: Kösel-Verlag, 1964), 174–79.

[9] Constable, 156.

The Law is temporary, and it is also eternal. Jesus perfectly obeyed the Law, and He is going to fulfill everything written between Genesis and Malachi. Because He provided the way of salvation, He broke down the barriers and tore down the veil between us and God. This relationship allows us to walk in the Spirit and to love others and begin to embrace Matthew 5:17.

Daily Word

Jesus sat down on a mountain with His disciples gathered around Him and poured out wisdom for everyday living as a disciple and follower of Christ. This sermon became known as the Sermon on the Mount, and in it, Jesus addressed issues of the heart. The disciples knew they were to love the Lord, but Jesus went further, teaching them to love their enemies, even pray for their enemies.

This may seem impossible. However, with Christ's unconditional love covering you, He equips you to love others, even your greatest, meanest, most selfish enemy. Today, ask the Lord to give you a heart of compassion and love for those unloving people in your life. Maybe someone has said an unkind word to you or to your kids. Begin by praying for them. Then ask the Lord to bless their socks off and overwhelm their life with Jesus' precious love! In praying for them, believe the Lord has a plan for their lives and will turn this difficult relationship around for good. As people observe you loving your enemy, you become a light on a hill and salt on the earth for Jesus. People will see something different in you—the love of Jesus. And maybe, just maybe, your love will draw someone to Jesus.

But I tell you, love your enemies and pray for those who persecute you, so that you may be sons of Your Father in heaven. —Matthew 5:44–45

Further Scripture: Proverbs 25:21; Romans 12:9–10; 1 John 4:7

Questions

1. Matthew 5:1–12 is commonly referred to as The Beatitudes. What does "beatitude" mean? Name the different ways that God is willing to bless believers from Matthew 5. Do these blessings apply to you? How?

2. Why do you think that God would bless you when people mock you or lie about you (Matthew 5:11–12)? Why does Scripture say that we should rejoice or be happy about that (1 Peter 4:13–14)?

3. In Matthew 5:14, Jesus told the disciples, "You are the light of the world." However, in John 8:12, Jesus said that He is the light of the world. Do you think this is a contradiction? Why or why not? What is Jesus saying to us in both of those passages (Matthew 5:14–16; John 9:5; Philippians 2:15)?

4. Why do you think that Jesus was taking the Old Testament Law one step further than what they had always heard (for example, with adultery/lust, murder) (Proverbs 6:25; Matthew 5:21–45; Colossians 3:5; 1 John 3:15)? What was Jesus the most concerned about in these passages?

5. If you bring a gift to the altar and remember that someone has something against you, what did Jesus say you must do first (Matthew 5:23–24)? Does this apply to you right now? If so, how do you plan on bringing about reconciliation to that relationship?

6. What did the Holy Spirit highlight to you in Matthew 5 through the reading or the teaching?

Lesson 6: Matthew 6

King: Earthly Possessions or Heavenly Treasures

Teaching Notes

Intro

We're in the process of studying the four Gospels—Matthew, Mark, Luke, and John. While John is called the spiritual Gospel, looking at Jesus from a unique perspective, Matthew, Mark, and Luke are synoptic Gospels, which means that they all look at stories that Jesus was involved with, but from different angles. Think of it this way: You're at a Dallas Mavericks basketball game and a call is made from the perspective of the referee; the Maverick player might have a different perspective, and the opponent player might have yet another perspective. The play still happened, but everyone saw it differently.

What we'll look at over the next several months will be different perspectives of who Jesus is. In Matthew, we'll see Jesus as a *King*. In Mark, we'll see Jesus as a *Servant*. In Luke and John, we'll see His identity differently. The joy is to continue to learn something new about Jesus. Yesterday we got stuck on one verse; think of what we learned from it. My prayer is that as you go through the Gospels, even if you've read them 100 times, God will continue to give you little golden nuggets that point to Christ.

Teaching

Matthew 6:1–8: Beginning in chapter 5, Jesus began to unfold His ministry through the Sermon on the Mount. Matthew 6 is a description of Jesus talking to the crowd that had gathered, about how to give and pray the right way, so people would not notice you.

Matthew 6:9–18: In Matthew 6:9–13, Jesus taught His listeners to pray by giving them the Lord's Prayer. Jesus explained that all this is based on forgiveness (vv. 14–15) and talked about how His followers should fast (vv. 16–18). The ultimate example is that of Jesus in the wilderness when He fasted 40 days and 40 nights.

Matthew 6:19–21: Wiersbe points out that "materialism will enslave the heart."[1] In verses 19–21, Jesus talked about possessions and recognized that money is not

---

[1] Warren W. Wiersbe, *The Bible Exposition Commentary: Matthew–Galatians* (Colorado

inherently evil (Proverbs 6:6–8). We need money to walk through everyday stuff, and it helps us take care of family (1 Timothy 5:8). Money also brings enjoyment, and having savings is a good thing (1 Timothy 4:4). Our goal should be to have enough money to bless our children, as well as our grandchildren, with an inheritance (Proverbs 13:22; 2 Corinthians 12:14).

On the other hand, money can be bad. The Lord knows when you've short-changed or mistreated people with money (James 5:2–5). And, "the love of money is a root of all kinds of evil, and by craving it, some have wandered away from the faith and pierced themselves with many pains" (1 Timothy 6:10). This means you have a divided heart . . . between the love of money and the love of God.

On the other side, how can we collect treasures for heaven (Matthew 6:20)? *Nelson's Commentary* states that "the ultimate destiny of our lives is either earthly or heavenly and the concentration of our efforts will reveal where our real treasure is."[2] This means there are rewards for faithful service . . . faithful work that actually deposits into heaven (1 Peter 1:14). So when we do things in secret while our focus is on *King* Jesus, that's when we receive heavenly rewards (Matthew 5:12; 6:6; 10:42).

Matthew 6:22–23: Sorg expressed the "heart is the center of the personality, and it controls the intellect, emotions, and will."[3] Wiersbe added that materialism does more than control the heart, it controls "the mind" as well.[4] So, we're moving from enslaving the heart to enslaving the mind with materialism. Jesus said the eye either lets the body be full of light or of darkness (vv. 22–23). So, if the light within you is darkness, how deep is that darkness? *Nelson's Commentary* says, "No muscle of your body can relax if your eye is uncomfortable."[5] If your eye is bad, it impacts everything. If you let a remote lens of darkness begin to creep in, the things of the world and earthly religion will begin to turn your mind dark. If you protect your eye and your mind from the darkness, then your eye and mind will be light. Understand that the eye is very similar to the heart in Scripture (Psalm 119:10, 18, 148). When you enslave your life with either light or darkness, then that's how you'll walk out your life.

Springs: David C. Cook, 1989), 27.

[2] Earl D. Radmacher, Ronald B. Allen, and H. Wayne House, eds., *Nelson's New Illustrated Bible Commentary* (Nashville: Thomas Nelson, 1999), 1152.

[3] T. Sorg, *The New International Dictionary of New Testament Theology*, s.v. "kardia," 180–84; Thomas L. Constable, *Expository Notes of Dr. Thomas Constable: Matthew*, 207, https://planobiblechapel.org/tcon/notes/pdf/matthew.pdf.

[4] Wiersbe, 27.

[5] Radmacher et al., 1152.

Matthew 6:24: Wiersbe finished his quote on materialism this way: "Materialism will enslave the heart, the mind, and the will."[6] Jesus said, "No one can be a slave of two masters, since either he will hate one and love the other, or be devoted to one and despise the other. You cannot be slaves of God and of money" (v. 24). Earthly material treasures become what the Scriptures say is "an idol or god of the human heart that is in conflict with the one true God."[7] That means we can become so driven by earthly treasure that we forget about being kingdom-minded. Being kingdom-minded means that what we do, what we have, goes to advancing the kingdom. Tasker described this as a type of slavery mentality and said that "single ownership and fulltime service are the essence of slavery."[8] You've got to decide if you're going to go after the will of man or the will of God.

Verse 25 follows: "This is why I tell you: Don't worry about your life, what you will eat or what you will drink; or about your body, what you will wear. Isn't life more than food and the body more than clothing?" *Nelson's Commentary* says, "To set one's heart upon material possessions or to worry about the lack of them is to live in perpetual insecurity and to deprive one's self of the spiritual blessings of God."[9] God knows what's on your heart, what you need, so you can begin to walk in "carefulness, cautiousness, and faith," knowing that God will show up. When we give in to anxiousness, we are assuming that God cannot take care of it and we'll have to do it ourselves (v. 26). Verse 27 explains why we don't need to worry. God looks after those who follow Him. In verses 28–29, Jesus reminded His listeners how great God's care of us is by comparing God's riches to those of King Solomon (2 Chronicles 9:3–4).

In verse 31, Jesus asked the disciples if they had enough trust in Him to not worry about where the next meal would come from (Matthew 8:26). Constable says, "It is not only foolish to talk like this, but it's pagan to fret about the necessities of life."[10] "The fretting disciple lives as an unbeliever (Gentile) who disbelieves and disregards God."[11] When we focus on the material things, we become idolaters. But seeking God's kingdom is putting Him first (Matthew 6:33). Wiersbe said "that the average person is crucifying himself between two thieves: the regrets of yesterday and the worries about tomorrow."[12] Constable said that God has given us enough grace "so we can deal with life one day at

---

[6] Wiersbe, 27.

[7] John MacArthur, *The MacArthur Bible Commentary* (Nashville: Thomas Nelson, 2005), 1311.

[8] R. V. G. Tasker, *The Gospel According to St. Matthew: An Introduction and Commentary* (Grand Rapids: Eerdmans, 1961), 76; quoted in Constable, 209.

[9] Radmacher et al., 1152.

[10] Constable, 212.

[11] Constable, 212.

[12] Wiersbe, 28.

a time. Tomorrow He will provide enough grace (help) for what we will face then."[13] I wrestled with that statement, thinking that I need the grace for tomorrow. But I don't. God gives us enough grace for today.

Closing

So how do we overcome worry? Wiersbe lays out three words that will give us the victory over worry. First, Wiersbe says to have enough *faith* to trust God (Matthew 6:30). Second, he says we must trust the *Father* to care for His children (Matthew 6:32). Third, he says to focus on putting God *first* as the priority in our lives (Matthew 6:33). Wiersbe summarizes it this way: "If we have *faith* in the *Father* and put Him *first*, He will meet our needs."[14]

Daily Word

The disciples continued listening to Jesus' teachings from the Sermon on the Mount. Jesus taught practical lessons about how to walk with God in giving, praying, fasting, and handling material items. And then Jesus said to these men, "Do not worry about your life." These disciples had just left their livelihoods and their families to follow Jesus. Can you imagine the thoughts going on in their minds about how they would eat, drink, or even have clothing? Yet Jesus continued to tell them that rather than worry, they were to seek first the kingdom of God and those things would be provided.

As a follower of Christ, you are to seek the Lord and pursue a life with Him above all other concerns in life. Jesus promises that when you seek Him first, all the things you truly need will be provided. Therefore stop worrying and remember—God's got it! He knows what you will eat or wear even before it happens. When you catch yourself worrying today, stop and say a prayer of thanksgiving for God's faithfulness and His promise to provide for you as you seek Him first.

But seek first the kingdom of God and His righteousness, and all these things will be provided for you. Therefore don't worry about tomorrow, because tomorrow will worry about itself. —Matthew 6:33–34

Further Scripture: Proverbs 3:5–6; Philippians 4:6–7; Colossians 3:1–2

---

[13] Constable, 213.

[14] Wiersbe, 28.

Questions

1. In Matthew 5:16, Jesus said to let your good deeds shine out for all to see; however, in Matthew 6:1, He said not to do you your good deeds publicly. What is the reason for Jesus saying these statements (Ephesians 5:8–9; 1 Peter 2:12)?

2. Money in and of itself is not evil. Matthew 6:24 says that you cannot serve two masters. What are some practical ways that money can be used for good (Proverbs 6:6–8; 13:22; 2 Corinthians 12:14; 1 Timothy 4:4; 5:8)? How can money be bad (Luke 12:13–21; 1 Timothy 6:10; James 5:2–5)?

3. Matthew 6 says to store up our treasures in heaven and that God will reward us for certain things. How can we tangibly store up treasures or rewards in heaven (Matthew 5:12; 6:6, 15, 20; 10:42; 1 Peter 1:14)?

4. Why did Jesus say in Matthew 6:14 that when we forgive others your heavenly Father will forgive you (Mark 11:25; Ephesians 4:32; Colossians 3:13)? Why is it important to God that we forgive others? Are there people in your life that need your forgiveness?

5. How does Jesus teach each of us to pray in Matthew 6:5–13 (2 Kings 4:33; Ecclesiastes 5:2; Romans 8:26–27)? Jesus mentioned getting away by yourself to pray, but is it also OK to pray in public? Why or why not (Luke 18:10–14; Ephesians 6:18; 1 Thessalonians 5:17; James 5:16)? No matter where we pray, who should always be the focus of our prayers?

6. What did the Holy Spirit highlight to you in Matthew 6 through the reading or the teaching?

Lesson 7: Matthew 7
King: The Choice of Life and Death

Teaching Notes

Intro

Today we're in Matthew 7. The first six verses of Matthew 7 are about being careful not to judge others. Verse 3 tells us that if we have something in our own eyes, we shouldn't point out what is in someone else's eyes. Yesterday, we talked about the importance of the eyes being able to let light into our lives but keeping out the darkness.

Teaching

In the verses we'll study today, Jesus talks about two of everything: two gates, two ways, two destructions (death), two groups of people, two houses, two builders, two fruits, two trees, two claims. I believe that it is essential for us to understand the choices that we have. We are constantly on a journey of choosing (Deuteronomy 30:19; Psalm 1:1–2; Jeremiah 21:8). Every day that we wake up, we have a choice—the way of life or the way of death. Which way do you want to choose to honor *King* Jesus? That's the backdrop of these verses.

Matthew 7:13–16: Jesus said there was a wide path that was easy to follow, which many people were going through, but that led to destruction (v. 13). *Nelson's Commentary* stresses that "the vast majority of people in the world have the same attitude as the scribes and Pharisees. They simplistically believe that their external works are what count."[1] Then, Jesus presented the other gate as narrow and the path as difficult, and he stated that few people will find it (v. 14). These passages are about the cost/reward of each way: Matthew 25:46; John 17:2; and Romans 9:22. The wide path leads to destruction. The narrow path leads to life. There's an obvious, real contrast between what He's asking us to do. Most people like easy messages and broad paths (Matthew 10:38–39; 16:24–25; John 15:18–19).

Many more people want to communicate the message of the broad path rather than the narrow one. That leads to verse 15: "Beware of false prophets who

---

[1] Earl D. Radmacher, Ronald B. Allen, and H. Wayne House, eds., *Nelson's New Illustrated Bible Commentary* (Nashville: Thomas Nelson, 1999), 1153.

come to you in sheep's clothing but inwardly are ravaging wolves" (Acts 20:29). They'll be the ones that say Jesus doesn't want you to suffer but wants you to get more stuff for happiness. MacArthur says that "these deceive not by disguising themselves as sheep, but by impersonating true shepherds."[2] They'll have messages that sound really, really good.

Peter wrote, "But there were also false prophets among the people, just as there will be false teachers among you. They will secretly bring in destructive heresies, even denying the Master who bought them, and will bring swift destruction on themselves" (Jeremiah 6:13–15; 2 Peter 2:1). How then will we judge the difference? There are two trees, those that bear fruit and those that do not (v. 16). MacArthur says that "false doctrine cannot restrain the flesh, so false prophets manifest wickedness."[3] Bad trees cannot produce good fruit.

Matthew 7:17–20: Good trees produce good fruit and life, but bad trees produces bad fruit and death (v. 17). "A good tree can't produce bad fruit; neither can a bad tree produce good fruit. Every tree that doesn't produce good fruit is cut down and thrown into the fire. So, you'll recognize them by their fruit" (vv. 18–20). The two gates and the two trees have parallel consequences. The wide gate and the bad fruit tree are both destroyed; the narrow gate and the good fruit tree give life. You have a choice to pursue the path of life, or the path of death (Jude 3–4). One of the issues in American society is that we're not even aware that there are false teachers out there. We take whatever we hear at face value, without testing the truth of the statement. That's the alarming part.

Matthew 7:21–28: In verse 21, those who are found to not have followed the will of God will have to depart (go away) from God. All these options lead away from life. Wiersbe explains that "the two ways [gates] illustrate the *start* of the life of faith; the two trees illustrate the *growth* and results of the life of faith here and now; and the two houses illustrate the *end* of this life of faith, when God shall call everything to judgment."[4] For verses 24–25, we can look at the first of two houses or two builders. The house was built on a good foundation of rock—it weathered the storm without damage. The people here heard and acted on what they heard. Verses 26–27 describe the other builder and house that was built on a terrible foundation of sand that could shift—it collapsed during the storm and was destroyed. These people heard and didn't act.

---

[2] John MacArthur, *The MacArthur Bible Commentary* (Nashville: Thomas Nelson, 2005), 1135.

[3] MacArthur, 1135.

[4] Warren W. Wiersbe, *The Bible Exposition Commentary: Matthew–Galatians* (Colorado Springs: David C. Cook, 1989), 31.

One commentator stated that the house could represent your religious life, the rain could imply divine judgment, and only the one built on the foundation of obedience to God's Word stands. In verse 28, when Jesus had finished the sermon, "the crowds were astonished at His teaching, because He was teaching them like one who had authority, and not like their scribes." Why were the crowds so astonished at His authority? The scribes and Pharisees did not teach their own ideas, instead "always quoting the various rabbis and experts in the law. Jesus needed no human teacher to add authority to His words, for He spoke as the Son of God."[5]

Jesus spoke with all authority, without referring to any other opinion (Mark 1:22). The more that I walk in dependence on the Holy Spirit, the more I speak with the authority that He gives me. The challenge is, will we walk in this authority that comes from the Spirit (Mark 1:22; 11:28)? When we believe that we have authority, we can walk on the narrow path, begin to experience good fruit, and can build our foundation on the *Rock*, when we believe we have *King* Jesus with us. We have nothing to fear any more. Luke 6:48: "He is like a man building a house, who dug deep and laid the foundation on the rock. When the flood came, the river crashed against that house and couldn't shake it, because it was well built." When we dig deep into the Word and into the cornerstone of Christ in our lives, nothing is going to shake us. No destruction will affect us. We will walk with this authority.

Closing

It's time that the church today begins to walk with this authority . . . that we actually have Christ in our lives and that we have been radically changed, so that people will want what we have. Let's continue to dig deep in the Word of God so that our foundation cannot be shaken.

Daily Word

In the middle of the Sermon on the Mount, Jesus told His disciples to not judge others. You can't love and judge at the same time. Think about that for a minute. When you judge someone, you have no idea what has happened to them during their day, in their past, or even throughout their upbringing.

Think about your own life, and remember the Lord loves you *and* the person you are judging equally. Jesus models how you are to love others with compassion. It's with this same love and compassion you are loved today. Jesus loves you unconditionally, and He asks you to love others with that same love. Today, every time you have a judgmental thought toward someone, ask the Lord to give you eyes to see what He sees and a heart to love them as He loves them.

---

[5] Wiersbe, 32.

> **Do not judge, so that you won't be judged. For with the judgment you use, you will be judged, and with the measure you use, it will be measured to you. —Matthew 7:1–2**
>
> Further Scripture: Mark 12:31; Romans 14:10; James 4:11

Questions

1. Has the Lord ever revealed to you that you had a log in your eye (Matthew 7:3–5)? If so, was it because you were trying to help get a speck out of someone else's eye?

2. In Matthew 7:12, Jesus taught the crowd to treat others the same way they wanted to be treated. Look at Matthew 25:31–46. Do you see this principle when Jesus taught about the sheep and the goats? Why were the "goats" called accursed, and sent to eternal fire?

3. Jesus talked about two gates in Matthew 7:13–14. Describe the two gates. In John 10:7 and 9, Jesus described Himself as what? Look at John 14:6. Do you think all these passages point to the same idea?

4. Twice in Matthew 7 (vv. 16 and 20) Jesus said, "you will know them by their fruits." What fruit would a good tree bear? (Galatians 5:22–23)

5. According to Matthew 7:21–23, who will enter the kingdom of heaven?

6. Matthew 7:24 says a wise man builds his house on the rock. What do you think this rock is (Psalm 62:2; 1 Corinthians 10:4)? In this passage, what makes this man wise? (James 1:22)

7. What did the Holy Spirit highlight to you in Matthew 7 through the reading or the teaching?

Lesson 8: Matthew 8
King: The Greatest Faith

Teaching Notes

Intro

Yesterday, we discovered that in order to be built on a solid rock foundation that cannot be shaken, we need a strong foundation in the Word of God. We believe that if you dig into the Word every day, this process can radically change your life.

Teaching

In Matthew 8, there are all kinds of stories of healing. The first four verses talk about a leper who was healed because Jesus touched him. Jesus interacted and engaged with the community. He commanded us to go into the world because He has given us authority. Jesus engaged the culture.

Matthew 8:5–13: In verse 5, Jesus engaged the culture. Jesus entered Capernaum and was interacting with the people there, when a centurion came up to Him. A centurion was a Roman military officer who was in charge of 100 soldiers. Carson said that many of these officers would have been of Phoenician (modern-day Lebanese) and Syrian background.[1] The centurion would have been the backbone of the military. Throughout the New Testament, when you read of a centurion, it's always a positive statement. Centurions are presented as having power under control, and a sense of meekness. This centurion who came to Jesus was able to say, "I need help." By pleading with Jesus, the centurion acknowledged that Jesus was in control.

This passage has a few surprises. The first surprise comes from verse 5. It surprises me that a centurion, a military man, would humble himself and plead with Jesus.

There are at least two surprises from verse 6. First, the centurion identified Jesus as "Lord." Most commentators would say the centurion was being polite

---

[1] Donald A. Carson, "Matthew," in *Matthew-Luke*, vol. 8 of *The Expositor's Bible Commentary*, ed. Frank E. Gaebelein and J. D. Douglas (Grand Rapids: Zondervan, 1983), 200; Thomas L. Constable, *Expository Notes of Dr. Thomas Constable: Matthew*, 238, https://planobiblechapel.org/tcon/notes/pdf/matthew.pdf.

with this title and wasn't referring to Jesus as deity. We've already identified that the centurion was willing to plead with Jesus. The next observation is that the centurion was pleading for his servant, which means that he recognized Jesus as an authority who had the power to help.

In verse 7, Jesus replied that He would come heal the servant, another surprise. The centurion simply asked for help and Jesus simply said yes. The Father wants to pour out good things to us. Here's where the rewards come from—when we intercede in prayer for someone else. This makes you want to talk to Jesus. We can come before the throne in humility because Jesus understands and hears our prayers.

The surprises continue in verse 8 when the centurion proclaimed his own unworthiness. MacArthur states that "Jewish tradition held that a person who entered a Gentile's house was ceremonially defiled."[2] The centurion recognized that as a Jew, Jesus would become defiled if He entered his home. It's kind of like outside the gate at the Old City in Jerusalem. The Muslims took over the Eastern Gate and they cemented up the gate. It's also known as the Golden Gate and is the gate the Messiah will ride through to restore the kingdom of God. Not only did the Muslims cement up the gate, but they put a cemetery before it because they knew that no priest would defile himself crossing through the cemetery. However, Jesus is not concerned with being unclean but instead wants to touch people's lives. When it's time for Jesus to return, He'll come through that cemetery.

A surprise from verse 8 is that the centurion believed that Jesus had the authority to heal his servant. Another surprise is that the centurion thought he wasn't worthy, but that Jesus was. He was willing to humble himself to get help for his servant. Jesus has no desire to pour out His mercy or His grace on our lives if we are not humble before Him. The centurion's response that he wasn't worthy was like John the Baptist's response to Jesus that he wasn't even worthy to untie His sandals (Mark 1:7; John 1:27). That's what Jesus is looking for.

In verse 9, a surprise is that the centurion, because he was a soldier, connected simply on the basis of authority. He recognized that Jesus' authority was greater.

In verse 10, Jesus was amazed. Where else in Scripture have you ever read the statement that Jesus was amazed? Jesus was amazed that the centurion had such great faith that He could command "Come," "Go," or "Do." It's a surprise! Scripture says that the one who postures himself to decrease while Christ increases in him will be elevated. Jesus pointed out that this Gentile had the greatest faith because he recognized what Jesus could do. And all the centurion did was to plead for his servant. Back in verse 6, the centurion didn't ask for

---

[2] John MacArthur, *The MacArthur Bible Commentary* (Nashville: Thomas Nelson, 2005), 1136.

Jesus' help. And in verse 8, he said to Jesus, "Only say the word, and my servant will be cured." I want to put back into our hearts and minds that Jesus is in the business of healing. It's His kingdom business. He has the authority and is in charge of the kingdom, so He can do whatever He wants.

In verse 11, Jesus described the gathering of Israel in heaven. This is a weird transition since Jesus had just complimented a Gentile for having the greatest faith. But the point of this verse is that when Israel comes together in heaven, the banquet will be not only for the Jews but also for the Gentiles (those from the east and the west) will be at the banquet, too. The religious leaders of that time thought that the kingdom of God and the Messianic banquet was only for the Jews. In verse 12, Jesus said "the sons of the kingdom will be thrown into the outer darkness. In that place there will be weeping and gnashing of teeth."

Jesus was challenging the Jews with an alternative perspective about heaven. And, He had just complimented a Gentile, indicating that Gentiles from all over would join the banquet in the kingdom (Isaiah 59:19; Malachi 1:11). Jesus said He didn't come to abolish, but to fulfill. "Fulfill" doesn't mean to come to an end, but to complete the process that has already been in place. Many of these prophetic words are still yet to unfold. The Messianic banquet—still in place. Jesus' name will be great among the nations, not just Israel—still in place. What bothered the Jews was that they thought this banquet was only going to be for them. The end of verse 12 says there will be weeping and gnashing of teeth. There are multiple places in the Scripture that talk about this (Matthew 22:13).

In the middle of this story, Jesus tells the Jews that the Gentiles can come to the table, too, if they have faith, and at the end, the servant was totally healed (v. 13). I believe that when we have a kingdom mindset, we can walk like the centurion and we can walk like Jesus. I want us to look at one verse and, through observation, move through the process of interpretation and land on application: "As you go, announce this: 'The kingdom of heaven has come near'" (Matthew 10:7).

When you walk with the presence of God, when you walk as Christ has changed your life, the kingdom of heaven has come near, and this is what you can do: "Heal the sick, raise the dead, cleanse those with skin diseases, drive out demons. You have received free of charge; give free of charge" (v. 8).

When we walk with this humility, understand that *King* Jesus has given us authority, and with the Holy Spirit within us, we can actually do what Christ does . . . heal the sick, raise the dead, cleanse those with skin diseases, cast out demons. What you've been given, you need to give away.

Closing

What I wanted you to do in this lesson was to slow down and consider what the Scripture is saying. Ultimately, what I take away from this lesson is that when you come to the table with Jesus, you can learn from Him, and then "Come," "Go," and "Do" just like Jesus did. We've all received free of charge and now it's our turn to give free of charge.

Daily Word

A centurion came to Jesus and asked Him to heal his servant who was lying at home paralyzed and in terrible agony. This Gentile commander in the Roman army amazed Jesus. He showed an unnecessary love toward his servant and displayed humility in the presence of Jesus, ignoring his own earthly position and ranking. And he displayed faith, believing Jesus could heal miraculously just by saying a word.

As a follower of Christ, empowered by the Holy Spirit, you have the strength to walk in love, humility, and faith, causing Jesus to be "amazed" by you today. No matter what you may be walking through, approach the situation with love, humility, and faith like the centurion. Maybe you too will be amazed at how the Lord will move through the situation!

Hearing this, Jesus was amazed and said to those following Him, "I assure you: I have not found anyone in Israel with so great a faith!" —Matthew 8:10

Further Scripture: Matthew 8:13; John 20:29; Colossians 1:10–11

Questions

1. When the leper approached Jesus, according to the Law, what should the man have done (Leviticus 13:45)? How did Jesus respond to this "unclean man" (Matthew 8:3)? How do you respond to those that our culture deems unclean?

2. Is it likely the centurion mentioned in Matthew 8:5 was a Roman and not an Israelite? Are you surprised that Jesus was immediately willing to go with this man to heal his servant? Why?

3. Jesus held up this centurion's faith as an example of great faith, not even found among the Israelites. What did this man understand that Jesus recognized as great faith?

4. It appears that Jesus was discouraging the scribes in Matthew 8:19–20 from following Him. Why do you think He did this?

5. The disciples obviously believed Jesus to be special, since they were committed to following Him. Why do you think they were amazed (Matthew 8:27) when the winds and seas obeyed Him, even though they had seen Him healing many people? (Matthew 8:16)

6. What did the Holy Spirit highlight to you in Matthew 8 through the reading or the teaching?

Lesson 9: Matthew 9
King: The Message of New Wineskins

Teaching Notes

Intro

As a quick review, remember that you will see different perspectives of Jesus as we move through the Gospels. The perspective from Matthew is of Jesus as *King*. In Matthew, we're going to begin to see that tension between the old way that was not working and waiting for the new to come into place.

Teaching

Matthew 9:1–8: Jesus entered his own town and began to heal. Some friends brought a paralyzed man before Him. When Jesus saw the faith of the friends, He told the paralyzed man that his sins were forgiven (v. 2). This is like the centurion asking Jesus to heal his sick servant. I believe Jesus healed the servant because of the centurion's faith, and I believe the same thing about the paralytic man. Jesus healed him in response to the faith of those who had brought the man to Jesus.

Matthew 9:9–13: These verses tell the account of Matthew's calling to follow Jesus. Jesus approached Matthew, who was still sitting in his tax office. When Jesus called him, he immediately got up and left his job (v. 9). I believe that word of Jesus' incredible acts had already spread around the country, and Matthew had heard the stories. He had been tracking with Jesus, watching, observing, and listening, and maybe even sitting under His teaching.

In verse 10, Matthew described how Jesus sat at his table with Matthew's guests—other tax collectors and sinners. The Pharisees questioned why Jesus was with these men (v. 11). Jesus replied, "Those who are well don't need a doctor, but the sick do" (v. 12). Then, He told them to learn what it meant to have mercy and compassion, not sacrifice, because he came for the sinners (v. 13).

This is the backdrop of Matthew 9—this spirit of arrogance and tension. Jesus was being questioned why He did things one way, while the religious leaders did things another way. Jesus was told they didn't like what He did, but He continued anyway. When we follow *King* Jesus, it is never going to look like the way of the religious. Ever. The reason we need revival in the church is that the spirit of religion needs to be broken off. Jesus desires mercy and compassion; He doesn't want our sacrifices and offerings only. Jesus came to call not the righteous but the sinners (v.13). It was in this context that Matthew started following Jesus.

Matthew 9:14: Verse 14 begins a transition to another time when the followers of John the Baptist questioned Jesus. John the Baptist's message was one of repentance, and the message needed to be clarified and changed over to the way Jesus did it. This time, John the Baptist's disciples questioned the practices of Jesus and His disciples. According to Luke 5:29–39, the Pharisees were with John the Baptist's disciples. Their question was about the religious practice of fasting and whether they were more religious since they fasted more than Jesus and His disciples did.

Israelites were required to fast for the Day of Atonement (Leviticus 16:29–30); the two fasting days each week were voluntary, although the Pharisees religiously practiced it (Luke 18:12). The question then can be understood as, "Jesus, why don't You and Your disciples fast the two days like us?" There's more evidence of fasting that God required in the Old Testament (Exodus 34:28; Leviticus 11:44–47). They were asked to fast from different types of animals, and for Nazarites like Samson, from certain things.

The Pharisees fasted twice a week as part of their religious mentality. This was their culture and a part of their religion. Kent Berghuis gives five categories of fasting: "(1) fasting as a sign of grief or mourning, (2) as a sign of repentance and seeking forgiveness for sin, (3) as an aid in prayer, (4) as an experience of the presence of God that results in the endorsement of his messenger, and (5) as an act of ceremonial public worship."[1] This was the lens that the disciples of John the Baptist had when they questioned why Jesus and His disciples didn't fast.

Matthew 9:15: You would think that the disciples of John the Baptist and those of Jesus would have been supporters of one another. In verse 15a, Jesus said, "Can the wedding guests be sad while the groom is still with them?" In other words, He asked, "Can the wedding guests—the sons of the Bridegroom, the disciples—be sad while they're with Me?" One of the reasons for fasting was grief or mourning. The verse continues that when Jesus is taken away, they will then fast (v. 15b). Jesus' words shook John's disciples' understanding. Yet, John the Baptist was named the best man (Isaiah 62:5; Hosea 2:20; John 3:29). *Nelson's Commentary* says, "The principle expressed here is that Jesus Christ has come to bring in

---

[1] Kent D. Berghuis, *Christian Fasting: A Theological Approach* (Dallas: Biblical Studies Press, 2007), 4.

a new dispensation altogether, which cannot be fitted into the forms of the old Jewish economy."[2] We're going to go from a period of rule of Law to God's grace.

Matthew 9:16–17: Jesus began to spell out what He was saying about grace through the example of old and new wineskins. Just as new cloth sewn onto old would not hold securely, the Jews had been following instructions for how to fast for a long time and could not see there was a new way. In verse 17, the focus is on "new" and "fresh." John MacArthur provides an explanation for these illustrations:

> Animal skins were used for fermentation of wine because of their elasticity. As the wine fermented, pressure built up, stretching the wineskin. A previously stretched skin lacked elasticity and would rupture, ruining both wine and wineskin. Jesus uses this as an illustration to teach that the forms of old rituals, such as the ceremonial fasting practiced by the Pharisees and John's disciples, are not fit for the new wine of the New Covenant era.[3]

The Pharisees were a small, isolated sect of about 6,000 Jews who had been separated and represented the "orthodox core." If there was any group that would hold on to the old garments or the old wineskins, it would be the Pharisees. But Jeremiah said there was a new covenant of grace that would not be like the covenant made with their ancestors, the covenant they broke even as God brought them out of the wilderness. God would put the new covenant "within them and write it on their hearts" (Jeremiah 31:33; Ezekiel 36:26–27). But that new spirit could not be put in the old rituals, the tablets, the 613 laws; into the old way of doing things. The new covenant changes that and begins with God's Spirit being within us. And the fact that when we're open to new wineskins, radical change can happen.

In Acts 19:2–5, Paul didn't write the disciples in Ephesus off for not being baptized by the Spirit, but instead he poured into them, teaching and doing ministry with them. He laid hands on them, the Holy Spirit came over them, and they began to speak in other languages and prophesy (Acts 19:6–7). Part of our calling is to walk with them and to set the religious free. In this case, because Paul invested time, 12 men got to experience the new covenant.

---

[2] Earl D. Radmacher, Ronald B. Allen, H. Wayne House, eds., *Nelson's New Illustrated Bible Commentary* (Nashville: Thomas Nelson, 1999), 1157.

[3] John MacArthur, *The MacArthur Bible Commentary* (Nashville: Thomas Nelson, 2005), 1139.

It was this event that led to the beginning of reviveSCHOOL, this example of studying daily for two years at the lecture hall of Tyrannus (Acts 9b–10), engaging in discussion, and learning about the kingdom of God so that all throughout Asia, both Jews and Greeks, could hear the message of Jesus.

Closing

The gospel is intended for tax collectors and sinners. The gospel is intended for Jews and Gentiles. We don't embrace the new wineskins for ourselves, but so that all have the chance to hear about the Lord and to be set free from the bondage of religion. When you study the Word of God on a regular basis, we believe that your entire community can be changed.

Daily Word

Jesus continued to go throughout the towns and villages, preaching the good news and healing people with diseases and sicknesses. As Jesus went out, He *saw* the crowds of people, and He *felt* compassion for them.

As a believer of Christ, you are to be Jesus' love to those around you. Do you *see* people and their needs around you, or do you quickly pass them by, busily making your way to your next event? Open your eyes to really *see* people like Jesus does, asking the Holy Spirit to guide your way. And when the Lord brings someone to your attention, what do you *feel*? Jesus *felt* compassion for the weary and worn out. Do you *feel* anything, or do you just pass them by, believing they can care for themselves or hoping someone else will take care of them?

People are messy, but as a follower of Christ, you are to *see, feel, and love* those around you. Jesus told the disciples to pray to the Lord of the harvest to send more workers because the harvest is abundant. Today, you can be an answer to Jesus' prayer. Open your eyes to *see* someone hurting, *feel* compassion toward them and put Jesus' *love* into action.

When He saw the crowds, He felt compassion for them, because they were weary and worn out, like sheep without a shepherd. —Matthew 9:36

Further Scripture: Zachariah 7:9–10; Matthew 9:37–38; Colossians 3:12

Questions

1. In the first few verses of Matthew 9, how did Jesus demonstrate that He had the power to forgive sins?

2. In Matthew 9:9, Jesus called Matthew to follow Him, and he did. When was your call to follow Jesus? Did you, as Matthew did, immediately respond in obedience, or did you resist for a time?

3. When Jesus was dining with tax collectors and sinners, He was criticized by whom? How did Jesus respond to their questions?

4. In verse 13, Matthew quoted Hosea 6:6. God's people had continued the law of sacrifice but had given up the knowledge of God and truth (Hosea 4:1). Do you know people who are religious and go through the motions, but are not walking with God or in the truth? (Romans 1:21–25)

5. How would you explain the illustrations Jesus used about cloth and wineskins to someone unfamiliar with these verses? (Matthew 9:16–17; 2 Corinthians 5:17)

6. Jesus instructed the two blind men who were healed not to tell anyone about what happened. Why do you think He did that?

7. When you hear about people's brokenness, or witness it firsthand, do you feel compassion, as Jesus did (Matthew 9:36)? Have you thought about praying for God to send out workers into His harvest? Have you considered that He may want to send you?

8. What did the Holy Spirit highlight to you in Matthew 9 through the reading or the teaching?

Lesson 10: Matthew 10

King: Jesus' Instructions for His Apostles

Teaching Notes

Intro

The one word we're using for the Book of Matthew is *King*. In Matthew 10, we'll see the beginning of the *King's* ambassadors. The role of the ambassador is to go out and do the *King's* business. Isaiah 6:8 says, "Then I heard the voice of the Lord say, 'Who shall I send? Who will go for Us?' I said, 'Here I am. Send me.'" This is a backdrop of Matthew 10.

Teaching

Matthew 10:1–4: Jesus pulled the disciples together and gave them authority "over unclean spirits, to drive them out and to heal every disease and sickness" (v. 2). The 12 disciples were all there, and through the authority and assignment given to them, they became apostles. MacArthur says, "Disciple means 'student,' one who is being taught by another. Apostles refers to qualified representatives who are sent on a mission."[1]

In chapter 10, Jesus was getting ready to send His disciples out to do business. This was an action plan for the 12 disciples to do ministry. How did these disciples receive authority? Jesus had authority to give. No other leader at this point had ever given authority to others. MacArthur explains that the reason this authority was given was so the disciples/apostles could "announce Messiah's arrival and authenticate Him plus His apostles who preached His gospel."[2] He told them to drive out *all* unclean spirits and to heal *every* disease and sickness. Jesus was getting ready for His kingdom to begin.

Matthew gave the names of the 12 disciples, always listing them in pairs. They were everyday guys. First, Simon and his brother Andrew. Next were James and John, brothers who were also called the Sons of Thunder. These four were all fishermen and they were Jesus' inner circle. Next, Matthew listed Philip and Bartholomew, and then Thomas and Matthew the tax collector (the author himself).

---

[1] John MacArthur, *The MacArthur Bible Commentary* (Nashville: Thomas Nelson, 2005), 1140.

[2] MacArthur, 1140.

Some scholars suggest Matthew and James the son of Alphaeus were brothers. James the son of Alphaeus was listed with Thaddaeus, whose other name was Judas. He may have chosen to use the name Thaddaeus so he would not be confused with Judas Iscariot. Finally, Simon the Zealot (because he was a former member of the Zealots) and Judas Iscariot.

Matthew 10:5–15: Verse 5 says, "Jesus sent out these 12 after giving them instructions." They were sent out in the pairs as we listed above. Those instructions (the game plan) continued through the remainder of chapter 10.

His instructions included:

1. Stay focused on the target audience, the Jews—"the lost sheep of Israel," not other nations or Samaria (Jeremiah 50:6; Matthew 15:24; John 4:22; Romans 1:16).
2. While going, announce the kingdom of heaven is near, MacArthur explains that "kingdom of heaven" refers "to the sphere of God's dominion over those who belong to Him. The kingdom is now manifest in heaven's spiritual rule over the hearts of believers and, one day, will be established in a literal earthly kingdom"[3] (Revelation 20:4–6). The responsibility included "going." Plummer said this:

> The charge, "as you go, preach," is another indication of the temporary character of these directions. There are to be 'field-preachers' moving on from place to place. No permanent organization is to be attempted. The sheep are all scattered, and the first thing is to awaken in them the desire for a shepherd and a fold. The Messiah and the Kingdom are ready when they are ready.[4]

One commentary I read suggested that these 12 men should have been leaders in Israel but instead became leaders of the church.

In Matthew 10:5–6, the kingdom of God will be ushered in, based on the sheep's response to Christ's ambassadors—His disciples/apostles. In the process, between Matthew 10 and Matthew 28, the Jews, however, kept refusing His offer. Then, in Matthew 28:18–20 the focus changed:

---

[3] MacArthur, 1124.

[4] Alfred Plummer, *An Exegetical Commentary on the Gospel According to St. Matthew* (London: Robert Scott Roxburghe House, 1909), 149.

> Then Jesus came near and said to them, "All authority has been given to Me in heaven and on earth. Go, therefore, and make disciples of all nations, baptizing them in the name of the Father and of the Son and of the Holy Spirit, teaching them to observe everything I have commanded you. And remember, I am with you always, to the end of the age."

It feels like Jesus changed the game plan, but still with all authority. The ambassadors of the *King* were given a new assignment with a larger scope: to "make disciples of *all* nations." Zechariah 12:10 says:

> "Then I will pour out a spirit of grace and prayer on the house of David and the residents of Jerusalem, and they will look at Me whom they pierced. They will mourn for Him as one mourns for an only child and weep bitterly for Him as one weeps for a firstborn."

God promises that Jesus' mission will come full circle, and that, while the Jewish people refused the gospel, eventually they will realize what they've rejected.

In verse 8, Jesus told the disciples that they were to heal the sick, raise the dead, and drive out demons, free of charge. They were not even carrying coins or their money belts. Luke 22:36 seems to contradict this: "Then He said to them, 'But now, whoever has a money-bag should take it, and also a traveling bag. And whoever doesn't have a sword should sell his robe and buy one.'" This difference was the audience. *Nelson's Commentary* explains the difference:

> The disciples' mission was short-term. In essence, they were to do a national religious survey to determine the people's response to Jesus as Messiah. For the 12 disciples to cover an area that is at most 75 miles by 125 miles would not take very long. Thus, they did not need extensive provisions.[5]

For Luke 22:36, Jesus sent out men for longer journeys that took them outside of areas of their own people. In these areas, they could not be assured of help as they journeyed.

---

[5] Earl D. Radmacher, Ronald B. Allen, and H. Wayne House, eds., *Nelson's New Illustrated Bible Commentary* (Nashville: Thomas Nelson, 1999), 1159.

Matthew records that for those on this journey who were not treated well, made to feel unwelcome, or shown a refusal to listen, they were to "shake the dust off [their] feet" as they left the house or town (vv. 13–14).

Wiersbe says that our message today is no longer that the kingdom of heaven is near, but rather that Jesus died for our sins.[6] From chapter 10 until chapter 28 in Matthew, the message was "the kingdom of heaven is at hand." But, in Matthew 28, there's a shift as the focus is turning to all people in all nations.

Closing

There's so much more in Matthew 10. We just scratched the surface. But the takeaway from this chapter is that we all have a job to do as His ambassadors. And, there will be a day when Christians will see something absolutely incredible—the Jewish people will turn to the Messiah.

Daily Word

As Jesus commissioned the disciples with authority, He said to them three times: Don't be afraid.

Today, as you go about your own day, as you live your life for Christ, guess what remains the same? Don't be afraid. Jesus will give you words to speak when you think you have nothing to say. Jesus will share everything with you and nothing will be hidden. Jesus is more powerful than anything or anyone. Jesus knows every hair on your head, and you are worth more than a sparrow, who Jesus also cared for. He loves you, child of God! So today, don't be afraid. You have all authority from Jesus because it has been given to you. Walk on and do not fear.

But even the hairs of your head have all been counted. So, don't be afraid therefore; you are worth more than many sparrows. —Matthew 10:30–31

Further Scripture: Isaiah 41:10; Psalm 56:3; 2 Timothy 1:7

Questions

1. What is the difference between a "disciple" and an "apostle"? Do you consider yourself to be one or the other or both? Why or why not?

2. What people group are the 12 disciples being sent to? Who are they *not* being sent to (Matthew 10:5–6; 15:24)? How is this different than Matthew 28:18–20?

---

[6] Warren W. Wiersbe, *The Bible Exposition Commentary: Matthew—Galatians* (Colorado Springs: David C. Cook, 1989), 37.

3. What are the specific things that Jesus instructed the 12 to do as they were sent out in Matthew 10:6–8? Are these things still applicable to you today? Have you witnessed any of these things happening in your lifetime?

4. In Matthew 10:34, Jesus said, "I did not come to bring peace, but a sword." What is the sword? How does this statement differ from Jesus' statements about peace in John 14:27 and John 16:33?

5. What does it mean to turn family member against family member in Matthew 10:35–36? (Micah 7:6; Matthew 10:37–39)

6. What did the Holy Spirit highlight to you in Matthew 10 through the reading or the teaching?

Lesson 11: Matthew 11
King: Was John the Baptist the Second Elijah?

Teaching Notes

Intro

The one word we're using for the Book of Matthew is *King*. Yesterday, in Matthew 10, Jesus charged His 12 apostles with a mission to take His message to the lost sheep of Israel, as well as to cast out demons and heal the sick.

Teaching

Matthew 11:1–3: As the disciples left to do what Jesus had assigned them to do, He also left to teach through the towns of Israel (v. 1). Everyone was on a mission at this time. John the Baptist, who was in prison, heard somehow what Jesus was doing. John the Baptist was put into prison for the accusations he had made against Herod and his wife (Luke 3:19–29). After Jesus heard about John's arrest, He left for Galilee (Matthew 4:12).

John the Baptist had a specific image in his mind of who Jesus was because his whole life had been dedicated to preparing for Jesus' coming. But as he sat in prison, he sent a message by his (John's) disciples to Jesus, asking for confirmation that Jesus was the One he had announced was coming, or was there someone else (v. 3). Why did John need this confirmation of Jesus' identity?

1. Jesus was in Galilee, not Jerusalem where a new king would have ushered in the kingdom.
2. John was confused. In Matthew 3:11–12, John recognized that he was unworthy to even touch Jesus' sandals.

But he expected Jesus to come with fire (Matthew 3:12), with authority and power. There's a lot of evidence that the Messiah was expected in Jerusalem:

> Psalm 118:26: "He who comes in the name of the Lord is blessed. From the house of the Lord we bless you."

> Mark 11:9b–10: "Hosanna! He who comes in the name of the Lord is the blessed One! The coming kingdom of our father David is blessed! Hosanna in the highest heaven!"
>
> Hebrews 10:37: "For yet in a very little while, the Coming One will come and not delay."

John was not confused because of a lack of faith but because what he expected was not taking place when he expected it.

Matthew 11:4–6: Jesus answered John's question by telling John's disciples to report to him what they had heard and seen of Jesus' work: "the blind see, the lame walk, those with skin diseases are healed, the deaf hear, the dead are raised, and the poor are told the good news" (v. 5). Jesus was going to gather witnesses and perform miracles so that John could be assured of Jesus' role as the Messiah.

> Isaiah 29:18–19: "On that day the deaf will hear the words of a document, and out of a deep darkness the eyes of the blind will see. The humble will have joy after joy in the Lord, and the poor people will rejoice in the Holy One of Israel."

This is a prophetic word from Isaiah about the Messiah, and Jesus was already walking out this prophecy. These are words that John the Baptist would have known, so Jesus performed all of these to make sure John understood the message. Isaiah 35:5–8 is an additional prophecy about the Messiah to come.

Matthew 11:7–10: As John's disciples left, Jesus began to preach to the crowd around Him. Jesus asked the crowd what had drawn them to the wilderness to hear John preach. Possibly, He made fun of the "soft clothes" working in palaces. Jesus emphasized that John was a prophet and more. Jesus then quoted Malachi 3:1 to point to John as the one who had come to prepare the way for Him. John the Baptist had fulfilled his responsibility to prepare the people for Jesus' coming.

Matthew 11:11–15: Jesus stated that no one was greater than John, but that "the least in the kingdom of heaven is greater than he" (v. 11). MacArthur says that "John was greater than the [Old Testament] prophets because he actually saw with his eyes and personally participated in the fulfillment of what they only prophesied."[1] Malachi prophesied that one was to come—John the Baptist. Now, we're in the kingdom of God and we can experience the prophetic word from the past, which makes us greater than John the Baptist. The lowest of the low ("the least") is now greater than John the Baptist.

---

[1] John MacArthur, *The MacArthur Bible Commentary* (Nashville: Thomas Nelson, 2005), 1143.

Verse 12b states, "The kingdom of heaven has been suffering violence, and the violent have been seizing it by force." MacArthur shares that John the Baptist, as a prophet crying out from the wilderness, aroused strong reactions from people.[2] John's message that the kingdom of heaven was near was met with such violence that John's beheading was requested by Herod's step-daughter as a birthday present (Matthew 14:6–12). This graphic description shows the tension between the prophets who were not backing down from their message of the One, Jesus, who was to come, and the enemy who would not back down either. And this will continue until the kingdom is actually ushered in. I will tell you that scholars have many different views on this; I've only presented one, so you're welcome to continue to dig into this.

Verses 13–14 state that "all the prophets and the Law prophesied until John; if you're willing to accept it, he is the Elijah who is to come." There is no verse so clear that, if the Jews would accept the message that the kingdom of heaven is near, the kingdom would start. All the Jewish people had to do was simply say "Yes!" If they receive the message, then John becomes the prophetic fulfillment of the "second Elijah" prophecy. So, the question is, Was John the Baptist the prophetic fulfillment of Elijah?

MacArthur provides this biblical evidence that John the Baptist is this fulfillment: Malachi 4:5–6; Matthew 11:14; 16:14; 17:3, 9; 27:47–49; Mark 8:28; 9:4; Luke 1:17; 9:28; John 1:21.[3] In Isaiah 40:3, John the Baptist proclaimed what his role was and, based on this evidence, MacArthur suggests that:

1. John the Baptist came in the "'spirit and power of Elijah,' and would have fulfilled prophecies, if they had believed."[4]
2. John partially fulfilled Malachi 4:5–6.
3. Malachi 4:5–6 will be fulfilled literally when the Jews embrace the message of the kingdom of God.

When that will happen, I don't know, but I hope I'll be alive to see it. Matthew 11:16 focuses on the Jews' rejection of Jesus as the Messiah.

Closing

That's a lot about John the Baptist as we cover Matthew 11, but my prayer is that some of this, at least a nugget, is new to you, and that all these pieces come together to paint a complete picture of the Messiah.

---

[2] MacArthur, 1144.

[3] MacArthur, 1144.

[4] MacArthur, 1226 (Mk 9:13).

Daily Word

In Jesus' prayer to His Father, the Lord of heaven and earth, He shared that truths are revealed to infants, not the wise and the learned. The Greek word for *infants* is literally, *babies*. Using the word for *babies*, Jesus meant humble and sincere. Therefore Jesus was saying humble and sincere seekers would know and find the truth.

You see, you don't need to be at the top of your class intellectually or even proud of how much knowledge you have. Rather, Jesus longs for you to come to Him willing to receive all He has for you. He reveals Himself to the person with the heart of a child, walking in humility and sincerely hungry for truth. As you approach Jesus in humility, He says the kingdom of heaven will be yours. Let go of feeling as though you need to have it all together, and instead, come as you are.

At that time Jesus said, "I praise You, Father, Lord of heaven and earth, because You have hidden these things from the wise and learned and revealed them to infants." —Matthew 11:25

Further Scripture: Matthew 5:3; Matthew 18:4; Mark 10:15

Questions

1. How and why is John the Baptist compared to Elijah in Matthew 11:14 (Matthew 17:10–13; Luke 1:17; John 1:21)? How do you think Malachi 4:5 ties together with Matthew 11:14—was John the Baptist fulfilling that prophecy, or is there still someone to come?

2. What does the phrase "whoever has ears, let them hear" mean (Matthew 11:15)? What happens if someone doesn't have these "ears"? Do you consider yourself to have the "ears" mentioned in this verse?

3. Why was John the Baptist uncertain about Jesus' identity in Matthew 11:1–6 when he had already been with Jesus (John 1:29–36)?

4. How is Matthew 11:5 a fulfillment of Isaiah 29:18–19; 35:5–6; 61:1–2?

5. What do you learn about Jesus from His words in Matthew 11:25–30? What truth about Jesus would you like to penetrate your heart today?

6. What did the Holy Spirit highlight to you in Matthew 11 through the reading or the teaching?

Lesson 12: Matthew 12
King: John the Baptist's Questions for Jesus

Teaching Notes

Intro

Yesterday, we looked at John the Baptist and the question of whether he was Elijah. In Matthew 11:14, we discovered that if the Jews had accepted the message that the kingdom of heaven was near, John would have become the prophetic fulfillment of the "second Elijah" prophecy. From Matthew 10 through chapter 28, the Jews continue to reject *King* Jesus. We're going to start in the middle of Matthew 12. Jesus is having constant interactions with the religious. He is talking about being the Lord of the Sabbath, about healing a man with a paralyzed hand, about serving as a Servant of the Lord, and about a house divided. We'll start in verse 38 and study the sign of Jonah.

Teaching

Matthew 12:38: In verse 38, some of the scribes and Pharisees asked for a sign from Jesus. It was a set-up. Stanley Toussaint states that, "Although their rejection of Him is certain, the scribes and Pharisees approach the *King* and in antagonistic unbelief seek a sign from Him."[1] The Jews did not believe that anyone could produce a sign at that time. MacArthur states that they wanted "a miracle on a cosmic scale."[2] Additional Scriptures on the request for signs are Luke 11:16 and 1 Corinthians 1:22. Unbelievers seek signs for signs' sake; believers seek signs for authentication. God at times granted signs for His people in the past, but He did it to strengthen their weak faith. Abraham, Joshua, Gideon . . . all needed signs for affirmation.

Matthew 12:39: Jesus answered their request by explaining that "an evil and adulterous generation demands a sign, but no sign will be given to them except the sign of the prophet Jonah." In the Pentateuch, our mind goes to how the Israelites constantly committed spiritual adultery (Isaiah 57:3–8; Jeremiah 3:10;

---

[1] Stanley D. Toussaint, *Behold the King: A Study of Matthew* (Grand Rapids: Kregel, 2005), 165.

[2] John MacArthur, *The MacArthur Bible Commentary* (Nashville: Thomas Nelson, 2005), 1164.

Hosea 7:13–16). Instead of giving them a miraculous sign, Jesus gave them the sign of Jonah.

Matthew 12:40: Jonah spent three days and three nights in the belly of the whale. Douglas O'Donnell explained that it's important to understand how the ancient Jews figured time: "A new day began after sunset (not at midnight), and part of a day was often counted as a whole day"[3] (Genesis 40; 1 Kings 20).

Jonah 2:3 references being in "the heart of the seas," and Psalm 46:2 talks about "the depths of the seas." Jesus said he would be in "the heart of the earth," referencing His own death and burial (Matthew 12:40). One of the problems is that while the Jews believed that Jesus really died (Luke 24:18–20), they didn't believe He came back to life.

Matthew 12:41: Jonah did not stay in the belly of the whale. If he had, the people of Nineveh would never have had the chance to hear his message and repent. Jonah had to "come back from the belly of the whale" in order for the Ninevites to repent. Jesus had to "come back from the belly of the earth to life" so we could have repentance. Jesus said that the men of Nineveh will stand in judgment of the Jews ("this generation") because they said, "Yes," to the message from Jonah (Jonah 3:5–10), when the Jews said, "No" to Jesus. Some would say that the message wasn't the same in both instances, because one generation later, the Ninevites went back to their former ways (Nahum 3:7–8).

Yesterday, we talked about John the Baptist being greater than the Old Testament prophets because he was walking out the fulfillment of their words. Even the least of those in the kingdom of heaven, however, are greater than John the Baptist, because we are walking out the prophetic word that he released.

So, why is Jesus greater than Jonah? Wiersbe states:

> He is greater in His person, for Jonah was a mere man. He was greater in His obedience, for Jonah disobeyed God . . . Jesus actually died, while Jonah's 'grave' was in the belly of the great fish. Jesus arose from the dead under His own power. Jonah ministered only to one city, while Jesus gave His life for the whole world. Certainly, Jesus was greater in His love, for Jonah did not love the people of Nineveh—he wanted them to die. Jonah's message saved Nineveh from judgment; he was a messenger of the wrath of God. Jesus' message was that of grace and salvation.[4]

---

[3] Douglas O'Donnell, *Matthew: All Authority in Heaven and on Earth* (Wheaton, IL: Crossway, 2013), 339.

[4] Warren W. Wiersbe, *The Bible Exposition Commentary: Matthew—Galatians* (Colorado Springs: David C. Cook, 1989), 43.

Matthew 12:42: "The queen of the south" was the Queen of Sheba, located at what the Israelites thought was the end of the world (Jeremiah 6:20). She came to hear the wisdom of Solomon and turned to God (1 Kings 10:1–10). Gentiles (Ninevites and the Queen of Sheba) were responding, but the Jews were not. Jesus told the Jews that He was greater than Solomon as well as Jonah. How was Jesus greater than Solomon? He was "greater in wisdom, wealth, and works."[5] "Jesus' kingdom offers much more than all of Solomon's glory. And, to sit at Christ's table and hear His words, and to share His blessings, is much more satisfying than to visit and admire the most spectacular kingdom, even that of Solomon."[6]

Jesus gave them biblical signs . . . through Jonah, through the Ninevites, through Solomon, and through the Queen of Sheba. And the Jews didn't want it. Because the Jews rejected the sign, we received God's blessing. One day, they will see Zechariah 12:10 come to fruition.

Closing

If you're trying to make a decision today, and you're asking for more signs, don't ask for signs to test Jesus. Only ask for a sign of affirmation for the next step.

Daily Word

As Jesus referenced the Pharisees' evil words, He gave the illustration of a tree being known by its fruit. He explained that a bad tree produces bad fruit, just as a good tree produces good fruit. The Pharisees spoke evil words about Jesus, which revealed the nature of their hearts.

It is important to remember the Lord is interested in your heart above all else, because what comes out of your mouth is an overflow of your heart. If the words of your mouth hurt others or are displeasing to the Lord, it may be time to do a heart check. What are you filling your heart with? When you fill your heart with things from the Lord, like truth from His Word, it will transform you. Set your heart daily on the Lord, and watch transformation take place in the words that come out of your mouth.

For the mouth speaks from the overflow of the heart. —Matthew 12:34

Further Scripture: Luke 6:45; Romans 12:2; Ephesians 3:16–17a

---

[5] Wiersbe, 44.

[6] Wiersbe, 44.

Questions

1. The Pharisees pointed out to Jesus that His disciples were breaking the law in Matthew 12:2. What law were they supposedly breaking? (Exodus 20:8)

2. In Matthew 12:7, Jesus quoted from Hosea 6:6 and said that if they had understood this verse, they would not have condemned the innocent. What did He mean by this? (Micah 6:6–8)

3. It is revealed in Matthew 12:10 that the Pharisees tried to set Jesus up so they could accuse Him. What was their motivation? How did this "trap" turn out?

4. What "sign" did Jesus say will be given, when asked for a sign by the scribes and Pharisees (Matthew 12:40)? Under the New Covenant, should we be asking God for signs?

5. According to Matthew 12:42, what did the Queen of Sheba come from the ends of the earth to hear (1 Kings 10:1–6)? Who is greater than Solomon? (Colossians 2:2b–3)

6. Who did Jesus say His mother and brothers were in Matthew 12:48–50? Does this give you confidence in who you are in Christ?

7. What did the Holy Spirit highlight to you in Matthew 12 through the reading or the teaching?

Lesson 13: Matthew 13
King: The Secrets of Parables

Teaching Notes

Intro

In the past few weeks, we've looked at *King* Jesus, and how the Jews continued to reject Him. While Matthew 13 is loaded with parables, today we're going to focus on how Jesus talked between these parables.

Teaching

Matthew 13:1–3: Verses like these show us how human Jesus was—sitting by the sea. Such a crowd surrounded Him that He got into a boat and taught those on the shore using parables. We're going to talk about parables today. What is a parable? Why are we talking about parables? Are they even necessary in the future?

Stanley Toussant says, "a parable is the act of placing one thing beside another so a comparison can be made between them."[1] *Nelson's Commentary* explains that a parable "utilized common scenes from everyday life to teach new truths about the kingdom."[2] Jesus told parables in such a way that some people grasped what He was saying, and others didn't have a clue.

Matthew 13:10–18: From this point on, Jesus only communicated with the crowds using parables (v. 34). The disciples asked Jesus why He was using parables (v. 10). Jesus replied that there were secrets that were given for the disciples to know "but it has not been given to them" (v. 11). The "them" could have been the Jews or those in the crowd. MacArthur said, "Jesus uses them to obscure the truth from unbelievers while making it clearer to His disciples."[3] To understand is to have been given a gift through the Holy Spirit. Because the Jews rejected the message, others are given a gift which is placed sovereignly on the elect. God is choosing who understands the parable, and who does not.

---

[1] Stanley Toussant, *Behold the King: A Study of Matthew* (Portland: Multnomah, 1980), 169.

[2] Earl D. Radmacher, Ronald B. Allen, and H. Wayne House, eds., *Nelson's New Illustrated Bible Commentary* (Nashville: Thomas Nelson, 1999), 1164.

[3] John MacArthur, *The MacArthur Bible Commentary* (Nashville: Thomas Nelson, 2005), 1147.

Why is this important? John the Baptist came to deliver the Word and the Jews rejected it. John finally found people who would receive the message. The word translated as "secrets" can also be translated as "mysteries." MacArthur explains, "'Mysteries' are those truths which have been hidden from all ages in the past and revealed in the New Testament."[4] Matthew 13:11 talks about the secrets that have been given to the disciples but not others.

In Luke 8:10, Jesus said: "The secrets of the kingdom of God have been given for you to know, but to the rest it is in parables, so that 'Looking they may not see, and hearing they may not understand.'" That fulfills the prophecy in Isaiah 6:9, "And He replied: Go! Say to these people: Keep listening, but do not understand; keep looking, but do not perceive."

Romans 11:25 explains specifically why the Jews do not receive the message, even today: "So that you will not be conceited, brothers, I do not want you to be unaware of this mystery: A *partial hardening* has come to Israel until the full number of the Gentiles has come in." This means that the Jews have had a hardening of their hearts so the message can come to the full number of Gentiles. This means that we have to understand this, but the Jews won't have any idea what this is all about. This partial hardening means that of the 8 million Jews in Israel, part of them (maybe 4 million) understand and the others do not and will stay that way until God's predetermined number of Gentiles have embraced the message of salvation.

Romans 16:25–26: "Now to Him who has power to strengthen you according to my gospel and the proclamation about Jesus Christ, according to the revelation of the mystery kept silent for long ages but now revealed and made known through the prophetic Scriptures, according to the command of the eternal God to advance the obedience of faith among all nations." There was a mystery that had been kept secret for a long time, but according to verse 26, it has now been made known through the prophetic Scriptures. For example, we know from the prophetic word that Jesus is going to return to the Mount of Olives, and that when His feet land there, the Mount of Olives will split. But we haven't seen that fulfilled. It's still a mystery. Same for the Jewish people who know that the Messiah is going to come, but they haven't been able to see that He is in front of them.

1 Corinthians 2:7 says, "On the contrary, we speak God's hidden wisdom in a mystery, a wisdom God predestined before the ages for our glory." When we release God's truth, it's not up to others to see if they respond. That's up to God's predetermined plan whether they will understand the message or not.

1 Corinthians 4:1: "A person should consider us in this way: as servants of Christ and managers of God's mysteries." Managing these mysteries as believers

---

[4] MacArthur, 1148.

means to know these well enough so that, for any mystery, we can explain it, experience it, and walk it out.

Ephesians 6:19: "Pray also for me, that the message may be given to me when I open my mouth to make known with boldness the *mystery* of the gospel." That means being able to explain with *boldness* that everyone sins, that sin leads to death, love comes in and can take away the sin. Through the death, Jesus' death on the cross, they can receive life.

In verse 12, Jesus explained that whoever has this knowledge, even more will be given. But, for those who do not have this knowledge, even more can be taken away. For this reason, Jesus uses prophecies. Isaiah's prophecy in Isaiah 6:9–10 is fulfilled through Jesus' teachings.

Matthew 13:34–35: Jesus told the crowds that He would only use parables to speak to them. This fulfilled the prophecy of the prophet Asaph who wrote Psalm 78:2: "I will declare wise sayings; I will speak mysteries from the past."

Matthew 13:44–46: The message throughout Matthew has been the constant rejection of Jesus by the Jews. In this parable, "treasure" is the first common object. The treasure was buried in a field, found, and reburied. The man who found the treasure sold everything he had to be able to buy the field in which the treasure was buried. For a Gentile, the treasure would represent Jesus and He is our salvation. But, since the Gentiles didn't have to earn their salvation, maybe the treasure was Israel and the Jews, who will one day accept Jesus' salvation (Exodus 19:5; Psalm 135:4). Maybe Jesus was communicating with the Jews that they were His special treasure and that He was already giving up everything for them.

Closing

In this context, I believe that Jesus was using parables to say, "You are My special people." Ask yourself: Are you a good steward and manager of these mysteries? And, can you communicate these mysteries clearly to others?

Daily Word

Jesus shared seven parables referring to the mystery of the kingdom of heaven. For believers, the kingdom of heaven is a treasure. Even if you sell everything you have and all that remains is this one treasure, the kingdom of heaven, it is enough. Christ's saving grace, redeeming power, righteousness, peace, joy, and eternity with Him are worth letting go of everything else.

Are you still hanging on to something that is preventing you from experiencing all of the kingdom of heaven? Ask the Lord to purge your heart today so you can freely enjoy all the kingdom of heaven has to offer. Let go of anything hindering you. Just let go. When you seek Jesus with all your heart, He will be found.

The kingdom of heaven is like treasure, buried in a field, that a man found and reburied. Then in his joy he goes and sells everything he has and buys that field. —Matthew 13:44

Further Scripture: Jeremiah 29:13–14; Matthew 6:33; Romans 14:17–19

Questions

1. What is a parable? What subject was Jesus speaking to the people about through the parables in Matthew 13? Why did He use parables (Ezekiel 12:2; Matthew 13:13)?

2. When reflecting on the parable of the sower in Matthew 13:3–8, have you experienced sowing "seed" in these different types of soil? When reading Jesus' explanation of the parable (vv. 18–23), how can you prepare your heart and mind to be the right kind of soil to bear fruit?

3. When you read the parable in Matthew 13:44, do you experience this kind of joy in your relationship with Christ? Do you think you've "sold all that you have" to embrace the kingdom of heaven?

4. When Jesus came to his hometown, they took offense at Him (Matthew 13:57). Do you find it difficult to share the gospel with those you knew or grew up with before coming to Christ? Do you find that those closest to you are less willing to hear what you have to say about the gospel message?

5. What did the Holy Spirit highlight to you in Matthew 13 through the reading or the teaching?

Lesson 14: Matthew 14
King: Walking on Water

Teaching Notes

Intro

When we look for *King* Jesus in this chapter, it's a little hard. The first section of the chapter covers John the Baptist's beheading, with the final verse recording that his disciples came to Jesus to tell Him what had happened (Matthew 14:1–12). It's like the end of an era. Then, the account of the miraculous feeding of 5,000 men is given (vv. 13–21). This was one of many of Jesus' profound miracles that is recorded.

Teaching

Matthew 14:22: After experiencing food multiplying, the disciples must have been excited for what they had seen Jesus do. Immediately after this miracle, Jesus "made the disciples get into the boat and go ahead of Him to the other side" (v. 22). Wiersbe gives an outline of 5 statements of how Jesus interacted with His disciples in the context of walking on the water.[1] Wiersbe's *Statement 1: "He brought me here."* God put us in this position. The obvious takeaway here is that when *King* Jesus puts us in a situation, we cannot expect smooth sailing (John 16:33). Jesus is constantly refining us to test us to look more like Him. Wiersbe says there are two kinds of storms that we could engage in—"storms of correction, when God disciplines, and storms of perfection, when God helps us grow."[2]

Matthew 14:23–24: Wiersbe's *Statement 2: "He is praying for me"* (Mark 6:48; Romans 8:34). Jesus knew their situation in the storm, and He interceded for them as He prayed on the mountain alone. The disciples were "over a mile from shore, battered by the waves" (v. 24).

---

[1] Warren W. Wiersbe, *The Bible Exposition Commentary* (Colorado Springs: David C. Cook, 1989), 51–52. (All five statements provided are from these pages.)

[2] Wiersbe, 51.

Matthew 14:25: Wiersbe's *Statement 3: "He will come to me."* About 3 in the morning, Jesus came walking to where the disciples were. Jesus will show up in our lives when we need Him. Since He's already been praying for us, He'll walk in knowing everything that is needed (2 Corinthians 1:8). Jesus will be our strength when we have nothing (Isaiah 43:2). Jesus will come at the right time. We have to receive Him.

Matthew 14:26–27: The disciples were terrified when they saw Jesus approach and thought He was a ghost (v. 26). Wiersbe's *Statement 4: "He will help me grow."* Jesus responded, "Have courage! It is I. Don't be afraid" (v. 27).

Matthew 14:28–31: Peter immediately said to Jesus, "Tell me to come to You" (v. 27). Jesus told him to come (v. 28). Wiersbe's *Statement 5: "He will see me through."* When Peter became overwhelmed with what he was doing, he started to sink and cried out to Jesus for help. Jesus immediately grabbed Peter's hand and asked, "You of little faith, why did you doubt" (vv. 29–31)?

Matthew 14:32–33: When Jesus and Peter climbed in the boat, the winds ceased, and "those in the boat worshiped Him and said, 'Truly You are the Son of God!'" The disciples worshiped Him, because they saw that He had come to them during this time. Maybe, they recognized the whole process unfolding.

Matthew 14:34–36: They landed at Gennesaret. The men there recognized Jesus and brought all the sick to Him. "They were begging Him that they might only touch the tassel on His robe. And as many as touched it were perfectly well" (v. 36).

Leon Morris suggests several lessons can be learned from this[3]:

1. If you follow Christ's commands (get in the boat), it doesn't mean you'll avoid the storms. In fact, in verse 24, the disciples were a long way from land, so they couldn't go back, and the wind was against them. They had to depend upon Jesus to carry them through.
2. Jesus knows the trouble (emotional, physical, spiritual), and because of that He knows how to rescue us.

Closing

Where is *King* Jesus in all of this? He's in charge. The minute we try to take care of ourselves, we refuse to allow *King* Jesus to be in charge and take care of us.

---

[3] Leon Morris, *The Gospel According to John*, rev. ed., The New International Commentary on the New Testament (Grand Rapids: Eerdmans, 1995).

Daily Word

The story of Jesus walking on water in the middle of a storm and calling out to Peter to join Him powerfully illustrates Jesus as King. Jesus had control and authority, even over the wind and the waves. As the storms began, Jesus was praying alone on the mountain. However, just when the disciples needed help, Jesus appeared to them walking on the water, telling them to take courage and not be afraid. Jesus reached out his hand to Peter and said to him, "You of little faith, why did you doubt?"

Just like the disciples, you will find yourself in the middle of a storm in life. Maybe even today, the winds of your storm are swirling around you. Jesus promises He is interceding for you. He will reach out His hand to help you. Today, take courage. Have the faith to walk out of the boat, trusting the Lord will be with you and will help you. Do not walk in doubt. Grab hold of the hand of Jesus and confidently walk in faith that He is with you!

Immediately, Jesus reached out His hand, caught hold of him, and said to him, "You of little faith, why did you doubt?" When they got into the boat, the wind ceased. —Matthew 14:31–32

Further Scripture: Isaiah 43:2; 2 Corinthians 1:8; 1 Timothy 6:15

Questions

1. In Matthew 14:1–12, why was John the Baptist beheaded? Do you think that John lived and died in vain? Why do you think that Jesus did not save him?

2. In Matthew 14:14, Jesus had compassion toward the group and healed their sick. What were the circumstances that caused Jesus to feel this way? Have you faced something and felt Jesus' compassion in your life?

3. Jesus fed the multitude of 5,000+ men, not counting women and children. Do you believe Jesus only wanted to give them physical food? Spiritual food? Why or why not? (Matthew 14:16–21)

4. There are rough patches in our lives called storms. In the storm of Matthew 14:24, Jesus was walking towards them. At one point, Jesus got in the boat and the storm calmed. Can you think of a time in your life where Jesus calmed you or your storm?

5. What did the Holy Spirit highlight to you in Matthew 14 through the reading or the teaching?

Lesson 15: Matthew 15
King: Interacting with Hypocrites

Teaching Notes

Intro

For the past 14 chapters, we've been talking about the Jews' rejection of Jesus as the *King*. Jesus sent His 12 disciples on a short mission trip around Israel, to go after the lost sheep of Israel (the Jews). In Matthew 14, there was a little break from the issues with the Jews. Jesus walked on the water to rescue His disciples from a storm, showing that He is always with us and knows our needs. In Matthew 15, we're back to arguing with the Jews.

Teaching

Matthew 15:7–9: In verses 1–6, Jesus was again interacting with the religious leaders. Jesus called them out on their teachings, and then called them hypocrites (v. 7). The leaders asked questions they knew Jesus wouldn't answer like they wanted. It was an ongoing set-up. Jesus got to the heart of their actions, saying: "These people honor Me with their lips, but their heart is far from Me . . . teaching as doctrines the commands of men" (vv. 8, 9b).

Matthew 15:10–11: We started this study in verse 7 to show how intense Jesus' rebuke of the religious leaders was. Then, He called the crowd together and told them to "Listen and understand: It's not what goes into the mouth that defiles a man, but what comes out of the mouth, this defiles a man" (vv. 10–11). The Pentateuch was all about clean and unclean food. But, with these words, Jesus confronted their religious belief, saying that it doesn't matter anymore what is eaten, because all food is clean (Mark 7:19; Acts 10:15).

MacArthur explains that "people might defile themselves ceremonially (under the old covenant) by eating something unclean, but they would defile themselves morally by saying something sinful."[1] This means we're more concerned about what we put in our mouths for food than we are about what comes out of our mouths (James 3:6).

---

[1] John MacArthur, *The MacArthur Bible Commentary* (Nashville: Thomas Nelson, 2005), 1153.

If anyone says that hell does not exist, then why would they need Jesus? Jesus came to save us from our sin and our death. You cannot say that hell no longer exists, then thank Jesus for dying on the cross for our sins. Hell sets the standard for so much, and if you're not careful, it will come straight out of your mouth.

Matthew 15:12–13: The disciples told Jesus that the Pharisees had taken offense at His words (v. 12). Jesus responded, "Every plant that My heavenly Father didn't plant will be uprooted" (v. 13).

Matthew 13:24–30 actually talks about this teaching through the Parable of the Wheat and the Weeds. It states that God clearly does plant things (Psalm 1:3; Isaiah 60:21). It also states that there are other things God does not plant.

Remember Matthew 13:34–36 when Jesus only spoke to the crowds in parables? In verse 36, the disciples asked Jesus to explain the Parable of the Wheat and the Weeds to them. Jesus explained these things:

- The sower of the good seed is the Son of Man (v. 37).
- The field is the world (v. 38).
- The good seed is the sons of the kingdom (v. 38).
- The weeds are the sons of the evil one (v. 38).
- The enemy who sowed the weeds is the Devil (v. 39).
- The harvest is the end of the age (v. 39).
- The harvesters are the angels (v. 39).

The weeds are gathered and burned at the end of the age. The angels will gather everything that causes sin and throw them into the blazing furnace. With this background, go back to Matthew 15.

Matthew 15:14: In the Parable about the Wheat and the Weeds, Jesus said to leave the weeds alone because they will be destroyed in the end. Jesus said the same thing in verse 14. Leaving them alone was the worst thing that could happen to them because it signaled abandonment by God.[2]

Matthew 15:15–16: Once again, Peter asked Jesus for an explanation of the parable. And, once again, Jesus questioned that they still lacked understanding.

Matthew 15:17–18: Here's the quote of all quotes from J. A. Bengel, an 18th-century scholar: "The filth of the draught [toilet] is not so great as is that of a human

---

[2] MacArthur, 1153.

heart not yet cleansed."[3] It relates to this verse. The filth in the toilet is disgusting, and yet it is nothing compared to things that can come out of the mouth (Psalm 119:11). What you put in your heart will come out (Psalm 101:3).

Matthew 15:19–20: From the heart can come all kinds of evil thoughts and actions. Jesus said these evils things are what defile a man, not eating with unwashed hands.

The question that comes from this is how do we work on our hearts? If we're taking care of our hearts, none of these things will be a problem. Douglas Shawn O'Donnell has what he calls the Parable of the Mouth, with nine things we can work on to take care of our hearts:

1. A broken and contrite heart (Psalm 51:17)
2. A circumcised heart (Romans 2:29)
3. A clean heart (Hebrews 10:22)
4. A pure heart (1 Peter 2:2)
5. A new heart (Ezekiel 36:26)
6. A sincere heart (Ephesian 6:5)
7. An obedient heart (Deuteronomy 11:13)
8. Believe from the heart (Ephesians 3:17)
9. That Christ dwells in the heart (Ephesians 3:17)

Closing

Our prayer is that the Messiah will dwell in your hearts. When that happens, all the things we've listed will flow from your heart.

Daily Word

As Jesus withdrew to the area of Tyre and Sidon, a Canaanite woman cried out, asking Jesus to heal her demon-possessed daughter. This mother was in great distress and had been walking through a terrible trial, and yet she found hope in Jesus. Jesus responded slowly in His answer to this unlikely candidate for healing. She was a Gentile and a pagan enemy of Israel. Even so, she humbly knelt before Jesus with strong faith that He could heal her daughter and pleaded with Him to help. Jesus saw her faith, saw her belief in Him, and restored her daughter.

---

[3] J. A. Bengel, *Gnomon of the New Testament*, vol. 1 (Eugene, OR: Wipf and Stock, 2016), 308; available at www.biblehub.com/commentaries/matthew/15-19.htm.

As you face trials in life and find yourself in distress, humbly come before Jesus. Don't assume you aren't a likely candidate or good enough for Jesus to help. He loves all people. Jesus may have a different time frame from the one you want, but sit before Him, talk with Him, and share your heart with Jesus the Messiah. The process of waiting and humbling yourself brings glory to the Lord. The Lord sees you and knows you. No matter what you face today, keep your faith in Jesus. He is your helper.

But she came, knelt before Him, and said, "Lord, Help me!" —Matthew 15:25

Further Scripture: Matthew 25:23; Hebrews 11:6; 1 Peter 1:7

Questions

1. What do you believe Jesus meant in Matthew 15:8–9? How does this correlate to Isaiah 29:13–14? Will God continue to move despite them? Why or why not?

2. What do you believe Matthew 15:11 means? Why were the Pharisees offended at this? Do you struggle with what comes out of your mouth?

3. In Matthew 15:19, what did Jesus list that comes from the heart? How does this describe verse 18?

4. Jesus refused to speak to the woman from Canaan when she wanted healing for her daughter. Why? In the end, why did He change His mind? Do you think you would chase after Jesus for something you wanted? Why or why not?

5. What did the Holy Spirit highlight to you in Matthew 15 through the reading or the teaching?

Lesson 16: Matthew 16

King: You Are the Christ!

Teaching Notes

Intro

In Matthew 15, Jesus had confronted the religious leaders for giving only lip service to God. In Matthew 16, Jesus addressed His disciples. First, He warned them to "beware of the yeast of the Pharisees and Sadducees" (v. 6). Though the disciples had heard Jesus confront those religious leaders, they didn't make the connection. Instead, they focused on the fact that none of them had brought bread for their next meal.

Teaching

Matthew 16:8–12: Jesus then focused His attention on the disciples by asking them, "You of little faith . . . don't you understand yet?" The disciples should have realized that Jesus wasn't talking about bread. After all, they had watched Jesus turn five loaves into food for 5,000 people and seven loaves into food for 4,000—with bread left over each time. Only when Jesus explained it clearly to them did they understand that He was warning them against the teachings of the Pharisees and Sadducees.

Matthew 16:13–14: Jesus led the disciples into the region of Caesarea Philippi, where He asked them, "Who do people say that the Son of Man is?" The disciples had been walking and teaching among the people, so they knew what the people thought about Jesus. They offered several opinions: John the Baptist, Elijah, Jeremiah, one of the other prophets.

How does American culture describe Jesus today? Muslims might say He was a great prophet. Some religions would say Jesus was an incredible teacher. The media might call Him an incredibly moral man and a great teacher. Others would say He's a great historical figure. But few would say He is the Messiah, because they think that sounds judgmental. But our job is to clearly communicate to the culture who Jesus is. To do this, we each need to decide who we think Jesus is.

Matthew 16:15–16: Then, Jesus asked the disciples a direct question: "Who do you say that I am?" Peter quickly answered, "You are the Messiah, the Son of the living God!" The term "Living God" implied the Old Testament name for God— Jehovah. Deuteronomy 5:26 asked, "For who out of all mankind has heard the voice of the living God speaking from the fire, as we have, and lived?" This living God cares for you. Take a moment to come up with one word to answer the question, "Who is Jesus to you?"

Matthew 16:17: Jesus said that Peter was blessed because God had revealed this truth to him. God can show up anytime in anyone's life and reveal who He is.

Matthew 16:18: Jesus then changed Simon's name to Peter, and said, "On this rock I will build My church, and the forces of Hades will not overpower it." Two similar words are used here: "petros" (Peter's name) means small stone, and "petra" ("this rock") means foundation. The foundation for the Church is Jesus Christ. First Peter 2:6 referred to Jesus as the "stone in Zion, a chosen and honored cornerstone." In Acts 4:11, Peter pointed out the Jews had rejected Jesus, who was indeed the cornerstone. In Ephesians 2:20, Paul explained that the Church was "built on the foundation of the apostles and prophets, with Christ Jesus Himself as the cornerstone." The Church, the "ekklesia" or "called out ones," are mentioned 114 times in the New Testament. The Church probably didn't involve a massive building where everyone gathered. It was about the "called out ones" who came together, took care of each other, then went back out to find the lost sheep.

Matthew 16:19: "I will give you the keys of the kingdom of heaven . . ." Once you have the keys you can lock or unlock something. The keys were a symbol of authority. Jesus gave the apostles authority on earth. What are we binding on earth? We are binding things on earth that aren't of the Lord, things that aren't meant to be free, things that are already bound in heaven. Whatever is loosed in heaven we can loose here on earth. Some examples are described in Matthew 10:8, where Jesus gave the disciples authority to heal people from sickness, raise the dead, free people from skin diseases and drive out demons. Jesus gave them authority to show God's power. Do we limit what we do on earth because we have such a narrow mindset of what heaven is like? (For example, do we say that we can't pray for healing?) May we gain confidence in our authority to do on earth what has been done in heaven.

Matthew 16:20: The disciples were told not to "tell anyone I am the Messiah" because it wasn't time to reveal to the world who Jesus was. He still had to suffer, die, and come back to life before His identity could be revealed.

Matthew 16:21–23: Jesus began to tell His disciples that He would go to Jerusalem and suffer. Jesus became more focused on fulfilling that calling in His life. Peter rebuked Jesus, whom he'd just identified as the Messiah, for saying such things. Nelson's Commentary[1] described Peter as the apostle whose quick actions often got him in over his head, such as trying to walk on the water from the boat to Jesus (Matthew 14:22–32) or promising never to deny Jesus (Matthew 26:35) or refusing to allow Jesus to wash his feet at the Last Supper (John 13:5–11). This time, Jesus turned to Peter and said, "Get behind Me, Satan!" Because Peter was not thinking about God's concerns, but man's. Jesus responded to him as He had to Satan during His temptation (Matthew 4:10).

Matthew 16: 24–26: For those disciples who want to focus on God's concerns, not man's, "must deny himself, take up his cross, and follow Me" (v. 24). To focus completely on Christ, you should be willing to lose your life.

Matthew 16:27–28: Jesus said, "The Son of Man is going to come . . . and then He will reward each according to what He has done." Some will not taste death before they see the Son of Man coming in His kingdom. The question for us is how do we do what Jesus just said? What tangible steps can we take?

Wiersbe said Jesus presented two approaches to life to His disciples:[2]

Deny yourself	or	Live for yourself
Take up your cross	or	Ignore the cross
Follow Christ	or	Follow the world
Lose your life	or	Save your life
Forsake the world	or	Gain the world
Keep your soul	or	Lose your soul
Share His reward and glory	or	Lose His reward and glory

To follow the *King* is hard; it requires perseverance and dealing with persecution. Or we can choose man's way, which is easier and more comfortable but also represents the wide way that leads to destruction. Choosing the narrow way is difficult and costly, but it leads to life.

---

[1] Earl D. Radmacher, Ronald B. Allen, and H. Wayne House, eds., *Nelson's New Illustrated Bible Commentary* (Nashville: Thomas Nelson, 1999), 1172.

[2] Warren Wiersbe, *The Wiersbe Bible Commentary: New Testament* (Colorado Springs: David C. Cook, 2007), 49.

Closing

The gospel is intended for tax collectors and sinners. The gospel is intended for Jews and Gentiles. We don't embrace the new wineskins just for ourselves, but so all have the chance to hear about the Lord and to be set free from the bondage of religion. When you study the Word of God on a regular basis, we believe that your entire community can be changed.

Daily Word

Jesus asked His disciples who people said He was. Since the disciples were out doing ministry, as they had been commissioned to do, they had answers to give to Jesus. Then Jesus looked at His disciples and asked them directly, "But . . . who do you say that I am?" The disciples had left everything and followed Jesus. They witnessed His miracles of healing, restoring, and providing for people. They walked with Him. Peter answered, "You are the Messiah, the Son of the living God."

Today, ask yourself that same question. As you receive Jesus in your own life and walk with Him, who do you say Jesus is? Your answer may change from day to day, depending on your experiences in life. Jesus may be your Savior, your Friend, your Strength, your Help, your Burden-Bearer, your Joy, or your Hope. Today, be ready to bear witness to others. You may be the only witness they have in life. Let your light shine before all men.

"But you," He asked them, "who do you say that I am?" —Matthew 16:15

Further Scripture: John 15:27; Acts 22:15; 1 Peter 3:15

Questions

1. In Matthew 16:1–4, why did Jesus call them an evil and adulterous generation? Have you ever found yourself looking at the signs instead of at Jesus?

2. What is leaven? How does it affect bread? Is bread what Jesus was talking about in Matthew 16:6–12?

3. When Jesus asked Peter, "Who do you say I am," Peter responded that Jesus was the Christ, Son of the living God. Jesus said He would build His church on this rock and hell would not prevail. How do these three verses, Matthew 16:18, Acts 4:11, and Ephesians 2:20, work together to describe this? What was the "rock" Jesus referred to?

4. Why did Peter rebuke Jesus in Matthew 16:22? Why did Jesus say to Peter, "Get thee behind me, Satan"? Jesus then told them to deny themselves, take up their cross and follow Him. How does this verse speak to you?

5. In Matthew 16:25–26, how do you lose your life, yet gain it? How do you think one would lose their soul if they gained the whole world?

6. What did the Holy Spirit highlight to you in Matthew 16 through the reading or the teaching?

Lesson 17: Matthew 17
King: His Transformation Before Men

Teaching Notes

Intro

As a former tax collector, Matthew focused on Jesus' authority and His role as a *King*. In Matthew 17, we can use one word for the entire chapter: *transfiguration—a metamorphosis*, to change or transform into a new form. Jesus did this in front of His disciples on a mountain. Stanley Toussaint defined it as "the confirmation of the reality of a future kingdom."[1] Through the transformation, Jesus showed Himself as He would be in the future, after His death, burial, and resurrection. His change would come in front of those who knew Him best.

Teaching

Matthew 17:1–3: Jesus took His inner circle of disciples up a high mountain: Peter, James, and his brother John (v. 1). Remember that every important occurrence with Jesus seems to happen on a mountain. The transformation possibly took place on Mount Hermon, which stood at 9,400 feet. Jesus' appearance was totally transformed; something radically changed. Wiersbe says the transformation points to four things: "The glory of His Person–His face shone and His physical appearance changed (v. 2); the glory of His kingdom–(vv. 4–5); the glory of His cross–(vv. 8–9); the glory of His submission–(v. 12b)."[2]

In verse 3, Jesus was joined by Moses, who represented the Law, and Elijah, who represented the Prophets. See Matthew 5:17: "Don't assume that I came to destroy the Law or the Prophets. I did not come to destroy but to fulfill." The visual picture of these three together reveals God's approval of Jesus as the fulfillment. Toussaint says that "The presence of the Old Testament saints with Christ in a glorified state is the greatest possible verification of the kingdom principles in the Old Testament."[3]

---

[1] Stanley Toussaint, *Behold the King: A Study of Matthew* (Grand Rapids: Kregel, 1980), 210–11.

[2] Warren W. Wiersbe, *The Bible Exposition Commentary: Matthew–Galatians* (Colorado Springs: David C. Cook, 1989), 60–61.

[3] Toussaint, 210–11.

Matthew 17:4: Peter always seemed to speak the obvious. He offered to build three tents for Jesus, Moses, and Elijah. Probably, Peter also wanted to remain in the presence of the Old Testament saints.

Matthew 17:5: God interrupted Peter while he was still speaking and announced "the glory of His kingdom": "This is My beloved Son. I take delight in Him. Listen to Him!" Matthew 3:17 has the same language at Jesus' baptism. Psalm 2:7 is a messianic prophecy that points to these specific words (Isaiah 42:1). This meeting on the mountain was the climax when Jesus' identity and His future kingdom were confirmed. Everything we've studied has pointed to the Messiah.

Matthew 17:6: When those who had seen this realized they were in the presence of the Lord, they fell down and worshipped God.

Matthew 17:7: The word "glory" means weight. When the Jews are in prayer, they are constantly rocking forward. So possibly, the weight of being in God's presence causes us to lean forward, and even fall down on our knees. Jesus immediately comforted them, saying, "Don't be afraid." They heard the voice of the Lord while on the mountain.

Matthew 17:8–9: When the disciples looked up, both Moses and Elijah were gone. Only Jesus, Peter, James, and John were left. Jesus began to establish "the glory of His cross," as they descended the mountain. Jesus told them not to tell anyone what they had seen until the prophecy had come true—that "the Son of Man is raised from the dead" (v. 9). Five times in Matthew, Jesus warned the disciples not to tell anyone about Him until God's timing was complete: Matthew 8:4; 9:30; 12:16; 16:20; 17:9.

Matthew 17:10–12: The disciples questioned why Elijah would come first (v. 10). Jesus responded that Elijah would still come (Malachi 4:5–6; Matthew 17:11). John the Baptist had brought the words of Elijah and had been rejected, so Elijah was still coming (v.12a). Jesus would take on "the glory of His submission" (v. 12b).

Each of the glories we've discussed—His person, His kingdom, His cross—are dependent upon the final role of submission, which means to cede one's own authority to that of someone else. There could be no future kingdom until Jesus actually gave up His life on the cross. James, the disciple on the mount with Jesus, was the first to die (Acts 12:1–2). John was jailed on the Isle of Patmos and placed in burning oil. He suffered, even though he lived the longest of any of the disciples. Peter suffered in Rome, was crucified upside down, and died. As the statement goes, "In order to experience life, you have to experience death."

Jesus was painting a picture for Peter, James, and John, of what would be required of them. They all gave up their lives for His gospel.

Peter explained the significance of Jesus' transformation with these words: "For we did not follow cleverly contrived myths when we made known to you the power and coming of our Lord Jesus Christ; instead, we were eyewitnesses of His majesty. For when He received honor and glory from God the Father, a voice came to Him from the Majestic Glory: This is My beloved Son. I take delight in Him! And we heard this voice when it came from heaven while we were with Him on the holy mountain. So, we have the prophetic word strongly confirmed. You will do well to pay attention to it, as to a lamp shining in a dismal place, until the day dawns and the morning star rises in your hearts. First of all, you should know this: No prophecy of Scripture comes from one's own interpretation, because no prophecy ever came by the will of man; instead, men spoke from God as they were moved by the Holy Spirit" (2 Peter 1:16–21).

Closing

The transfiguration radically changed Peter and drove him to the place where he was ready to give up his own life for the cause of the gospel. Why? Because Peter realized that death will always lead to life.

Daily Word

Jesus took Peter, James, and John up on a high mountain where they witnessed Jesus physically transform in front of them. And if that wasn't enough of an experience, Moses and Elijah appeared and talked with Jesus. Suddenly, God the Father spoke from heaven and proclaimed three revealing points: Jesus is the Son of God, the Father loves Jesus, and we must listen and obey Jesus. After God the Father spoke, the disciples fell facedown and were terrified. Not only was Jesus transformed, but Peter, James, and John's lives were also transformed as they went away with Jesus.

As a follower of Christ, God gives you the gift of the Holy Spirit and transforms your life as you spend time in His presence. You may be thinking, *Wait. I believe in Jesus, but I'm not feeling transformed.* As an example for you, Jesus intentionally went away to a mountain to spend time with the Father. Today, get away from the busy, the routine and the chaos. Spend time alone with the Lord, earnestly asking the Lord to transform you more and more into His image. As you make spending time with the Lord a regular routine, He promises His Spirit will transform your heart.

**He was transformed in front of them, and His face shone like the sun. —
Matthew 17:2**

Further Scripture: Psalm 139:23–24; Romans 12:2; Ephesians 4:22–23

Questions

1. What does it mean to be "transfigured"? What things happened when Jesus
   was transfigured? (Matthew 17:2)
2. How would you explain Matthew 17:10–13? How does the coming of Elijah
   point to the Messiah? (Malachi 4:5)
3. Why did Moses and Elijah appear in Matthew 17:3? (Matthew 5:17)
4. Why was the person with seizures not healed when the disciples prayed for
   him (Matthew 17:14–20)? How much faith do you need to have in order to
   pray for someone to be healed (Romans 12:3)? What do you conclude when
   you pray for someone and they aren't healed?
5. What was Jesus trying to convey to Peter about the temple tax in Matthew
   17:24–27? What does it mean that the "children are exempt"? How is this
   relevant to you today?
6. What did the Holy Spirit highlight to you in Matthew 17 through the reading or the teaching?

Lesson 18: Matthew 18
King: Having Childlike Faith

Teaching Notes

Intro

Any time we study Scripture, we get to see the unfolding, invisible kingdom that we operate within. In Matthew 18, there is a major unveiling of kingdom principles.

Teaching

Matthew 18:1: I read this verse as the disciples, asking hopefully, "What makes someone great in this kingdom? How do we become great in the kingdom of heaven?"

Matthew 18:2–5: A little child, maybe five or six, was placed in the midst of the disciples. Jesus said they must be "converted," which means to turn away or to turn toward—to turn away from what is not of God and toward God in order to enter His kingdom.

Many Scripture passages speak clearly about having the wisdom of God rather than the wisdom of the world (1 Corinthians 1–2). That means we are to be willing to start over like a child. A child has no standing in places of authority, no great knowledge, and no great strength (1 Corinthians 1:18–25). Since God's lowest thoughts are greater than the highest thoughts of men, we enter the kingdom understanding that our limited capabilities are childish compared to the Master. We must rely on God teaching us to bring us to understanding. In verse 5, the words "receive one" (NASB) refer to taking by the hand one who is seeking God.

Matthew 18:6: There will always be those who come with no knowledge of spiritual life, no knowledge of Christian living, and no compass for life direction. Therefore, whoever humbles himself like this child is the greatest in the kingdom. We are to use a new believer's "childish" endeavors as teaching points, not places to expose their lack of understanding. If we who are walking in the way of Christ bring only reprimand to young "student" believers, they will tire of the discipline and walk away. If we cause that, we have misunderstood the Master's mission and have thwarted the "path of citizenship."

Matthew 18:7–9: Some Bible versions interpret offenses as temptations, and others as stumbling blocks. To be offended means that something has come against your version of the truth. We who are born of the Spirit still live within the confines of a sinful world that will be offensive to us. We will be offensive to those who don't understand our truth. But if we are the one who causes another to stumble, we have not cared enough for others to see how we have brought reproach to the kingdom and peril to a person (Galatians 5:13).

This is an indicator of how seriously we should view sin as a "transgression." Can anyone imagine cutting off your hand or foot, or plucking out your eye because it causes you to follow a sinful practice? However, the painful reminder of what is at stake is the essence of these verses.

Matthew 18:10: This verse seems to indicate that we have personal "guardian" angels. It would also give strong indication that we must make sure that those who are working and guarding the "little ones" are getting our cooperation and they do not find us sending conflicting messages to those learning about the kingdom.

Matthew 18:11: Our call is not to happiness, self-preservation, or self-sufficiency. Our call is to do the will of the Father, like Christ who came to seek and save that which was lost. What was lost? Spirit life that makes us eternal spirit beings. Jesus had one mission—to return the world to the original truth of His love for us and our ability to love Him.

Matthew 18:12–14: These three verses give us a "one another" aspect of the gospel. Does the peril of the journey keep us from rescuing a fallen one? Does the satisfaction of the 99 who are safe hold us in the position of safety? Whether it involves personal cost, time, or energy, the truth of the gospel is "God is not willing that any should perish but that all should come to repentance" (2 Peter 3:9).

Matthew 18:15–16: This passage must in one sense start backwards from verse 17 to qualify what kind of sin or offense your brother has against you. To merit telling the church, the sin must be something that violates the tenants of faith in the church and brings reproach to God. This is not personal preference; this is not a tattletale type of offense. We must qualify what we are talking about (Galatians 5:19–20).

We must keep it as private as possible to keep the possible shame or reproach from becoming widespread. The goal is always repentance. After time has passed, with no turning, the desire to see the individual restored compels us to take another person or two with us to make sure the matter was handled with proper understanding. And we must allow time for the matter to be resolved, if possible.

If there is no contrition, the matter is to come to the church so that all may understand there are lines drawn for kingdom behavior. We simply know we are not operating in the sphere of faith together and cannot have the fellowship we once had in the Spirit.

Matthew 18:18–19: These two verses do not mean that anything we decide to call important or sinful is a demand to God to make it so. We are to be sons and daughters of the kingdom which would indicate that the laws of heaven are our utmost priority. With that in mind, we draw lines on the earth as far as what we believe concerning kingdom living. When we forgive or remit sins, it means heaven will not keep record. If we demand a payment for personal transgression that is truly sinful practice and we need to see the signs of true repentance, that will be honored also. We don't dictate our faith, we learn it. Faith comes by the hearing of the Word of God and we function under its governance.

Matthew 18:20: This verse indicates that if the reason for our "assembly" is Him, Jesus will be the overseer and participant in our gathering. The purpose of the group is what matters.

Matthew 18:35: There are two facts in this passage that cause us to see what is represented to us by "the debt." The first debt is obviously ours to God. There is no way to pay it, He has the right to call us on it. We have nothing to offer and cannot begin to think of even offering anything meaningful to Him.

The second debt can only mean, in comparison, the little infractions that others owe us in offense or in some other form of indebtedness. There is no eternal weight to what is owed us. We can only enjoy beauty of this relationship by the mercy of our Redeemer. Therefore, forgiveness is to be a light matter to us, indicating that anytime we are offended, we must take into "account" what we have been forgiven, and then offer forgiveness in relationship to our personal debt.

This would also indicate there is a punishment for those who walk in unforgiveness. Scripture is replete, or well supplied, with passages that would indicate this as one of the "biggies" for the believer.

Closing

This "one another" chapter should be a barometer of the measure of our unity with Christ. If we say, "He is Lord," we lead with our lives and walk among the little ones as Christ did. We gladly forfeit our rights to our life to become the conduit of His love to others. We desire to restore anyone who stumbles and do our best not to be a cause for anyone to stumble. If there are those who stumble, we seek to redeem and restore. If we are the object of offense, we must view it with the eyes of the cross—"Father, forgive them." They don't truly understand what they are doing.

Daily Word

Jesus instructed the disciples to live differently from the way the world lives. He told them to forgive not just seven times but seventy-seven times seven; in other words, to forgive as many times as necessary. Jesus told a parable that illustrated to the disciples that if those who don't forgive will be forever tortured for not forgiving a fellow brother or sister.

Forgiveness. Some of you may run from that word. However, forgiveness is the key to your belief in Jesus. When you confess your sins to Jesus, He is faithful and forgives you fully from all unrighteousness. His death on the Cross covered your sins. You are forgiven forever. You are loved unconditionally. In addition, Jesus says you are to love others, just as He loves you. And yet when it comes to forgiving one another, you make excuses, you run from it, and you avoid it. But it never goes away; bitterness may even set in. Today, ask the Lord to help you to forgive.

Forgiveness doesn't come from your own strength but from the unconditional love and grace you receive from the Father. So walk it out by trusting and obeying all He is asking you to do in faith. Jesus promises His peace will be with you.

Then Peter came to Him and said, "Lord, how many times could my brother sin against me and I forgive him? As many as seven times?" "I will tell you, not as many as seven," Jesus said to him, "but 70 times seven. . . . So My heavenly Father will also do to you if each of you does not forgive his brother from his heart." —Matthew 18:21–22, 35

Further Scripture: Ephesians 1:7–8; Colossians 3:13; 1 John 1:9

Questions

1. How do you personally become "like a little child" in faith (Matthew 18:3)? What would the opposite of being "child-like" look like?

2. What does Matthew 18:6–7 reveal about what God thinks of causing someone to stumble? How can you guard yourself against causing others to stumble? (1 Corinthians 10:32–33; Philippians 2:3)

3. In what way have you been the "one sheep" that God has left the 99 for?

4. Have you ever followed the pattern of instruction in Matthew 18:15–17 to deal with sin in the church? How did the situation resolve?

5. What does it mean to truly forgive someone? How many times should you forgive someone who has offended you? How serious is dealing with unforgiveness? (Matthew 18:21–35; Ephesians 4:32; Colossians 3:13)

6. What did the Holy Spirit highlight to you in Matthew 18 through the reading or the teaching?

Lesson 19: Matthew 19

King: Getting Rid of Distractions

Teaching Notes

Intro

Matthew, also called Levi, was a tax collector, and it seems like money was a favorite subject for him. We're going to look at money today, because dealing with money is difficult when you're following Jesus. Matthew 19 begins by looking at questions on divorce (vv. 1–12), blessing the children (vv. 13–15), and then we get to our passage today when the rich young ruler talked to Jesus about getting into heaven. The story of the rich young ruler is in all three synoptic Gospels: Matthew 19:16–22; Mark 10:17–22; Luke 18:18–23. That means that all three see the story from different perspectives.

Teaching

Matthew 19:16–20: Matthew wrote that "someone" came up to Jesus. He did not identify the man as a rich young ruler, as some of the other gospels did, but instead presented the man humbly. The man asked Jesus what *good* he needed to do to have eternal life (v. 16). Eternal life means to continue on forever in God's presence. It's the opposite of eternal punishment. The word "good" has no absolute standard, so how can anyone truly know what it means to *do good*. Morris said that "it was no ordinary teacher who could answer that question."[1] Jesus responded, "Why do you ask Me about what is good? There is only One who is good. If you want to enter into life, keep the commandments" (v. 17). This makes it looks like Jesus was pointing to eternal life through works. The young man then asked which commandments he needed to keep (an interesting thought since they are all God's commandments). Jesus began to quote the sixth commandment—don't murder, the seventh commandment—don't commit adultery, the eighth commandment—don't steal, the ninth commandment—don't give false witness, the fifth commandment—honor your father and your mother, and finally, you need to love your neighbor as yourself—not one of the original Ten Commandments (vv. 18b–19) (Leviticus 19:18; Deuteronomy 6). Based on

---

[1] Leon Morris, *The Gospel According to Matthew* (Grand Rapids: Eerdmans, 1992), 490.

not breaking these commandments, in verse 20 the young man asked what he still lacked (Romans 3:20–22; 8:3–4; James 2:10).

Matthew 19:21: Jesus said if the man wanted to be perfect, he needed to sell everything he had, give it to the poor, and then he would have treasures in heaven (v. 21). Matthew 9:9 shows that Matthew walked away from everything to follow Jesus. He had to understand the young man's struggle.

The thing that's wrong in the American church today is that we want to follow Jesus, but we want to keep everything. We want our feet in both worlds—the Jesus world and our comfortable lifestyles.

Matthew 19:22: The young man left Jesus grieving because he had many possessions. At least he was honest about what he could not do. He did not fake his response. Luke 9:57–62, gives three examples of people who wanted to follow Jesus but couldn't pay the price of the commitment. Distractions of stuff are killing the American church. We all have things in our lives that become distractions that pull us away from Jesus (Romans 8:7; 1 John 5:3).

Matthew 19:23–24: Jesus turned to His disciples and explained that it was hard for a rich person to enter the kingdom of heaven. He told them it would be easier for a camel to go through the eye of a needle than for a rich person to enter the kingdom of God (vv. 23–24). Nelson's Commentary provides several interpretations for "the eye of the needle." One interpretation points to the difficulty of threading a camel hair rope through the eye of a needle; another suggests the camel trying to get through a small gate in the city wall of Jerusalem named "the eye of the needle." A third interpretation is that Jesus described an actual camel, the largest animal in Palestine, trying to squeeze through the actual tiny eye of the needle. All three interpretations draw attention to the extreme difficulty a rich man could have.[2]

Matthew 19:25–26: The disciples were astonished, because a rich man was seen as someone who had been spiritually blessed. They asked, "Then who can be saved?" (v. 25). In verse 26, Jesus responded with the true word of hope for believers: "With men this is impossible, but with God all things are possible" (Mark 10:27).

Matthew 19:27–30: Peter said that the disciples had already walked away from everything to follow Jesus. He asked, "So what will there be for us?" (v. 27). Jesus

---

[2] Earl D. Radmacher, Ronald B. Allen, and H. Wayne House, eds., *Nelson's New Illustrated Bible Commentary* (Nashville: Thomas Nelson, 1999), 1177.

responded that they would be rewarded in the Messianic Age when the Son of Man sits on His glorious throne with them sitting on the 12 thrones that are beside Him (v. 28). Then Jesus pointed out that all those who had left houses and family and fields behind to follow Him would receive 100 times as much when they inherited eternal life (v. 29). Jesus said, "But many who are first will be last, and the last first" (v. 30). Matthew 20:16 is a bookend to this teaching in Matthew 19: "The last shall be first and the first shall be last."

Closing

Mark Twain said, "It ain't these parts of the Bible that I can't understand that bother me, it's the parts that I do understand."

When you radically trust God for your life, when you give up everything in your life to follow Jesus, you will be set free. Missionary Hudson Taylor said "he had never succeeded in making a sacrifice for God. Every time he gave up anything for God, he received so much blessing that he felt himself better off rather than worse off for having given up whatever it was."

My takeaway: What am I holding onto that prevents me from radically following Jesus? When I'm willing to give up everything, I will experience God in a supernatural new way in my life.

Daily Word

Jesus continued teaching the disciples about the kingdom of heaven and explained it is easier for a camel to go through the eye of a needle than for a rich person to enter heaven. Why is it so hard for a rich man to enter the kingdom of heaven? From an earthly perspective, the rich man doesn't technically need to trust in Jesus. He is able to do life on his own and in his own strength. But God is full of grace and love, and Jesus promised the disciples that with God all things are possible.

God looks at the heart and knows when a person trusts and believes in Jesus as Lord and Savior. Therefore, even if you have all the riches you want, but your heart is set on Christ, it is possible for you to enter His kingdom. Jesus wants your heart to trust fully in Him. Today, is there anything you are trusting in more than God? He desires for you to keep your heart surrendered to Jesus the *King*, ensuring that He is the God of all your life. If you are to boast in anything, boast in Jesus!

"Again, I tell you, it is easier for a camel to go through the eye of a needle than for a rich person to enter the kingdom of God." . . . But Jesus looked at them and said, "With men this is impossible, but with God all things are possible." —Matthew 19:24, 26

Further Scripture: Psalm 20:7; Ephesians 2:8–9; Colossians 3:2

Questions

1. In Matthew 19:14, why did Jesus rebuke the disciples? Do you see this pointing to our dependence on our Father? Why or why not?

2. In verse 21, Jesus told the young ruler to sell all he had, and he would have treasures in Heaven. What do you believe the treasures are that await those who believe? How does that compare to the treasures mentioned in Exodus 19:5; Deuteronomy 28:12; and Proverbs 2:4?

3. When the warning was given in Matthew 19:23–24 about the rich, do you think that warning is for those rich in finances or in another area? Why?

4. In verse 29, Jesus says whatever you have given up—family and/or land—you will receive a hundredfold. How does this speak to you? Do you think He meant the reward will be here on earth or in heaven? Why?

5. What did the Holy Spirit highlight to you in Matthew 19 through the reading or the teaching?

Lesson 20: Matthew 20
King: The Last Shall Be First

Teaching Notes

Intro

In chapter 20, Jesus, the *King*, instructed His disciples regarding the right attitude for service. In a word, Jesus instructed them to become *Christlike*.

Teaching

Matthew 20:1: Jesus began with a parable about a landowner needing workers. The first word "For" connects this parable to the end of chapter 19 and to Peter's question in verse 27. Jesus continues His response to Peter from Matthew 19:28–30 with this parable. This parable is bracketed with the statement, "the first will be last, and the last first" (Matthew 19:30; 20:16).

Matthew 20:2–7: The harvest needed to be gathered quickly, and these verses express the typical urgency surrounding the harvest. The landowner continued to return to the market to find more workers, promising to pay them "whatever is right." The workers hired later in the day would have expected to receive considerably less pay than a full day's wages. In Jesus' time, the work day was roughly 6:00 a.m. to 6:00 p.m., and the hours were numbered one through 12.[1] That means the third, sixth, ninth, and eleventh hours were 9 a.m., noon, 3 p.m., and an hour before sunset, or 5 p.m., respectively. The landowner agreed to pay each worker a denarius for a full day's wage. It's important that we are careful in our attempts to discern who these full-day workers, or any of the other groups of workers, represented (such as those who have known Christ most of their lives, or have been especially faithful opposite those who are not so faithful).

Matthew 20:8–12: Jewish law mandated laborers had to be paid the same day they worked, and wages were often only ample for that day's needs (Deuteronomy 24:14–15). When the work day ended, the landowner instructed his foreman to pay the workers, beginning with the last hired and ending with the first hired.

---

[1] Donald A. Carson, *Matthew-Luke*, vol. 8 of *The Expositor's Bible Commentary*, ed. Frank E. Gaebelein and J. D. Douglas (Grand Rapids: Zondervan, 1983), 428.

Those hired last received a full day's wage—one denarius. When the workers who had begun at 6 a.m. received one denarius, they complained that they had been paid the same as those who had come much later.

Honest evaluation: How many of us would be happy if we worked all day and someone who worked just the last hour received the same pay that we did? The workers complained that it was not fair that those who came later had been paid the same.

"These last men put in one hour, and you made them equal to us who bore the burden of the day and in the burning heat!" (v. 12). Their complaint shows both comparison and entitlement, and it's like Peter's statement in Matthew 19:27, which basically says "What about us? This isn't fair."

Matthew 20:13–16: Myron Augsburger says that "friend" was an expression Jesus used three times in Matthew, and each time, the person addressed was wrong (Matthew 22:12; 26:50).[2] The NASB version translates verse 15 as, "Or is your eye envious because I am generous?" Jesus used it to show the root of the problem was the workers' perspective. It was wrong because they had made an agreement for the rate of pay in advance. Wiersbe says, "We should not serve Him because we want to receive an expected reward, and we should not insist on knowing what we will get."[3] If we serve Christ only for the benefits (temporal and eternal), then we will miss the best blessings He has for us. Augsburger explains that the points in a parable must support and clarify the primary intent, and they must move to that conclusion: (1) The calling to service is in direct relation to the need; (2) the reward for service is a gracious meeting of our needs; and (3) the integrity of service will respect the integrity of grace in meeting needs equally.[4]

Matthew 20:17–19: Jesus foretold His death and resurrection to His disciples. The title "Son of Man" associates the Messiah with suffering. He would be "mocked, flogged, and crucified" (v. 19). The Greek tense of all three verbs showed that it was an anticipated fact.

Matthew 20:20–28: Wiersbe identifies the "mother of Zebedee's sons" as Salome.[5] The sense is that Salome was the one behind the request, promoting

---

[2] Myron Augsburger, *The Preacher's Commentary: Matthew* (Nashville, Thomas Nelson, 1982), n.p.

[3] Warren W. Wiersbe, *The Bible Exposition Commentary: Matthew–Galatians* (Colorado Springs: David C. Cook, 1989), 74.

[4] Augsburger, n.p.

[5] Wiersbe, 75.

her sons. In Mark 10:35–45, the brothers make the request. She asked that her sons would be placed at Jesus' right and left in His kingdom. They dared to believe the promise Jesus had given about sitting on thrones (Matthew 19:28) so their act was one of faith.[6] While Jesus spoke of a cross, they were interested in a crown and special thrones.

Wiersbe notes several things that were wrong in the request. First, it was born in ignorance, because they didn't understand what they were asking. James was the first disciple to be martyred, and John would endure hard times on Patmos. Second, it had a lack of heavenly direction, and was based on worldly and selfish thinking, seeking glory for themselves. Third, the request was of the flesh, motived by pride, reminiscent of Satan's offer to put Jesus on his throne (Matthew 4:8–11). Jesus responded by predicting their martyrdom.[7] The reaction of the other disciples gave Jesus a teachable moment about leading by serving one another.

Salome was at the cross when Jesus was crucified and shared His sorrow and pain. Instead of two thrones on His right and left, she saw two thieves on crosses. It takes an infusion of the Divine heart into the human heart for us to begin to see what the kingdom of God is all about.

Matthew 20:29–34: These verses hold the last compassionate healing before Jesus entered Jerusalem. Jesus demonstrated His expectations to His disciples as He became a servant to two rejected, blind beggars. They asked Him for healing, and they were specific in their request (James 5:13–16).

In our tradition, we anoint and pray for healing until one of the following occurs: (1) They get healed in this life; (2) Jesus returns; or (3) they are healed in heaven. In *Jesus Shaped Life*, Mike Breen said that if healing does not happen, at least when Jesus returns, He will find us doing what He told us to do.[8] It is a declaration of war! The Messianic significance of this miracle is its fulfillment of Isaiah's prediction (Isaiah 29:18–19; 35:5–6).

Closing

Wiersbe says this chapter contains things that are difficult to receive and to practice:

- If we love the things of this world, we cannot love God supremely.
- If we are not yielded completely to His will, we cannot obey Him unreservedly.

---

[6] Wiersbe, 74–75.

[7] Augsburger, n.p.

[8] Mike Breen, quoted in Bob Rognlien, *A Jesus Shaped Life: Discipleship and Mission for Everyday People* (Gx Books, 2016).

- If we seek glory for ourselves, or if we compare ourselves with other believers, then we cannot glorify Him.

We cannot acknowledge Jesus as our *King* unless we love Him supremely, obey Him unreservedly, and glorify Him completely. The *King* instructed His followers then, and now, regarding the right attitude for service. And Jesus is not done—tomorrow He enters Jerusalem as a *King* riding on a donkey on the very day the Passover lamb is selected to be sacrificed (Matthew 21).

Daily Word

Jesus was leaving Jericho when two blind men cried out, asking Him for mercy and to open their eyes. Even as Jesus was on the way to the next place of ministry, He took the time to stop and ask what they wanted. He showed compassion and touched their eyes so they could see.

In the same way, Jesus has stopped and showed you compassion because of His great love for you. If your eyes have been opened by His love and mercy in your own life, then you can show that same compassion to someone along your way. Today, take the time to show someone the same mercy and compassion Jesus showed the blind men.

There were two blind men sitting by the road. When they heard that Jesus was passing by, they cried out, "Lord, have mercy on us, Son of David!" The crowd told them to keep quiet, but they cried out all the more, "Lord, have mercy on us, Son of David!" —Matthew 20:30–31

Further Scripture: 2 Corinthians 1:3; Titus 3:5; 1 Peter 2:10

Questions

1. Matthew 20 starts with the Parable of the Laborers in verses 1–16. When you read this, would you feel the same way as the first set of workers did in verse 12? Why or why not? What do you think Jesus was conveying in these verses?

2. When someone comes to the saving knowledge of Christ at a young age, is their reward greater than someone who accepts Christ late in their life? Why or why not?

3. Why do you think Jesus told His disciples multiple times that He would be betrayed and crucified? If you were in the disciples' place, how do you think you might have reacted?

4. In Matthew 20:22, Jesus talked about a cup. What do you believe this is a picture of? Then, in verse 23, He said we will drink of the same cup as He did. What does this mean to you?

5. In Matthew 20:26–27, Jesus talked about the first and last, and servanthood. In your life, think of an example of how this was modeled correctly and also how it was modeled incorrectly.

6. What did the Holy Spirit highlight to you in Matthew 20 through the reading or the teaching?

Lesson 21: Matthew 21
King: Hearing the Voice of the Holy Spirit

Teaching Notes

Intro

To summarize, the words we've established for each book of the Bible so far are: Genesis=*Seed*; Exodus=*Deliverer*; Leviticus=*Atonement*; Numbers=*Rock*; and Deuteronomy=*Prophet*. Those five words cover the Pentateuch. For Matthew, that one word is *King*. No other chapter in Matthew emphasized Jesus as the *King* more than chapter 21. This chapter is the only time in which Jesus set up an event to bring attention to Himself.

Teaching

Matthew 21:1–3: Jesus and His disciples made the 17-mile journey from Jericho to Jerusalem. On the Mount of Olives, Jesus sent two disciples to go into the village to find a donkey and colt tied there and told them to bring them back to Him. Notice, Jesus told these disciples they would see the animals "at once." Jesus began to give radical ways to trust the voice of the Holy Spirit. John 10:14–16 says:

> I am the good shepherd. I know My own sheep, and they know Me, as the Father knows Me, and I know the Father. I lay down My life for the sheep. But I have other sheep that are not of this fold; I must bring them also, and they will listen to My voice. Then there will be one flock, one shepherd.

This is the beginning of the process of sanctification—of growing in the Lord through the Holy Spirit. Jesus had already prepared the owner's heart to allow the disciples to take the animals (v. 3).

We can trust the Holy Spirit's voice: "Whenever they bring you before synagogues and rulers and authorities, don't worry about how you should defend yourselves or what you should say. For the Holy Spirit will teach you at that very hour what must be said" (Luke 12:11–12).

And, we can trust God to give us directions of what to say: "Yahweh said to him, 'Who made the human mouth? Who makes him mute or deaf, seeing or blind? Is it not I, Yahweh? Now go! I will help you speak and I will teach you what to say'" (Exodus 4:11–12).

Matthew 21:4–5: The preparation and the instructions led the disciples to walk out the prophecy of both Isaiah 62:11 and Zechariah 9:9. When you hear from the Holy Spirit, He has already prepared you for what He sends you to do. Trust His voice and walk it out. Verse 5 points directly to Jesus as the *King*. A king riding on a donkey represents humility. A king riding a horse represents authority. Jesus had to come in humility as *King* (1 Kings 1:33; Zechariah 9:9b), before He could return on a white horse as *King* (Revelation 19:11).

Matthew 21:6–8: The disciples did exactly as Jesus instructed. They heard the voice of the Holy Spirit and responded in faith. They didn't need a meeting to figure out what to do. There is freedom in following the Holy Spirit's voice. By following directions and bringing back two animals, they played a part in preparing the way for the *King*. We should not minimize the importance of anything the Holy Spirit asks us to do. God can use any of us at any time to accomplish His will.

They laid their own robes on the animals; they gave up everything for Him to sit on the colt—a wild, unridden animal (Psalm 8:6–7; Mark 11:7; John 12:14). Jesus was in control of everything, even a wild animal that had never been ridden. The crowd began to spread their personal robes on the road for Jesus to ride over. When two gave up their robes, so did everyone in the crowd (v. 8). This all started because they trusted the voice of the Lord, they walked out the prophecy, they went in obedience, and they gave everything up . . . because they believed the *King* was coming. The human side of the people wanted Jesus to be a political king.

Matthew 21:9–10: The crowds went before Jesus and after Him, quoting praises from Psalm 118:25–26 to Jesus. The palm branches spread on the road anticipate the coming of the Millennial Age when on the day of the Lord the kingdom will be implemented. The people saw that Jesus was a part of the lineage of David the king (Matt 1:1). The word *Hosanna* means, "Save us now!" The people shouted out to Him, expecting Him to save them from the political conditions they were in. They didn't view Him as the Messiah. From Matthew 10 and through Matthew 28, the disciples were told to go out and find the lost sheep of Israel, but they were rejected all along the way. That's why in Matthew 28, the whole mission is changed, and all the Gentiles were added to the lost sheep. When Jesus entered Jerusalem, many believe He went through the Sheep Gate, which was where the sheep were brought into Jerusalem for sacrifice. That creates an amazing picture of Jesus as the ultimate sacrifice.

The word "shaken" in verse 10 can be interpreted as: being moved, being stirred (What is going on?), or being deeply disturbed. The third interpretation is probably most correct, because the people of Jerusalem questioned who Jesus was, and the crowds kept saying, "This is the prophet Jesus from Nazareth in Galilee!" They were distraught because they knew Him and where He had come from. When people hear the Holy Spirit's voice, when they walk out those instructions, when they enter a city and call out the name of Jesus, the city *will be* shaken!

Closing

It is our job to prepare the way for the *King*. I pray that the Holy Spirit would begin to show us what we each need to do to prepare His way, to show us His next steps. May we be obedient to the message we hear today.

Daily Word

As Jesus and the disciples approached Jerusalem and came to Bethphage on the Mount of Olives, Jesus spoke directly to the disciples, giving them specific actions to go and do. The disciples trusted His voice. They listened even though they were receiving seemingly random instruction to go get a donkey and a colt belonging to someone else. They gave everything up, even the robes off their backs, and proclaimed the name of Jesus, saying, "Hosanna in the highest heaven!" And because of their obedience, the city was shaken as *King* Jesus rode in on a colt.

This act of obedience was the disciples' role in preparing the way for Jesus. You too have a role in preparing the way for *King* Jesus. Today, ask the Lord what your role is as Jesus makes His return. Listen to His voice, and go in obedience. Just as the disciples had an impact for the glory of the coming *King*, so will you as you walk it out, trusting and obeying the voice of the Lord.

The disciples went and did just as Jesus directed them. They brought the donkey and the colt; then they laid their robes on them, and He sat on them. —Matthew 21:6–7

Further Scripture: Matthew 21:10; Luke 9:23; John 10:27

Questions

1. Jesus knew that He would be handed over to the Romans to be mocked, flogged, and crucified (Matthew 20:19). Why did He choose to make such a triumphant and public entry into Jerusalem (Zechariah 9:9; Matthew 21:2–5)?

2. Jesus gave very specific instructions to His disciples about obtaining the donkey and its colt. Do you think the Disciples understood why they were asked to do that? What does this teach you about obeying the Lord?

3. Why was Jesus angry when He entered the temple (Isaiah 56:7; Jeremiah 7:11; Matthew 21:12–13)? Was Jesus focused on those who were buying, selling, or both? Even after this happened, did it distract Him from continuing to do ministry (Matthew 21:14)? What causes you to get distracted from ministering to others?

4. What were the chief priests' and the scribes' reaction to seeing Jesus' wonderful miracles (Matthew 21:15)? What were they upset about and how did Jesus respond?

5. How do you think the chief priests and the elders of Israel reacted when Jesus asked them if they had ever read the Scriptures (Matthew 21:42)? What was their reaction after they realized He was talking about them in the parable, not to mention, the prophecy that was fulfilled concerning Himself?

6. What did the Holy Spirit highlight to you in Matthew 21 through the reading or the teaching?

Lesson 22: Matthew 22
King: All Are Invited; Few Will Accept

Teaching Notes

Intro

The Word of God is a revelation of God's kingdom that is to come, that has been unseen, but is becoming visible to us, even as we walk out in that kingdom. When John the Baptist preached that the kingdom was coming, he was preaching not just the gospel of Jesus Christ, but His kingdom as well.

Every kingdom has to have a defined territory, a government (king), laws, and law enforcement (Ephesians 6:12). Every kingdom has its own language and culture and even attitude. So, we can begin to look at the kingdom of God using these principles—what it looks like, where its boundaries are, and where is the place of authority. We are to learn as citizens of the kingdom what this authority looks like. All these things are revealed in God's Word. I believe the currency of God's kingdom is time, and what He calls us to do with His time.

Teaching

Matthew 22:1–4: Jesus told another parable about the kingdom of heaven using a wedding. The king issued invitations to those under his authority and he expected them to obey his summons. But they did not come (vv. 1–3). The king had done all the work and preparation for the wedding. He sent out more servants but the invitees "made light of it." Their response reflected their heart toward the king.

Matthew 22:5–7: The invitees went their own ways (v. 5). The rest of the invitees seized the servants, "treated them outrageously and killed them" (v. 6b). The king responded with troops and punishment (v. 7).

The king sent his servants with invitations. The invitations were refused, so he sent his servants again. The servants were treated badly and murdered. What does this represent? It's easy to see what happened here. On the Mount of Transfiguration, God sent Moses, who brought the ways of God–the Law, and Elijah, who represented the Prophets. The Jews, the invited, refused the invitation. We'd like to picture the crown as solid gold and beautiful, but instead the crown was one of thorns and of suffering. The mother of the Sons of Zebedee asked for her sons to have the honor of being seated on thrones by Jesus. But Jesus was crucified between two thieves, on a cross with the title "*King* of the Jews." The ones who didn't recognize Jesus as such were the Jews.

Matthew 22:8: Those the king found unworthy measured their worth for the wedding based on their value to the king. The king measured their worth on the fact that they didn't see the value of their invitation or what their presence was worth to the kingdom.

Matthew 22:9–14: The king sent his servants out to invite everyone they could find, "both bad and good." All the guests had to do was come because the preparations had been completed. When the king entered, he saw a guest who had not put on a wedding garment. When the king asked the guest why, the guest was speechless.

In verse 14, Jesus explained that many are "called," but few are "chosen." That statement only makes sense if we look at the Greek words. The word "called" is from the Greek word for "invited," and the word "chosen" is from the Greek word for "belong." Therefore, verse 14 is best understood as, "For many are invited, but few belong." This makes sense, when we put it in the perspective of the kingdom with boundaries, laws, and law enforcement. If you want the benefits of the kingdom, you would follow the dictates of the king. You would be interested in the very things the king was offering. Those in the kingdom know the benefits . . . an army to protect us, a common language, laws for our good, an economy together. The people in this passage wanted to do their own thing, in their own way, and in their own time. Jesus was marching to the cross, and He wanted His followers to understand what His kingdom is about. In the old days, a flag would fly over the castle when the king was there and be taken down when he left. Jesus' message was that the *King* was present in His house and had invited everyone to come, but not everyone would accept His invitation.

Matthew 22:23–32: The Sadducees came to Jesus to try to entangle Him in a difficult question. Jesus responded to their question with, "You are deceived, because you don't know the Scriptures or the power of God" (v. 29). The Greek word *dunamis* is the power of the Holy Spirit. Jesus used the word *dunamis* here to explain how much the Sadducees didn't understand the power of God because they did not believe in resurrection. In verse 32, Jesus quoted God, saying, "I am the God of Abraham and the God of Isaac and the God of Jacob? He is not the God of the dead, but of the living." This went straight to the heart of who the Sadducees were . . . the children of Abraham, Isaac, and Jacob. So, were these patriarchs just dead and gone? If so, what was the beauty of having their heritage?

Jesus was saying that these men are still alive, because God is the God of the living and these patriarchs are part of God's plan to come.

Matthew 22:33–40: The crowds were amazed by how Jesus silenced the Sadducees. When the Pharisees heard what happened, they joined together. One of them, a lawyer, then questioned Jesus, asking which commandment was the greatest. Jesus responded, "Love the Lord your God with all your heart, with all your soul, and with all your mind. This is the greatest and most important command. The second is like it: Love your neighbor as yourself. All the Law and the Prophets depend on these two commands."

Matthew 22:41–45: Then Jesus asked the Pharisees whose Son the Messiah would be. They answered, "David's." Jesus asked, "How is it then that David, inspired by the Spirit, calls Him 'Lord,'" and then quoted Psalm 110:1. David's prophecy was way beyond the understanding of the Pharisees (who were supposed to know the Scriptures). The Pharisees were unable to answer Him because they realized that everything Jesus had been teaching was aimed at the religious people who wouldn't accept the *King* because they had their own ways.

Closing

When we come to that place, where our position causes us not to follow the edicts of the *King*, then we are the ones who will sit in jeopardy and be judged for it, and it will be a terrible judgment to come.

Daily Word

A king gave a wedding banquet for his son. However, those who were invited didn't want to come. Even after being summoned a second time, those who were invited paid no attention, going away to mind to their farms and businesses. Finally, the king extended the invitation to everyone, both good and evil people in the kingdom. The banquet filled with guests. One man came dressed in clothes that were disrespectable for the king's wedding banquet, and he was cast out.

In a similar way, the Lord your God is welcoming you into the kingdom of heaven through faith in His Son Jesus. Your response to the invitation reveals your heart. Do you have a need for Jesus the King in your life? Are you too consumed or overly interested in building your own kingdom through your career? Have you said yes to the invitation from Jesus but in your heart mocked the concept of Jesus as your Lord and Savior? Jesus says, "Love the Lord your God with all your heart, with all your soul, and with all your mind." All are welcome into the kingdom of heaven. Will you say yes in your heart?

For many are invited, but few are chosen. —Matthew 22:14

Further Scripture: Matthew 22:29; Romans 1:5–6; Revelation 17:14

Questions

1. Why did Jesus say at the end of the Parable of the Great Feast that many are called but few are chosen (Matthew 20:16; 22:14 (NKJV); Revelation 17:14)? Was this a choice of the guest not to come to the wedding party? Why or why not? What was the *King's* solution (Matthew 22:9)?

2. Jesus had been accusing and exposing the religious leaders (Matthew 9:4; 12:3–8). What was the plot against Jesus in Matthew 22:15–22? How did Jesus respond?

3. Name one difference between the Pharisees and the Sadducees. (Matthew 22:23; Galatians 1:14)

4. The Sadducees tried to trap Jesus with a theological question. What two things did Jesus point out about them? (Matthew 22:24–29)

5. What does it mean to love the Lord your God with all your heart, all your soul, and all your mind (Deuteronomy 6:5; 8:6; 10:12; Micah 6:8; Matthew 22:37; Romans 12:1)?

6. What did the Holy Spirit highlight to you in Matthew 22 through the reading or the teaching?

Lesson 23: Matthew 23

King: Jesus' Lamentations Over Jerusalem

Teaching Notes

Intro

We are in Matthew's account of what we know as Holy Week. Jesus was teaching in the temple courts. He had silenced the Sadducees on the question of the resurrection, and had debated with the Pharisees on the Greatest Commandment and the Messiah. Now, we are going to see Jesus warn the religious leaders of their hypocrisy in His last public message. These were serious warnings described as scathing denunciation and angry castigation (reprimanded severely). It was a fit response to the hypocritical questioning meant to trap Jesus rather than to hear Him. Jesus was direct, pointed, blunt, and yet full of lament and concern for the righteous.

Teaching

Matthew 23:1–3: Then Jesus spoke to the crowds and His disciples. Wiersbe wrote, "They had a false concept of righteousness (vv. 2–3)."[1] There were about 6,000 Pharisees with many more who were "followers." The name "Pharisee" means to "separate." They were obsessed with tiny, minute details of the law. The legalism traps they fell into came from an incorrect focus on Leviticus 21 and 22.

To the Pharisees, righteousness meant outward conformity to the Law of God. They ignored the inward condition of the heart. Jesus was critical of the Pharisees because they were close to truth and had much in common with the teachings of Jesus. It was the legalistic observance of the Torah commands and hypocrisy of certain rabbinical leaders that Jesus was critical of.

Matthew 23:4–6: Wiersbe said that the Pharisees "had a false concept of ministry"[2] (v. 4). To the Pharisees, ministry meant handing down laws to the people, adding to their burden. Jesus came to lighten men's burden (Matthew 11:28–30). Legalistic religions always seem to make burdens heavier.

---

[1] Warren W. Wiersbe, *The Bible Expository Commentary New Testament: Matthew–Galatians* (Colorado Springs: David C. Cook, 1989), 83.

[2] Wiersbe, 83.

Wiersbe wrote that the Pharisees also "had a false concept of greatness."[3] This is the only mention of phylacteries (enlarged boxes that sat on the head and arm) in the New Testament. Their tassels were blue and white cords worn on the outer garments (Numbers 15:36; Deuteronomy 22:12). The hypocrites would lengthen their tassels, because the more noticeable the tassel, the more spiritual they seemed. To them, success meant recognition and praise from men.

Matthew 23:7–10: Rabbi literally means, "my great one," and can also be used for "my master" or "my teacher." It became a title of respect used for the Torah scholars by everyone. Also, this title was associated with greatness. Jesus warned His disciples to avoid titles that would set them apart or above the community of faith.

Matthew 23:11–12: Compare Matthew 23:11 with the almost identical wording in Matthew 20:26–28. The greatest is the person who serves others. The hypocrites demanded to be served and respected. Jesus' attitude was one of painful sorrow that the Pharisees were blinded to God's truth and to their own sins.

Wiersbe wrote, "Perhaps the best way to deal with these seven (or eight) 'woes' is to contrast them with the eight beatitudes found in Matthew 5:1–12. In the Sermon on the Mount the Lord described true righteousness; here He describes false righteousness."[4]

Matthew 23:13–14: The poor in spirit enter the kingdom, but the proud in spirit keep themselves out and even keep others out. Instead of mourning over their own sins, and mourning with widows, the Pharisees took advantage of these people in order to rob them.

Matthew 23:15–22: The Pharisees were out to win others to their legalistic system. They could not introduce those around them to the living God. The Pharisees were blind to the true values of life. Their priorities were confused. The Pharisees would take an oath and use some sacred object to substantiate that oath—the gold in the temple, or a gift on the altar. They left God out of their priorities.

Matthew 23:23–24: The Pharisees had rules for every area of life, yet they ignored the important things. They tithed everything, right down to their pantry of mint, dill, and cumin. Their tithing was only a smoke screen, distracting people from noticing that they neglected the more important matters of the law—justice, mercy, and faithfulness (Deuteronomy 10:12–13; Micah 6:8).

---

[3] Wiersbe, 83.

[4] Wiersbe, 84.

Matthew 23:25–28: Jesus used two illustrations, the cup and planter, and the sepulcher. These illustrations are both essentially saying the same thing. It was possible to be clean on the outside, and at the same time, defiled on the inside.

Matthew 23:29–33: By calling them serpents (vipers), Jesus was equating them to Satan. Gehenna is interchangeable with the word "hell" here. Gehenna is a valley surrounding Jerusalem's Old City, from the west and south, currently known as Ben Hinnom. It was a place where the kings of Judah sacrificed their children by fire and was deemed cursed (Jeremiah 7:31; 19:2–9). In rabbinic literature and Scripture, Gehenna is a destination of the wicked.

Matthew 23:34–36: All the righteous blood that was shed will be charged to the Pharisees, from the death of Abel (Genesis 4:8) at the hand of Cain to the last martyr in the Hebrew Bible, Zechariah. The Hebrew Old Testament is arranged in a different order than our English Old Testament, making Zechariah the last martyr listed there (2 Chronicles 24:20–22).

Matthew 23:37–39: Jesus lamented Israel's destruction. "Lament" is a verb that means to feel or express great sorrow or regret. Stuart Briscoe wrote, "Matthew's inclusion of the lament is definitely to show that the prophecy of Jesus was not given in a spirit of vindictiveness."[5] It is a picture of love, tender care, and willingness to die for the sins of the world including Israel.

Stuart K. Weber wrote, "But they were not willing. Even Jesus does not force compliance. What grief this must have caused him. What a demonstration of love, that he would subject his emotion to our wills, allowing himself to experience pain and suffering at our rebellious whim. That is authentic love."[6]

Closing

Jesus turned and walked away from the temple, but His words rang in the ears of the disciples. They were moved to ask, "When will this happen and what will be the sign of your coming?" (Matthew 24:3). Jesus answered their questions in what we tend to call the Olivet Discourse, from the Mount of Olives just outside Jerusalem. That topic comes tomorrow.

Today the *King* wants to you to know that righteousness must begin with the inner person, not with external obedience alone.

---

[5] D. Stuart Briscoe, (Nashville: Thomas Nelson, 1987), n. p.

[6] Stuart Weber, *Holman New Testament Commentary: Matthew* (Nashville: Broadman & Holman, 1999), 382.

Daily Word

Jesus spoke to the crowds and His disciples about the Pharisees and the scribes. He described their outward appearance and how they liked to *look* religious. They liked to have the *proper place* at the banquets. They liked having a *status greeting* as Rabbi, thinking they deserved honor. Jesus pointed out that these things were not what was important.

Your designer, well-put-together outfits are not important. Your official title is not important. Your corner office with expensive furniture is not important. Jesus wants your heart. He wants your heart surrendered to Him because Jesus said the humbled will be exalted. Blessed are the poor in spirit, for theirs is the kingdom of heaven. Stop trying so hard. Sit and purify your heart. Stay in a place of humility, and as the Lord sees your heart, you will be exalted into the kingdom of God!

The greatest among you will be your servant. Whoever exalts himself will be humbled, and whoever humbles himself will be exalted. —Matthew 23:11–12

Further Scripture: Matthew 5:3; Matthew 23:37b; James 4:10

Questions

1. Why was Jesus adamant about obeying what the religious leaders said, but not to following their example? (Matthew 23:2–7)

2. In Matthew 23, Jesus gave many "Woe to you" statements. What were the reasons He said these things to the scribes and Pharisees? (Matthew 23:13–16, 23, 25, 27, 29)

3. Read Matthew 23:12. What does this verse mean to you? Is this promise for here on earth, for eternity, or both? (Psalm 138:6; Proverbs 29:23; Isaiah 57:15; James 4:6)

4. Jesus is more concerned with the heart than our outer appearance (1 Samuel 16:7; Psalm 15:2; Matthew 5:8). What are some things that we can slip into to get the attention of man rather than God? How can we correct this?

5. God has always desired and still desires His children to turn to Him, but we often turn to other things. How do you sense the love and compassion of God in Matthew 23:37? Jesus was grieving over Jerusalem, but He also gave hope. Where is the hope found in verse 39 of this chapter? (Romans 11:26)

6. What did the Holy Spirit highlight to you in Matthew 23 through the reading or the teaching?

Lesson 24: Matthew 24
King: Signs of the End Times

Teaching Notes

Intro

In Matthew 24, Jesus shared with His disciples the signs of His return. There are many perspectives on these verses. We'll deal with a couple of them. We're going to unpack the Scriptures and let God's Word speak for itself. The end goal of this lesson is for you to be prepared for the return of *King* Jesus.

Teaching

Matthew 24:1–2: Jesus brought up the coming destruction of the temple complex (AD 70). Not only does this refer to the destruction of the temple, but of the rip in the veil at Jesus' death.

Matthew 24:3–8: Later, the disciples asked Jesus when these things would happen and what signs would be seen. Jesus warned them to watch out for those who would deceive them—the false messiahs (v. 5). Many have come in the past, claiming to be the Messiah. Jesus said these false messiahs would deceive many. He also said there would be wars and rumors of wars, but the end would not come yet (v. 6). And, famine and earthquakes would happen (v. 7). These would all be birthing pains (v. 8). All these signs tell us to get ready.

Matthew 24:9–14: Then would come persecution of the disciples and even death. Those who call on the name of Jesus will be hated and betrayed. False prophets will deliver prophetic words that lead many of the hearers astray. Lawlessness and chaos will increase and spread. "The one who endures to the end will be delivered." We are to stick with it! Because of endurance to the end, the good news of God's kingdom will be proclaimed throughout the world.

Let's go to the end times here: The 144,000 will be the ones delivering the message during this time. They will be Jewish evangelists (Revelation 7:4). That's 12,000 from each of the 12 tribes. Their goal will be literally to preach the kingdom of God. Those who endure will be able to support these Jewish evangelists.

Matthew 24:15–22: Verse 15 is like a bomb just dropped. As the gospel is going forth, "the abomination that causes desolation" (the antichrist) will come in and take over in the second half of the seven-year period of peace. He will stand in the holy place meant for God. Daniel 9:24–27 talks about the signs discussed in Matthew 24. One week in these verses stands for 7 years. The timeline for 490 years is divided into three sections and looks like this:

> *First 7 Weeks (49 years):* The city of Jerusalem will be rebuilt.
> *Second 63 Weeks (434 years):* The Messiah will come and die for the sin of the world.
> *Last Week (7 years):* For the first three-and-a-half years, the prince will make an agreement with the Jews for a time of peace, and then the antichrist will come in and take over (2 Thessalonians 2:3–4).

The antichrist will sit in God's sanctuary and proclaim that he is god. When we see a seven-year peace agreement in Israel, and one of the leaders who initiates that agreement sits himself in God's sanctuary and declares he is god, we will know that Jesus hasn't come back yet. The third segment of years we have not seen yet. When this takes place, those in Judea must flee to the mountains without even getting their own things (vv. 16–18). It will be difficult for pregnant women and mothers of small children (v. 19), or in the winter or on the Sabbath (v. 20). When that peace agreement is made, we can begin to expect the end times to unfold. There will be great tribulation unlike anything the world has ever seen before, and no one would survive if the days of the tribulation were not limited because of the elect (vv. 21–22).

Matthew 24:23–28: During the tribulation, false messiahs and false prophets will show up again (vv. 23–24). Jesus emphasized not to be deceived or drawn in by these false messengers (vv. 25–26). Everyone will see the coming Messiah, not just a few, and it will come suddenly or at any time (v. 27)! At some point, there will be a gathering of people to battle at Armageddon, and the carnage will be horrific (v. 28). Before the Son of Man comes, there will be massive fighting.

Matthew 24:29–31: After this craziness in the tribulation, the sun, moon, and stars will be changed, and the Son of Man will appear in the sky with "power and great glory" (vv. 29–30). He will appear on a cloud in the same way as when He left in Acts 1. The peoples of the world will mourn as they see Him. His angels will go out with trumpets to gather His elect from around the world (v. 31).

1. The rapture of the church will take place at some point. We must be ready at any time.

2. The leader of ten European nations will make a seven-year peace agreement with Israel. That leader can be the antichrist (Daniel 9:26–27). When that happens, we should all get ready.

3. After three years, the antichrist (the abomination of the desolation) is going to break the agreement (Daniel 9:27).

4. The antichrist will move to Jerusalem and set up his image in the temple (2 Thessalonians 2:4).

5. The antichrist will begin to control the world to worship him, and at that time, God will send a great tribulation.

6. The nations will gather at Armageddon and will fight the antichrist. At some point, we will see the sign of Christ coming to fight the antichrist in Israel.

7. *King* Jesus will return to earth, defeat His enemy, be received by the Jews, and establish His kingdom.

8. Then Jesus will reign for 1,000 years.

Closing

This is obviously a very brief overview. What is important is to know that you shouldn't bank on the rapture pulling you out so you won't have to endure the tribulation. What is important is for us to be prepared and able to endure until the end.

Daily Word

The disciples asked Jesus, "What will be the sign of Your coming and of the end of the age?" And Jesus responded: persecution, lawlessness, false messiahs, false prophets, wars and rumors of wars, famines, earthquakes, nation will rise up against nation and kingdom against kingdom, and many will betray one another and hate one another. These events are the beginning of birth pains, just like a mom contracting and laboring before delivering a newborn baby.

The world will go through a similar labor before Jesus' return. So don't be alarmed when these events happen around you but rather recognize Jesus' return is near! Don't live in fear. Take notice of the birth pains occurring, and live with the hope you have in Christ.

Today, take the opportunity to proclaim God's love to the world as you prepare for the return of Christ.

See that you are not alarmed, because these things must take place, but the end is not yet. . . . All these events are the beginning of birth pains. —Matthew 24:6, 8

Further Scripture: Matthew 24:14; Mark 13:32; 2 Peter 3:10

Questions

1. Consider Matthew 24:36 and 42. What is the balance between "not knowing the times" and "keeping watch"? (Matthew 25:1–13; Luke 12:56)

2. What events/things precede the Messiah coming back? Where are we in the procession of events?

3. How can you practically apply the instruction in Matthew 24:45–51 to your own life?

4. How does Matthew 24 spark urgency in your own heart, and how do you act upon that urgency?

5. What did the Holy Spirit highlight to you in Matthew 24 through the reading or the teaching?

Lesson 25: Matthew 25
King: Sheep, Goats, and Brethren

Teaching Notes

Intro

The goal for yesterday's lesson in Matthew 24 is to get ready for the end times. Matthew 25:1–13 is the Parable of the Ten Virgins and talks about some who will be prepared and some who will not. Verses 14–30 talk about the Parable of the Ten Talents. The question is this: How are we using the talents we've received for His glory? There's no heavier topic than what we'll talk about today.

The Bible talks about two judgments:

1. The Judgment of the Nations—it has no mention of the resurrection and is the judgment for those who are alive. Within this are three groups: sheep, goats, and brethren.
2. The White Throne Judgment—it is for nonbelievers and the wicked, and we'll cover that later.

Teaching

Matthew 25:31: This takes place before the Messianic Kingdom (the 1,000-year reign) and after the battle of Armageddon. This judgment is after the seven-year period of peace and the coming of the antichrist.

In verse 31, when the Son of Man comes with His angels (Daniel 7:13–14), He will sit on His throne of His glory. The people of all nations will come together before Him, just as a shepherd separates his flocks (often with both sheep and goats together). In this context, the sheep are believers, and the goats are unbelievers. I want to paint a picture of sheep with the following verses:

> Matthew 10:16: "Look, I'm sending you out like sheep among wolves."
> John 10:14: "I am the good shepherd. I know My own sheep, and they know Me,"
> John 10:16: "But I have other sheep that are not of this fold; I must bring them also, and they will listen to My voice. Then there will be one flock, one shepherd."

> Psalm 79:13: "Then we, Your people, the sheep of Your pasture, will thank You forever; we will declare Your praise to generation after generation."
>
> Ezekiel 34:17: "The Lord God says to you, My flock: I am going to judge between one sheep and another, between the rams and male goats."

The sheep will be placed on His right and the goats on His left. The right symbolizes favor; the left symbolizes disfavor. Nelson's Commentary points out that sheep and goats can be herded together, but that at some point, they have to be separated.[1]

Matthew 25:34: The sheep will inherit the kingdom that has been prepared for them, by the *King*. It comes first and foremost by the sheep's faith in the *King*.

> Ephesians 1:4: "For He chose us in Him, before the foundation of the world, to be holy and blameless in His sight."
>
> Romans 8:29: "For those He foreknew He predestined them to be conformed to the image of His Son, so that He would be the firstborn among many brothers."

Matthew 25:35–40: These verses describe the sheep serving or their fruit. The time frame of this happening is for the people who are alive during the tribulation, that did these things for the brethren—the believing Jews. The sheep ask when they did these things (vv. 37–39). The *King* responds, "Whatever you did for one of the least of these brothers of Mine, you did for Me" (v. 40). This then is the third people group—the brethren.

The sheep served the brethren during the tribulation: The believing Jews are the recipients of the 144,000 sharing the gospel who trust Jesus with their lives. Because this group does not have the mark of the beast on them, they are unable to buy or sell, to make money, or to feed or care for their families. Therefore, the Gentiles step in and provide care for them, at great risk to their own lives.[2] The Gentiles were prepared to provide help. "Their motive was not for reward, but sacrificial love."[3] This means that believers who are still around in the end times should be taking care of these Jews.

---

[1] Earl D. Radmacher, Ronald B. Allen, and H. Wayne House, eds., *Nelson's New Illustrated Bible Commentary* (Nashville: Thomas Nelson, 1999), 1192.

[2] Warren Wiersbe, *Exposition Bible Commentary: Matthew–Galatians* (Nashville: Thomas Nelson, 1989), 93.

[3] Wiersbe, 93.

Matthew 10:40: "The one who welcomes you welcomes Me, and the one who welcomes Me welcomes Him who sent Me." The disciples were sent first to the lost sheep of Israel, but they welcomed Him not. So the message went to the Gentiles. Now, these Gentiles are to take care of the brethren who have come to believe in Jesus.

Matthew 25:41–45: Those on the left are cursed and are sent into the eternal fire. They were more concerned about themselves and their own needs than helping the brethren.

Matthew 25:46: Those on the left will go away into eternal punishment, while those on the right receive eternal life. "Eternal" = forever, never stops. "Eternal punishment" = eternal hell. Don't buy into the idea that hell is not a real place.

Descriptions of hell in Scripture:

- fire that never goes out (Matthew 3:12)
- shame and eternal contempt (Daniel 12:2)
- their worm does not die, and the fire is not quenched (Mark 9:44)
- torment . . . agony in this flame! (Luke 16:23–24)
- flaming fire (2 Thessalonians 1:8)
- the smoke of their torment will go on forever (Revelation 14:11)
- Death and Hades were thrown into the lake of fire (Revelation 20:14)

Closing

Let's prevent the goats from even being goats. Let's represent *King* Jesus now so people will be prepared to be sheep. Embrace *King* Jesus who is the resurrection, the truth, and the life. Only through *King* Jesus can we live on the right side of the *King*.

Daily Word

Jesus instructed the disciples to be alert and ready for the day He would return. He clearly advised them to live faithfully with what they had been given, not comparing or complaining about the gifts, talents, and treasures entrusted to them. Jesus simply wanted those gifts used for His glory.

How would you live if you knew Jesus were returning next week? Would you hide under a rock and sleep away the days? No way! The joy of the Lord is your strength! As He instructed the disciples, Jesus instructs you to live life intentionally because of the eternal hope found in Him. It may mean studying your Bible to learn more about Jesus' love for you as you prepare to live with Him forever. It may mean sharing your hope and faith in Jesus with those you love, regardless of feeling nervous or fearful. Living intentionally may look like using your gifts of hospitality, teaching, or serving unashamedly in faith. No more hiding your gifts or living in fear. When you live life fully, with all the Lord has given you, Jesus says, "Well done, good and faithful servant! I will now put you in charge of more!" Today, don't delay. Ask the Holy Spirit to guide you to live life to the fullest and prepare you to be ready for the return of Jesus the King!

**Therefore be alert, because you don't know either the day or the hour.
—Matthew 25:13**

Further Scripture: Galatians 5:25; Ephesians 3:20; 1 Peter 4:10

Questions

1. What was the difference between the foolish and wise virgins/bridesmaids (Matthew 25:1–13)? How were they the same? What was the reward for the bridesmaids who were ready and what was the punishment for those where weren't? How can you be ready for the return of Christ?

2. In the Parable of the Talents in Matthew 25:14–28, how many talents were given to each servant? How did the master react to the different outcomes? What does Jesus teach us about not comparing results in ministry?

3. Why did the master not like what the last servant did with his talent (Matthew 25:24–30)? How does the Lord feel about laziness (Proverbs 12:27; 20:4; Ezekiel 16:49; Romans 12:11)? Do you think the penalty was too severe? Why or why not?

4. Jesus was about to be crucified. What was He speaking about in Matthew 25:31–34? How are these statements of prophecy found in the Old Testament and future prophecy? (2 Samuel 7:12–13; Ezekiel 20:38; Daniel 7:13–14; 1 Thessalonians 4:16)

5. When we serve others, how are we actually serving Christ (Matthew 25:35–40)? What can you do around your neighborhood, school, or work to serve others more effectively?

6. What did the Holy Spirit highlight to you in Matthew 25 through the reading or the teaching?

Lesson 26: Matthew 26

King: Giving Everything to Jesus

Teaching Notes

Intro

The last few lessons have been tense, ramping up with a macro look at the information about the end times. Today, we'll use a micro look at the human side of these events. Matthew 26 begins with Jesus telling His disciples that there will be a plot to kill Him (vv. 1–5).

Teaching

Matthew 26:6–9: Bethany was a small village on the Mount of Olives, where the house of Simon was, who was possibly the father of Lazarus, Mary, and Martha. Simon suffered from a "serious skin disease," probably leprosy. The only cure for leprosy was the touch of God. This is the crazy backdrop of the anointing that's going to take place, in preparation for the *King* (Mark 14:3–9; John 12:1–8). While there, a woman (based on other accounts it was Mary, the sister of Martha and Lazarus) came with a jar of expensive oil. According to John 12:3, Mary had "a pound of fragrant oil–pure and expensive nard." The perfume was worth 300 denarii (John 12:5). Biblical scholars suggest that 300 denarii was what most workers earned in a year. Mary poured it over Jesus' head and feet, while the disciples questioned her sacrifice.

When we think of Mary, we can use the phrase "radical brokenness." Wiersbe points out that Mary is mentioned three times in Scripture, always at the feet of Jesus: (1) Mary sat at His feet and listened to Him teach—Luke 10:38–39; (2) after the death of her brother, she sat at His feet and grieved (John 11:28–32); (3) and she worshiped at His feet as she anointed Him with perfume (John 12:3).[1] People who are broken are attracted to truth—to the feet of Jesus. Mary anointed Jesus' head and His feet and wiped His feet with her hair (John 12:3). She gave up all of her finances and then gave up "her glory" before the *King* (1 Corinthians 11:13). She gave everything she had in preparing the *King*.

---

[1] Warren Wiersbe, *The Bible Exposition Commentary: Matthew–Galatians* (Nashville: Thomas Nelson, 1989), 94.

Our question should always be, "What can I do to prepare for the *King*?" The disciples, however, were the complete opposite and became indignant at Mary's actions. In John 12:4–5, Judas is identified as the one with the most issues about the cost of the perfume. Why did Judas care? He was in charge of the finances, and possibly he thought Jesus would be the political king and he would rise in power with Him.

In John 17:12, Jesus called Judas the "son of destruction," which is also the "son of waste." Judas had every opportunity to turn his life around, but instead, he opened it up to Satan (John 13:2). Judas spent three years as a disciple and was given power in the process, but somewhere along the way, he ignored the truth. When he began to express his emotions and his concerns, he took them to the religious authorities, not to Jesus. He gave up nothing but accepted 30 pieces of silver instead. "After Judas ate the piece of bread, Satan entered him. Therefore, Jesus told him, 'What you're doing, do quickly'" (John 13:27). This doesn't mean that Judas was the martyr, because he could have said no. The prophecies continued to point to someone close to the Messiah who would betray Him (Psalms 41:9; 55:12–14). Judas had the choice to turn his brokenness to the Lord, and instead, he turned to Satan.

Matthew 26:10–13: Jesus responded that Mary had done a noble thing for Him in preparing Him for burial. By giving up a year's worth of wages, and by letting her hair down to use on Jesus' feet, Mary truly prepared the way for the *King*. Mark 14:3b has this description: "A woman came with an alabaster jar of pure and expensive fragrant oil of nard. She broke the jar and poured it on His head." That's the picture of how we should all come to the Lord—not with timidity, but with boldness, ready to give up everything to Jesus.

Once the bottle was broken, the bottle could not be recorked or reused. Whether Mary knew it or not, what she did is a picture from the Old Testament. Second Kings 9:6 says: "Then take the flask of oil, pour it on his head, and say, 'This is what the Lord God of Israel says: "I anoint you king over Israel."'" The young prophet poured the oil on the king's head. Because of the oil on his head, Jehu was prepared in the way of a king. Wiersbe said that since Mary had listened to Jesus' teaching, she knew He would soon die, and that "His body would not need the traditional care given to the dead because His body would not see corruption (Psalm 16:10; Acts 2:22–28)."[2]

There are two kinds of people—the Marys and the Judases. Based on Matthew 25, Mary is a sheep and Judas is a goat. Mary was taking care of Him, which is a foreshadowing of taking care of the brethren. Judas took care of himself. Jesus said that everyone who heard about His death would also hear about how Mary

---

[2] Wiersbe, 94.

gave up everything to prepare Jesus for His death (v. 13). Can you imagine if she had been worried about what others thought of her actions?

Matthew 26:14–16: Judas went to the chief priests and asked what they would give him if he turned over Jesus to them. They paid him 30 pieces of silver, and he began to look for an opportunity to betray Jesus. The account of Judas' betrayal is in the rest of Matthew 26:47–51. Mary kissed the *King* in worship; Judas kissed the *King* in betrayal. Mary, in her brokenness prepared the way; Judas, in his pride prepared the way.

Closing

Douglas Sean O'Donnell wrote: "Mary loved Jesus above all . . . Mary also loved Jesus with costly love . . . She loved Jesus for who He said He was."[3] My prayer is this: Don't try to work your way out of what God is asking you to do. If you do that, you're going the way of Judas.

Daily Word

While Jesus reclined at a table in Simon's house, a woman came to Him with an alabaster jar of very expensive, fragrant oil. She poured the oil over His head. Jesus received this sacrificial offering as way of preparing Him for burial, something the disciples did not fully understand at the time. The disciples witnessed this scene from a logical viewpoint, upset to see the woman "waste" an expensive amount of perfume. But Jesus understood the woman's heart. He honored her for breaking the jar and pouring the oil over Him. It was an act of love and devotion to Jesus the King and fulfilled the Scriptures.

As you offer your heart to Jesus, are you holding anything back? Release the things you feel like you need control over: your future, your children, your finances, your health, or your schedule for the day. Today, pour out your broken heart before the Lord and say, "Jesus, have it all!" Even if it doesn't make sense, offer the Lord all you are and all you have in faith. The Lord will bless you as you worship Jesus the King with a broken heart.

I assure you: Wherever this gospel is proclaimed in the whole world, what this woman has done will also be told in memory of her. —Matthew 26:13

Further Scripture: 2 Kings 9:6; Psalm 51:16–17; Psalm 62:8

---

[3] Douglas Sean O'Donnell and R. Kent Hughes, *Matthew: All Authority in Heaven and on Earth* (Wheaton, IL: Crossway, 2013), 766–68.

Questions

1. Who was the woman that poured the jar of perfume on Jesus (Matthew 26:7; John 12:3)? Why were some disciples upset about this (John 12:4–6)? How did Jesus feel about what she did to Him?

2. In Matthew 26:21, while Jesus and the disciples were having the Passover meal, Jesus mentioned how one of them would betray Him. After just receiving 30 pieces of silver to betray Jesus, why do you think that Judas would ask if he was the one (Matthew 26:25)? Could Jesus have been giving Judas a chance to repent with his response?

3. What was the new covenant that Jesus introduced to the disciples during the Passover meal (Jeremiah 31:31, 33–34; Ezekiel 36:26–27; 2 Corinthians 5:21; Hebrews 9:14–15)? How is this better than the old covenant?

4. What do you notice that Jesus did on the night before He was to be crucified (Matthew 26:30)? How important would you say singing praises to God is to Him (Psalms 100; 113)? Think of a time in your life that was stressful and filled with anxiety. Were you able to sing praises to the Lord during those circumstances? Could you do it now if hard times were to come?

5. Jesus knew that Peter would deny Him and that the disciples would desert Him, yet He still desired them to pray for Him. What was He trying to teach them about prayer (Psalm 43:5; Matthew 6:13; 26:38, 41)? How many times did Jesus ask God the Father to take this cup from Him? How consistent are you with your prayer life?

6. What did the Holy Spirit highlight to you in Matthew 26 through the reading or the teaching?

Lesson 27: Matthew 27

King: Fulfillment of Crucifixion Prophecies

Teaching Notes

Intro

All of Matthew is about the *King*. Yesterday, we looked at how Mary and Judas both had roles in preparing the way for the *King*. Today, we look at the crucifixion. Matthew 27 has 66 verses.

Teaching

Matthew 27:1–10: Jesus was handed over to Pilate and Judas returned the 30 pieces of silver to the chief priests and elders and took his own life. Verse 4 shows that in Judas' heart, he knew he had messed up. Even the chief priests recognized the 30 pieces of silver were blood money, so they bought a potter's field with it (vv. 6–7).

Matthew 27:11–14: Jesus was asked by the governor, "Are You the *King* of the Jews?" Jesus answered, "You have said it." From His birth in Matthew 1 through the end of Matthew, Jesus is presented as the *King* of the Jews.

Matthew 27:15–26: Pilate asked the crowd if they wanted Jesus or Barabbas to be released. The crowd called, "Crucify Him!" They kept shouting those words when Pilate asked more questions. Pilate washed his hands and said he was innocent of Jesus' blood (the same conversation Judas had with the religious leaders in verse 4). The people answered, "His blood be on us and on our children!"

Matthew 27:27–31: Pilate handed Jesus over to be crucified. What did that look like? MacArthur says it was a form of execution that had originated with the Persians, Phoenicians, and Carthaginians to the Romans. The goal was to keep the victim alive as long as possible (most lasted for days) while inflicting pain. Plus, the legs gave out, so the victim couldn't breathe, so breaking the legs brought a quicker death. The nails were driven through the instep and wrists, which was not fatal but extremely painful[1] (John 19:31).

---

[1] John MacArthur, *The MacArthur Bible Commentary* (Nashville: Thomas Nelson, 2005), 1182.

> Galatians 3:13: "Christ has redeemed us from the curse of the law by becoming a curse for us, because it is written: Everyone who is hung on a tree is cursed."

Matthew 27:32–34: This shows Jesus' humanity in the pain He experienced and being too weak to carry His 200-pound cross (Hebrews 4:15). Simon from Cyrene was forced to carry the cross for Jesus (v. 32), and he later became a believer. Golgotha (Skull Place) was located outside the city gates. Jesus was on the cross when they gave Him wine mixed with gall (v. 34), which would have eased His pain. This was prophesied in Psalm 69:21. Jesus refused it. Why? Two possible reasons:

1. Luke 23:43 records that Jesus ministered to one of the others on the cross, so maybe He wanted to be able to do that clearly without any physical hindrance.
2. Proverbs 31:6 suggests that maybe Jesus wanted to embrace the pain.

Matthew 27:35–37: The soldiers cast lots for His clothes and put a sign over His head that charged Him: *This is Jesus, the King of the Jews*. When combined with evidence in the other Gospels (Mark 15:26; Luke 22:38; John 22:38), the sign read: *This is Jesus of Nazareth, the King of the Jews*. This shows both the humanity and the divinity of Christ.

Matthew 27:38–44: Isaiah 53:12 has the prophecy of being between the thieves on the crosses. The people walking by—the crowd, the chief priests, the scribes, and elders—mocked Him as the *King* of Israel. Even the criminals taunted Jesus as well.

7 Crucifixion Prophecies Jesus came to fulfill:

1. God will forsake His own Son in His time of agony (Psalm 22:1; Matthew 27:46; Mark 15:34).
2. Christ will be scorned and ridiculed (Psalm 22:7,8; Matthew 27:39–40; Luke 23:35).
3. Christ's hands and feet will be pierced (Psalm 22:16; John 20:25,27; Acts 2:23).
4. Others will gamble for Christ's clothes (Psalm 22:18; Matthew 27:35, 36).
5. Not one of Christ's bones will be broken (Psalm 34:20; John 19:32, 33, 36).
6. Christ will be betrayed by a friend (Psalm 41:9; John 13:18).

7. Christ will be given vinegar and gall (Psalm 69:21; Matthew 27:34; John 19:28–30).[2]

Closing

All of this is to show how it points to the Messiah. The Old Testament points to the Messiah. The New Testament points to the Messiah. Matthew 27 shows Christ's on-going fulfillment of prophecy. The *King* will suffer in order for us to be set free. My prayer is that we don't forget the pain Jesus went through for us to have life. And Jesus' fulfillment doesn't end at the cross. That's tomorrow!

Daily Word

Jesus unjustly died on the Cross. Although the crowd hailed, "This is Jesus, the King of the Jews," putting Jesus to death did not make sense according to the laws of the time. However, Jesus' death was the will of the Father, who gave up His only Son so that whoever believes in Jesus would have eternal life. Jesus went through physical pain. He was mocked. He was pierced for our transgressions and bruised for our iniquities. He suffered, both physically and emotionally. In those final moments, the prophecies were fulfilled as Jesus died. He suffered much so that we could be set free and live eternal life.

Today, reflect and give thanks for the pain Jesus suffered on the Cross. It's hard to linger in the rawness of the pain Jesus endured for our sins. It'd be easier to move on to the fact that yes, Jesus was resurrected! But don't miss the pain He suffered. It was real. You may like to skip over your own pain and move on to happier times. But the truth is, everyone suffers. Everyone endures pain. Jesus, the King of kings, is your Savior. He understands and can sympathize with your pain. He was willing to endure the suffering and death for you, beloved child of God. As you press into the pain Jesus suffered and the pain in your own life, the Lord promises He is with you. He will help you endure the pain. And from that pain, you are promised a resurrected life. Our hope is found in Christ alone!

When the centurion and those with him, who were guarding Jesus, saw the earthquake and the things that had happened, they were terrified and said, "This man really was God's son!" —Matthew 27:54

Further Scripture: Isaiah 53:5; John 3:16; Hebrews 4:15–16

---

[2] MacArthur, 1182.

Questions

1. Can you see the prophecy of Isaiah 53:3 being fulfilled in Matthew 27:1–2? Why or why not?

2. In Matthew 27:5–10, Judas returned the 30 pieces of silver to the chief priests. Why couldn't they put this money into the temple treasury? In Zechariah 11:12–13, what messianic prophecy is fulfilled in this New Testament passage?

3. Read Matthew 27:12–14. What prophecy spoken by Isaiah 53:7 is fulfilled? Could you keep silent if you were being unjustly accused?

4. There are at least 12 messianic prophecies from three different Old Testament books fulfilled in Matthew 27. If you were reading this for the first time, do you think that fact would convince you Jesus is the Son of God? (Psalm 22:1, 7–8, 16, 18; 31:5; 38:11; 69:21; Isaiah 50:6; 53:1–3, 7, 9, 12; Zechariah 11:12–13)

5. A crown of thorns was put on Jesus (Matthew 27:29). In Genesis 3:18, thorns were part of the curse as a result of sin. Do you think this crown was symbolic of Jesus becoming a curse for us? (Galatians 3:13)

6. Matthew 27:51 reports that the veil of the temple was torn in two from top to bottom. What does this veil represent (Hebrews 10:20)? What does Jesus' death open up the way to (Hebrews 10:19–20)? Do you walk in this confidence?

7. Jesus quoted from Psalm 22:1 when He cried out to God asking why He had forsaken Him. Do you think He really was forsaken by God at that moment? (Matthew 28:7; Luke 1:33; Ephesians 1:19–21)

8. What did the Holy Spirit highlight to you in Matthew 27 through the reading or the teaching?

Lesson 28: Matthew 28
King: Go and Tell of the Risen Lord!

Teaching Notes

Intro

This is the last lesson in Matthew. Yesterday, we looked at the arduous ordeal Jesus endured on the cross, but today, we'll see how His story ended well because of His resurrection. The Apostle Paul wrote a lot about Jesus' resurrection, stating that without the resurrection, Jesus would have been just another man (Romans 6:4). The resurrection was necessary for Him to take His place as our *King*, our Messiah, our Savior. We can trust that Christ is no longer in the grave (Romans 8:34).

Teaching

Matthew 28:1–4: "After the Sabbath" refers to sundown on Saturday, or what some have referred to as the dawn of Sunday morning. This means we're looking at the period from sundown on Friday until the dawn of Easter Sunday. Constable states that the two Marys "apparently did not know that the Sanhedrin had posted a guard at the tomb."[1] They were focused on their task of anointing Jesus' body. There was a violent earthquake as an angel appeared suddenly and rolled the stone from the tomb entrance and sat on it (v. 2). Luke 24:4 shows that there were actually two angels. In Matthew 27:51, the earthquake marked the death of Christ. At the point of the resurrection there was, again, an earthquake. In verse 3, the angel had the appearance of holiness; his robe was white as snow (Matthew 17:2; Acts 1:10). One commentary suggests that the guards were so shaken that they passed out (v. 4).

Matthew 28:5–10: The angel told the women that he knew they were looking for Jesus who had been crucified, but not to be afraid (v. 5)! The angel pronounced, "He is not here! For He has been resurrected, just as He said" (v. 6). When did Jesus say this? (Matthew 12:40; 16:21; 17:9, 23; 26:32, all point to Jesus' death, burial, and resurrection after three days. The disciples had to think beyond the bad news of the crucifixion and death to be able to embrace the good news of

---

[1] Thomas L. Constable, *Expository Notes of Dr. Thomas Constable: Matthew*, 704, https://planobiblechapel.org/tcon/notes/pdf/matthew.pdf.

Christ's resurrection (v. 7). Christianity is dependent upon the resurrection, not just the death. But we have to experience death to find true life (Matthew 10:39; 16:25; 28:6).

The angel invited the women to come see the empty tomb and to personally experience Jesus' resurrection (v. 6b), before they were told to go tell His disciples (v. 8). All of us have to experience Jesus' resurrection personally before we too can go and tell others about it. Sadly, we tend to live like Jesus is still in the tomb and He's not coming out. However, when we come and see that "He is not here!" we can go and tell others about Him.

Then, the angel told the women to go and tell the disciples the news (v. 7). The women left with "fear and great joy" (v. 8). Jesus met them along their way with the customary greeting, "Good morning!" (v. 9). The women held Jesus' feet and worshipped Him. They came looking for His body and left immediately to tell the disciples Jesus had risen. Jesus' appearance to them was not necessary because they were already on their way as an act of faith. But Jesus chose to bless them with His presence, and they worshipped Him. Jesus told the women to tell the disciples to go to Galilee and they would see Him there. That was not an easy trip and a distance of 100 miles. It was the location Jesus had told them in Matthew 26:32.

This began Jesus' post-resurrection appearances. He showed up to the women. He showed up in Jerusalem and Judea. He showed up in Galilee. He showed up in Jerusalem again.

When the disciples heard the story, Peter and John ran back to the tomb to see what the women had seen (John 20:4–7). Finding Jesus' burial garments was like finding "a cocoon."[2] His clothes were perfectly wrapped, but He was not there.

Matthew 28:11–15: As the disciples were on their way to Galilee, the guards reported what had happened to the chief priests (earthquake, angels, passing out). Nelson's Commentary points out that this was an actual assignment for the guards.[3] The religious authorities came up with a plan to say that Jesus' disciples had stolen His body while the soldiers slept, and they paid the soldiers hush money to keep them silent about the truth (v. 12). The plan makes no sense because a guard sleeping at his post was sentenced to death (Acts 12:19; 16:27). Further, if they were sleeping, how did they know the story of what had happened? And, when did the disciples get so strong that they were able to move the stone? In verse 14, the religious leaders even promised to cover for the soldiers if

[2] Warren Wiersbe, *The Bible Exposition Commentary: Matthew–Galatians* (Colorado Springs: David C. Cook, 1989), 105.

[3] Earl D. Radmacher, Ronald B. Allen, and H. Wayne House, eds., *Nelson's New Illustrated Bible Commentary* (Nashville: Thomas Nelson, 1999), 1202.

the governor found out about the missing body. The soldiers took the money and spread the story that Jesus' body was stolen. According to verse 15, the story was still being spread among the Jews.

Matthew 28:16–17: Hughes asked several interesting questions in his commentary on these verses. First, why did only 11 go to Galilee? He pointed out that the number 11 is imperfect, according to Scripture, and so wondered why the remaining disciples had not added another. He suggested that "perhaps it was because they thought the Jesus-as-Messiah train ride had stopped for good at the cross."4 Hughes also questioned why the disciples were sent to Galilee and suggested that this 100-mile journey was a "faith walk," which would take trust.5 Another possibility is that Jesus didn't want to return to Jerusalem yet because they had rejected Him. A third question Hughes asked was why Jesus met His disciples on a mountain. Hughes emphasized that Jesus began His ministry at the Sermon on the Mount (Matthew 4:12).6

When the disciples saw the resurrected Jesus, they worshipped Him (v. 17a). But it was not just the 11 who saw Him. Paul recorded 500 people seeing Him at one time (1 Corinthians 15:6). Possibly this is where those who doubted came from (v. 17b).

Matthew 28:18–20: Remember that the disciples had been sent out to the lost sheep of Israel (the Jews), but they had rejected Him. He now gave them a new mission. First, He emphasized that "all authority has been given to Me in heaven and on earth" (v. 18). God was declaring both His humanity and His divinity. Then Jesus told them, "Go, therefore, and make disciples of all nations."

How were the disciples to make disciples? First, by going. We cannot make disciples without going out to them. Second, by baptizing them. Baptism can happen at any time and any place with water, when someone believes in the death and resurrection of Christ. Ordination is not required to baptize a new believer. In the name of the Father, the Son, and the Holy Spirit, we should be baptizing new believers all the time. Third, by teaching them everything that Christ has commanded us to teach. And we can remember, Jesus is always with us, even to the end of the age.

Closing

King Jesus is now ruling and reigning over our lives. We have a commission to talk about Jesus wherever we go.

---

4 Douglas Sean O'Donnell and R. Kent Hughes, *Matthew: All Authority in Heaven and on Earth* (Wheaton, IL: Crossway, 2013), 906.

5 O'Donnell and Hughes, 907.

6 O'Donnell and Hughes, 907.

Daily Word

"Come and see . . . Jesus has been resurrected, just as He said He would be!" the angels proclaimed. They instructed Mary Magdalene and the other Mary to go and tell what they have seen and heard. As the women went on their way, they met Jesus along the path. After worshipping Jesus at His feet, He too told them to go and tell. Then the disciples saw Jesus resurrected just as He foretold to them. And although they worshipped Him, some still doubted what they saw. Had Jesus truly been resurrected?

Just like the disciples, Jesus is alive in you! He has told you to *go and tell* others about His great love. Will you worship Him and go, or will you continue to doubt the Jesus you have seen alive in your life? Today move from doubt to faith, and live for Christ just as He commanded His disciples! Jesus promises He will be with you always, even to the end of the age.

When they saw Him, they worshiped, but some doubted. . . . "Go, therefore, and make disciples of all nations, baptizing them in the name of the Father and of the Son and of the Holy Spirit, teaching them to observe everything I have commanded you. And remember, I am with you always, to the end of the age." —Matthew 28:17, 19–20

Further Scripture: Psalm 96:3; Galatians 2:20–21; Revelation 14:6–7

Questions

1. Describe the angel who came from heaven and rolled away the stone from the tomb (Matthew 28:3). Compare this to the description of Jesus in Matthew 17:2. Explain why they are similar.

2. The guards were so afraid of the angel that they became like dead men, but the women who came to the tomb were told not to be afraid (Matthew 28:4–5). How did the women respond? (Matthew 28:8)

3. The angel told the women that Jesus had risen, just as He said. When did Jesus say this? Matthew 12:38–41; 16:21; 17:23; 20:19; 26:32)

4. When Jesus appeared to the women in Matthew 28:9–10, He told them to not be afraid. Do you think, even though the angel told them that Jesus had risen, the sight of Him scared them? Would you have been afraid?

5. Do you think that when the disciples headed to Galilee, like Jesus instructed through the women (Matthew 28:10), it demonstrated their faith that He was indeed raised to life? If so, how does that explain verse 17, that upon seeing Him, some were doubtful?

6. When Jesus told the disciples to make disciples of all the nations, why was this significant? (Matthew 10:5–6)

7. What did the Holy Spirit highlight to you in Matthew 28 through the reading or the teaching?

Lesson 29: Mark 1

Servant: Teaching with Authority

Teaching Notes

Intro

As we continue our study of the Gospels, we're moving into the Gospel of Mark. It is a picture of Jesus as *Servant*. The Gospel was written by John Mark, and in Acts 12:12, the house of John Mark's mother is shown as a place of prayer. Therefore, Mark brought a unique perspective on prayer to his Gospel. When there's a praying mother, it tends to carry over to her children. On the first missionary journey, Barnabas and Saul (also called Paul; Acts 13:9) took John Mark with them (Acts 12:25). Furthermore, John Mark was Barnabas's cousin (Colossians 4:10). John Mark had a rich spiritual legacy.

John Mark also had some problems. He couldn't finish the missionary journey and returned home early, creating a split between Barnabas and Paul (Acts 13:13; 15:38–40). Even though John Mark bailed on Paul, he is identified as one of Paul's coworkers (Philemon 24) and was still useful in the ministry (2 Timothy 4:11). Also, John Mark and Peter had a close discipleship relationship (1 Peter 5:13).

John Mark wrote his gospel two to three decades after the resurrection, probably from Rome, because it was written to Roman believers who were Gentiles. Throughout the Gospel of Mark, Jesus is portrayed as the "suffering *Servant*"; "For even the Son of Man did not come to be served, but to serve, and to give His life—a ransom for many" (Mark 10:45). Throughout this Gospel, Jesus' human emotions were shown (Mark 1:41). As the suffering *Servant*, Jesus was moved with compassion for people and could connect with them (Mark 1:41; 3:5). Jesus had both human emotions and physical limitations: He became tired (Mark 4:38), hungry (Mark 11:12), and disappointed (Mark 8:12).

Teaching

Mark 1:1–8: The first 8 verses herald the coming of the Messiah through prophecy (vv. 2–3) and through John the Baptist preparing the way (vv. 4–8). John Mark's stories are often much shorter than what we read in Matthew.

Mark 1:9–15: John Mark documented Jesus' baptism by John the Baptist (vv. 9–11) and Jesus' temptations in the wilderness (vv. 12–13). Then, John Mark stated that John the Baptist was arrested, and Jesus went to Galilee to begin His ministry (v. 14).

Mark 1:16–20: Jesus began to call His disciples.

Mark 1:21–22: Jesus began His ministry in Capernaum of Galilee. One common thread in the book of Mark is that Jesus always went to the synagogue to teach. (Mark 2:13; 4:1–12; 6; 10–12; 14.) Capernaum was an important and prosperous fishing village located on the northwest shore of the Sea of Galilee and on a major road. Its location became an essential component to Jesus' headquarters. Those in the synagogue were astonished with His teaching because He taught "as one having authority" (v. 22). Jews were used to rabbis quoting other rabbis, using oral tradition. Jesus spoke as the Truth Himself; His message was a new perspective for His hearers. One commentary said that Jesus spoke with directness and forcefulness, while still being personal. In fact, 42 percent of the Gospel of Mark is specifically referencing His teaching.[1]

Mark 1:23–24: Just then, a man with an unclean spirit entered the synagogue. The demon (the unclean spirit) recognized Jesus as both human and divine as "the Holy One of God!" MacArthur interpreted the demon's question as, "Why do you interfere with us?"[2] *Nelson's Commentary* states that 20 percent of all of Jesus' miracles "involved Jesus helping those troubled by demons."[3] If you do ministry every day, as you continue to proclaim the gospel, you will face demonic activity. Jesus spent almost a quarter of His time dealing with demons because He had compassion for those people who were being attacked by demons.

A synagogue was started every time there were at least ten men in a community. *Nelson's Commentary* explains what would be found in first-century synagogues:

- *Elders*: those who regulated the policies of the synagogue.
- *A ruler*: one appointed by the elders to take care of the building and planning of services.

---

[1] Earl D. Radmacher, Ronald B. Allen, and H. Wayne House, eds., *Nelson's New Illustrated Bible Commentary* (Nashville: Thomas Nelson, 1999), 1208.

[2] John MacArthur, *The MacArthur Bible Commentary* (Nashville: Thomas Nelson, 2005), 1199.

[3] Radmacher et al., 1209.

- *A minister*: one who tended the sacred scrolls, attended the lamps, and kept the building clean, as well as teaching the children to read and administering lashes of punishment.
- *A delegate*: a capable person who was chosen by the ruler before the service to read Scripture, lead prayer, and preach to the congregation (a temporary office). Jesus served as a delegate in the Nazareth synagogue (Luke 4:16–30).
- *An interpreter*: a person who could translate the Hebrew Scriptures since most Jews spoke Aramaic.
- *Almoners*: two or three people who received money taken up to meet the needs of the poor.[4]

Since Jesus spent so much time teaching in synagogues, He would have encountered and interacted with people in all of these positions. Paul also entered every community and went straight to the synagogue. The interactions with the religious authorities often took place in synagogues. The service began with the reading of the Shema (Deuteronomy 6:4–9), a speaker would lead a time of prayer as they faced Jerusalem with their hands extended, and then a chosen speaker would stand and read a section of the Law, which the interpreter translated, and a section of the Prophets, which was also translated. The delegate then preached the commentary and sermon. Afterward, the priest announced the benediction, and the congregation concluded with "Amen."[5] This becomes an underlining audience throughout Mark.

Mark 1:25–28: The man with the unclean spirit interrupted Jesus' teaching. Jesus rebuked the demon saying, "Be quiet!" (or "Be muzzled!") and commanded him to leave the man (v. 25). The demonic spirit came out, and the man began trembling with convulsions (v. 26). Dealing with demonic spirits gets messy! The people in the synagogue were amazed at what they had seen and began to argue about what had happened and about Jesus teaching with authority (v. 27). Word spread based on what people had seen in the synagogue—because Jesus had cast out the demonic easily (v. 28). When you walk with authority and power, the spirit of religion will push back, but people will be hungry to hear the message.

Mark 1:29–34: After the synagogue, Jesus, Simon, James, John, and Andrew went into Simon and Andrew's house. Jesus served Simon Peter's mother-in-law by healing her (vv. 29–31) (yes, Simon Peter was married; 1 Corinthians 9:5).

---

4 Radmacher et al., 1208.

5 Radmacher et al., 1208.

That evening, people quickly began to bring the sick and the demon-possessed to Jesus for healing. They came so quickly that the whole town gathered at the door (vv. 32–33). Jesus cast out the demons but "did not permit the demons to speak, because they knew Him" (v. 34). This is an exact picture of the *Servant* that we're after.

Closing

Look at Mindi's incredible painting for the book of Mark. Remember, there is one painting per book of the Bible. Look especially at the hand—the power of Christ is brought through the hand that healed the sick and cast out the demons. He touched Simon Peter's mother-in-law and she became well. Christ, the suffering *Servant*, is willing to engage anyone and everyone at any time to draw them closer to Him.

Daily Word

Jesus knew His mission: to preach the good news of God, which is that truth is fulfilled, the kingdom of God has come near, and all must repent and believe in the good news (Mark 1:15). He went out teaching in full authority. At one point, in the midst of teaching, healing, and driving out demons, He went away alone early in the morning to pray. His disciples soon found Him, saying, "Everyone's looking for You!" Jesus responded, "Let's go. This is why I have come!"

Jesus is God in human form. It's important to remember He is fully human. He knew His mission and calling, and He has delegated this same mission and calling to your life. Just like Jesus, you will have busy seasons. You will have demanding times where everyone is looking for you.

Therefore, Jesus models the importance of getting away from all the activity to pray. He also models a positive, "let's go!" attitude when it's time to get back to the mission. Today, take time to pray and seek the Lord. And when it's time to get back to work, practice saying, "Let's go! This is what God has called me to." Work not in your own strength but from the strength and power of the Holy Spirit, equipping you for each step on your mission.

And He said to them, "Let's go on to the neighboring villages so that I may preach there too. This is why I have come." —Mark 1:38

Further Scripture: Philippians 2:13; Colossians 1:28–29; 2 Timothy 1:9

Questions

1. Why did Jesus go into the wilderness for 40 days? Why was He tempted by Satan? Do you think this was necessary? Why or why not?

2. The first disciples, Simon and Andrew, were fishing when Jesus told them to follow Him and He would make them fishers of men. Do you think you would have dropped everything to follow someone you didn't know? Why or why not?

3. In Mark 1:25, Jesus stopped the demon from speaking of who He was. What do you think the reasoning behind this was? Jesus demonstrated authority over demons (Mark 1:27; Luke 4:36). Do we have this same authority? (Luke 10:17; John 14:12)

4. In verses 40–45, Jesus was moved with compassion and healed a man with leprosy. He told the healed man to go before the priest to be examined and to pay the offering. Why didn't Jesus want him telling anyone? If you had been healed by Jesus, would you have been able to remain quiet? Why or why not?

5. What did the Holy Spirit highlight to you in Mark 1 through the reading or the teaching?

Lesson 30: Mark 2

Servant: The Authority to Forgive Sin

Teaching Notes

Intro

Our one word for Jesus in the book of Mark is *Servant,* to help us understand Mark 10:45: "For even the Son of Man did not come to be served, but to serve, and to give His life—a ransom for many." In Mark 1, Jesus' early success emerged as people began to show up at His door to seek healing and the casting out of demons. However, with favor and success usually comes opposition. In Mark 2, that opposition begins.

Teaching

Mark 2:1–4: Jesus returned to His headquarters after having been away for a while (v. 1). So many people gathered to hear Jesus teach that it was standing room only (v. 2). Then four men arrived who were "almost frantic to get their paralyzed friend to Jesus so Jesus would heal him."[1] They didn't care about the crowd and found a way to get their friend through the roof above Jesus' head (v. 4). MacArthur explains that most first-century homes had flat roofs where the inhabitants could rest during the day and sleep on hot nights that were accessed by external staircases. The roof would have been built with wet clay over slabs of dried clay to seal the roof against rain coming through. "The paralytic's friends took him up to the top of such a house and dug out the top coat of clay. . . until they made enough room to lower him down into Jesus' presence."[2] The four friends were so concerned about the paralytic that they didn't care how much work it took or how much damage was created as they brought their friend to Jesus. Wiersbe said that the friends didn't just pray for their friend, "they did not permit the difficult circumstances to discourage them."[3]

---

[1] Thomas L. Constable, *Expository Notes of Dr. Thomas Constable: Mark*, 61, https://planobiblechapel.org/tcon/notes/pdf/mark.pdf.

[2] John MacArthur, *The MacArthur Bible Commentary* (Nashville: Thomas Nelson, 2005), 1200.

[3] Warren Wiersbe, *The Exposition Bible Commentary: Matthew–Galatians* (Colorado Springs: David C. Cook, 1989), 115.

Mark 2:5–7: When the friends broke through the roof, they lowered the paralytic down to Jesus. He looked down at the man lying before Him and said, "Son, your sins are forgiven" (v. 5). The Jews believed that any disease or affliction was caused by some sin. But, in John 9:1–3, Jesus clearly stated that this belief was not true. How completely does God forgive repentant sinners? MacArthur provides five verses that show how much God can forgive sin:

- Psalm 103:12: God removes transgressions as far as the east is from the west.
- Isaiah 38:17: God will cast sins behind His back.
- Isaiah 43:25: God remembers sins no more.
- Micah 7:19: He casts sins into the depths of the sea.
- Colossians 2:13–14: God nailed a certificate marked "paid in full" to the cross.[4]

Some of us don't believe that God can completely remove our sins because they are so huge or so many. But God forgives them *all*!

The scribes (lawyers) had the responsibility to check out these new teachings to make sure they were biblically correct. They heard Jesus forgive the paralytic's sins and they heard blasphemy. Either they didn't recognize Jesus as the Messiah, or they did not believe that the Messiah could forgive sin. Constable points out that the scribes and Pharisees would later condemn "Jesus to death for what they considered blasphemy"[5] (Mark 14:61–64). The accusation of blasphemy always led to trouble.

Wiersbe says that Jesus *looked down* on the body of the paralyzed man, *looked around* at the scribes and Pharisees who had come to spy, and *looked within* "to the critical spirit in their hearts and knew that they were accusing Him of blasphemy."[6] Jesus understood with the "omniscient mind of the Savior"[7] what they were thinking (v. 8). In verse 9, Jesus asked which was easier—to say your sins are forgiven or to say pick up your mat. In some contexts, it would be easier to say the sins are forgiven because it can't be proven. Jesus then told the paralytic to pick up his mat and go home to prove that He had authority to forgive sin (vv. 10–11). There's tension in proving who Jesus is. The paralytic immediately got up and left the room while the others watched (v. 12). Most of the people there wanted to see a miracle from God.

---

[4] MacArthur, 1201.

[5] Constable, 63.

[6] Wiersbe, 115.

[7] MacArthur, 1201.

Mark 2:13: Jesus went out again by the sea and the crowd came to Him and He taught them. What you're going to see is that everything just continues to take off.

The title *Son of Man,* in verse 10, points to the picture of Jesus as a *Servant.* MacArthur states that "Jesus used this term for Himself to emphasize His humiliation."[8] With the title *Son of Man,* Jesus was saying that He was with His hearers and that He was a part of them. The title implies that Jesus was both the divine Messiah and the representative of man. *Son of Man* was used 14 times in the book of Mark alone. Over time, the *Son of Man* will show His suffering (Mark 2:28; 8:31, 38; 13:26, 32).

Closing

"So, from the very beginning of the story Jesus walks a tightrope—under constant threat—and must evade incriminating charges until the right time. His narrow escape from such a serious charge (blasphemy) early in the story contributes significantly to the tension and suspense in this conflict."[9] Jesus was constantly working out His humanity and His divinity. In this story of the paralytic, Jesus put Himself into an environment where He could bring about physical healing but restore spiritually as well. The Son of Man has the authority on earth to forgive the sins of man. People wanted to be around the *Servant,* the *Son of Man,* who could set them free.

Here's my request for this lesson: If you're the paralytic in this story, reach out to friends and let them know you need help. If you're the friend in this story, reach out to someone who is hurting and let them know you're there for them. That's how we begin to understand the *Son of Man* as the *Servant.*

Daily Word

Levi hosted a dinner at his home for Jesus and the disciples. The dinner party also included tax collectors and sinners—in other words, people who specifically violated God's law. As the scribes and Pharisees questioned Jesus about His decision to associate with this part of the community, Jesus reminded them of His purpose. Jesus came to seek the lost. Jesus came to save people from their sins, not to look down on them. Jesus came to dwell among the sinners.

As a believer in Christ, you are called to be Jesus' love to sinners. You aren't called to live in holy church huddles. You aren't called to remain inside the church building on Sunday mornings and Wednesday nights and only share God's love

---

[8] MacArthur, 1201.

[9] David M. Rhoads and Donald M. Michie, *Mark as Story: An Introduction to the Narrative of a Gospel* (Philadelphia: Fortress, 1982), 187.

in your small groups or Bible study class. Those times are great for encouraging the body of Christ. However, as a child of God, you are called to *go out*. You are called to live among sinners and reflect Jesus' love. He promises to empower you, to give you strength, and give you the words to say when you go out as His witness. Today, ask the Lord to give you eyes to see the "sinners and tax collectors" in your community. Then go sit with someone you normally wouldn't. Invite a family over to your home who doesn't go to your church. Go out of your way to love someone like Jesus does. You are a light of the world.

When Jesus heard this, He told them, "Those who are well don't need a doctor, but the sick do need one. I didn't come to call the righteous, but sinners." —Mark 2:17

Further Scripture: Matthew 1:21; John 1:14; Acts 13:47

Questions

1. Four men made a hole in the roof so they could lower a paralyzed man down to Jesus (Mark 2:3–5). Why did Jesus forgive the man's sins instead of saying that he was healed? Do you think these meant the same thing back then? Why or why not?

2. Why do you think tax collectors and disreputable sinners carried the same stigma? Do they still?

3. Read Mark 2:21–22. Can you think of any examples in your own life that relate to these parables?

4. Meditate on Mark 2:27. What does this say to you? How do you explain this verse?

5. What did the Holy Spirit highlight to you in Mark 2 through the reading or the teaching?

Lesson 31: Mark 3

Servant: Facing Opposition in Ministry

Teaching Notes

Intro

We've moved from the study of Matthew and the picture of Jesus as the *King* to our study of Mark and the picture of Jesus as the *Servant*. In Mark 3, we'll see how Jesus was not afraid to interact with people. Because He went amidst the people, many began to follow Him.

Teaching

Mark 3:1–6: In the first six verses, Jesus went back to the synagogue and saw a man who had a paralyzed hand. Jesus restored the man's hand.

Mark 3:7–12: As Jesus continues to do ministry, people are following Him everywhere. There is a great multitude from Judea, Galilee and everywhere, who followed Jesus, listened to His teaching, and watched Him heal the sick and cast out unclean spirits.

Mark 3:13–19: Jesus begins calling the 12 and naming them apostles: Simon Peter, James and John (the Sons of Thunder), Andrew, Philip and Bartholomew, Matthew and Thomas, James the son of Alphaeus, and Thaddaeus, Simon the Zealot and Judas Iscariot. They were to be with Him, preach the gospel, and have authority to cast out demons. If Satan is real (and we believe he is), then his demons are still alive and active. We, like the disciples (v. 15), have the authority to drive out demons as well. It's this tension of good and evil that is the backdrop for the verses to come (Ephesians 6:12). Matthew 10:8 records Jesus' instructions: "Heal the sick, raise the dead, cleanse those with skin diseases, drive out demons. You have received free of charge; give free of charge."

Mark 3:20–21: Jesus returned home, still followed by the crowd so that Jesus couldn't even eat (v. 20). Constable refers to these verses as an opposition "sandwich" of sorts, which shows two specific areas of opposition Jesus faced.[1]

---

[1] Thomas L. Constable, *Expository Notes of Dr. Thomas Constable: Mark*, 91, https://planobiblechapel.org/tcon/notes/pdf/mark.pdf.

The first part of the "sandwich" is the bottom bun and represents opposition from Jesus' family (v. 21). The family wanted to "restrain" (that is, take custody and take charge, or arrest and put in restraints) Jesus because "He's out of His mind." His family had journeyed 30 miles from Nazareth out of concern for Him—out of both love and ignorance (Acts 26:24; 2 Corinthians 5:13). Remember from our four month study of the Pentateuch that all the Jews understood, was the Law and the traditions built around it. Jesus was doing things and teaching things that didn't fit into their understanding of the Law. And the people were leaving the synagogues to hear what He had to say and to watch what He did. When we continue to take leaps of faith, we too should expect opposition from our families.

Mark 3:22–26: Moving to the "meat" part of the sandwich, Constable called this opposition from the enemies.[2] This opposition went straight for the jugular—calling Jesus out and making it personal. The scribes said Jesus had Satan (Beelzebub) in Him. *Nelson's Commentary* outlines eight pagan gods in the New Testament. Beelzebub was "a heathen god considered by the Jews to be the supreme evil spirit."[3] They were calling Jesus out as the ultimate evil spirit. Other pagan gods from the New Testament are:

- Diana: Roman goddess of "the moon, hunting, wild animals, and virginity."
- Hermes: "the Greek god of commerce, science, invention, cunning, eloquence, and theft."
- Mammon: "the Aramaic word for riches, personified by Jesus as a false god."
- Moloch: "National god of the Ammonites whose worship involved child sacrifice."
- Remphan: "An idol worshiped by Israel in the wilderness."
- Twin Brothers: "In Greek mythology, the twin sons of Zeus."
- Zeus: "the supreme god of the ancient Greeks."[4]

The scribes also accused Jesus of driving out demons because He was the ruler of the demons. Jesus knew this was a completely stupid accusation and asked them: How could Satan drive out Satan (v. 23)? Then, Jesus continued to

---

[2] Constable, 91.

[3] Earl D. Radmacher, Ronald B. Allen, and H. Wayne House, eds., *Nelson's New Illustrated Bible Commentary* (Nashville: Thomas Nelson, 1999), 1212.

[4] Radmacher et al., 1212.

make His point with the statements that a kingdom divided against itself, and a house divided against itself, cannot stand (vv. 24–25). And if Satan rebels against himself and is divided, he cannot stand but is finished (v. 26)!

Mark 3:27–30: Jesus then approached the religious from a different direction. He said no one could rob a strong man's house unless he first binds up the strong man (v. 27). This statement makes sense when you realize the strong man is Satan, and Jesus is there to tie up and get rid of Satan's works. 1 John 3:8 says: "The one who commits sin is of the Devil, for the Devil has sinned from the beginning. The Son of God was revealed for this purpose: to destroy the Devil's works." The role of Jesus is to always go after Satan.

In verse 28, Jesus told the scribes that "people will be forgiven for *all* sins and whatever blasphemies they may blaspheme." Then, Jesus called them out for what they had said about Him: "But whoever blasphemes against the Holy Spirit never has forgiveness, but is guilty of an eternal sin" (v. 29)—because they were saying, "He has an unclean spirit" (v. 30). What Jesus was saying to the scribes was that because of what they had said about Him, they had just committed an eternal sin. The scribes were saying that Satan was controlling Jesus. Jesus responded that He had the Holy Spirit in Him and on Him, but the scribes said that was an unclean spirit. They had committed the unforgiveable sin—blasphemy against the Holy Spirit. These scribes were willfully choosing to be irreverent to God. One commentary says blasphemy can be understood as, "a type of sin, predominantly in speech, that is hostile, malicious, injurious, and derogatory to God." Another way to look at this blasphemy against the Holy Spirit is "one's preference for darkness even though it has been exposed to light (John 3:19). Such a persistent attitude of willful unbelief can harden into a condition in which repentance and forgiveness, both mediated by God's Spirit, become impossible"[5] (Matthew 12:31–32; Hebrews 10:29).

At Jesus' baptism in Mark 1:10, as soon as Jesus came out of the water, He experienced "the heavens being torn open and the Spirit descending to Him like a dove." Therefore, the scribes had to decide whether the Holy Spirit that came upon Jesus was of God or the enemy.

Mark 3:31–35: The rest of the opposition "sandwich" is found in these verses. Jesus' mother and brothers had finally arrived in Capernaum. They sent word to Him and then called to Him (v. 31). But Jesus knew why they were there—to restrain Him. Jesus looked at the people around Him and asked, who were His mother and brothers (v. 33). Then Jesus said His family were those who did the

---

[5] John D. Grassmick, "Mark," in *The Bible Knowledge Commentary: New Testament*, ed. John F. Walvoord and Roy B. Zuck (Wheaton: Scripture Press, 1983), 117; quoted in Constable, 94.

will of God (v. 35). That means, whoever didn't try to stop Him from doing the will of God . . . of preaching the Word and driving out demons . . . those were His family.

Closing

If you're doing ministry, you should expect opposition. In fact, if you're not facing opposition, you're probably not doing ministry. If you are preaching the gospel *and* casting out demons, you should expect opposition because when this happens, you'll rub people the wrong way. Romans 8:14 says, "All those led by God's Spirit are God's sons." As we do these things, we are part of God's family.

Daily Word

After seeing Jesus preach, heal, and cast out demons, the crowds continued to follow Him. He went up to a mountain and appointed twelve apostles to partner with Him to preach and to have authority to drive out demons. Then He returned home, and still the crowds followed Him. Jesus' ministry was busy, and He was in high demand. He even had a team around Him to walk out His mission. However, when Jesus went home, His own family tried to restrain Him and said that Jesus was "out of His mind." Jesus' family didn't welcome Him and say, "Welcome home and put Your feet up. You are doing amazing work of Your Heavenly Father, and we support You." No, even Jesus, the servant of God, received opposition and accusations about His ministry from His own family.

Can you relate? As you study God's word and live your life for Christ, have you found those closest to you giving you a hard time? You are promised as you walk with Jesus that you will face opposition. So today, be strong. Remember who you are in Christ and what He has called you to. Greater is He who is in you than He who is in the World.

When His family heard this, they set out to restrain Him, because they said, "He's out of His mind." —Mark 3:21

Further Scripture: Romans 8:31–32; Ephesians 6:12; Philippians 1:27–29

Questions

1. Did the Pharisees' plot in Mark 3:6 give you more understanding as to why Jesus would keep instructing people to "not tell others about Him" (Mark 3:12)? Why did Jesus instruct people to not tell others about Him? (Matthew 9:30; Mark 1:43–44)

2. What do you practically think Mark 3:11 looked like? How is it that the evil spirits knew who Jesus is, but others were unable to accept Him as the Son of God? (Acts 19:15)

3. How do you think Jesus chose the 12 that would become His disciples (Mark 3:13–14)? What is the difference between "calling" and "appointing"?

4. Do you know anyone that casts out demons? Have you or anyone you know accused someone in a similar way as the teachers of the law accused Jesus in Mark 3:21–22?

5. How can you discern someone who is casting out demons in Jesus' name versus Satan's?

6. What does "blaspheming against the Holy Spirit" mean (Mark 3:29)? How would you explain this verse to someone? Can someone be forgiven if they blasphemed against the Holy Spirit before accepting Christ?

7. What did the Holy Spirit highlight to you in Mark 3 through the reading or the teaching?

Lesson 32: Mark 4

Servant: Walk in Faith and Not Fear

Teaching Notes

Intro

In Mark 3, we looked at the opposition Jesus faced from His own family and from His enemies while His ministry was growing. Crowds of people followed Him, as He preached and cast out demons. However, His family thought He was out of His mind and wanted to restrain Him. The scribes felt what Jesus was doing didn't fit into their religious box, so they accused Him of being from Satan. Jesus explained that Satan couldn't cast himself out and pointed out that the scribes had blasphemed against the Holy Spirit—the one unforgiveable sin. The chapter ended with Jesus' statement that His family were those who did the will of God. That backdrop is important for chapter 4, because the crowds continued to grow and needed more from Him. He must have been getting exhausted, but He kept going.

Teaching

Mark 4:1–9: Jesus started teaching by the sea when a large crowd gathered around Him. Jesus moved to a boat and taught one of His most famous parables—The Parable of the Sower. Jesus described the sower throwing out seeds on different types of soils with drastically different results. Then He explained that the way people receive the gospel is very similar to how the soil accepts the seed.

Mark 4:10–20: Jesus talks about why He uses parables, explaining the kingdom of God in this way. He said some people will understand and some won't. In His parables, Jesus used everyday objects to make a spiritual point, and to communicate to both believers and nonbelievers. Then Jesus would break down the meaning of the parable to His disciples.

Mark 4:21–32: Mark included three more parables in this chapter. The first was about putting a light on a lampstand so the light could be seen (vv. 21–25). The second was about growing seed and its harvest (vv. 26–29). The third was about the impact of the tiny mustard seed (vv. 30–32).

Mark 4:33–34: Jesus only taught the crowds using parables but He explained everything to the disciples.

Mark 4:35–41: Wiersbe points out that "God's Servant, Jesus Christ, is the Master of every situation and the Conqueror of every enemy."[1] After a day of teaching, Jesus told the disciples to take the boat across the sea, possibly to get some time away from the crowds (vv. 35–36). The Sea of Galilee is eight miles wide, 700 feet below sea level, and surrounded by mountains that rise from 3,000 to 4,000 feet about sea level. The sea experiences cool evenings. As the boat started across the sea, other boats followed. When the storm came (v. 37), all of the boats would be spared. Sometimes Jesus wants us to go through storms to refine us to become more like Him.

Verses 37–38 show Jesus' humanity as He slept soundly during the storm, even as the boat began to fill with water. The disciples were crying for help while Jesus slept. Hiebert explained that the disciples' reaction "was a cry of distrust, but one often matched by believers today in difficult circumstances when they feel that the Lord has forsaken them."[2] The disciples were fishermen who knew the storms on Galilee, and they expected Jesus to fix things. As Jesus slept during the storm, they became frightened. Unbelief begins to create fear. When people experience fear, they become frozen. And, when they become frozen, they no longer walk by faith. And when they stop walking by faith, their faith becomes stagnant and dead. Jesus told His disciples that they had no faith (Hebrews 3:12).

In verse 39, Jesus "rebuked" the storm. One commentator wrote, "In the calming of the storm (4:35–41) his 'rebuke' of the wind and 'muzzling' of the waves are phrased in the language of exorcism, recalling the power of God over chaos at creation. Both episodes are effected solely by the word."[3] Jesus was ceasing all the evil activity by telling it to stop. Jesus, the Creator, could speak to the seas because He had created them (Hebrews 1:2). Jesus asked the disciples (v. 40), "Why are you fearful? Do you still have no faith?" Over and over, Jesus' disciples showed timidity and a lack of trust. That should give us hope. As we do ministry with people, as we pour into communities, Sunday School classes, discipleship groups, small groups, and our families, and wonder why they're not getting it, remember that the disciples didn't get it either (Mark 7:18; 8:17–21).

---

[1] Warren Wiersbe, *The Exposition Commentary: Matthew–Galatians* (Colorado Springs: David C. Cook, 1989), 124.

[2] D. Edmond Hiebert, *Mark: A Portrait of the Servant* (Chicago: Moody, 1974), 115; quoted in Thomas L. Constable, Expository Notes of Dr. Thomas Constable: Mark, 112, https://planobiblechapel.org/tcon/notes/pdf/mark.pdf.

[3] James R. Edwards, "The Authority of Jesus in the Gospel of Mark," *Journal of the Evangelical Theological Society*, 37:2 (June 1994): 223; quoted in Constable, 112.

Fear paralyzes people. If you don't have a healthy perspective of who Jesus is, the fear from the storms will overwhelm you. But when you have a proper perspective of the storms and who Jesus is in them, you almost welcome the storms because then God is refining you more and more. God uses these moments to make us look more like Him for His glory.

In verse 41, the disciples were terrified and asked who Jesus is that even the wind and sea would obey Him. They didn't have a clue who Jesus was or what He could do. They were more afraid of the storm until they saw Jesus control nature. When we go through storms, we can see how big God is and how He is in control. Psalm 89:8–9: "Lord God of Hosts, who is strong like You, Lord? Your faithfulness surrounds You. You rule the raging sea; when its waves surge, You still them." Jesus can do this just as God does. It shows Jesus' divinity, and it proves that we can trust Him in the storm.

Mike Query offers reasons why we don't walk by faith:

1. We're afraid (Exodus 3:11). God responds, I'll be with you (v. 12).
2. We might get pushback (Exodus 3:13). God responds, It's not about you (vv. 14–15).
3. The people are the problem (Exodus 4:1). God responds, I Am is bigger than people (vv. 2–9).
4. I'm not talented enough (Exodus 4:10). God responds, I'll make up for whatever you lack (vv. 11–12).[4]

Closing

We have a lot to learn from the disciples being in the storm. It's all about the perspective of the storms, that we are being refined by them to walk in faith and not in fear.

Daily Word

Jesus and the disciples left the crowd and went into a boat on the Sea of Galilee. Suddenly, a fierce windstorm came upon them, and their boat filled with water. The disciples reacted to the storm in fear and accused Jesus of not caring for them. Jesus simply stood up, rebuked the wind, and said to the sea, "Silence! Be still!" Immediately, the storm ceased.

---

[4] Mike Query, "5 Excuses We Make for Not Following God," Bay Area Christian Church, https://bacc.cc/5-excuses-we-make-for-not-following-god/.

At some point in life, you will find yourself in an unexpected "storm on the sea." It may be a sudden car accident, a financial crisis, a sickness of a child or loved one, or a depression that won't go away. Will you respond in fear, like the disciples, or in faith? Fear is a lack of confidence in God whereas faith is a trust in God. Jesus asked the disciples, "Why are you fearful? Do you still have no faith?" Even in the middle of the crisis, Jesus can *calm the storm* and bring peace to you. He can make the hard things more doable. He can bring joy to your sadness. He will always provide. And He can bring a peace that passes all understanding. Turn to Him in the middle of your storm, with faith that He is with you and will bring you peace.

He got up, rebuked the wind, and said to the sea, "Silence! Be still!" The wind ceased, and there was a great calm. Then He said to them, "Why are you fearful? Do you still have no faith?" —Mark 4:39–40

Further Scripture: Psalm 46:1–2; Psalm 107:28–30; 2 Thessalonians 3:3

Questions

1. Why did Jesus use parables? Do you think that you would have understood the parables in Mark 4? Or would you have asked questions like those the disciples asked?

2. Look at Mark 4:24–25; what does this mean to you? Can you think of an example or a time when you have seen this?

3. In Mark 4:35, Jesus got in the boat to go to the other side. In this context, why do you think He went to the other side?

4. In Mark 4:39, Jesus calmed the storm. How does this point to Jesus as God? (Psalm 89:8–9; 104:7)

5. In verse 40, Jesus addressed the issue of no faith. Look at the following verses: Matthew 15:28; 21:21; Mark 5:34; 2 Corinthians 5:7; Hebrews 11:6. What do all these verses have in common? How do you feel about the amount of faith that you have?

6. What did the Holy Spirit highlight to you in Mark 4 through the reading or the teaching?

Lesson 33: Mark 5
Servant: The Touch of the *Servant*

Teaching Notes

Intro

Mark 4 ended with Jesus pointing out His disciples' lack of faith during the storm and their amazement at what they had seen Jesus do. Mark 5 focuses on how Jesus interacted with the people.

Teaching

Mark 5:1–20: After the storm in chapter 4, the boat came ashore on "the other side of the sea." As soon as Jesus stepped out of the boat, a man with an unclean spirit came to Him. Jesus probably hadn't gotten enough rest, but He had gotten what He needed. As soon as we get rest, be prepared to do more ministry. Jesus cast the unclean spirits into a herd of 2,000 pigs who ran down the steep bank, entered the sea, and drowned. Jesus' ministry didn't stop.

Mark 5:21: The rest of chapter 5 records Jesus' interactions with two very different people—Jairus, an important synagogue official who was well to do, and an unnamed woman who was bankrupt from seeking medical care. Jesus performed a double miracle with these two and showed that He does not show favoritism. The gospel is meant for *all!*

Mark 5:22–24: Jairus came up to Jesus, "fell at His feet and kept begging Him" (vv. 22–23) for help. How does a religious leader get to this point? Obviously, Jairus felt desperate for his daughter and knew Jesus could give her life. Kent Hughes pointed out that desperation is a prelude to grace.[1] Desperation allows us to realize we need something more than ourselves. Jesus went with him, followed again by a large crowd pressing against Jesus. Notice that as the *Servant*, Jesus *walked with* Jairus and *spent time with* him.

---

[1] R. Kent Hughes, *Mark: Jesus, Servant and Savior* (Wheaton, IL: Crossway, 2015), 125.

Mark 5:25–32: A woman who had been bleeding for 12 years approached Jesus. Because of the bleeding, she was considered ceremonially unclean, and anyone who touched her would be considered unclean as well (Leviticus 15:25–27). She had "endured much under many doctors" (v. 26) and spent everything she had trying to be cured. According to Kent Hughes, some of medical treatments she would have experienced include:

- Carrying a piece of barleycorn found in the droppings of a white female donkey.
- A special drink she would hold while someone came behind her to scare her.[2]

This is an example of Jesus wanting to heal in a different way than the traditional practices of medical care.

The woman pressed into the crowd surrounding Jesus. What would the woman have touched? She would have touched one of the four tassels on Jesus' robe (Numbers 15:37–40). Her faith motivated her to seek out Jesus: "If I can just touch His robes, I'll be made well!" (v. 28). Her faith motivated her to act. Funny, when we have faith in Christ, we sit down, but faith should always lead to action. Faith doesn't just mean forgiveness of sin but that we walk out our faith. Augustine wrote, "The flesh will press in, but the faith will touch." Verse 29 records that the woman was instantly healed—after 12 years and just one touch. Because Jairus asked for healing for his daughter, another was also healed.

That's an important picture for us. As we walk out our faith, whether in reviveSCHOOL or at a job or a ministry, we're constantly walking among people whom we should bring to Jesus. And we don't have to wait until we find nine buddies to do it. One person at a time . . . one day at a time . . . Jesus wants us to find those people who desperately need Him and bring them to Him.

At once, Jesus realized that power had gone out of Him (v. 30). He asked who had touched Him, an interesting question since He already knew. He wanted the person to acknowledge the healing. The disciples couldn't believe He even asked such a question because the pressing crowd was so large (v. 31).

Mark 5:33–34: As Jesus looked over the crowd, the trembling woman came and fell at Jesus' feet (v. 33). Her action of worship was the same as Jairus' action. They both realized they needed Jesus. The woman told Jesus her story.

Jesus responded with a kind of adoption ceremony. This was the only time Jesus referred to anyone as "daughter," and He did it here to welcome her into the family of God because of her faith. He told her to go in "peace." The word

---

[2] Hughes, 123–24.

"peace" in Israel is a very common word, *shalom*. According to Constable, *shalom* is explained as, "not just freedom from inward anxiety, but that wholeness or completeness of life that comes from being brought into a right relationship with God."[3] Jesus said in Mark 3:35: "Whoever does the will of God is My brother and sister and mother."

Mark 5:35–43: While Jesus was still speaking, people from Jairus's house arrived with news that his daughter was dead. They questioned why Jairus would continue to bother the Teacher (v. 35). Jesus overheard their words and responded, "Don't be afraid, only believe" (v. 36). Faith always trumps fear—don't walk in fear, but walk in faith. Jesus walked on to Jairus' house with only Peter, James, and John. From Matthew 17:1–2 and 26:37, we know these same disciples were with Jesus on the Mount of Transfiguration and in the Garden of Gethsemane. Jesus took His inner circle with Him so they could see something special.

At Jairus' home, paid mourners were "weeping and wailing loudly" (v. 38b). Even the poorest husband had to hire two flute players and one female to wail when his wife died.[4] Jesus asked why they were making such a commotion over the dead, because the child was only asleep (v. 39). The people started to laugh, so Jesus sent them all outside. Then Jesus, His three disciples, and Jairus entered where the child was. Jesus took the child by the hand—Jesus the *Servant* was not afraid to touch the unclean, the demon possessed, or the sick and inflicted who needed life. Jesus said to the child, "*Talitha koum!*" which means, "Little girl, I say to you, get up!" (v. 41). And the girl got up and walked. She was 12 years old. Interesting coincidence . . . the woman had been bleeding for 12 years and the child was only 12 years old? God showed that no matter how young or old, or how long an illness or hardship had been endured, Jesus can still heal. When the people saw her, they were utterly astounded, or "out of their minds with great amazement."[5] In verse 43, Jesus told the witnesses not to tell anyone what had happened, and that the child needed food.

Jesus wanted to continue to do ministry and walk among the people and with them. If the story were told, of Jairus's daughter, His ability to move about would have been even more difficult.

---

[3] Hugh Anderson, *The Gospel of Mark* (Greenwood, SC: Attic Press, 1976), 154; quoted in Thomas L. Constable, *Expository Notes of Dr. Thomas Constable: Mark*, 124, https://planobiblechapel.org/tcon/notes/pdf/mark.pdf.

[4] H. Van der Loos, *The Miracles of Jesus*, Novum Testamentum series, vol. VIIII (Leiden, Netherlands: E. J. Brill, 1965), 568; quoted in Constable, 126.

[5] John D. Grassmick, *In The Bible Commentary: New Testament*, eds. John F. Walvoord and Roy B. Zuck (Wheaton, IL: Scripture Press, 1983), 126; quoted in Constable, 128.

Closing

What do we do with a dad who only wanted his daughter healed or a woman who was so tired of living under constant affliction, and just wanted to see healing? The answer is simple: *Jesus is the only way!* Satan's goal was to go after the father through his daughter and to go after the woman who had been afflicted for 12 years. John 10:10 says that, "A thief [Satan] comes only to steal and to kill and to destroy. I have come so that they may have life and have it in abundance." John 11:25–26 affirms that Jesus is life!

Daily Word

A woman who suffered from bleeding for twelve years had faith and believed if she could just touch Jesus, she would be made well. Just as she believed in faith, as soon as she touched Him, her body was cured. Even though a crowd surrounded Jesus, He sensed power had gone out from Him. When He realized the woman had touched Him, He said to her, "Daughter, your faith has made you well. Go in peace and be free from your affliction."

Do you understand this woman's pain and struggle? She had been untouchable for years because of her affliction. And now, because of her faith and the touch of Jesus, she was healed. Do you need a touch from the Lord today? What does it look like for you to reach out in faith and touch Jesus? Quiet yourself and pray. Humbly repent and ask the Lord to take away your pain and set you free. Share your affliction and burden with a trusted person. No matter the depth of sin or the span of years you have carried this burden, release it today. Reach out and touch Jesus. His power is greater than all your fear and doubt. Have faith and praise the Lord for His love for you and for the hope you have in Him.

Then the woman, knowing what had happened to her, came with fear and trembling, fell down before Him, and told Him the whole truth. "Daughter," He said to her, "your faith has made you well. Go in peace and be free from your affliction." —Mark 5:33–34

Further Scripture: Jeremiah 17:14; Philippians 4:7; James 5:15–16

Questions

1. In Mark 5:6, what do you notice that the demon-possessed man did immediately when he saw Jesus? How do you see Jesus' authority over the demons? (Philippians 2:10)

2. Why do you believe the people, after seeing a demon-possessed man healed, would plead for Jesus to leave them alone (Mark 5:17; Luke 8:37)? What did the man immediately start doing after he was healed? (Mark 5:20)

3. How do you see the humility and faith in Jairus in Mark 5:22–23? Do you believe this was why Jesus honored his request (James 4:10; 1 Peter 5:5)? How do you think Jairus felt when, instead of being in a hurry to heal his daughter, Jesus stopped to heal the woman?

4. Has there been a time in your life when you or someone you know was healed because of your faith? What about a time when, with the same faith, Jesus chose not to heal? How did you handle it?

5. In Mark 5:40, Jesus was laughed at and ridiculed, but He was not deterred from doing the will of the Father. Have you ever been in a situation in which you have been laughed at or mocked for following God? Was there evidence afterward that the Lord was working in that situation? How did those who were mocking respond?

6. What did the Holy Spirit highlight to you in Mark 5 through the reading or the teaching?

Lesson 34: Mark 6
Servant: Giving God What We Have

Teaching Notes

Intro

Yesterday, we talked about how Jesus with His Servant attitude engaged and ministered to the community and healed people who were desperate for true healing and life. In Mark 6, Jesus returns to His hometown of Nazareth and faces questions from the people there (vv. 1–6). Then, Jesus sends His 12 disciples out in pairs with authority over unclean spirits. He commissioned them to go out and gave them instructions for what to do as they went (vv. 6b–13). Jesus was ramping up His ministry. As this was happening, John the Baptist was beheaded by King Herod. When his disciples heard about what happened, they came to get his body and place it in a tomb, burying the one who had physically come to prepare Jesus' way (vv. 14–29).

Teaching

Mark 6:30–44: The apostles returned to report to Jesus all they had done on "their tours of ministry."[1] Jesus took them away to a remote place to rest. This seems to be the pattern: pour in . . . pour in . . . rest. Unfortunately, I'm afraid in ministry today, we try to keep a steady pace and balance. But Jesus went hard, full throttle, and then He rested, and started it again. Because they had not even had time to eat, He took them to an area near Bethsaida to let them get filled up again (Luke 9:10). Jesus may have taken them away because of the death of John the Baptist, possibly to mourn, or because of the potential of political unrest.

Rest is essential in ministry. Many burn out. Some are in the boat with Jesus but spend their time bailing out water. They were being dependent upon themselves rather than Jesus. Vince Havner said, "If you don't come apart and rest, you will come apart."[2]

---

[1] Earl D. Radmacher, Ronald B. Allen, and H. Wayne House, eds., *Nelson's New Illustrated Bible Commentary* (Nashville: Thomas Nelson, 1999), 1218.

[2] Vince Havner; quoted in Warren Wiersbe, *The Bible Exposition Commentary: Matthew–Galatians* (Colorado Springs: David C. Cook, 1989), 131.

They went by boat (a four-mile trip), but the people saw them leave and ran to meet them there (as much as eight miles) (v. 33). The people were so hungry to hear Jesus they ran after Him. As Jesus stepped ashore, a "huge crowd" awaited them, and "He had compassion on them." Compassion will always lead to action (v. 34). Mark 1:41 shows the depth of Jesus' compassion: "Moved with compassion, Jesus reached out His hand and touched him. 'I am willing,' He told him. 'Be made clean.'" A true servant has compassion; compassion leads to action (Exodus 34:6; Numbers 27:17).

Jesus began to teach the huge crowd. But "when it was already late," the disciples showed fake compassion saying, "This place is a wilderness, and it is already late" (v. 35)! Their idea was to send the people away so they could purchase food for themselves.

Why fake compassion? First, they were ready to send them away to have time to find food for themselves (v. 36). Second, they asked if they should collect money to buy the food for the crowd (v. 37). Two hundred denarii were about eight months of wages and would have been a seemingly impossible amount to spend on the people.

This was a heart condition for the disciples. Wiersbe compared the disciples to a church committee trying to figure out how to feed the homeless: "With that approach, they would have made ideal committee members!"[3] This is a church issue: we throw money at people or we send them away, instead of thinking what can happen when God shows up.

Jesus presented another option, asking, "How many loaves do you have" (v. 38) (John 6:9)? The five loaves and two fish were either a problem or a solution. Jesus had the disciples divide the people into groups of hundreds and fifties on the green grass. Looking down on this scene, one could have seen multitudes of people waiting to be fed or seen how God had put this together by using one lad who gave everything up to be used by Jesus.

In verse 41, Jesus took the food, looked up to heaven (showing His dependence on God in a posture of prayer), broke the bread, and gave it to His disciples. He kept giving food to the disciples to dispense to the crowds until everyone had his or her fill (v. 42).

Wiersbe points out that "we are not manufacturers; we are only distributers."[4] Not only was everyone satisfied, but there were 12 baskets full of leftovers. And the 5,000 men were only part of the crowd because women and children were not counted. Some speculate the crowd at 7,000–8,000 people, while others suggest as many as 20,000. God blessed in abundance.

---

[3] Wiersbe, 132.

[4] Wiersbe, 132.

Closing

Sometimes you just need to trust the Lord with what you have and let Him multiply it. My hope and my prayer is that wherever we are, we will always depend upon the Lord. And all of this started because Jesus had compassion on those who had a need. Compassion will always lead to action.

Daily Word

Jesus and the disciples went away again to rest and get refreshed. But once again, the crowds came. Even so, Jesus had compassion on them and began to teach them many things. They were spiritually hungry for His teachings. However, as evening came, they were also physically hungry. Rather than send them away to the nearby villages, Jesus took what He had—five loaves of bread and two fish—and blessed the food. Miraculously, all 5,000 ate and were filled, with leftovers filling twelve baskets.

There may be times in your life when you look around and wonder, *How am I going to make it?* Look to Jesus. Ask Him to provide all of your needs for today. He cares for you, and He says to not worry about tomorrow because tomorrow has enough worries of its own. As you seek first His kingdom and His righteousness, He will provide for you both spiritually and physically. He is the God of miracles!

Everyone ate and was filled. Then they picked up 12 baskets full of pieces of bread and fish. —Mark 6:42–43

Further Scripture: Psalm 81:10; Matthew 6:34; Philippians 4:19

Questions

1. Why do you think that Jesus' own hometown of Nazareth scoffed at Him and refused to believe in Him? Why would Jesus not do many miracles there (Hebrews 11:6)? Have you ever been guilty of not honoring the gifts and callings of someone because he or she was just a "commoner" to you?

2. As Jesus was sending out the 12 disciples, what did He give them the authority to do? What was their message?

3. The disciples in Mark 6:13 were casting out demons, healing many sick people, and anointing them with oil. Who was this practice of anointing people generally reserved for? (Exodus 29:7; 1 Kings 19:16; 2 Kings 9:6; James 5:14)

4. Why would King Herod believe Jesus was John the Baptist who had been raised from the dead? Why would others believe He was Elijah (Malachi 3:1; 4:5–6; Mark 6:17–27)? Herod was clearly sinful for what he had done. Do you think it's hard to see who Jesus really is when we are stuck in sin? Why or why not?

5. What do you think was going through the minds of the disciples when Jesus said for them to give the people something to eat (Mark 6:37)? What does God's provision always start with (Matthew 6:31–33; Mark 6:38; Philippians 4:19)? How have you seen God provide for you or others that couldn't have happened any other way except for God?

6. What did the Holy Spirit highlight to you in Mark 6 through the reading or the teaching?

Lesson 35: Mark 7

Servant: The Touch of Jesus

Teaching Notes

Intro

Yesterday we looked at the feeding of the 5,000 men. An event we didn't get to cover was Jesus walking on the water. In Mark 7, we'll be looking at the traditions of the elders. The congregation I grew up in shaped my life, and God used it to radically call me to Him. I'm not knocking that congregation, but there were traditions that were not taken from Scripture but were what we'd grown up with. The first 23 verses in Mark 7 deal with questions about why things were done in different ways than had been done traditionally. In verse 24, Jesus began to talk with a young woman with a demonic spirit.

The synoptic Gospels each show Jesus through a different lens. In Mark there are several parables about healings, and stories that are not included in the other Gospels. For example, Mark 4:26–29 contains the parable of the growing seed. Today's story of healing the deaf and mute man is only in the gospel of Mark. Another one is of the blind man healed in Mark 8:22–26, and the final one is the parable of an absent homeowner found in Mark 13:34–37.

Teaching

Mark 7:31–32: Usually, Jesus' interactions were with the Jews, so anytime He had an encounter with a Gentile, it was always different. Jesus was on a road trip that could have taken weeks or even months. He left Tyre, went by Sidon to the Sea of Galilee, and then through the Decapolis (the ten cities east of the Jordan). This was not an easy journey, and it wasn't the straightest path. In Decapolis, people brought Him a deaf man with a speech impediment (he could not hear and could not be understood). They begged Jesus "to lay His hand on him" (v. 32). Ben Witherington says this may suggest "he was a Jew, since laying on of hands was a Jewish practice."[1] Grassmick states that "Defective speech usually results

---

[1] Ben Witherington III, *The Gospel of Mark: A Socio-Rhetorical Commentary* (Grand Rapids: Eerdmans, 2001), 234.

from defective hearing, both physically and spiritually."[2] This could have been a possibility.

Mark 7:33: Jesus took the man away from the crowd. Mark recorded that Jesus did this repeatedly as He healed people. This goes against the way we are wired in the U. S. where we seek attention. Jesus as the *Servant* was the complete opposite. He took this man aside for privacy. Yesterday, we talked about how compassion always leads to action. If you have a servant mentality, you'll have compassion. This passage is a radical picture of Jesus the *Servant*, who touched this man in places no people would have touched. Jesus touched the man's ears, probably full of earwax, and then touched the man's tongue. There's nothing kosher about what Jesus did. It was totally unclean. Maybe this was a form of sign language Jesus was doing by touching the ears since the man could not hear.

Luke 5:12 records Jesus touching a man covered with leprosy. With Jesus, a simple touch can radically change a life. We cannot be afraid of how someone smells, looks, is dressed, or if they are covered in tattoos. It doesn't matter because each person is made in God's image.

Mark 7:34: Looking up to heaven was another sign language, showing that Jesus depended on the God of heaven. Jesus sighed deeply for carrying the weight or burden of caring for the man. Then Jesus said, "Ephphatha" which meant "Be opened!" Jesus walked through a process of healing the man using visual signs and then spoke only two words—"Be opened!" Kent Hughes states this is a model for ministry: Jesus looked up to heaven in dependence on God (v. 34); He sighed with compassion (v. 34); He touched the man, taking action (v. 33); and walked with authority, because He believed that God would heal the man (v. 34).[3] His Word says God can show up at any time. He is the same yesterday, today, and tomorrow. We need to take the healing hand of Christ, walk it out, and see what we can do! Let the ears hear; let the mouth actually begin to speak.

Mark 7:35: The man was instantly healed. He could hear. His speech difficulty was removed. He began to speak clearly.

Mark 7:36: Then Jesus ordered them to "tell no one, but the more He would order them, the more they would proclaim it." Think about it . . . the man who had difficulty speaking wasn't able to now keep silent! MacArthur explains,

---

[2] John D. Grassmick, "*Mark*," in *The Bible Knowledge Commentary*, eds. John F. Walvoord and Roy B. Zuck (Wheaton: Scripture Press, 1983), 136.

[3] R. Kent Hughes, Mark, volume 1: *Jesus, Servant and Savior* (Preaching the Word) (Wheaton, IL: Crossway, 1989), 178.

"Although Jesus ministered to Gentiles as the need arose, His intention was not to have a public ministry among them."[4]

Mark 7:37: "They were extremely astonished and said, 'He has done everything well! He even makes deaf people hear, and people unable to speak, talk!'" That phrase, *He has done everything well!* takes me back to Genesis 1:31: "God saw all that He had made, and it was very good."

This was the real deal; Jesus was doing amazingly well. Matthew 15:31 says: "So the crowd was amazed when they saw those unable to speak talking, the deformed restored, the lame walking, and the blind seeing. And they gave glory to the God of Israel." Jesus depended upon the Lord, had compassion for others, took action, and walked with authority. The Gentiles began to notice and give glory to the God of Israel.

How do we take this spiritually? I keep going back to the saying, "he who has ears to hear." One commentator observed that every time Jesus addressed those with ears, it was because He had been giving them the Word. He was speaking to them and then asking if they were hearing Him. I'm not talking about the physical side of speaking and hearing, but of the spiritual side. Jesus said, "Anyone who has ears should listen" (Matthew 11:15; Mark 4:9, 23)! Jesus is saying He wants us to listen and be in tune to what He is saying.

The Parable of the Sower is a parable we haven't taught on. The website www.GotQuestions.org says this about the parable: "Some hear but they don't ever let it take root; some hear but reject it because of persecution and trial; some hear the Word and they allow themselves to understand and accept it and it begins to transform them and to bear fruit." How you hear and receive the Word is actually what you will get from it. The Word of God says you can completely tune out the Holy Spirit and never let Him speak to you.

If you hear the Word of God and are not changed by it, you're more like the seven churches in Revelation. Every time there is a word of encouragement in Revelation, there is the command that "anyone who has an ear should listen to what the Spirit says to the churches" (Revelation 2:29). The unforgiveable sin is to blaspheme the Holy Spirit. If the Holy Spirit is talking to you and you reject the Spirit, it's really hard to hear from the Lord. Each time the same statement is made to these churches (Revelation 2:11, 17, 29; 3:6, 13, 22). John 10:27–28 says, "My sheep hear My voice, I know them, and they follow Me. I give them eternal life, and they will never perish—ever! No one will snatch them out of My hand." And Mark 4:24 says, "Then He said to them, 'Pay attention to what you hear. By the measure you use, it will be measured and added to you.'"

---

[4] John MacArthur, *The MacArthur Bible Commentary* (Nashville: Thomas Nelson, 2005), 1223.

Closing

A deaf man experienced Christ and was able to read His lips, feel His touch, and eventually, hear His voice. Spiritually, we need to be in tune to what the Holy Spirit is saying to us.

Daily Word

Jesus exemplifies servanthood. He lived out His compassion for people with action. When a deaf man who also had speech difficulty was brought to Him, Jesus didn't shy away. Rather Jesus modeled to His disciples how to do ministry. First He depended upon the Lord. Then He loved and had compassion for the man. Jesus took action by touching him, and He ministered with authority from the Lord. Through the ministry and power of Jesus, the deaf man was healed, his ears were opened, and he also began to speak clearly.

Friend, as you see the needs of others, remember you do not carry their burdens and ailments on your own. Seek the Lord for His power, His authority, and His compassion. You are able to do all things through His strength at work within you. You will get weary if you try to do ministry by your own strength and in your own flesh. If ministry and people's needs are weighing you down right now, take a deep breath, and look to heaven. Ask the Lord for help. Then put your compassion into action and watch God's grace become sufficient.

**So He took him away from the crowd privately. After putting His fingers in the man's ears and spitting, He touched his tongue. Then, looking up to heaven, He sighed deeply and said to him, *"Ephphatha!"* (that is, "Be opened!").
—Mark 7:33–34**

Further Scripture: Isaiah 49:10; Matthew 11:28; 2 Corinthians 12:9

Questions

1. When the scribes and Pharisees questioned Jesus about why His disciples did not observe the traditions of the elders, what Old Testament verse did Jesus quote to them? (Mark 7:6–7; Isaiah 29:13)

2. What do you think it meant to honor God with their lips, but their hearts were far away from Him?

3. What did Jesus accuse the scribes and Pharisees of in Mark 7:9? What example did He use to make His point? (Mark 7:10–13)

4. According to Mark 7:20–23, Jesus taught that the things that defile a man come from where? What examples did He list?

5. What actions did Jesus perform in Mark 7:33–34 to heal the man who was deaf and had a speech impediment? Do these seem strange to you?

6. Why do you think Mark 7:34 notes that Jesus looked up to heaven with a deep sigh when He spoke to the deaf man's ears to be opened?

7. What did the Holy Spirit highlight to you in Mark 7 through the reading or the teaching?

Lesson 36: Mark 8
Servant: Take Up Your Cross

Teaching Notes

Intro

Jesus was not afraid to engage the people and to interact with the people as a *Servant*. This chapter contains a key verse for Christians. The reality is that when we follow Jesus, it will not be easy.

Teaching

Mark 8:1–10: Again, the large crowd that had gathered around Jesus for three days had nothing to eat. And again, this was not a problem but a potential. Jesus wanted the disciples to trust Him, to depend on Him in every walk of the ministry. This crowd numbered 4,000 men, and Jesus used seven loaves and a few small fish to feed them all with seven baskets of food left over. God kept saying to His people: trust Me, I am the Bread of life.

Mark 8:11–21: When the Pharisees began to argue with Jesus and demand a sign to test Him, Jesus and the disciples got in a boat and went to the other side. As they sailed, Jesus commanded, "Watch out! Beware of the yeast of the Pharisees and the yeast of Herod" (v. 15). While the disciples focused on their lack of bread, they didn't understand Jesus' message. In other words, the Pharisees and Herod had some issues the disciples needed to be aware of, so Jesus warned them to beware of the Pharisees, the religious, and the opposition.

Mark 8:22–26: These verses describe Jesus healing a blind man. This story is exclusive to the Gospel of Mark. And in this instance, Jesus healed the man in two stages. After Jesus healed the man, He told him to go straight home without even going into the village, which implied Jesus instructed him not to tell anyone what had happened.

Mark 8:27–33: These verses recount Peter's confession of the Messiah. Jesus asked the disciples, "Who do people say that I am?" (v. 27). The disciples said some people thought Jesus was John the Baptist, Elijah, or one of the prophets, such as

Isaiah, Jeremiah, or Moses. When Peter answered, "You are the Messiah!" (v. 29). Jesus told the disciples they couldn't tell anyone He was the Messiah. Jesus then predicted His death, burial, and resurrection after three days (v. 31). Jesus didn't hide these events from His disciples.

Peter drew Jesus aside and began to rebuke Him. The most recent mention of "rebuke" was when Jesus rebuked the wind and the rain while they were in the boat during a storm on the sea of Galilee (Mark 4:39). Now Peter rebuked Jesus. Why? Peter didn't want this to happen even if Jesus would be resurrected. Each of us has to answer these questions: Do I really believe in this chapter in the Bible? Do I believe in Jesus' death, burial, and resurrection? Do I really believe what He has called me to?

Jesus looked at the disciples and rebuked Peter (v. 33), "Get behind Me, Satan, because you're not thinking about God's concerns, but man's!" Peter's problem was that he was focused on man's concerns, not God's. This is an ongoing battle that we face every day. If we only see the problems, we'll never see the potential. We'll never experience faith. We'll never experience God working in our lives. We'll never experience the resurrection of the situation. Peter didn't want to deal with it, and the American church doesn't want to experience the suffering, to experience the resurrection that God has for us. Wiersbe said that this was just what Satan was after . . . the disciples "were following Satan's philosophy (glory without suffering) instead of God's philosophy (suffering transformed into glory)."[1]

Mark 8:34: Jesus summoned the whole crowd, not just the disciples, and said to them, "If anyone wants to be My follower, he must deny himself, take up his cross, and follow Me."

What does "follower" mean to you? A follower goes along behind someone. If Jesus goes left, you go left. If you are a follower, you do what Jesus does. So why do we pick and choose what we do? For example, *I'll read this part of the Bible, but not this.* We will not be ready for the end times if we don't embrace Mark 8:34. Jesus is preparing us for anything radical that is coming. I believe we will be part of the end times. If the Apostle Paul said it, we should say it as well.

Jesus gave three specific instructions in this statement that deserve further study. The first instruction was "Deny yourself." What does that mean? It might mean denying yourself pleasure or denying yourself things of this world. It doesn't mean you hate yourself. It means giving full control to Jesus by surrendering completely to Him. John MacArthur said this reveals an important spiritual truth: "Those who pursue a life of ease, comfort, and acceptance by the world will not find eternal life. On the other hand, those who give up their lives

---

[1] Warren Wiersbe, *The Bible Exposition Commentary: Matthew–Galatians* (Colorado Springs: David C. Cook, 1989), 140.

for the sake of Christ and the gospel will find it."[2] You cannot put the things of this world before Christ.

The second instruction was "Take up your cross." This means we must make some form of sacrifice and demonstrate the willingness to do whatever it takes to become dead to our own will. We must be willing to suffer, to be rejected, and to be killed . . . to follow Christ and how He lived His life. The suffering and death component fits in this. Are we willing to go there? Jesus' disciples ended up actually doing that.[3] Matthew, the tax collector with a comfortable home, was impaled by spears in Ethiopia. James (who once wanted to be the greatest) was thrown off a wall and clubbed to death. Jude was crucified by magi in Persia. John was boiled in tar and exiled to an island of Patmos. Matthias (the disciple who took Judas' place) was stoned and beheaded. Philip was hung upside down by iron hooks. Peter, who didn't want Jesus to be killed, was, according to tradition, crucified upside down by Nero. These guys didn't get it while Jesus was alive, but when the Spirit of God came, something happened, and they became willing to take up their cross. When truth is really, really hard, we initially reject it. Then the Spirit of God kicks in, and we come to accept it. Doubting Thomas was stabbed with a spear in India. James the Lesser was beheaded in Palestine. Simon was crucified in Persia (just like Jude). Andrew was crucified on an X-shaped cross in Greece. Bartholomew was flayed to death by a whip in Asia Minor. All of these men were crucified because of the gospel. They believed this message was so life-giving that they embraced Mark 8:34. This message still applies today. In 2 Peter 1:16, Peter said, "We did not follow cleverly contrived myths . . ." No one would die for a myth or a fable. If you really want to be a follower, you have to surrender everything that gets in the way of following Jesus. You have to be willing to die for the sake of the gospel. But until persecution comes, it's really hard to gauge whether or not you can do this.

The third instruction was "Follow Christ." How many times are we asked to give up everything and walk in His steps? In Mark 2:14, Jesus called Matthew (also called Levi, son of Alphaeus; Matthew 9:19) to follow Him. Following Jesus doesn't mean sitting still. You have to get up and share the gospel. You don't worry about where to lay your head; you don't worry about your bills. In Mark 10:21, Jesus told the rich young man to sell everything and then *follow* Him. There is more to do than just accepting Jesus as Savior—we have to follow Him. We have to walk out our faith by following Jesus wherever He leads. Obviously, getting to this point in your faith is a process that takes time.

---

[2] John MacArthur, *The MacArthur Bible Commentary* (Nashville: Thomas Nelson, 2005), 1225.

[3] MacArthur, 1225.

Mark 8:35–38: Only by losing our lives for the sake of Jesus and the gospel can we save them. And if we are ashamed of Jesus and His words, then He will also be ashamed of us "when He comes in the glory of His Father with the holy angels" (v. 38).

Closing

All of this, recorded in verses 35–38, would not be an issue if we live out Mark 8:34. Where are you in all of this today? Peter initially had a problem. It was all about himself, rather than about the Lord. But when you flip it, this works.

Daily Word

Peter took Jesus aside and attempted to convince Jesus to stop speaking about His upcoming death to the disciples. Jesus rebuked Peter and firmly said, "Get behind me, Satan." And it was over. The enemy's intention to persuade Jesus to not suffer and die was easily diffused by the truth.

You may find yourself in a situation you know is not from the Lord. You may feel temptation creeping in to overtake you. The thoughts and lies in your head may feel so overwhelming that you don't want to get out of bed in the morning. In these moments, stand firm and know the Lord your God is with you. Remember, you have authority in the name of Jesus to say out loud, "Get behind me, Satan!" As you submit to the Lord, the enemy will flee. Remember to focus on God's promises and the truth in His Word. Jesus had to walk His authority out, and so will you. Walk in confidence—Jesus is at work within you!

But turning around and looking at His disciples, He rebuked Peter and said, "Get behind Me, Satan, because you're not thinking about God's concerns, but man's!" —Mark 8:33

Further Scripture: Luke 10:19; James 4:7; 1 John 2:14

Questions

1. For the second time, Jesus fed a large crowd with some loaves of bread and a few fish (Mark 6:35–42; 8:2–9). What similarities were in the two accounts? What differences?

2. After both of these situations, the Scripture mentions the disciples' hearts being hardened. What does this mean to you?

3. Jesus seemed to connect the disciples' lack of seeing or understanding with a hardened heart. Have you seen anyone's hardened heart cause a lack of

understanding about what God was doing in their life? What can cause a hardened heart?

4. When reading the account in Mark 8:22–25, do you find it hard to understand why the man was only partly healed when Jesus first touched him? Do you know of any other accounts of Jesus healing people and then asking them if they were healed?

5. When Jesus addressed the crowd in Mark 8:34, He called them to take up their cross and follow Him. Do you think they understood what that meant?

6. What did the Holy Spirit highlight to you in Mark 8 through the reading or the teaching?

Lesson 37: Mark 9

Servant: A Servant of All

Teaching Notes

Intro

To be a follower of Christ, you have to deny yourself, take up your cross, and follow Him. While you might consider this a wheel of death, it is actually a wheel of life. When you exemplify these characteristics, you are a true disciple of Christ.

Teaching

Mark 9:2–13: Six days after telling His followers to deny themselves, take up their cross, and follow Him, Jesus took Peter, James, and John "up on a high mountain by themselves to be alone" (v. 2). Peter, James, and John were Jesus' inner circle of disciples. On this mountain, these three disciples witnessed Jesus' transfiguration and saw Him talking with Moses and Elijah. We covered this event in an earlier lesson in Matthew, so we'll move past it this time.

Mark 9:14–29: These verses record another demonic interaction. Remember Jesus sent His disciples out to cast out demons, and here we see Him doing it Himself, not as Satan or as Beelzebub, because that doesn't make sense, but because He is God, and He has authority from God to set people free.

Mark 9:30–32: Prior to His command in Mark 8:34, we saw the first prediction in Mark that Jesus was going to die. There are a total of three predictions in the Gospel of Mark; this is the second one. In verse 30, Jesus and the disciples "made their way through Galilee." Jesus had this message only for His disciples. "The Son of Man is being betrayed into the hands of men. They will kill Him, and after He is killed, He will rise three days later" (v. 31a). Even though the disciples didn't understand His statement, they were afraid to ask Him about it.

Mark 9:33–34: Then they came to Capernaum. When the disciples gathered with Jesus in the house (no specific house was named, but it could have been Peter's house or even a house Jesus "rented"), Jesus asked what they were arguing about on the journey, totally aware they had not included Him in on the conversation. "Arguing" means this was a major problem—a serious discussion. They were silent because they had been arguing about who was the greatest. They missed the whole point of humility. In Matthew 5:3, Jesus said, "The poor in spirit are blessed, for the kingdom of heaven is theirs."

Mark 9:35: Whenever Jesus sat down, He had something important to say. "If anyone wants to be first, he must be last of all and servant of all." As described in Mark 8:34, following Christ means being a servant to others. Being a follower of Christ is countercultural. Commentator Henry Swete said, "The spirit of service is the passport to eminence in the Kingdom of God for it is the spirit of the Master Who Himself became *diakonos panton* ['servant of all']."[1] If you want to gain access to the kingdom of God, then you serve. As followers of Christ, believers must deny themselves, take up their cross, and follow Him. This required mentality places self, last to become a servant to all. Our one word for the Gospel of Mark is *Servant*. Jesus came as a servant, and this is the lifestyle He wants us to have. John the Baptist said, "He must increase, but I must decrease" (John 3:30). That goes against everything our culture teaches us. Life is not about us; it's about Him. If no one knew what you did, would you still do it because Jesus asked you to? Compare this verse with Mark 10:45. At that point, Jesus begins exalting you.

The word used as "servant" is the Greek word *diakonos*, which describes somebody who serves willingly without being forced. You might fake it, but God totally knows your heart and motives (Psalm 139:2). Make this your prayer, "Lord give me a heart to put others first." According to 1 Chronicles 28:9, God searches our hearts and knows our thoughts. Jesus asks us to serve, and to serve well.

Brad Archer described seven characteristics of a godly servant.[2]

- *A servant is humble.* Philippians 2:3–8 says Jesus "humbled Himself by becoming obedient to the point of death—even to death on a cross." He is our example of a humble servant.
- *A servant prepares.* In 1 Timothy 4:7b, Paul said "train yourself in godliness." How can we do that? Skip to verse 15 to see what Paul said. "Practice these things; be committed to them, so that your progress may be evident to all."

---

[1] Henry Barclay Swete, *The Gospel According to St. Mark* (London: Macmillan, 1905), 205; quoted in Thomas L. Constable, *Expository Notes of Dr. Thomas Constable: Mark*, 203, https://planobiblechapel.org/tcon/notes/pdf/mark.pdf.

[2] Brad Archer, "Seven Marks of a Godly Servant," Unlocking the Bible, May 27, 2016, https://unlockingthebible.org/2016/05/seven-marks-of-a-godly-servant/.

- *A servant perseveres.* In Luke 12:35–36, the servants remained ready for service even though they didn't know when the master would return. Likewise, we are to be ready and waiting, to serve the master.

- *A servant serves where needed.* In 1 Corinthians 9:19, Paul said, "I have made myself a slave to everyone, in order to win more people." When we serve wherever needed, we have the chance to win people to Christ.

- *A servant serves (or not) as God directs.* Romans 8:28 says God works all things together to those who are called. When you've been called, you just go. It doesn't have to make sense. You do as God leads.

- *A servant expects to suffer.* Matthew 10:24–25 and Mark 8:34 say that as servants of Christ, we should not be surprised when we suffer for our faith.

- *A servant is not ashamed.* In 2 Timothy 2:15, Paul said, "Be diligent to present yourself approved to God, a worker who doesn't need to be ashamed, correctly teaching the word of truth." When we're doing the work, God has given us to do, then we won't be quiet or ashamed if we're correctly teaching the word of truth.

Pray for God to show you how to work on these things so that you begin to display these characteristics of a godly servant. As you read 1 Peter 5:6, consider how you might humble yourself under God's mighty hand.

Closing

In Mark 9:37, Jesus took a child in His arms and said, "Whoever welcomes one little child such as this in My name welcomes Me." Why did I make this random comparison? The word "child" and "servant" is the same word in the Aramaic language. You must have the heart of a child to effectively serve others. You willingly serve anybody without showing any favoritism. When you willingly put others before yourself, when you deny yourself, take up your cross, and follow Jesus, when you have the mentality of "servant of all," then Jesus gets the glory.

Daily Word

As the disciples walked along their way, they argued. Although Jesus wasn't with them, He asked them what they had been arguing about. They remained silent and didn't answer, but Jesus knew. He knew their thoughts before they even had them. The disciples argued about who was the greatest. Jesus sat them down like a parent talking to children and spoke clearly. If you want to be the greatest, then serve one another. Don't seek to be the first, seek to be the last.

As a follower of Christ, you are called to walk in humility, thinking of others more highly than yourself. When you serve others, you point people to Jesus, not to yourself. And that's the whole point: to glorify Jesus and His power and strength at work within you. Next time you have the option to go first, pause for a second, and let someone else go ahead of you. In doing this, the Lord will honor you. He sees your heart and knows your thoughts.

Sitting down, He called the Twelve and said to them, "If anyone wants to be first, he must be last of all and servant of all." —Mark 9:35

Further Scripture: Psalm 139:1–3; John 3:30; James 4:10

Questions

1. Read Mark 9:1. To what do you think it refers?

2. Both Moses and Elijah talked with Jesus during His transfiguration. Although both the Law and the prophets were represented here, what did God instruct the disciples to do? (Mark 9:7; Hebrews 1:1–2)

3. When asking Jesus for help, the man with the son in Mark 9:17–24 used the words, "If you can do anything, have compassion on us and help us." Did this sound like the man had much faith that Jesus could heal his son? How did Jesus respond to the father? What did the man then request of Jesus?

4. If someone desires to be first, what did Jesus say would happen? (Mark 9:35; 10:43–45)

5. How can your hand, foot, or eye cause you to stumble? Would you choose to lose a body part in order to "enter life"? (Mark 9:43,45)

6. What did the Holy Spirit highlight to you in Mark 9 through the reading or the teaching?

Lesson 38: Mark 10
Servant: True Servanthood

Teaching Notes

Intro

To be a follower of Christ, you have to deny yourself, take up your cross, and follow Him. While you might consider this a wheel of death, it is actually a wheel of life. When you exemplify these characteristics, you are a true disciple of Christ. Mark 10:45 is the key verse of the entire Gospel of Mark, and we'll end with it today. Mark 10 begins with a discussion about divorce (vv. 1–12), and then moves to blessing the children (vv. 13–16). Mark then presents the encounter with Jesus and the rich young ruler (vv. 17–22), which we've already covered in Matthew. Mark also covers possessions in the kingdom of God (vv. 23–31).

Teaching

Mark 10:32–34: This is the third prediction Jesus gave of His coming death in the Gospel of Mark. Jesus and His disciples were on the road going to Jerusalem. Verse 32 says that "those who followed Him were afraid." Jesus took His 12 disciples aside and began to tell them about His coming death. In verse 33, Jesus described what would happen in Jerusalem: "The Son of Man will be handed over to the chief priests and the scribes, and they will condemn Him to death." Then, He gives details; "they will mock Him, spit on Him, flog Him, and kill Him, and He will rise after three days" (v. 34). This is the third time Jesus gave them this message. Mark 10:33 uses the same language as the first two.

> The first prediction was in Mark 8:31: "Then He began to teach them that the Son of Man must suffer many things and be rejected by the elders, the chief priests, and the scribes, be killed, and rise after three days."

> The second prediction was in Mark 9:31: "For He was teaching His disciples and telling them, 'The Son of Man is being betrayed into the hands of men. They will kill Him, and after He is killed, He will rise three days later.'"

Mark 15:17–20 is the confirmation of the mocking mentioned in Mark 10:34: "They dressed Him in a purple robe, twisted together a crown of thorns, and put it on Him. And they began to salute Him, 'Hail, King of the Jews!' They kept hitting Him on the head with a reed and spitting on Him. Getting down on their knees, they were paying Him homage. When they had mocked Him, they stripped Him of the purple robe, put His clothes on Him and led Him out to crucify Him." This was also foretold in the Old Testament (Psalm 22:6–8; Isaiah 50:6).

Mark 10:35–37: Mark provides an odd transition here. In Matthew 20:20, the mother of James and John approached Jesus to ask Him for something special. In Mark's account, James and John went to Jesus and said, "We want You to do something for us if we ask You" (v. 35). Jesus responded with, "What do you want Me to do for you?" (v. 36). After Jesus had just explained all He would endure in Jerusalem, they asked to sit at His right and left hands to get some of that "glory" (v. 37).

MacArthur wrote, "This incident reveals yet again the disciples' failure to grasp Jesus' teaching on humility. Ignoring the Lord's repeated instruction that He was going to Jerusalem to die, the disciples still thought that the physical manifestation of the kingdom was about to appear, and they were busy maneuvering for the places of prominence in this kingdom."[1]

However, the disciples knew more than we give them credit for knowing. In Matthew 19:28 Jesus said to them, "I assure you: In the Messianic Age, when the Son of Man sits on His glorious throne, you who have followed Me will also sit on 12 thrones, judging the 12 tribes of Israel." In Matthew 20:20–22, the disciples were asking where their assigned seats were. John 14:13 says, "Whatever you ask in My name, I will do it so that the Father may be glorified in the Son." The disciples may have been asking what the kingdom in the end times would look like and what their role in it would be.

Mark 10:38–39: Jesus explained that they didn't know what they were asking. Were they able to drink the cup of God's wrath that carries the sin of mankind? Were they ready to immerse themselves in the full suffering that He faced? Both brothers answered, "We are able" (v. 39). Jesus answered that they were . . . they would drink the cup and be baptized with the same baptism Jesus faced. In Acts 12:2, King Herod killed James with the sword. James drank the cup, for the sake of the gospel, and was immersed in the suffering component of the baptism. John was sent into exile on the island of Patmos because of the gospel (Revelation 1:9). Their response to Jesus was correct.

---

[1] John MacArthur, *The MacArthur Bible Commentary* (Nashville: Thomas Nelson, 2005), 1233.

Mark 10:40–41: Jesus responded that the positions at the table were not His to give. MacArthur says, "Honors in the kingdom are bestowed not on the basis of selfish ambition, but because of divine sovereign will."[2] How God has orchestrated it is up to God (v. 40). The other disciples became indignant (jealousy, maybe) with James and John asking for priority seating (v. 41).

Mark 10:42–45: Jesus explained that the world had rulers who had power over their subjects, and men want power over others, but the kingdom of God was based on the opposite position: humility and servanthood. Christians don't ask for these positions (v. 42). Think of all the people in America with high influence who are being called out for sexual sin and for being abusive to women and people under their authority. That is the way of the world, not the way of the kingdom of God.

It's important in Christian ministry to be careful, to not draw upon your own power, but to allow the Holy Spirit to be the one in charge. Jesus said, "On the contrary, whoever wants to become great among you must be your servant, and whoever wants to be first among you must be a slave to all" (vv. 43–44). One commentator said there is no place in the body of Christ for domineering leaders. Gould wrote, "Here is the paradox of the Kingdom of God. Instead of being lords, its great ones become servants, and its chiefs the bond-servants of all."[3] Mark 9:35 affirms, "Sitting down, He called the Twelve and said to them, 'If anyone wants to be first, he must be last of all and servant of all.'" (1 Peter 5:3–6 talks about not lording power over those who have been entrusted to you.)

In 3 John 1:9–10, John described a situation in which a member of the church was striving for his own glory within the church: "I wrote something to the church, but Diotrephes, who loves to have first place among them, does not receive us. This is why, if I come, I will remind him of the works he is doing, slandering us with malicious words. And he is not satisfied with that! He not only refuses to welcome the brothers himself, but he even stops those who want to do so and expels them from the church." When we become refined by Jesus, we begin to embrace and become His Word. We begin to live out what it means to be a servant. Jesus said, "For even the Son of Man did not come to be served, but to serve, and to give His life—a ransom for many" (v. 45).

"*Ransom* refers to the price paid to free a slave or prisoner; *for* means 'in place of.' Christ's substitutionary death on behalf of those who would put their

---

[2] MacArthur, 1233.

[3] Ezra P. A. Gould, "A Critical and Exegetical Commentary on the Gospel According to St. Mark," International Critical Commentary series (Edinburgh: T. & T. Clark, 1896), 202; quoted in Thomas L. Constable, *Expository Notes of Dr. Thomas Constable: Mark*, 230, https://planobiblechapel.org/tcon/notes/pdf/mark.pdf.

faith in Him is the most glorious, blessed truth in all of Scripture."[4] All of this means Christ gave His life as a ransom in place of and for us. Romans 4:25 says, "He was delivered up for our trespasses and raised for our justification." Romans 5:6–8 summarizes it this way: "For while we were still helpless, at the appointed moment, Christ died for the ungodly. For rarely will someone die for a just person—though for a good person perhaps someone might even dare to die. But God proves His own love for us in that while we were still sinners, Christ died for us!"

Closing

The only way for Christ to get to this point, of being our ransom, was for Him to be willing to give up His life as *Servant* (Romans 6:3; 1 Corinthians 15:3; 2 Corinthians 5:21; Galatians 1:4; 1 John 2:6). When you're willing to serve without any personal satisfaction but because God asked you to, you're beginning to understand Mark 10:45.

Daily Word

James and John asked Jesus to seat them at His right and left in His glory. In response to this request, Jesus taught the disciples a lesson on power and the struggle of desiring a place of honor. He pointed out that people in high positions like to exercise power over others. In contrast, a follower of Jesus is great by becoming a servant. Rather than being served like royalty, it means serving others, even giving your life for the sake of others. This was the purpose of Jesus' life—He came to serve and give His life so others could live forever.

In a similar way, you too are not called to fame, riches, power, and position, but you are called to serve. If you are asking yourself how to love a family member, how to deal with a spouse, or how to bless your coworkers, start by asking the Lord how to serve them. Begin by humbling yourself, like Jesus, and serve the people God has put in your life regardless of what you think you deserve. By doing so, you will honor the Lord.

On the contrary, whoever wants to become great among you must be your servant, and whoever wants to be first among you must be a slave to all. For even the Son of Man did not come to be served, but to serve and to give His life—a ransom for many. —Mark 10:43–45

Further Scripture: Romans 5:6–8; 1 Peter 5:3–6; 1 John 2:6

---

[4] MacArthur, 1233.

Questions

1. Why did Jesus refer back to what Moses commanded (Mark 10:3)? How was what Moses taught about divorce different from what Jesus taught? (Deuteronomy 24:1)

2. How do you receive the kingdom of God like a child? (Mark 10:14–15)

3. Why did Jesus not want the rich man to call him "Good Teacher" (Mark 10:17–18)? How hard is it for the rich to enter the kingdom of God?

4. What would you have felt if you were the disciples hearing the words Jesus spoke about His death? (Mark 10:32–34)

5. When have you asked something akin to what James and John asked Jesus in Mark 10:35–45? What was their motivation for asking this? How does Jesus respond to you when you ask Him to do something that isn't in His will?

6. What did the Holy Spirit highlight to you in Mark 10 through the reading or the teaching?

Lesson 39: Mark 11

Servant: Producing Fruit

Teaching Notes

Intro

Yesterday, we looked at Jesus' prediction that He would die, be buried, and on the third day come back to life. In fact, Jesus made that prediction three times in the Gospel of Mark. James and John responded to Jesus' prediction by asking if they could sit at His right and left, in places of honor. Jesus responded that if they wanted to get to that place, they would have to be willing to endure the suffering He would endure. Jesus said it wasn't about being first, but it was about being last. Mark 11:1–11 covers Jesus' triumphal entry into Jerusalem, which we've already talked about. Verse 11 says, "And He went into Jerusalem and into the temple complex." He looked around, checked it out, and then went out to Bethany.

Teaching

Mark 11:12–14: This is the beginning of another "sandwich" of content. We'll look at the fig tree, then the events at the temple, and then the fig tree again. The next day Jesus left Bethany to go back to Jerusalem, and He was hungry (v. 12). This highlights Jesus' humanity. He saw a fig tree with leaves and went to see if it had fruit on it because He was hungry (v. 13). However, there was no fruit on the tree because "it was not the season for figs." Jesus said, "May no one ever eat fruit from you again!" (v. 14). The season for figs was May or June, and Passover was in March or April, so they weren't even in the right season. However, in March, there are a number of buds that should be apparent that are edible. In April, the leaves appear, and later the fruit appears. When Jesus came up to the fig tree, He expected to find little, edible buds, but He found nothing. He wanted something to eat and found nothing.

Many commentators see this as a spiritual illustration about Israel. Normally, a fig tree is a symbol of Israel's peace, prosperity, and provision (Micah 4:4; Zechariah 3:10). Now pause this story, and we'll come back to it.

Mark 11:15–16: Jesus returned to the temple complex and "began to throw out those buying and selling in the temple" (v. 15). He had been there the night before, "looking around at everything," and decided then what He was going to do the next day (v. 11). When Jesus arrived, He began immediately and "overturned the money changers' tables and the chairs of those selling doves and would not permit anyone to carry goods through the temple complex" (vv. 15b–16). The temple complex was the high holy place and, "by cleansing the temple, Jesus clearly claimed authority equal to God who first filled this place with His glory."[1] Jesus walked in a new authority (2 Chronicles 5:13–14). Jesus began to flip upside-down all things that were being done within the temple complex–the animals being sold for sacrifice, the money that had to be exchanged into temple currency to be able to make an offering, and even those who transported goods across the complex.

The moneychangers had an important role at the temple because people were coming from so many places and cultures who needed to exchange their currencies. The opportunity to make money off that need was great. Doves were sold to the poor for sacrifice, and the poor were being ripped off too. Rodney Cooper says Jesus demanded that people didn't cut through the temple as a short cut because the temple was a holy, consecrated place in which to worship the Lord.[2] They were treating it like a convenience store. It had to be chaotic before, and especially after, Jesus cleared the temple.

Mark 11:17: In the middle of the chaos, Jesus began to teach, using two Old Testament prophets, Isaiah and Jeremiah. Isaiah 56:7 says, "I will bring them to My holy mountain and let them rejoice in My house of prayer. Their burnt offerings and sacrifices will be acceptable on My altar, for My house will be called a house of prayer for all nations." Notice: A house of prayer for *all nations!* Jeremiah 7:11 says, "'Has this house, which is called by My name, become a den of robbers in your view? Yes, I too have seen it.' This is the Lord's declaration." Instead of a house of prayer, it had become a den of robbers. In verse 17, Jesus pulled these two ideas together and accused those who listened, of turning God's house of prayer into a den of thieves. The Gentiles could only worship in the outer court, and the Jews were pushing them out of that area with all the animals they were selling for sacrifice and the moneychangers. Brooks says, "With the conversion of the court of the Gentiles into a bazaar with all its noise and commotion and stench, they were deprived of the only place in the temple where they could

---

[1] Earl D. Radmacher, Ronald B. Allen, and H. Wayne House, eds., *Nelson's New Illustrated Bible Commentary* (Nashville: Thomas Nelson, 1999), 1228.

[2] Rodney Cooper, *Holman New Testament Commentary: Mark* (Nashville: Broadman & Holman, 1991), Kindle location 4373.

worship. By clearing out the traders Jesus literally and symbolically provided a place for Gentiles in the temple of God."[3]

The Jews had pushed out the Gentiles (John 1:10–12). Jesus moved everything out of the way to welcome the Gentiles (Acts 13:46–47). Cooper says the temple had become a refuge of unjust people, and the Jews felt secure in God's acceptance because of rituals and laws.[4] Because of who they were, the Jews felt they could get away with anything they wanted. But the temple was becoming like the fig tree with no foliage.

Mark 11:18–19: The chief priests and scribes heard Jesus teaching with authority, and they were afraid of Him and wanted to destroy Him. Jesus had to leave the city at night for safety.

Mark 11:20–22: The next day Peter noticed that the fig tree Jesus had cursed the day before had "withered from the roots up" (v. 20). Jesus told him to "Have faith in God."

How does all this fit together? Cooper says the religious system had many leaves but no fruit, and the surface piety was seen in the tithes, prayers, and fasts.[5] The rituals were keeping out women, lepers, blind beggars, and those with demons, in order to make the religious elite look good. The foliage offered much promise but *no* fulfillment. As a fig-less tree could not satisfy Jesus' hunger, neither could a religious system satisfy our spiritual hunger. When are we going to realize the system is broken? Obviously, the temple is no longer standing, so the Jews get a little grace here. But consider the church today. How are we becoming a religious system that is broken and not producing fruit?

Romans 11:11 says, "I ask, then, have they stumbled in order to fall? Absolutely not! On the contrary, by their stumbling, salvation has come to the Gentiles to make Israel jealous."

Mark 11:23–26: How do we fix the broken system? Through more prayer and forgiveness in the church.

Closing

You want to know how to produce fruit today? By having faith that our prayers will be answered. It's that simple.

---

[3] James A. Brooks, *Mark: An Exegetical and Theological Exposition of Holy Scripture* (Nashville: Broadman & Holman, 1991), 186.

[4] Cooper, Kindle location 4381.

[5] Cooper, Kindle location 4400.

Daily Word

Jesus spotted a fig tree with leaves in the distance, but when He got closer, He saw it had no fruit. It just looked good on the outside. In a similar way, Jesus became upset when He entered the Temple complex and found this place of worship had become more like a market than a sanctuary. Both the Temple complex and the fig tree looked good on the outside, but upon closer inspection, there was no evidence of fruit in either.

Jesus said to the disciples, "Have faith in God." That's the bottom line . . . have faith. When you have faith in God, you are connected to Jesus. The more you abide in Jesus, the more fruit you will bear. Be careful of only looking like a Christian on the outside while on the inside not connected to Jesus. Maybe you go to church on Sundays, but the rest of the week, you don't even think about living life with Christ and there's no fruit evident of a life abiding in Him. Jesus wants you to walk in faith daily with Him. In doing so, you will be able to move mountains.

The next day when they came out from Bethany, He was hungry. After seeing in the distance a fig tree with leaves, He went to find out if there was anything on it. When He came to it, He found nothing but leaves, because it was not the season for figs. —Mark 11:12–13

Further Scripture: Matthew 21:43; John 15:5; Galatians 5:22–23

Questions

1. The Pharisees told anyone who saw Jesus to tell them so that they could arrest Him (John 11:57). How do you see the courage of Jesus in Mark 11:7–11 despite these threats?

2. God is not pleased when we have the appearance of fruit but actually have no fruit at all. What's the difference between bearing no fruit and bearing bad fruit? (Matthew 7:16–20; Mark 11:13–14)

3. What did Jesus say His Temple would be called and who was it for (Isaiah 56:7)? What did Jesus mean by remarking that they had turned the temple into a den of thieves? (Jeremiah 7:11)

4. What did Jesus say was the reason for the fig tree miracle (Mark 11:21–22)? Who should always be the object of our faith (Romans 3:26; Galatians 3:26; Hebrews 11:6)? Does this mean if we have enough faith God will do any-thing we ask (Mark 11:23–24)? Why or why not? (1 Corinthians 2:5; 13:2; 1 John 5:14)

5. Was Jesus evading the question the religious leaders asked Him in Mark 11:28–30? If not, why did He respond that way? Does it seem the religious wanted to know the truth about who Jesus was?

6. What did the Holy Spirit highlight to you in Mark 11 through the reading or the teaching?

Lesson 40: Mark 12

Servant: The Parable of the Vineyard

Teaching Notes

Intro

Mark 12 gives us an opportunity to study another parable today. A parable uses an everyday object to teach a spiritual lesson.

Teaching

Mark 12:1: A man planted a vineyard and put a fence around it. He then "dug out a pit for a winepress and built a watchtower" (v. 1). The owner leased it out to some farmers and left. The vineyard, the fence, the pit, a watchtower, and the people in the story, are objects for the parable. A watchtower was there as a look-out post, a shelter, and tool storage.

MacArthur explains, "The owner made an agreement with men he believed were reliable caretakers, who were to pay a certain percentage of the proceeds to him as rent."[1] The rest of the money went to the tenant farmers. The image of a vineyard was very common in the region. MacArthur says, "The hillsides of Palestine were covered with grape vineyards, the backbone of the economy."[2] When the backbone of the economy is doing well, the entire country is doing well. When the backbone breaks, the entire country suffers. The vineyard was used as a symbol for Israel, both good and bad (Psalm 80:8–16; Jeremiah 2:21). Jesus used Isaiah 5:1–2, 7 as the basis for this parable about Israel (the vineyard) and God (the owner).

Mark 12:2–5: A slave showed up to collect some of the fruit of the vineyard, but they mistreated him and sent him away with nothing (vv. 2–3). Then, the owner sent a second slave who was treated shamefully (v. 4). The owner sent several others who were mistreated and/or killed, and then, he sent many others, some of which were killed (v. 5). Wiersbe says that, "If Mark 12:2–5 covers the three years when the fruit was not used, then it was in the fourth year that the beloved

---

[1] John MacArthur, *The MacArthur Bible Commentary* (Nashville: Thomas Nelson, 2005), 1240.

[2] MacArthur, 1240.

Son was sent."[3] Therefore, these slaves represent the prophets who had been released to proclaim a message from God, and they constantly pointed to the coming Messiah. In this parable, God was sending people to speak to the tenant farmers (who represent the Jewish religious leaders in this parable). Repeatedly, the religious leaders refused to hear the message from the prophets.

Nelson's Commentary points out that "this story illustrates the immense patience God had with Israel."[4]

Mark 12:6–8: The owner (God) had one more person to send—His Son (v. 6). The tenant farmers recognized the son as the heir and decided to kill him so they would receive his inheritance (v. 7). MacArthur says "the vinedressers were greedy" and "wanted the entire harvest and the vineyard for themselves."[5] The tenants wanted everything for themselves, so they killed the son and threw him "out of the vineyard" (v. 8). Jesus too was put outside the gates (Hebrews 13:12–13). Three times in Mark, Jesus predicted His own death, burial, and resurrection. In this parable, Jesus showed that it was already taking place. The fourth year was "the year when the fruit was devoted to the Lord (Leviticus 19:24)."[6] This makes the coming of the Son as an offering devoted to the Lord even more significant.

Mark 12:9–11: "Therefore, what will the owner of the vineyard do?" (v. 9). He will destroy the farmers and give the vineyard to others. The destruction of the farmers took place in AD 70 when Rome destroyed the temple. MacArthur explains that giving the vineyard to others was being "fulfilled in the establishment of Christ's church and its leaders, who were mostly Gentiles"[7] (Psalm 118:22–23).

Mark 12:12: Jesus told a parable about a vineyard, and this time, the religious leaders understood the parable.

The vineyard represents the Jews. Why did God give the vineyard to the Jews and not us? John Piper states "the Jews have priority over the Gentiles, as the chosen people of God" (Genesis 12:1–3; Exodus 19:6; Deuteronomy 14:2; Nehemiah 9:7; Amos 3:2). Second, Piper states "the Jews have a priority over the

---

[3] Warren W. Wiersbe, *The Bible Exposition Commentary* (Colorado Springs: David C. Cook, 1989), 151.

[4] Earl D. Radmacher, Ronald B. Allen, and H. Wayne House, eds., *Nelson's New Illustrated Bible Commentary* (Nashville: Thomas Nelson, 1999), 1230.

[5] MacArthur, 1240.

[6] Wiersbe, 151.

[7] MacArthur, 1240.

Gentiles as guardians of God's special revelation—the Old Testament Scriptures" (Romans 3:1–2; 9:4). Third, Piper states "the Jews have a priority over the Gentiles in that the Messiah Himself, Jesus, came first as a Jew to the Jews" (Matthew 10:5–6; 15:24; Romans 1:3; 9:5). Fourth, Piper states "the Jews have a priority over Gentiles in that salvation is from the Jews" (John 4:22).[8]

John 1:11–12 says: "He came to His own, and His own people did not receive Him. But to all who did receive Him, He gave them the right to be children of God, to those who believe in His name." Because of rejection (Mark 12:9), God will destroy the farmers and give the vineyard to others. Romans 11:11–12 explains who the others are—the Gentiles. Romans 11:25 summarizes this: "So that you will not be conceited, brothers, I do not want you to be unaware of this mystery: A partial hardening has come to Israel until the full number of the Gentiles has come in."

Closing

In all of this, God had a plan. Despite the rejection of the prophets and the rejection of His Son, God had a plan that included the Gentiles—*us*!

Daily Word

Jesus and the disciples were at the temple treasury. Jesus watched as individuals dropped their money into 13 trumpet-shaped chests used for the worshippers to place their freewill offerings. Jesus saw the rich people offering large sums of money, and He also saw a widow offering a small amount of two tiny coins. But Jesus saw more than people putting money into the treasury, He saw their hearts as they gave. Even though the amount the widow gave was physically worth very little, spiritually, the gift of her heart was greater than all the others.

Jesus had previously shared with the disciples that the greatest commandment was to love the Lord their God with all their heart, soul, mind, and strength. The widow put this love of the Lord, her God, into action. As you give your money, time, or talent to the Lord, give from a place of loving Jesus with all you have. He doesn't call you to give just because it's a duty or a law. No, He wants you to give because of your love for Him. And because you love Jesus, you love others. Therefore, it is a *joy* to give with all you are and with all you have. Today, check your heart. Are you giving from a heart that loves Jesus or because you feel it's your Christian duty?

---

[8] John Piper, "To the Jew First, and Also to the Greek," Desiring God, July 5, 1998, https://www.desiringgod.org/messages/to-the-jew-first-and-also-to-the-greek.

And a poor widow came and dropped in two tiny coins worth very little. Summoning His disciples, He said to them, "I assure you: This poor widow has put in more than all those giving to the temple treasury." —Mark 12:42–43

Further Scripture: Matthew 6:21; 2 Corinthians 8:1–3; 2 Corinthians 9:7

Questions

1. Jesus spoke to a Jewish audience about the vineyard because they knew the vineyard was used in the Old Testament as a picture of what? (Isaiah 5:1–7)

2. Which Old Testament verse was Jesus quoting in Mark 12:10–11? How did the religious leaders react to the parable of the wicked vinedressers? How should we respond when we are convicted about something by the Holy Spirit? (John 16:8; Acts 17:30; Hebrews 4:12)

3. Why did those trying to trap and arrest Jesus compliment Him in Mark 12:14? Was this compliment sincere? Why or why not?

4. Jesus stated that the Sadducees did not know the Scriptures or the power of God. Why is it important that we know Scripture and understand the power of God?

5. Why was Jesus so impressed with how much the poor widow gave in the collection box? (2 Samuel 24:24; 2 Corinthians 8:12)

6. What did the Holy Spirit highlight to you in Mark 12 through the reading or the teaching?

Lesson 41: Mark 13

Servant: Watch! Be Alert!

Teaching Notes

Intro

So far in our study of the Gospels of Matthew and Mark, we haven't studied the same content more than once. However, Mark 13 is almost verbatim the same as Matthew 24, so we don't have a choice. I prayed through this and asked God how to make Mark 13 different. His response was, "Don't!" As we walk through Mark 13, we'll begin to look at what the end times will look like so we can know how to be ready for His return.

Teaching

Mark 13:1–2: When one of the disciples pointed out the massive stones of the temple, Jesus responded that not one stone would be left upon another. Jesus was referring to the coming destruction of the temple in AD 70. This has already happened.

Mark 13:3–6: Verses 3–8 give "signs of the end of the age," or the indicators that the end is coming closer. Jesus sat on the Mount of Olives looking across the Kidron Valley to the temple complex. He was with four of His disciples: Peter, James, John, and Andrew (v. 3). They asked privately about the signs that would come before the end times (v. 4). Jesus responded to first watch out for those who would deceive them (v. 5). Jesus said that many would come and claim to be from Him, but they would be lying and would deceive many (v. 6). This included *false messiahs and false prophets* (Matthew 7:15; Acts 20:28–31).

Mark 13:7–8: Jesus then continued with additional signs: *wars and rumors of wars* would come, but don't be afraid, the end is not yet come (vv. 7–8a). There will also be *earthquakes and famines* which are signs of the beginning of the end (v. 8b).

Mark 13:9–13: Persecutions will also be experienced, so Jesus' followers must be on guard (v. 9). Jesus' followers will be arrested and mistreated, but they must be His witnesses to all nations (v. 10). His followers don't have to worry about what they will say then, because the Holy Spirit will speak for them (v. 11). Families will fight each other and betray each other, even unto death (v. 12). Everyone will hate followers of Jesus, "but the one who endures to the end will be delivered" (v. 13). One commentator said this is stage 1 and the beginning. There will be a leader of ten European nations who will make a seven-year peace agreement with Israel.

Mark 13:14–20: Stage 2, which begins after three-and-a-half years, is described in verses 14–23. The "abomination that causes desolation" is also referred to as "*the great tribulation*" (Daniel 9:27). The antichrist will be the individual who establishes the peace agreement, and after three-and-a-half years, he will break the agreement and will move to Jerusalem. There, the antichrist ("man of lawlessness") will set up his own image in the temple that is rebuilt in Jerusalem (2 Thessalonians 2:3–4). He will sit in God's sanctuary proclaiming himself as god. We need to be on guard, watching! Other names for the antichrist include: "the coming prince," Daniel 9:26; "beast" or "first beast," Revelation 13:1; and "horseman" on a "white horse," Revelation 6:2.

At the three-and-a-half-year time frame, you and the church had better be ready. Where should you go? Mark 13:14 says "those in Judea must flee to the mountains." Verses 15–16 mean to flee, without trying to gather your stuff together. Those who are pregnant and nursing, will struggle physically when they flee (v. 17). Jesus instructed His disciples to pray that the antichrist would not come in winter so His followers would not struggle in the weather (v. 18).

When this begins, all hell will break out: "For those will be days of tribulation, the kind that hasn't been from the beginning of the world, which God created, until now and never will be again. Unless the Lord limited those days, no one would survive. But He limited those days because of the elect, whom He chose" (vv. 19–20).

Mark 13:21–23: In stage 3, there are more *false messiahs and false prophets*. Verse 23 emphasizes what believers are to do: "And you must watch! I have told you everything in advance."

Mark 13:24–27: After the tribulation, "the sun will be darkened, and the moon will not shed its light; the stars will be falling from the sky, and the celestial powers will be shaken" (vv. 24–25). *The Son of Man (Christ) will return* in clouds and everyone will see Him. In Acts 1:11, Jesus said He would return in the same way He left in His ascension. He will send out His angels to gather His elect from every corner of the earth.

Mark 13:33–37: "Watch! Be alert! For you don't know when the time is coming" (v. 33).

Closing

I've never been more convinced than I am right now that Jesus is coming back! We are getting that much closer to the end times. All of these pieces keep falling into place. I want the church to be ready for the coming of the Messiah. He is coming back. We need to be alert!

Daily Word

Jesus prepared His disciples for the end times. In this chapter, He encouraged them seven times with the same message: watch out, don't be alarmed, be on watch, be alert. He wanted the disciples to be aware and watch for signs of the end, but He didn't want them to be afraid. Jesus prepared them, telling them everything they needed to know in advance.

Just as the disciples were to have this attitude in preparation for the end times, so are you as a follower of Christ. As you go about your day, are you watchful for signs of the end and living life with this eternal, hopeful perspective? No matter what may happen, be it earthquakes, wars, persecution, or false prophets, you are to be on guard while not alarmed. Remember, you have the hope of salvation. Walk in confidence, asking the Lord for wisdom to discern your days. Today, trust Jesus regardless of the circumstances or events happening around the world. Jesus prepared you about what would happen, so don't be afraid. The Lord is with you!

And you must watch! I have told you everything in advance. —Mark 13:23

Further Scripture: Luke 12:35–36; 1 Corinthians 16:13–14; Revelation 16:15

Questions

1. In Mark 13, Jesus was explaining what is to come at the end of the age. Do you believe that we are living in the end times? Why or why not? Use Scripture to back up your answer.

2. Jesus said to be "on guard" and "alert" in verse 33. What do you think that looks like?

3. As Christians, do we have to face the trials and tribulations that Christ was talking about? Why or why not?

4. In Mark 13:14, Jesus spoke about the end times and "the abomination that causes desolation." What is that and how does it connect to the following three verses? (Daniel 9:27; 11:31; 12:11) Has this prophecy been fulfilled?

5. Verse 26 says that everyone will see the Son of Man coming in the clouds. How do you think that will be possible?

6. What did the Holy Spirit highlight to you in Mark 13 through the reading or the teaching?

Lesson 42: Mark 14

Servant: Stay Awake and Pray!

Teaching Notes

Intro

In the Gospel of Matthew, we looked at Jesus as the *King*. In the Gospel of Mark, we looked at Jesus as the *Servant*. Everything Jesus said in Mark shows that in order to be the *King*, He had to come as the *Servant* (Psalm 78:70–72). Mark 10:45 is the theme verse of the entire book of Mark and supports this understanding of Jesus as the *Servant*: "For even the Son of Man did not come to be served, but to serve, and to give His life—a ransom for many." Jesus Christ, the *Servant*, gave up His life for you and for me. In chapters 14–16, we'll be looking at how we can serve Jesus.

Teaching

Mark 14:1–26: Verses 1–2 reveal the plot to kill Jesus, and verses 3–11 describe Jesus' anointing in Bethany. Verses 12–16 describe the preparations that were made for the Passover feast. Verses 17–21 give the account of Jesus foretelling that one of the disciples would betray Him by turning Him over to the opposition. Then in verses 22–26, the disciples share the Lord's Supper with Jesus. That's the backdrop for today's study.

Mark 14:27–31: After the supper was concluded, Jesus and the disciples headed to the Mount of Olives. While they walked, Jesus told them, "All of you will run away, because it is written: "I will strike the shepherd, and the sheep will be scattered" (v. 27). Jesus emphasized that all the disciples would run away when trouble came. Then, He told them, "But after I have been resurrected, I will go ahead of you to Galilee" (v. 28). He was telling them that after they scattered and ran away, they would be able to meet Him in Galilee. Peter denied that he would ever flee, "even if everyone runs away" (v. 29). Jesus said, "I assure you, today, this very night, before the rooster crows twice, you will deny Me three times!" (v. 30). But Peter kept insisting that he'd die with Jesus before he left Him, and the other disciples agreed (v. 31). So, how did the servants of the ultimate *Servant* serve Him?

Mark 14:32–36: The name "Gethsemane" is only mentioned twice in Scripture, here and in Matthew 26:36. This was Jesus' regular place to go (John 18:1). Judas also knew where Jesus would be. The name "Gethsemane" means "olive press." Rodney Cooper wrote that, "Symbolically, Jesus would now be pressed hard concerning the fulfillment of His mission as the 'sacrifice' for our sins."[1] Jesus told His disciples to stay and pray. Then He took Peter, James, and John with Him further into the garden (vv. 32–33). Jesus' humanity is clearly seen here, as He was "deeply distressed and horrified" (v. 33b). He needed the emotional and physical support of His inner circle. He needed moral support. Jesus knew exactly what He was about to experience. Peter, James, and John were alone with Jesus three times: on the Mount of Transfiguration, at the healing of Jairus' daughter, and in Gethsemane (Philippians 3:10).

MacArthur explains the word "horrified" (NIV "troubled") "refers to a feeling of terrified amazement. In the face of the dreadful prospect of bearing God's full fury against sin, Jesus was in the grip of terror."[2] In verse 34, Jesus said, "My soul is swallowed up in sorrow—to the point of death." I think Jesus was distraught because He was about to bear the sin of the world (2 Corinthians 5:21). MacArthur says that "Jesus' sorrow was so severe that it threatened to cause His death at that moment"[3] (Luke 22:44). He was taking on everything—all past, present, and future sin. All He asked of His friends was to stay awake with Him (v. 34). In verse 36, Jesus wasn't asking if He could get out of what was to come, "but if it were possible in God's plan."[4] Jesus was asking if there was another way to fulfill God's plan. "The hour" (v. 35) refers to "the time of His sacrificial death as decreed by God. It included everything from the betrayal, to Jesus' trials, the mockery, and His crucifixion."[5] (Jesus used "the hour" throughout His ministry: John 2:4; 7:30.) Jesus had waited on this hour to come and now asked God if there was another way (v. 35b). This intercession is mentioned in Hebrews 5:7: "During His earthly life, He offered prayers and appeals with loud cries and tears to the One who was able to save Him from death, and He was heard because of His reverence." *Abba* was the term for Daddy or Father. Jesus may not have liked what He was required to do, but He willingly did what He was asked (v. 36).

---

[1] Rodney Cooper, *Holman New Testament Commentary: Mark* (Nashville: Broadman & Holman, 2000), Kindle location 5580.

[2] John MacArthur, *The MacArthur Bible Commentary* (Nashville: Thomas Nelson, 2005), 1252.

[3] MacArthur, 1252.

[4] MacArthur, 1252.

[5] MacArthur, 1252.

Mark 14:37–43 Jesus returned for the first of three times and found His closest friends asleep. They were unable to stay awake even for one hour (v. 37). Jesus told them again to pray and emphasized that "the spirit is willing, but the flesh is weak" (v. 38). MacArthur pointed out that "the disciples needed to learn that spiritual victory goes to those who are alert in prayer and who depend on God and that self-confidence and spiritual unpreparedness lead to spiritual disaster."[6] When we are so confident that we don't feel we need to turn to God, we are headed toward spiritual disaster.

Jesus prayed a second time, voicing the same concerns to God, and then came back to find the disciples asleep again. Jesus went a third time to pray and again found the disciples still asleep. Jesus said, "the time has come. Look, the Son of Man is being betrayed into the hands of sinners" (v. 41). The predictions were not the reality. Jesus told His disciples to get up and go with Him to meet His betrayer (v. 42). While Jesus was speaking to His disciples, Judas arrived with the chief priests, scribes, and elders (v. 43).

Closing

As servants of the Most High God, we need to learn how to pray and to be on watch.

> Colossians 4:2–4: "Devote yourselves to prayer; stay alert in it with thanksgiving. At the same time, pray also for us that God may open a door to us for the message, to speak the mystery of the Messiah, for which I am in prison, so that I may reveal it as I am required to speak" (Luke 11:8; 18:4–5).
>
> 1 Thessalonians 5:17: "Pray without ceasing" (NASB 1995).
>
> Romans 13:11: "Besides this, knowing the time, it is already the hour for you to wake up from sleep, for now our salvation is nearer than when we first believed."

How do we get ready? Stay awake and pray!

Daily Word

Jesus prayed to His Father in the Garden of Gethsemane. He told His disciples to sit nearby and pray. Three times Jesus found the disciples asleep. And three times Jesus asked them, "Couldn't you stay awake?"

---

[6] MacArthur, 1252.

As you await the return of Christ, devote yourselves to prayer and stay alert. Jesus warned that the Spirit is willing, but the flesh may be weak. Therefore you must continue to pray. It sounds simple, but the disciples fell asleep and couldn't stay awake for even an hour. As a follower of Christ waiting for His return, how is your prayer life? Spend time in prayer, and watch how it gives you strength for the day.

Stay awake and pray so that you won't enter into temptation. The spirit is willing, but the flesh is weak. —Mark 14:38

Further Scripture: Romans 13:11; Colossians 4:2; 1 Thessalonians 5:17

Questions

1. Why were the disciples so upset in verses 3–5? At this time, do you think they still failed to see who Jesus really was? Why or why not?

2. In verses 27–31, Peter said he would not deny Jesus even unto death. Why was Peter not able to keep his promise? Is this a promise you could have made and kept? Why or why not?

3. Why did Jesus ask Peter, James, and John to stay awake while they were with Him in Gethsemane? (Mark 14:32–41)

4. What did the Holy Spirit highlight to you in Mark 14 through the reading or the teaching?

Lesson 43: Mark 15

Servant: Jesus Is Crucified and Buried

Teaching Notes

Intro

In Mark 14, Jesus had two words for His disciples in the Garden of Gethsemane: "Stay awake." Three times, Jesus said this, and on the third time, Jesus said, "I am being betrayed." Then, Judas showed up in the Garden of Gethsemane and Jesus was handed over to the authorities.

Teaching

Mark 15:1–5: As soon as morning came, the chief priests, elders, scribes, and the whole Sanhedrin tied Jesus' hands and delivered Him to Pilate. When Pilate asked Jesus if He was King of the Jews, Jesus answered, "You have said it" (Matthew 26:25). As the chief priests continued to accuse Jesus of many things, He said nothing more.

Mark 15:6–15: At the festival, Pilate's custom was to release a prisoner. It came down to two choices: Jesus or Barabbas. The crowd chose to release Barabbas. After the release, Pilate asked, "What do you want me to do with the one you call the King of the Jews?" And the crowd screamed, "Crucify Him!" Pilate wanted to know why, but they shouted again, "Crucify Him!" To satisfy the crowd, Pilate had Jesus flogged and handed Him over to be crucified.

Mark 15:16–20: Three times, Jesus had predicted that He would be killed, buried, and resurrected. In the process, He would be mocked, flogged, and spit on. These verses confirm that Jesus lived out all the prophecies concerning the ways He said He would suffer.

Mark 15:21–32: These verses record the actual Crucifixion of Jesus.

Mark 15:33–41: When it was noon, darkness came over the whole land until three in the afternoon. Jesus was on the cross and died. Remember, Mark 10:45 said that this was Jesus' end goal. "For even the Son of Man did not come to be served, but to serve." Jesus served by giving His life as a ransom for many. As Jesus breathed His last, the crowd tried to understand what had just taken place.

Mark 15:42–43: Now that Jesus was dead, the essential connection between His death and His resurrection was His burial. The Crucifixion actually took place on Friday, which is why we call it Good Friday. It was now evening, so the Sabbath had begun. Joseph of Arimathea boldly asked Pilate for Jesus' body. Arimathea was a town about 20 miles northwest of Jerusalem. Joseph was a well-known, prominent member of the Sanhedrin, which was known for wanting to get rid of Jesus.

Go back to Mark 15:1 where the chief priests, elders, scribes, and the whole Sanhedrin arrested Jesus and handed Him over to Pilate. Was Joseph a part of this? John 19:38 revealed that Joseph "was a disciple of Jesus—but secretly because of his fear of the Jews." Luke 23:50–51 says Joseph was a righteous man who had not agreed with the Sanhedrin's plan to turn Jesus over. Scripture always said Joseph looked forward to the kingdom of God. Why was this important? This dictated his actions in burying Jesus. As a secret disciple of Christ who disagreed with the Sanhedrin's actions, he boldly approached Pilate and asked for Jesus' body. This took radical courage because going to Pilate indicated he was in alignment with Jesus who was crucified. Joseph was willing to "deny himself, take up his cross, and follow [Jesus]" (Mark 8:34). Joseph was willing to be identified with Jesus and was willing to die in order to receive the body of Jesus.

Mark 15:44–45: Pilate was surprised Jesus was already dead. Pilate asked the centurion if Jesus was already dead because crucifixion was a long, arduous, suffering process. Pilate gave the corpse to Joseph (this is the only time Jesus' body was described as a corpse). Wessel said that it was also unusual to give the corpse of a person condemned for treason to anyone but a near relative.[1] Maybe Pilate knew Jesus wasn't guilty of treason, so he gave His body to Joseph. Maybe Pilate knew who Jesus really was.

Mark 15:46: Joseph took Jesus down from the cross, wrapped His body in linen, and placed Him in a tomb cut into the rock. Joseph then rolled a stone in place to cover the opening. The Garden Tomb is one of two locations where tradition says Jesus was buried. The tomb has two chambers inside; Jesus' body was laid in the inner chamber.

John 19:38–42 says Nicodemus, also a member of the Council, helped Joseph with the burial. (In John 3:1–2, Nicodemus had met with Jesus in the evening.)

---

[1] Walter W. Wessel, "Mark." In *The Expositor's Bible Commentary: Matthew–Luke*, vol. 8, ed. Frank E. Gaebelein and J. D. Douglas (Grand Rapids: Zondervan, 1984), 784.

Nicodemus brought about 75 pounds of myrrh and aloes. They wrapped Jesus' body in linen clothes and aromatic spices according to the customs of the Jews. They laid His body in a tomb, in the garden where no one had ever been placed.

Maybe this was the first time Joseph revealed himself as a follower of Jesus. In John 7:45–50, Nicodemus defended Jesus when the chief priests and Pharisees wanted to know why the temple police hadn't arrested Jesus. Wiersbe says, "We must not think that these two men suddenly decided to bury Jesus, because what they did demanded much preparation."[2] He suggests these men had studied the prophecies in the Scriptures and, "led by the Spirit," figured out that Jesus would die at Passover. Isaiah prophesied the Messiah would be buried in a rich man's tomb. Someone had to step up and pursue prophecy. Joseph and Nicodemus did this because they were "looking for the kingdom of God," had studied Isaiah 53:9, and chose to be part of it. They fulfilled the burial customs of the day. Normally, the body would have been washed, anointed with spices (which Nicodemus brought), wrapped in cloth and bound with burial bandages, and the face covered with a separate cloth. Joseph and Nicodemus served Jesus who, at that point, was a dead body.

Mark 15:47: Mary, the mother of Jesus, and Mary Magdalene watched where Jesus' body was placed. The women who had supported Jesus in His ministry prepared oils and spices to anoint His body after the Sabbath was over. His body wasn't there, but they were prepared and ready.

What can we learn about serving Jesus from this account?

1. The servants were prepared. They looked forward to the kingdom of God. One theory (unproven) was that they hid in the tomb during the time when the Sanhedrin demanded Jesus' crucifixion.[3]
2. They knew the Word. They were familiar with the prophecies of the Old Testament and saw them fulfilled in Jesus' death.
3. They were bold.
4. They made sacrifices. They were willing to deny themselves, take up their crosses, and follow Jesus.
5. They exercised good stewardship. Joseph and Nicodemus were good stewards of their material possessions.
6. They had radical faith.

---

[2] Warren Wiersbe, *The Bible Exposition Commentary: Matthew–Galatians* (Colorado Springs: David C. Cook, 1989), 134.

[3] Wiersbe, 134.

Joseph and Nicodemus looked forward to the kingdom of God by burying Jesus' dead body because they believed He was going to live again.

Closing

We need to become good stewards of our possessions to prepare for the coming of the *King*.

Daily Word

Jesus not only faced physical pain before His Crucifixion, He endured emotional pain as well. People passed by and yelled insults, the chief priests with the scribes mocked Jesus, and even the criminals crucified alongside Jesus taunted Him. Jesus endured it all until His death on the Cross.

As followers of Christ, persecution for your faith will come. As you live boldly for Jesus in this culture, be prepared for insults, mocking, and taunting. Jesus endured the emotional and physical pain by keeping His eyes on His mission from the Father. Sometimes, emotional suffering hurts more than physical pain. May you live your life in such a way that people will know the Jesus inside you, even if it means enduring hardship, suffering, and persecution. Even then, be courageous—Jesus has conquered the world!

In the same way, the chief priests with the scribes were mocking Him to one another and saying, "He saved others; He cannot save Himself! Let the Messiah, the King of Israel, come down now from the cross, so that we may see and believe." Even those who were crucified with Him were taunting Him. —Mark 15:31–32

Further Scripture: John 15:18; John 16:33; 2 Timothy 3:12

Questions

1. In Mark 15:2–3, Jesus responded to Pilate's question, and then the chief priests accused Him of many things. What were some things they accused Him of? (Mark 14:58, 64; Luke 23:2, 5; John 19:7)

2. Pilate knew that the chief priests handed Jesus over to him out of envy. What were they envious about?

3. The chief priests used their influence to move the crowd to favor Barabbas. Do you use your influence to move people toward faith in Jesus?

4. In Mark 10:34, Jesus told the 12 that He would be mocked, spit on, scourged (flogged), and killed. According to Mark 15, did all these things happen? How did Jesus know they would?

5. At what time of day was Jesus crucified? At what time did He die? How long did He suffer on the Cross? How do you see this suffering as an act of supreme love?

6. What did the Holy Spirit highlight to you in Mark 15 through the reading or the teaching?

Lesson 44: Mark 16
Servant: Jesus is Alive!

Teaching Notes

Intro

Mark 16 is the final chapter of the Gospel of Mark. Yesterday in Mark 15, Joseph and Nicodemus prepared Jesus' body for burial. But a dead Savior does no good—He would be just a normal, everyday man. But Jesus is more than that. Romans 4:25 said Jesus was delivered up for our sins (trespasses), but He was raised for our justification. In 1 Corinthians 15:1–8, Paul clarified the gospel. Christ died for our sins, He was buried, and He was raised from the dead according to the Scriptures.

Today, we're going to talk about Jesus' appearances after His resurrection. Jesus appeared to many people (1 Corinthians 15:5–8). Our one word for Mark is the word *Servant*. In the first 13 chapters, we talked about the ways Jesus served us. Then we talked about the ways the disciples could have served Jesus. In Mark 14, while in the Garden of Gethsemane with Jesus, they could have stayed awake and prayed. In Mark 15, after Jesus was crucified, Joseph and Nicodemus buried His body.

Rhoads and Michie said, "In the final scenes in Jerusalem, the minor characters especially exemplify the admonition to be 'servant of all.'" Earlier Jesus served others. Now, in His time of need, others served Him. Simon the Leper received Jesus in his house. A woman anointed Him with ointment worthy of a year's salary. Simon of Cyrene took up His cross. Joseph took His body from the cross and buried Him. A group of women went to the tomb to anoint Jesus after His death. These actions of service for Jesus were done by people who courageously sacrificed and risked something—money, arrest, reputation—to carry them out. These minor characters served Jesus because they saw how Jesus served them.[1]

Teaching

Mark 16:1: When the Sabbath was over, the women brought spices to anoint Jesus' body. They were ready to serve a dead body.

---

[1] David Rhoads, Joanna Dewey, and Donald Michie, *Mark as Story* (Minneapolis: Fortress, 1999), 132.

Mark 16:2–3: They went to the tomb at sunrise, all the while wondering who would roll away the stone from the entrance of the tomb. They weren't strong enough to move the stone. They weren't thinking about the Roman soldiers, but about caring for Jesus' body. Matthew 27:62–66 describes why Roman soldiers guarded Jesus' tomb. The Pharisees had asked Pilate to secure the tomb because "while this deceiver was still alive, He said, 'After three days I will rise again.'" They wanted to make sure the disciples couldn't steal the body and then claim that Jesus had risen from the dead. So, Pilate had sealed the tomb and placed guards before it.

Mark 16:4–5: *Surprise #1*: The stone had been rolled away. *Surprise #2*: The women entered the tomb and were amazed and alarmed when they saw a young man (an angel) dressed in a white robe. Luke 24:4 says two men (angels) "stood by them in dazzling clothes."

Mark 16:6: *Surprise #3*: The angel delivered the message that Jesus had risen from the dead. Did the women expect to hear this message? No. How do we know? They had taken spices to complete the burial customs. They had full expectation that Jesus' dead body would still be in the tomb.

Mark 16:7–8: The angels told the women to go and tell Jesus' disciples, and Peter, that Jesus was going ahead of them to Galilee. Before His death, Jesus had told them He would meet them in Galilee after His resurrection (Mark 14:27–28). So, the women ran from the tomb. Mark recorded that initially they told no one because they were afraid.

Mark 16:9–10: By comparing this account with John 20, we learn that the women ran to tell Peter and John, and then ran back to the tomb. Jesus appeared to Mary Magdalene at the tomb because she stayed there while the other women ran to the disciples. Who was the first person that Jesus appeared to? A woman. Mary Magdalene then reported to the disciples who were mourning and weeping. In another Gospel it says Jesus appeared to the other women as well (Matthew 28:9). Luke 24:34 says Jesus appeared to Peter. Over the course of 40 days, Jesus appeared to many people.

Mark 16:11–13: The disciples didn't believe Mary Magdalene's report. Jesus then appeared "in a different form to two of them" walking in the country. This was when Jesus talked with two believers on the road to Emmaus, which was covered in more detail in Luke 24:13–22. These believers reported this to the disciples, but they didn't believe this account either.

Mark 16:14: Later, Jesus appeared to the 11. At this point, Judas had committed suicide after betraying Jesus, and they had not yet added Matthias. Jesus rebuked their hardness of heart and unbelief. How many times had they refused to believe those who had seen Him after His resurrection? How many times did Jesus say these events would happen? In Mark 8:31, Jesus told them the Son of Man must suffer . . . and then rise again. The message didn't stop with His burial. In Mark 9:31, Jesus told them a second time what would happen. Mark 10:32–33 records the third time Jesus told them what would happen to Him. Mary Magdalene reported she had seen Jesus and they refused to believe her.

If you don't let the resurrection sink in, His death and burial are pointless to who we are in Christ. He has defeated all the weight of the sin of the world past, present, and future. He carried and bore the curse of the law according to Galatians 3:13. All of that was wiped away through the resurrection. The disciples had forgotten what God had told them.

Mark 16:15–16: Jesus told them, "Go into all the world and preach the gospel to the whole creation." This included Jews and Gentiles. Everybody needs to hear that Jesus died, was buried, and has come back to life. Jesus also said, "Whoever believes and is baptized will be saved, but whoever does not believe will be condemned." The emphasis is on belief, not baptism, because those who don't believe are condemned (not those who aren't baptized). Salvation comes through faith, through belief. Baptism is an incredible way to outwardly express your inner faith in Jesus' death, burial, and resurrection. The best way to serve Jesus is to go and tell somebody the gospel.

Mark 16:17–18: Jesus described some signs that would accompany those who believe. They would drive out demons and speak in new languages (we'll come back to the next two). They would lay hands on the sick, who would get well (v. 18b). The Holy Spirit wants to move through us to see these things happen. Verse 18 also describes picking up snakes. This doesn't mean we should go looking for snakes (Matthew 4:7 says don't test God). But if you're sharing the gospel and for some reason you have to pick up a snake, don't worry; it won't harm you. If you drink anything deadly, it won't harm you. As you continue to advance the kingdom of God, to tell the message of the death, burial, and resurrection of Jesus, you'll be fine.

Mark 16:19–20: Right after speaking to them, Jesus was taken up to heaven and sat down at the right hand of God. Jesus, in a miraculous way, is no longer in the tomb. The disciples went out and preached everywhere the message of Jesus' death, burial, and resurrection. Jesus is alive! The Lord worked with them and confirmed their words through the accompanying signs just described.

Closing

The Great Commission is found in Matthew 28:18–20; Mark 16:15–18; Luke 24, John 20; and Acts 1. When Jesus' servants began to realize that Jesus had gone through death, burial, and resurrection, they could not contain the good news any longer. We cannot contain this good news any longer; we have to go out and preach who Christ is. My challenge to you is this: Don't stay quiet any longer—go tell people He's alive!

Daily Word

The women arrived at Jesus' tomb early in the morning with spices to anoint His body. Instead of finding His body in the tomb, an angel met the women and shared the news that Jesus had been resurrected and gone ahead of them to Galilee. Just as Jesus had promised, He would see the women again! As the women went away from the angel, they were so bewildered with the news that Jesus was alive they didn't say anything as they went on their way.

Have you ever seen God move in such a big way that it took a while for the miracle to sink in? Maybe your body was healed, the Lord provided finances for something that seemed impossible, you passed a test you felt certain to fail, or your difficult marriage turned around in a moment. Just like the women who witnessed the miracle of Jesus' resurrection, sometimes it takes a while to articulate the power and amazement of Jesus in your life. But just as the women eventually shared the amazing news of Jesus' resurrection, the Lord will give you words and opportunities to go into all the world and share about His miraculous power in your life!

So they went out and started running from the tomb, because trembling and astonishment overwhelmed them. And they said nothing to anyone, since they were afraid. —Mark 16:8

Further Scripture: Matthew 7:28; Acts 3:11–12; Romans 15:18–19

Questions

1. Why do you think the angel in the tomb specifically mentioned Peter?
2. In Mark 14:28, Jesus told the disciples that after He had been raised, He would go ahead of them into Galilee. Why do you think He chose Galilee? Did any of the disciples expect Him to be raised from the dead?
3. The disciples heard reports from several sources that Jesus was alive, and they did not believe them. What two things did Jesus reproach them for? Why

do you think their hearts were hard? Do you wrestle with a hardened heart when difficult times come?

4. One of the signs that will accompany those who believe is that they can pick up serpents and not be harmed. Where in the New Testament do we read such an account (Acts 28:3–6)? Do you think this sign could also be symbolic for the authority we have over the serpent from Genesis 3? (Revelation 12:9–11)

5. What did the Holy Spirit highlight to you in Mark 16 through the reading or the teaching?

Lesson 45: Luke 1

Son of Man: The Angel Announces
the Birth of Two Sons

Teaching Notes

Intro

Welcome to the study of the Gospel of Luke, the third of the synoptic Gospels. Luke was a doctor who wrote this account for Theophilus, a Roman dignitary. Theophilus was possibly a believer from Caesar's household who turned to Christ about AD 60–61. Luke probably wrote this from Rome during Paul's imprisonment. Paul talked to Luke about his life, which Luke recorded in this Gospel.[1]

Our phrase for the Gospel of Luke is *Son of Man*. We'll be talking about Jesus' humanity as we study Luke's account. Jesus opened the table for all. We'll see the rich, the poor, the sick, and the healthy. Jesus was not afraid to engage any one of them, but invited all to come to Him.

The characteristics of a physician include being smart and looking for the details. Luke brought these characteristics to his research and writing. He emphasized the details as he told the story. Luke is volume 1, which flows into Acts, which is volume 2. Luke tried to explain scenarios that the Gentiles didn't understand about Jewish culture.

Teaching

Luke 1:1–4: Luke dedicated his writing to Theophilus. He carefully investigated the events and wrote them in an orderly sequence so his reader could understand why he believed what he believed.

Luke 1:5–25: Gabriel predicted to Zechariah and Elizabeth the birth of their son, John the Baptist. The angel was sent from the Lord to explain that John the Baptist's role would be to prepare the way for the coming Messiah. This event was the backdrop for Mary to receive her message from the angel. Zechariah and Elizabeth's son was considered miraculous because they were beyond the age of

---

[1] John MacArthur, *The MacArthur Bible Commentary* (Nashville: Thomas Nelson, 2005), 1264–1265.

childbearing. This event was in preparation for another miracle. For five months, Elizabeth kept herself in seclusion.

Luke 1:26: In the sixth month of Elizabeth's pregnancy, the angel Gabriel was sent by God to Nazareth. Nazareth was a small town about 70 miles north of Jerusalem. The town held a low reputation and is not mentioned in the Old Testament. When Philip later told his brother Nathanael that he had found the Messiah, who was the son of Joseph from Nazareth, Nathanael responded by asking if anything good could come out of Nazareth (John 1:43–46). That was the mentality about this town.

Luke 1:27: An angel appeared to a virgin named Mary, who was engaged to Joseph from the house of David. A virgin has not had sexual relations, so Mary had not had relations with Joseph. We don't often consider the magnitude of being engaged during that time. The engagement was legit (legally binding), and Mary was already committed, or "married," to Joseph. The key point is that Joseph was listed as from the house of David. In 2 Samuel 7:12–16, God told David that He would establish David's kingdom and throne forever. The Jews knew that the Messiah would come through the lineage of David.

Luke 1:28: The angel addressed Mary as "favored woman." In that period of time, women were not viewed very highly or allowed to have a prominent role. God chose this virgin named Mary, to bring about the birth of the Messiah. We have to wonder if the women of that time thought about the possibility of being the mother of the Messiah.

Luke 1:29: Mary was deeply troubled by the angel's statement. Gabriel told her to rejoice before telling her why.

Luke 1:30: The angel told Mary not to be afraid for she had found favor with God. Twice, Mary was told she had found favor with God. Keep in mind that even though she was a virgin, she was still a sinner, not because of sexual sin but because no one is perfect. Yes, she was chosen as the mother of the Messiah, but that doesn't mean we worship her. God chose her to be the vessel to bring about the coming Messiah.

Luke 1:31: The angel told Mary, "You will conceive and give birth to a son and you will call His name Jesus." Yeshua means, "Lord is Salvation." This would fulfill the prophecy of Isaiah 7:14, "The virgin will conceive, have a son, and name him Immanuel," which means "God with us."

Luke 1:32: Gabriel provided more descriptions of who Jesus would be and emphasized that God would give Him the throne of His father David. Again, fulfillment of prophecy (2 Samuel 7:12–16) was revealed.

Luke 1:33: Gabriel said Jesus would reign over the house of Jacob forever. The prophecies of the Pentateuch are fulfilled in Jesus. Daniel 2:44 said this kingdom would never be destroyed but would endure forever.

Luke 1:34: Mary asked, "How can this be, since I have not been intimate with a man?" Luke covered the practicalities. Mary was pure, so how could she conceive a child?

Luke 1:35: Gabriel explained that the Holy Spirit would overshadow her. Throughout Luke's writings, the role of the Holy Spirit was emphasized. He began by describing the power of the Holy Spirit in Jesus' birth.

Luke 1:36: Gabriel then gave Mary a sign, "Consider your relative Elizabeth who conceived a child in her old age and is now in her sixth month."

Luke 1:37: "For nothing will be impossible with God." Gabriel emphasized the prophecies of the Messiah would be fulfilled in Mary. This statement of God's power and ability was repeated in Matthew 19:26, when Jesus said, "With men this is impossible, but with God all things are possible." Mark 10:27 recorded the same statement. Your impossible situations may involve your marriage, kids, finances, school situations or friends. When left up to us, nothing will happen. But with God, all things are possible as long as it aligns with the Word of God. In America, believers constantly try to do things in our own strength. In reality, we need to give God room to work in our lives. God wants to work through us, but many times we just don't want to come to the table.

The prophet Jeremiah also said, "Nothing is too difficult for You" (Jeremiah 32:17). After Jeremiah recounted the wonders God had done to bring Israel out of Egypt and into the Promised Land, God confirmed, "I am Yahweh, the God of all flesh. Is anything too difficult for Me?" (Jeremiah 32:27). Give the difficult situations in your life to God and trust Him to show up. Pray, "Help my unbelief. Lord, please show us how big You are."

Luke 1:38: Mary demonstrated how to respond, when God asks us to do the impossible. Mary said, "May it be done to me according to your Word." Mary wanted to do what God wanted in her life based on what the Scripture said. Then, the angel left her.

Closing

Verse after verse in Scripture talks about how big God is and how He does the impossible. It's like God delights in parting the Red Sea, opening the Jordan River so millions walk through, and turning water to wine. These events show people didn't do the impossible, God did.

Once you're promised the impossible, respond by saying, "I'm in." Then God will get the glory.

Daily Word

God sent the angel Gabriel to a young virgin named Mary. He shared with her the news, "Do not be afraid, Mary, for you have found favor with God. Now listen: You will conceive and give birth to a son, and you will call His name Jesus. Therefore the Holy One to be born will be called the Son of God." Then the angel reminded her of this truth: "Nothing will be impossible with God." Mary responded in humility and surrender, saying, "I am the Lord's slave. May it be done according to your word."

No matter what you face today, no matter the magnitude of your responsibility, your calling, or your trial, believe these truths for your own life: do not be afraid, God sees you, His favor is upon you, you have a purpose, and nothing will be impossible with God.

Today, walk with the Lord, having the same faith and humility as Mary. The Lord has a plan for you, and He makes the impossible *possible*!

For nothing will be impossible with God. —Luke 1:37

Further Scripture: Isaiah 41:10; Jeremiah 32:17–18; Matthew 17:20

Questions

1. To whom was Luke writing? Why do you think he wrote to him specifically (Acts 1:1)? How would you feel if you were Elizabeth or Zechariah, and heard about who your child would become?

2. How did Zechariah's response and Mary's response differ when the angel of the Lord brought the news of their children to them? Do you think you would have responded to the news more like Zechariah or Mary?

3. Who/what was the "Morning Star" or "Rising Star" mentioned in Luke 1:78–79? (Malachi 4:2)

4. Did Luke 1:32–33 refer to Solomon or Jesus? How did Solomon foreshadow Christ? (1 Chronicles 22:9–10, 29:23–25; Isaiah 9:7)

5. What did the Holy Spirit highlight to you in Luke 1 through the reading or the teaching?

Lesson 46: Luke 2

Son of Man: Understanding Jesus' Humanity

Teaching Notes

Intro

Matthew portrayed Jesus as *King*. Mark portrayed Jesus as *Servant*. Luke portrayed Jesus as the *Son of Man*. How is Jesus the *Son of Man*? He's the son of Mary, but He's also tied to humanity. Jesus became human to redeem mankind.

Jesus' birth fulfilled the words of Isaiah 7:14, "Therefore, the Lord Himself will give you a sign: The virgin will conceive, have a son, and name him Immanuel." The disciple John stated, "In the beginning was the Word" (John 1:1), and then clearly explained, "The Word became flesh and took up residence among us" (v. 14). Jesus came to earth to invite us to the table. Jesus knows us so well, and He wants to put everything before us. Jesus will connect with us wherever we are, if we will just come to the table. This is possible because a young virgin named Mary gave birth to the Messiah.

Teaching

Luke 2:1–7: These verses provided some of the details concerning the birth of Jesus. Mary had a son and named him Jesus (v. 7).

Luke 2:8–20: The shepherds were some of the first messengers of the good news. After the shepherds followed the angels' instructions and traveled to Bethlehem to see the Messiah, Luke reported, "After seeing them, they reported the message they were told about this child" (v. 17). Whoever heard their report was amazed.

Luke 2:21–24: On the eighth day, Jesus was circumcised. He was the Son of Man, so He was like us in human form. The name Jesus was given by the angel. Immanuel means "God with Us," and Yeshua means "The Lord is salvation." Both point to Jesus' work to bring about salvation.

Luke 2:25–38: Simeon was a righteous and devout man. The Holy Spirit had promised that he wouldn't die before "he saw the Lord's Messiah" (v. 26). When Joseph and Mary brought Jesus to the temple for the first time, Simeon took the

Child in his arms and praised Him (vv. 29–32). "At that very moment," Anna, a prophetess, also "began to thank God and to speak about Him to all who were looking forward to the redemption of Jerusalem" (v. 38).

The remainder of Luke 2 painted a picture of Jesus as a human child by focusing on His boyhood. Jesus' father was a carpenter. Some say woodworking; others say working with stone and rock because Nazareth had more rocks than trees. Joseph's occupation was revealed in Matthew 13:55, when the people in Jesus' hometown responded to His public ministry by wondering, "Isn't this the carpenter's son?" As a child, Jesus had a family: Mary, Joseph, and brothers, James, Joseph, Simon, and Judas, and sisters as well.

Luke 2:39–40: Jesus' family returned to Galilee to the town of Nazareth. Jesus "grew up and became strong, filled with wisdom, and God's grace was on Him." *Nelson's Commentary* said this described the growth of Jesus' human nature, not His divine nature.[1] He was fully God the moment He was born on earth. This indicated He was growing into humanity to experience what you and I experience.

Luke 2:41–42: Every year, Jesus' family traveled to Jerusalem for the Passover festival. Passover, Feast of Pentecost (Shavuot), and the Feast of Tabernacles were celebrated in Jerusalem. The Passover festival came from Exodus 23. They went to Jerusalem to celebrate what God had done in Egypt. Even Jesus celebrated as a young boy with His parents. When Jesus was 12, they went up to Jerusalem according to the custom of the festival. At the age of 12, boys received intensive instruction in preparation for the age of responsibility, which was 13. At 13, Jesus was accepted into the religious community as a man required to keep the law.

Luke 2:43–46: "After those days were over," refers to Exodus 23, where the one-day feast was followed by the weeklong feast of unleavened bread, a seven- to eight-day period. The family journeyed toward home, but Jesus "lingered" in Jerusalem. The larger the traveling party, the easier it was for this to happen. This was a seven-hour walk, a day's journey, with many people. Mary and Joseph looked for Jesus among relatives and when they didn't find Him, they panicked. After three days, they found Jesus in the temple complex listening to the teachers and asking questions. He wasn't drilling them. He was a little boy, as a human, learning among the rabbis. Consider Psalm 119:99–100: "I have more insight than all my teachers because your decrees are my meditation. I understand more than the elders." What an awesome picture of humility. Jesus submitted

---

[1] Earl D. Radmacher, Ronald B. Allen, and H. Wayne House, eds., *Nelson's New Illustrated Bible Commentary* (Nashville: Thomas Nelson, 1999), 1254.

to listening even though He knew more than the teachers. We need to surround ourselves with people teaching the Word based on the Word so we can soak up the Word.

Luke 2:47–50: Jesus had theological discussions as a 12-year-old. All who heard Him were astounded at His understanding and His answers. His parents were astonished, and Mary said, "Why have You treated us like this? Your father [Joseph] and I have been anxiously searching for You." Mary's anxiety came out. Jesus wondered why they were searching because He "had to be in My Father's [God's] house." According to *Nelson's Commentary*, Jesus meant He was doing the work of the Lord or He was supposed to be here.[2] Joseph and Mary didn't understand. How many times did the disciples fail to understand? Luke 9:45 describes the same mentality. The disciples didn't understand this statement and were afraid to ask Jesus about it.

Luke 2:51–52: Jesus, being obedient to his parents, went down to Nazareth. His mother kept all these things in her heart. What things do you think was she processing? Jesus didn't get kicked out of synagogue; He was welcomed. He was having full conversations; He impressed and amazed everyone who was there. Mary had so much to process: she knew what Gabriel had said; she knew that Jesus was the Son of God, the *Son of Man*, God with us. Jesus wasn't being disobedient by staying in Jerusalem. Now He honored the Ten Commandments by honoring His parents. Luke ended by saying, "Jesus increased in wisdom and stature, and in favor with God and people."

Closing

We know about Jesus' childhood from Scripture. He grew up strong and filled with wisdom. God's grace was on Him, and He found favor with God and people. Over and over, commentators point out that Jesus grew as a human, but He didn't stop being God. John MacArthur said Jesus "submitted the use of His divine attributes to the will of the Father."[3] Jesus submitted to the Father, God, and allowed God to show Him when to use these abilities. "Christ was therefore subject to the normal process of human growth, intellectually, physically, spiritually, and socially."[4] He constantly gave up His divine attributes to the Father and continued to grow as a human.

Luke wrote of moments in time when omniscience was on display; moments when God allowed Jesus to use His "God power." Everything was always in

---

[2] Radmacher et al., 1254.

[3] John MacArthur, *The MacArthur Bible Commentary* (Nashville: Thomas Nelson, 2005), 1280.

[4] MacArthur, 1280.

submission to the Father, as evidenced by His statement, "I don't know the times" (Matthew 24:36). While here on earth He gave the use of divine attributes over to the plan of the Father. At times, God released His omniscient powers. It wasn't until after the resurrection that Christ truly resumed His full divine knowledge and power.

This was the boyhood of Jesus. Luke 3 included an awesome picture of God the Father stating His approval of His Son while Jesus was here on earth. The boyhood of Jesus included His parents and several brothers and sisters. Jesus increased in wisdom and stature while a human here on earth as the *Son of Man*.

Daily Word

Jesus wasn't just born with all wisdom and favor as an infant. Over the years, He sat and listened to scholars and teachers of the Mosaic Law. He asked them questions, and He was obedient to His parents. With time, Jesus increased in wisdom, stature, and in favor with God and people.

Like Jesus, you will continue to grow in wisdom as you spend time in the Word of God, discussing Scripture with other believers, and living obediently to the Lord. The Lord doesn't expect you to have it all together the moment you say yes to Him. You don't have to have it all together because His grace is sufficient in your weakness. Continue to place yourself in positions where you will grow in Christ. Walk with perseverance and endurance, pressing on to know Him more.

And Jesus increased in wisdom and stature, and in favor with God and with people. —Luke 2:52

Further Scripture: Hebrews 5:12–14; James 1:2–4; 1 Peter 2:2–3

Questions

1. Caesar Augustus decreed that a census be taken of the Roman Empire. How did God use this to fulfill the prophecy of Micah 5:2?

2. When the shepherds went to see what the angels told them about, they had no address or specific location. What clue did they have to find baby Jesus?

3. According to Leviticus 12, how many days after Jesus' birth did they go to the Temple for purification (Luke 2:22)? What took place during this visit to the temple that was significant?

4. Although Joseph and Mary knew that Jesus was not like other children, Luke 2:33 said they marveled at the things that were said about Him. Why do you think they did so?

5. Luke 2:40, 52 described Jesus' development from infant to child. What do you think was meant by the phrase, "the grace of God was upon Him"?

6. What did the Holy Spirit highlight to you in Luke 2 through the reading or the teaching?

Lesson 47: Luke 3
Son of Man: The Genealogy of Christ

Teaching Notes

Intro

In Luke 3, we'll talk about the lineage of Christ. The beautiful part is that we'll see Jesus' connections to humanity. Jesus' lineage goes all the way back to Adam.

Teaching

Luke 3:1–20: These verses tell the story of the Messiah's herald. John the Baptist paved the way for Jesus. The transition statement in verse 20 revealed that John was locked up in prison.

Luke 3:21: "When all the people were baptized, Jesus also was baptized." In Matthew 28:19, Jesus said, "Go . . . make disciples . . . baptizing them . . ." If Jesus was baptized, and He instructed us to baptize people, then that's what we should do. For some reason, we don't talk about baptizing people. As a follower of Jesus, (1) make sure you're baptized. Baptism doesn't save you, but it is an outward expression of inner faith. (2) Baptize other people, even if you've never done it, because Jesus commanded it.

Luke 3:22: The Holy Spirit descended on Jesus, the *Son of Man*. God clearly described Jesus as "My Son." As Jesus began His ministry, He was baptized and visibly anointed from heaven. He was about 30 years old, which seemed to be the age that many people began their ministry. In Genesis 41:46, Joseph was 30 years old when he entered the service of Pharaoh king of Egypt. Had Joseph and Jesus done other work? Certainly, but this was the turning point when God clearly anointed Jesus for ministry. In 2 Samuel 5:4, David was 30 years old when he began his reign as king, and he reigned 40 years. Ezekiel 1:1 said that in his thirtieth year, Ezekiel the prophet saw the visions of God and began to walk out those visions. According to Numbers 4:3, at the age of 30, priests began to work at the tabernacle. So at about the age of 30, Jesus began His priesthood ministry.

Luke 3:23: Jesus was "thought to be" the son of Joseph, son of Heli. Perhaps this phrase meant that Joseph had "adopted" Jesus, which would have been important. Joseph would have legally been Jesus' father, taking on Jesus as his son. Matthew 1:16 said that Jacob fathered Joseph, the husband of Mary. You can trace Joseph's line back to David. Commentators offer different ways to explain the difference in Luke and Matthew's account of Joseph's father. Boch pointed out that this could be Mary's lineage or could be the result of the custom of Levirate marriage in the ancient Mideast, which permitted the widow of a childless man to marry his unmarried brother. The child of the second marriage was considered the legal son of the deceased man.[1]

Luke 3:24–27: These verses listed 17 names of men that we know nothing about. We recognize some, like Zerubbabel, who was head of tribe of Judah when the Israelites returned from Babylonian captivity under Cyrus the Great, in Ezra 2:2. *Luke 3:28–30*: "Son of Judah." While not Judah, the son of Jacob, he was probably a descendant of the tribe. Why is this important? In Genesis 49:10, Jacob's blessing included "the scepter shall not depart from Judah." The tribe of Judah was the tribe of the king's lineage. Revelation 5:5 described Jesus as, "the Lion from the tribe of Judah, the Root of David." As Jesus began His ministry, He fulfilled these prophecies.

Luke 3:31–33: We see names in this portion of Jesus' genealogy that we recognize. Jesus was from the lineage of David as described in 2 Samuel 7:12–13: "I will raise up after you your descendant . . . I will establish the throne of his kingdom forever." Every one of these guys had an important role in Scripture. Boaz was the main male figure in the book of Ruth. Jesus' ancestry was essential to His identity. Now the son of Judah is the direct descendant of Jacob. Leah, whom Jacob didn't even like (Jacob preferred Rachel), was Judah's mom. An interesting comparison was that Gabriel showed up to Mary of Nazareth, the town no one respected. With God anything is possible. He could use anyone to point people to the Messiah.

Luke 3:34: Through this verse, Luke confirmed that Jesus was the son of Abraham, who was the son of Terah, the son of Nahor.

Luke 3:35–36: Luke continued tracing the generations to show that Jesus was the son of Shem, son of Noah. Jesus was connected to Noah.

---

[1] Darrell L. Bock, *Luke*, The IVP New Testament Commentary Series (Downers Grove, IL: IVP Academic, 2010), 80–81.

Luke 3:37–38: Luke also showed that Jesus was the son of Seth, the son of Adam, the son of God. Jesus was tied to the son of Adam. Fitzmeyer said this ending was truly one of a kind.[2] Why did Luke tie this together? In Acts 17:28, Paul said, "For in Him we live and move and exist . . . for we are also His offspring."

Why is it important that Jesus was connected to Adam? This is essential to understanding the *Son of Man*. In all other religions, their gods are distant, somewhere else. You can't touch them or feel them. In Luke's Gospel, you see a God who can actually connect with us. The *Son of Man* came to connect with you and me. Romans 5:12–17 said, "Therefore, just as sin entered the world through one man, and death through sin." Through Adam, sin and death became reality for all people. Sin was in the world before the Law; the Law was essential to understanding sin. In verse 15, Paul wrote, "But the gift is not like the trespass. For if by the one man's trespass the many died, how much more by the grace of God and the gift overflowed to the many by the grace of the one man, Jesus Christ." Because of one trespass, many died. From Adam's sin came judgment, condemnation, and death. From the gift—God's grace in Jesus Christ—came justification, overflow of grace, righteousness, and life.

1 Corinthians 15:21 begins with the phrase, "For since death came through a man," meaning that death came through the one bite Adam took of the forbidden fruit. Paul then continued, "The resurrection of the dead also comes through a man." Paul said, "a man," and the lineage of Jesus gives proof of His humanity. Paul continued to emphasize this point in verse 22: "For as in Adam all die, so also in Christ all will be made alive again," and in verse 45: "The first man Adam became a living being; the last Adam became a life-giving Spirit." When you begin to understand these passages, they tie into Luke 3:23–38. The first and the last; that's exactly what you see in the genealogy of Jesus in the Gospel of Luke. Through this we see the bigger picture.

Closing

Jesus came to give life, not death. He came to give righteousness and grace, He did not come to bring judgment, condemnation or death. He's coming to make you alive in who He is. Jesus is giving a life-giving message that can radically change your life. Don't stay in the posture of a bitten apple. Christ wants to restore who you are, just come to the table. He wants to help you fix what you've done. He wants to restore, to bring you back to life in Christ.

---

[2] Joseph A. Fitzmyer, *The Gospel According to Luke I-IX* (New York: Doubleday, 1970), n.p.

Daily Word

John the Baptist, the miraculous son of Zechariah and Elizabeth, traveled around the River Jordan, preaching a baptism of repentance for the forgiveness of sins. Three different people groups asked, "What then should we do?" They wondered if perhaps John was the Messiah who had been foretold. But John corrected them, saying One was coming who was more powerful and would baptize people with the Holy Spirit and fire.

There was a hunger and humility in the question, "What then should we do?" The people knew they needed repentance. They knew they needed to take action and make a heart change. John knew they would find ultimate fulfillment through the Savior of the world. Jesus would come to save them from their sins, and then His fire would begin to transform their hearts.

Today, ask the Lord in humility, "What then should I do?" Is there something in your life you need to repent of in order to create a pure heart and make a real life change? Or maybe the Lord has you going through a trial to purify your heart. Ask the Lord, listen to His voice, and He will reveal to you what you should do. Remember, He loves you and, by faith, His grace is enough.

Tax collectors also came to be baptized, and they asked him, "Teacher, what should we do?" . . . John answered them all, "I baptize you with water, but One is coming who is more powerful than I. I am not worthy to untie the strap of His sandals. He will baptize you with the Holy Spirit and fire." — Luke 3:12, 16

Further Scripture: Psalm 51:10; Malachi 3:3; 1 Peter 1:7

Questions

1. When Luke wrote this chapter, why do you think he included all the details about the leaders of different regions and the year of the reign of Tiberius Caesar?

2. John the Baptist used the term "brood of vipers" when addressing the crowds in Luke 3:7. What do you think he meant by this?

3. Look at Luke 3:9 and 17. Do you think that what was burnt in fire was the same in both verses? Why or why not?

4. What do you think it means to be baptized with the Holy Spirit and fire? (Luke 3:16)

5. Why do you think the genealogy in Luke is different from the one in Matthew? (Matthew 1:1–16, Luke 3:23–38)

6. What did the Holy Spirit highlight to you in Luke 3 through the reading or the teaching?

Lesson 48: Luke 4

Son of Man: The Temptation of Christ

Teaching Notes

Intro

The theme of the Gospel of Luke: Jesus is the *Son of Man*. Luke portrayed the humanity of the *Son of Man*, who was sent to redeem humanity after the fall. Luke 4:1–13 covered Jesus' temptation by Satan in the wilderness. How did Jesus overcome this temptation? By the Word of God.

Teaching

Luke 4:14–15: Luke said that Jesus, filled with the Spirit, returned to Galilee after being tempted in the wilderness. He taught in their synagogues and was "acclaimed by everyone." In other words, everybody liked Him: other rabbis, teachers, and the Jewish people. They had no problem with Jesus at this point in His ministry. Nothing He had said had stirred the pot.

Luke 4:16: Jesus came back to Nazareth "where He had been brought up." He entered the synagogue "as usual." Everyone was accustomed to seeing Jesus come into the synagogue. But on this day, Jesus announced His calling. Mark and Matthew cover the event, but in much shorter accounts. For background on this event, let's talk about seven elements or parts in a Jewish synagogue service (similar to an order of worship):[1]

1. An invocation for God's blessing, and maybe some singing from Psalms 145–150.
2. Reciting traditional Hebrew confessions, such as the Shema in Deuteronomy 6:4–9 or Deuteronomy 11:13–21.
3. Prayer (pulled from a collection of 18 prayers).
4. Prescribed readings from the Law (Torah) and the Prophets.

---

[1] Warren Wiersbe, *The Bible Exposition Commentary: Matthew–Galatians* (Colorado Springs: David C. Cook, 1989), 184.

5. Brief sermon on the reading given by someone in that synagogue or a visiting rabbi.

6. Benediction given by the priest. Otherwise, a layman would pray and bless the people, such as the blessing in Numbers 6:24–26.

7. The meeting was dismissed.

Hebrews 10:19–25 encourages us to draw nearer to God. Specifically, verse 25 urges us not to stay away from our worship meetings. This is the only statement in the New Testament encouraging people to gather in worship. Although the disciples didn't prescribe it, they modeled it.

Luke 4:17: Jesus read from the scroll of Isaiah from the prophets (#4 above). Jesus then revealed the mission of the Messiah.[2]

Luke 4:18–19: Jesus' mission was described in Scripture, which Jesus read from Isaiah 61:1–2. But Jesus didn't finish reading verse 2. Why? It was all about God's timing. This was the first stage, not the second stage. Jesus had come to "proclaim the year of the Lord's favor" (Isaiah 61:2a; Luke 4:19), but "the day of our God's vengeance" (Isaiah 61:2b) would come later.

Luke 4:20–21: Jesus rolled up the scroll and returned it to the attendant, then He sat down and everybody focused on Him. Jesus then said, "Today as you listen, this Scripture has been fulfilled." Jesus said He had fulfilled what Isaiah had written hundreds of years earlier. Imagine being in the synagogue that day and hearing Jesus' words. In His Sermon on the Mount, Jesus had proclaimed, "Don't assume that I came to destroy the Law or the Prophets. I did not come to destroy but to fulfill" (Matthew 5:17). Whenever Luke emphasized "today" it was a big deal. In Luke 2:11, he emphasized, "Today a Savior was born." In Luke 5:26, the people who witnessed Jesus' miracles said, "We have seen incredible things today!"

The mission of the Messiah was just beginning. Jesus had many things before Him:[3]

> *He came to preach the gospel to the poor.* This wasn't just the financially poor but included all those who were poor in spirit (Matthew 5:3),

---

[2] Thomas L. Constable, *Expository Notes of Dr. Thomas Constable: Luke*, 111, https://planobiblechapel.org/tcon/notes/pdf/luke.pdf.

[3] Earl Radmacher, Ronald B. Allen, and H. Wayne House, eds., *Nelson's New Illustrated Bible Commentary* (Nashville: Thomas Nelson, 1999), 1257.

who would humble themselves and listen to the gospel. April 2, 1739, was the first time John Wesley decided to leave the church building and go out to preach the good news to the poor. He left everything they had been doing, left the building, and went to find the people who were open to the gospel.

He came to proclaim freedom to the captive. Nelson's Commentary said Jesus was going to find the prisoners, referring to all the people who were in bondage. Bondage comes in many forms—money, Satan, guilt. Jesus came to set them free. We have to change things up and go find the people. We have been anointed to do this.

He came to bring recovery of sight to the blind. This could be talking about physical sight. In the Gospels, Jesus did the miraculous. Luke 7:22 says Jesus physically restored sight to the blind. Jesus wanted to see physical sight be restored. He also wanted them to begin to see the spiritual world. In Acts 26:18, Paul said that Jesus had sent him to "open their eyes so they may turn from darkness to light and from the power of Satan to God." Jesus' role was to open their eyes.

He came to set free the oppressed. Oppressed meant crushed, broken in pieces, weighted down by the world, the flesh, the enemy, until you feel broken. Jesus didn't fail at taking away that weight. He urged people to, "Come to Me, all of you who are weary and burdened, and I will give you rest" (Matthew 11:28).

He came to proclaim the year of the Lord's favor (v. 19). The year of the Lord's favor was the Year of Jubilee. It was the seventh and fiftieth years when Israel's debts were cancelled, and slaves were freed. Jesus said He came to cancel all their debt—their spiritual debt to give them a fresh start. Up to this point in His ministry, Jesus had not stirred the pot—until this day. *Nelson's Commentary* said, "Jesus offers a total cancellation of spiritual debt and a new beginning to those who respond to His message."[4]

As we draw nearer to the end times, to the coming of the Messiah, we need to know the Word of God so we can pursue prophecy. There might be parts we are to play in the end times, but we can't because we don't know the Word of God.

---

[4] Radmacher et al., 1257.

Luke 4:22–24: Although they spoke well of Jesus, they also began to question who He was. Jesus knew they were wondering if He would do the same things in Nazareth that He had done in Capernaum. He knew they were mocking Him. And He responded: "No prophet is accepted in his hometown."

Luke 4:25–27: Jesus' next words stirred the pot even more. He reminded them that there were many widows in Elijah's day. But Elijah was not sent to the widows in Israel but to a widow in Zarephath. God sent the prophet to a Gentile because the widows in Israel wouldn't receive him. Likewise, in Elisha's time, many in Israel had skin diseases but none healed—only Naaman the Syrian. Jesus meant the message was not only for Israel, but also for the Gentiles.

Luke 4:28–30: "When they heard this, everyone in the synagogue was enraged." They drove Jesus out of town, intending to hurl Him over the cliff. But Jesus passed right through the crowd and went on His way. It was all about timing.

Closing

Jesus' mission is to the poor, the prisoners, the blind, and the oppressed—to set them free. His message of freedom is for both Jews and Gentiles. Jesus came to walk this out. The question is, will we do the same?

Daily Word

Jesus spent forty days fasting in the wilderness. The devil seized this time to tempt Jesus in three specific ways. Each time, Jesus resisted the temptation by quoting Scripture, and the devil departed from Him for a time.

Every day, you will face temptation. The enemy's purpose is to steal, kill, and destroy. The devil prowls around like a lion seeking to devour anyone along the way. How will you stay strong and not give in? The Word of God says to resist the devil, and he will flee from you. Combat each temptation with the truth found in God's Word. Identify the lies from the enemy and replace the lie with the truth. If the devil says you are not good enough, say out loud, "I am perfectly and wonderfully made." If the enemy says you are all alone, say out loud, "I am not alone, the Lord my God is with me wherever I go." Spend time with Jesus, and read His Word so that you will have the truth on your heart. The Holy Spirit promises to guide you in all your ways as you walk with Him.

And Jesus answered him, "It is said: Do not test the Lord your God." After the Devil had finished every temptation, he departed from Him for a time. —Luke 4:12–13

Further Scripture: John 10:10; 1 Peter 5:8; James 4:7

Questions

1. How did Jesus respond when He was tempted by Satan? Why did Jesus respond in this way? Do you know the Word well enough to be able to defend against temptations?

2. Why would the Holy Spirit lead Jesus into the wilderness to be tempted? (Luke 4:1–2; Hebrews 4:15)

3. Does it surprise you that Satan knows Scripture (Luke 4:9–11)? How did he twist Scripture and take it out of context?

4. What does it mean to "test or tempt the Lord your God" (Exodus 17:1–7; Deuteronomy 6:14–16; Malachi 3:10; Luke 4:12)? Is it ever appropriate to test God? What must we do to safeguard ourselves with the truth and not be deceived by the twisting of Scripture (Psalm 119:11; 2 Timothy 2:15)? How did Jesus respond after the devil had finished tempting Him?

5. Which Old Testament Scripture did Jesus say He fulfilled? How did the people respond?

6. What did the Holy Spirit highlight to you in Luke 4 through the reading or the teaching?

Lesson 49: Luke 5

Son of Man: Jesus Calls His First Disciples

Teaching Notes

Intro

In this lesson, we're talking about the mission of the Messiah. In Luke 4, Jesus stood in the synagogue and read from the scroll of Isaiah, announcing His mission to those who heard Him. Now, Jesus began His ministry by calling His first disciples.

Teaching

People were now intrigued by Jesus. No longer was Jesus just the childhood boy of Joseph and Mary, or a sibling to his brothers and sisters. Jesus had declared who He was.

Luke 5:1: The crowd pressed in, like crowds or the paparazzi around a celebrity, because they wanted to hear God's Word. Jesus was standing by Lake Gennesaret, also called the Sea of Galilee or Lake of Tiberius, which is a large freshwater lake over 690 feet below sea level. It was the main source of water and commerce for the region of Galilee.[1] Jesus delivered the Sermon on the Mount while overlooking the Sea of Galilee. Capernaum, Jesus' headquarters, was on the sea. Many other events in Jesus' ministry took place on the Sea of Galilee.

Luke 5:2–3: Jesus saw two boats at the shore and fishermen washing their nets. This implied they had spent the day fishing and were cleaning up because they were done for the day. Jesus got into one of the boats, and asked Simon to put out from the shore. Jesus sat down and taught from the boat to control the crowds. There was no lighting, no sound, no cameras—just pure acoustics. The Sea of Galilee was a natural amphitheater and remains so even today. It was customary for Jewish teachers and rabbis to sit down while teaching (Luke 4:20). In Matthew 5:1, when Jesus saw the crowds, "He sat down, His disciples came to Him. Then He began to teach." Jesus sitting down to teach was significant.

---

[1] John MacArthur, *The MacArthur Bible Commentary* (Nashville: Thomas Nelson, 2005), 1285.

Luke 5:4: After speaking to the crowds, Jesus told Simon, "Put out into deep water and let down your nets for a catch." Jesus urged this professional fisherman to go back out to fish even though their entire previous night had been unfruitful. MacArthur said: "Normally the fish that were netted in shallow water at night would migrate during the daylight hours to waters too deep to reach easily with their nets, which is why Peter fished at night. Peter, no doubt, thought Jesus' directive made no sense, but he obeyed anyway, and was rewarded for his obedience."[2]

Luke 5:5: Peter explained their last trip was done and they were cleaning up. Nevertheless, Peter then said, "But at Your word, I'll let down the nets." Boch said Peter had just declared his trust in Jesus.[3] *Nelson's Commentary* said this was "Peter's statement of faith."[4] Peter showed his faith by dropping the net into the water. Faith always leads to dropping the net. Peter's trust began his transition from fisherman to a follower of Christ. James 2:14 says, "What good is it, my brothers, if someone says he has faith but does not have works?" James implied that when you have faith, you exercise what you believe. James went further and said that faith without works is dead (v 17). If Peter said yes but never dropped the net, then he didn't have faith. How does the church show faith today?

Wiersbe said it was possible that "at least seven of the disciples were fishermen."[5] What were the skills of fishermen? Those fishing skills would have included knowing where to fish, how to tie knots, and which bait to use. Wiersbe pointed out that fishermen needed some form of courage, patience, and determination, a great deal of faith that this would actually work, the willingness to work together (to get nets into boats), and the ability to develop skills fast enough to get the job done quickly and efficiently.[6] It also took flexibility and adaptability.

Luke 5:6: Because Peter obeyed Jesus' command, even when he didn't think it made sense, "they caught a great number of fish, and their nets began to tear." It was a miraculous catch. All were amazed (v. 9). Jesus had commanded them to fish differently at a different time. We are on mission with Jesus and we can't quit. Second Chronicles 15:7 says, "But as for you, be strong; don't be discouraged, for

---

[2] MacArthur, 1285.

[3] Darrell L. Bock, *Luke*, The IVP New Testament Commentary Series (Downers Grove, IL: IVP Academic, 2010), n.p.

[4] Earl D. Radmacher, Ronald B. Allen, and H. Wayne House, eds., *Nelson's New Illustrated Bible Commentary* (Nashville: Thomas Nelson, 1999), 1259.

[5] Warren Wiersbe, *The Bible Exposition Commentary: Matthew–Galatians* (Colorado Springs: David C. Cook, 1989), 150.

[6] Wiersbe, 150.

your work has a reward." God will honor your faithfulness even when it doesn't make sense. Galatians 6:9 reminds us, "So we must not get tired of doing what is good, for we will reap at the proper time if we don't give up." The full catch came because they didn't quit but instead put their full trust in His command. They spent time with Jesus, and He poured out His blessings. Isaiah 50:10 says, "Who among you fears the Lord . . . Let him trust in the name of Yahweh; let him lean on his God." When we lean on God, He will respond. But it's almost never our timing, it's His.

Luke 5:7: They signaled their partners, probably James and John the sons of Zebedee, to come help them. They filled both boats so full that they were in danger of sinking. James and John were business partners and now they became spiritual partners. Peter invited others to experience Jesus' blessings. We should invite others so they can also experience the blessings. Wiersbe pointed out that the fishermen became channels of blessing who shared what God had done for them with others.[7]

Luke 5:8: Boch said Peter realized this was more than just a great day of fishing, so we now see Peter's confession and fear.[8] Peter fell at Jesus' knees and said, "Go away from me, because I'm a sinful man, Lord!" Peter articulated his shame over his own sin. When you spend time with Jesus, you recognize who you are. Isaiah made a similar confession, "Woe is me for I am ruined because I am a man of unclean lips . . . and because my eyes have seen the King, the Lord of Hosts" (Isaiah 6:5). Sometimes we don't see our sinful state because we don't spend time with Jesus.

Luke 5:9–11: All were amazed at the catch of fish they took. So were James and John, Simon's partners. Jesus told them, "Don't be afraid. From now on you will be catching people!" Jesus switched their careers, which soon led to others getting involved. The men brought their boats to land, left everything, and followed Him.

Closing

When we spend time in the boat, Jesus speaks to us, and God overwhelms us with His blessings. When we spend time in His presence, we realize our sinful state. Then, when we realize who Christ is, others will say, "I want that."

Boch pointed out what Peter didn't realize; admitting one's inability and sin is actually the best prerequisite for service. One can then depend on God.

---

[7] Wiersbe, 150.

[8] Bock, 100.

Peter's confession became his resume for service.[9] Humility becomes the elevator to spiritual greatness.

Because of humility, we begin to understand what we can't do. Humility is the only way to greatness. We want to catch the fish ourselves, but the reality is, when we say we can't catch the fish, Jesus begins to use us. Keep going because Jesus will honor you and what you're doing when you serve Him.

Daily Word

As Jesus ministered and performed miracles, people were drawn to follow Him and give Him praise. From the fishermen to the man with a serious skin disease, from the paralyzed man to the tax collector, at some point Luke described each of them in a *lowly position—a place of humility*. But, as they each witnessed Jesus' power, *they got up*. They were impacted by Jesus in such a way it caused them to get up and follow Him or get up and testify to others about His power.

As believers of Jesus, this is a model for you to follow as you enter Jesus' presence, seeking His power and healing touch in your own life. Today, enter into a place of humble worship and adoration with Jesus. As you experience His power and strength in your life, get up and proclaim it to others. The power of Jesus is not for us to contain; it's for us to get up and share with others!

After this, Jesus went out and saw a tax collector named Levi sitting at the tax office, and He said to him, "Follow Me!" So, leaving everything behind, he got up and began to follow Him. —Luke 5:27–28

Further Scripture: Luke 5:25; James 4:10; 1 Peter 5:6

Questions

1. What was Peter's reaction when he realized what had happened with the fish? How did this show he gave Jesus credit for providing the catch? What did Peter, James, and John leave behind to follow Jesus?

2. What was Peter's great statement of faith in Jesus' word (Luke 5:5)? What is Jesus asking you to do that requires this same faith in His word?

3. According to the Law regarding leprosy described in Leviticus 13, why was it odd that Jesus touched the man? Why do you think that Jesus was willing to heal him?

---

[9] Bock, 100.

4. What did Jesus do first for the man who was paralyzed? How did this show His deity? (Isaiah 43:25) What did He do to further prove to them that He had the authority on earth to forgive sins?

5. What was Jesus' response to the scribes and Pharisees who complained that He ate with tax collectors and sinners? Do you intentionally spend time with unbelievers in order to share your faith?

6. What did the Holy Spirit highlight to you in Luke 5 through the reading or the teaching?

Lesson 50: Luke 6

Son of Man: Finding Rest in
the Lord of the Sabbath

Teaching Notes

Intro

Even though we can take a Sabbath to rest, we still have to give Him all of our thoughts, all of our anxieties, and all of our woes, as well. So how do we get better at finding our rest in Him? In Israel, the Sabbath is such an important day of rest that they will get angry if tourists carry cameras over their shoulders.

Wiersbe says that the Sabbath is "the sanctity of the seventh day" and "was a distinctive part of the Jewish faith."[1] In America, we talk about going to church, but we don't really think about the sanctity of the day itself. The Sabbath was clearly "a sign between [God] and the nation" of Israel (Nehemiah 9:13–14).[2] The word "Sabbath" simply means to rest. Wiersbe notes that some rabbis taught that the Messiah would not come until Israel had learned how to perfectly keep the Sabbath as a holy day. "The Sabbath speaks of rest *after* work and relates to the law, while the Lord's Day speaks of rest *before* work and relates to grace."[3] Everything in Israel revolves around the Sabbath. This is the backdrop for our study in chapter 6.

Teaching

Luke 6:1–5: Verse 1 states that Jesus and His disciples passed through the grain fields on a Sabbath. As they moved through, the disciples did three things: they picked the heads of some of the wheat, rubbed them with their hands, and ate them. What they did was not for profit but only to eat. The Pharisees questioned why the disciples were doing what was unlawful on the Sabbath (v. 2).

The religious leaders knew that eating on the Sabbath was not illegal. Every-thing the Pharisees asked Jesus had to do with the Law (Matthew 12:12, 19:3,

---

[1] Warren Wiersbe, *The Bible Exposition Commentary: Matthew–Galatians* (Colorado Springs: David C. Cook, 1989), 189.

[2] Wiersbe, 189.

[3] Wiersbe, 190.

22:27, 27:6). A religious spirit causes a constant state of criticism and holds onto legalism.

Jesus responded to their question with an example from the Old Testament, of David entering the house of God and eating the sacred bread, which was unlawful for all but the priests (vv. 3–4; 1 Samuel 21:1–6). The sacred bread was also called "showbread." MacArthur wrote, "The consecrated bread of the Presence consisted of 12 loaves baked fresh each Sabbath, which was usually eaten only by the priests"[4] (Leviticus 24:8–9). David and his men were hungry and were fed by this showbread. Then, Jesus told them He was the "Lord of the Sabbath," Lord over the very thing they were trying to protect (v. 5). Jesus trumps the Law.

MacArthur states "the Sabbath laws do not restrict deeds of necessity (Matthew 12:3–4); service to God (Matthew 12:5–6); or acts of mercy (Matthew 12:7–8)."[5]

Luke 6:6–11: "On another Sabbath [Jesus] entered the synagogue and was teaching" when He saw a man "whose right hand was paralyzed" (v. 6). The scribes and the Pharisees watched Jesus carefully to see if He would heal on the Sabbath "so they could find a charge against Him" (v. 7). Jesus knew what the religious leaders were thinking (Luke 5:22), so He told the man with the paralyzed hand to stand up and come over to Him (v. 8). Jesus then asked the scribes and the Pharisees if it was legal to do good on the Sabbath (v. 9). He looked at them and then told the man with the paralyzed hand, "Stretch out your hand." The man did as Jesus asked, and when he stretched out his hand, his hand was restored" (v. 10). The religious leaders, however, were filled with rage, not joy for the healed man, and began to discuss what they might do to Jesus (v. 11; Matthew 23:6–7). The word "rage" can be understood as having senseless wrath. For Luke, this incident was the beginning of the religious authority's persecution of Jesus.

Closing

Joseph Mattera suggests ten signs for those who have a religious spirit:

1. They judge other people by their appearance.
2. They try to earn God's love and salvation.
3. They try to conform to outward holiness without inner transformation.
4. They are always critical of other people's walk with God.
5. Their closest Christian relationships are based on ministry activities.

---

[4] John MacArthur, *The MacArthur Bible Commentary* (Nashville: Thomas Nelson, 2005), 1145.

[5] MacArthur, 1145.

6. They perform Christian duties but have no passion for God.

7. They desire position and honor in the church more than honor from God.

8. They are rooted in the lifestyle of Christianity instead of in Christ.

9. They know about the truth of Jesus but not the way of Jesus.

10. They project righteousness but inwardly are filled with anger and resentment.

When we are in this position of a religious spirit, we can never find rest in the Lord. When we live in these ten, we never get to experience Psalm 37:7: "Be silent before the Lord and wait expectantly for Him; do not be agitated by one who prospers in his way, by the man who carries out evil plans."

Daily Word

The Pharisees began to question Jesus about properly honoring the Sabbath. Jesus incorporated rest in the midst of an ongoing ministry schedule and demanding crowds. It may not have fallen on a specific day or hour, but Jesus still took time to rest and spend time with His Father. This is the heart behind the Sabbath. And yet Jesus' actions were judged from the outside as being unlawful.

As believers, you are no longer tied to the law of the Sabbath. The Lord wants you to rest in Him and abide in Him. If you are busy judging others or even yourself, wondering if you are resting "enough" or doing "enough," you will miss the whole meaning of Sabbath. Be at rest with Jesus as your rock and your salvation. Trust in Him. Take time to rest in Him away from others so you will be filled with His love and grace to jump right back into life and ministry as the Lord leads. When you serve from a place of rest and through the power of the Holy Spirit, it gives the Lord glory. Try it. Take a deep breath and rest today.

Then He told them, "The Son of Man is the Lord of the Sabbath."
—Luke 6:5

Further Scripture: Psalm 37:7; Psalm 62:5–8; Luke 6:12

Questions

1. Why did the Pharisees say the disciples' actions were not lawful in verse 2? How does Jesus respond? How do you view the Sabbath?

2. In verse 11, were the Pharisees truly full of rage over Jesus healing on the Sabbath or do you think that there was a much deeper meaning? What do you think that meaning was?

3. How do you think the disciples felt to be chosen to be one of the 12 apostles?

4. Verse 45b says that "out of the abundance of the heart, the mouth speaks." What do you think the meaning of this is?

5. Why did Jesus say to have a house built on a solid foundation? Have you always had a firm foundation, or have you had to rebuild?

6. What did the Holy Spirit highlight to you in Luke 6 through the reading or the teaching?

Lesson 51: Luke 7

Son of Man: Showing Compassion
One Person at a Time

Teaching Notes

Intro

In the Gospel of Luke, we're looking at Jesus as the *Son of Man*. Jesus shows Himself as the *Son of Man* by being part of humanity and coming down to earth. John 1:14 says, "The Word became flesh and took up residence among us. We observed His glory, the glory as the One and Only Son from the Father, full of grace and truth." The Son of Man took up residence with us. Chapter 7 begins with the story of the Centurion's faith (vv. 1–10). Then, it covers the story of the widow's son, our main text for today, as we look at Jesus' interaction with the dead.

Teaching

Luke 7:11–14: Jesus and His disciples were on their way to the town of Nain, located about 20 miles southwest of Capernaum, on the northern slope of Mt. Moriah, and on the eastern side of the Jezreel Valley (where we will talk about Elisha later in our studies). Today this town (now spelled Nein) has a population of 200. As Jesus walked up to the gate of this tiny town, a dead man was being taken out in a coffin (v. 11).

Note that Jesus was always about the timing. John 11:9 says, "'Aren't there 12 hours in a day?' Jesus answered. 'If anyone walks during the day, he doesn't stumble, because he sees the light of this world.'" John 13:1 says, "Before the Passover Festival, Jesus knew that His hour had come to depart from this world to the Father." Jesus understands timing. When you trust the voice of the Holy Spirit, you will always understand every step is His (Psalm 119:105).

Nelson's Commentary describes the funeral procession that Jesus would have seen. First, the procession was coming out of the town gates to the cemetery located outside the town. Funerals took place the same day as the death so that no house would become unclean by keeping a dead body there overnight. The body would have been anointed before the procession began, and the processional would have included almost everyone in the small town.[1] The loss of the widow's only son would have brought the town to the funeral (v. 12).

As believers, we should be pouring into widows (Deuteronomy 27:19; Psalms 68:5; 146:9; James 1:27). Jesus saw the widow who had lost her only son and had compassion for her (v. 13). "His mother's only son" is parallel to Luke 8:42 and Jairus's only daughter, and Luke 9:42 and the story of the man's only daughter who was "at death's door." Jesus has a compassion for those who would lose their only children. Because of that compassion, He told the widow not to cry (Hebrews 4:15–16).

The word "compassion" is what changed Time to Revive. It led me into a study on compassion that focused on four words: love, listen, discern, and respond. These four words grew out of studying Jesus' compassion in Scripture. Jesus walked up to the coffin and touched it, something no one else would have done because it made Him unclean for seven days (Numbers 19:11). Jesus not only touched the coffin, but the coffin was open, so Jesus touched the dead son's body (v. 14). Out of His compassion for the widow, Jesus said, "Young man, I tell you, get up!" Everything Jesus did was out of His love and compassion. For us as believers, our prayer must be, "Lord, increase my compassion so I can love the widows and those who are unclean." What extremes are we willing to go through to love people for the sake of the gospel?

Luke 7:15–17: "The dead man sat up and began to speak, and Jesus gave him to his mother" (v. 15). Don't you wonder what the resurrected son said? We see Jesus do this in Scripture only two other times: Jairus's daughter (Luke 8:40–56) and Lazarus (John 11:38–44). Note that the young man's response was immediate, and so was Jesus' giving the young man to his mother. Every time Jesus touched someone, there was an immediate response: Simon Peter's mother-in-law got up immediately (Luke 4:39); the skin disease immediately left the man (Luke 5:13); and the paralytic man rose immediately (Luke 5:25). One of the things I wrestle with is that we don't see the work of Christ and respond immediately!

"Then fear came over everyone, and they glorified God" (v. 16b). The demonstration of supernatural power always leads to glorifying God. The people identified Jesus as "a great prophet." First Kings 17:17–24 explains the idea of Elijah as the great prophet and the double-mantle of Elisha. Second Kings 4:32–37 shares the story of a widow's son who died and came back to life. Jesus was reminding the crowds of what God could do. The people were saying that God had sent help, perhaps another prophet, and maybe some of them thought Jesus was the Messiah.

---

[1] Earl D. Radmacher, Ronald B. Allen, and H. Wayne House, eds., *Nelson's New Illustrated Bible Commentary* (Nashville: Thomas Nelson, 1999), 1263.

Verse 17 shares that the news of Jesus was spreading throughout Judea. Great multitudes were showing up to hear Jesus speak, and the word went out to the entire Jewish region. Jesus sent His disciples out with the instructions to "heal the sick, raise the dead, cleanse those with skin diseases, drive out demons. You have received free of charge; give free of charge" (Matthew 10:8). Mathew 10:8 doesn't exist unless we love the people first. We have to have the same compassion that Jesus had for the widow outside the gates.

Closing

To love someone, you have to first go out of your way because Jesus first went out of His way for us (1 John 4:19). Set your needs aside, you cannot ignore people (1 Thessalonians 3:12).

If you want to have an impact on the people around you, you must first and always start with love. As you love on people, the relationship will morph into listening. We need to listen to their questions and listen to their stories (Proverbs 18:2, 13). Listening then leads to discernment–what is God leading us to do with the person we've encountered (Proverbs 20:5)? Ask the Holy Spirit to help you understand what the person is sharing with you, and then respond as you are led (Colossians 4:5–6).

I believe this progression can happen for all of us, but as Jesus showed, it happens one person at a time.

Daily Word

Jesus traveled to a town called Nain with His disciples and a large crowd. As they were walking, Jesus noticed a coffin being carried out. Inside the coffin was a dead man, the only son of a widow. In the midst of large crowds coming and going, Jesus saw the widow and had compassion for her. Jesus went to the coffin and told the dead man to get up. The man got up, and Jesus gave him back to his mother.

Jesus saw a widow crying even though He was in the middle of a large crowd of people, and He had compassion for her. But He didn't stop there; He discerned the situation and took action by responding to a need. As a believer, you are called to do the same. As you go on your way today, open your eyes to *see* the needs of others and to *love* them like Jesus. *Ask* the Holy Spirit to lead you in how to respond with *action*. When every person takes time to love people like Jesus, it could change the world!

When the Lord saw her, He had compassion on her and said, "Don't cry."
—Luke 7:13

Further Scripture: Psalm 103:13; 2 Corinthians 1:3–4; 1 John 3:17

Questions

1. In verses 1–10, no greater faith had been seen in all Israel. What happened in these verses, and how do you think your faith measures up? Could you have more? (Matthew 17:20)

2. How is verse 28b possible? What does it mean? (Malachi 3:1, Matthew 20:16)

3. Jesus told the woman her faith has saved her and to go in peace. How did she exhibit faith?

4. What did the Holy Spirit highlight to you in Luke 7 through the reading or the teaching?

Lesson 52: Luke 8
Son of Man: Jesus Casts Out Demons

Teaching Notes

Intro

The phrase *Son of Man* can be a tough one to grasp, so we've tried in the Luke study to focus on Jesus as the *Son of Man*. But sometimes Luke moves to show Jesus' omnipotent power. This lesson today looks at how Jesus submitted His will to the Father, while He demonstrated His power over demons. Luke 8 begins by looking at the women who supported Jesus' ministry (vv. 1–3), then moves to The Parable of the Sower (vv. 4–8), a statement of why He taught with parables (vv. 9–10), and an explanation of the Parable of the Sower (vv. 11–15). Luke then discussed what it means to be the light (vv. 16–18), he looked at Jesus' relationship with His family (vv. 19–21), and then shared another account of the storm at sea (vv. 22–25).

Teaching

Luke 8:26–39: Jesus and His disciples sailed across the southeastern shore of Galilee to Gerasenes. As Jesus got out of the boat onto land, a demon-possessed man from town met Him (vv. 26–27a). Notice that the demon-possessed man came to Jesus; Jesus did not have to find the man. In ministry, you may encounter demons, but you don't need to hunt them out.

The man who approached Jesus had lived in the tombs outside the town for years, and he wore no clothes (v. 27b). According to Matthew 8:28, there were two demon-possessed men who approached Jesus. *Nelson's Commentary* says, "The man is a pawn in a cosmic battle that pits the authority of the two sides against each other."[1] The man fell down before Jesus and asked in a loud voice, "What do You have to do with me, Jesus, You Son of the Most High God? I beg You, don't torment me!" (v. 28). The demon's confession sounds like the language of Luke 1:31–32 (The Son of the Most High God). But it wasn't said in worship.

Wiersbe outlines the characters of demons. First, they have faith; they totally understand who Jesus is (James 2:19). Second, they believe in a future judgment

---

[1] Earl D. Radmacher, Ronald B. Allen, and H. Wayne House, eds., *Nelson's New Illustrated Bible Commentary* (Nashville: Thomas Nelson, 1999), 1267.

(Matthew 8:29) and that they will be subjected to torment in the future; and they also believe in a future place of torment (Luke 8:31).[2] Demons are fallen angels. When Satan left Heaven, he took one-third of the angels with Him. These are the fallen angels, and because they know they will be placed in the great abyss, they will create hell on earth until that time. These minions of Satan want the same thing he does . . . to steal, kill, and destroy every person on earth. I think one of the biggest downfalls of the church today is that we don't talk about the fact that we're in a battle. We don't talk about the fact that we're up against an enemy who uses the demonic to come against us. That's why Paul said to put on the armor of God to defeat him (Ephesians 6).

The demons had seized the man, over and over, even though he was under guard and restrained (v. 29). Then Jesus asked the man his name, to which he responded "Legion," because there were so many demons in him. A legion was a Roman military designation of 6,000 soldiers, which "suggests this is a spiritual battle."[3] When you find yourself interacting with a demon, do not be afraid to speak to it (in the name of Jesus) and even ask its name, because of the power and authority we have within us. The demons begged Jesus not to banish them into the abyss (v. 31).

How did Jesus recognize the man was demon-possessed? Here are the symptoms from Dr. Luke: (1) disregard for personal dignity (naked); (2) social isolation (pulls back from other people); (3) unclean shelter; (4) recognition of Jesus' identity (when you mention the name of Christ before a demon, you'll see some manifestation of fear); (5) demonic control of speech; (6) might see shouting or random outbursts; and (7) has great strength. This does not include all the symptoms, but it gives us the lens to see what Jesus saw in this encounter that allowed Him to identify the demonic. Unfortunately, most Christians don't even look for the demonic because, frankly, we're afraid to go there. Yet there is nothing to fear. They came and met Jesus; they begged for permission not to be put into the abyss and were ready to negotiate for extra time not in the abyss. In verse 32, a large heard of pigs were feeding (Mark said there were about 2,000 pigs). Jesus gave them permission to go into an unclean environment—the pigs. The pigs rushed down the hill and were drowned in the sea. The Jews understood the abyss as a watery deep below the earth, and the pigs had no value. It's interesting that the demons chose a different water prison. The demons were drowned but would still face the future judgment.[4]

---

[2] Warren W. Wiersbe, *The Bible Exposition Commentary: Matthew–Galatians* (Colorado Springs: David C. Cook, 1989), 202.

[3] Wiersbe, 1267.

[4] Thomas L. Constable, *Expository Notes of Dr. Thomas Constable: Luke*, 200, https://planobiblechapel.org/tcon/notes/pdf/luke.pdf.

When the herdsmen saw what happened, they ran to tell people in the town and in the countryside (v. 34). The people came down to see what happened and found Jesus and the man, whom the demons had left, dressed and sitting at Jesus' feet. They were amazed and afraid of what they saw (v. 35). Jesus set the man free from *all* the demons, not just some of them. Jesus said in Luke 4 that He wanted to set the captives free. When someone has been set free from demons, he is a new creation and the old things are gone (2 Corinthians 5:17). Out of fear, *all* the people in the region asked Jesus to leave, thinking there was no way that could have come from God (v. 37). Jesus, without reaction, got in the boat to leave when the freed man said he wanted to go too. But Jesus told the man to return to his home and tell all that God has done for him (v.38). Marshall described this as "a paradigm of what conversion involves: the responsibility to evangelize."[5]

Jesus didn't take the man with Him because He was focusing on pouring into to the 12 disciples. Instead, Jesus sent the man to go tell the people in his own community, because that was the way the gospel would spread (v. 39).

Closing

Charles Spurgeon said that when the man was sitting at Jesus' feet, it was clearly an identification of faith in Christ and a form of submission, he was ready to serve Christ. True conversion means that people are truly set free from everything that enchains them.

To close out, let's look at seven things we can use with demoniacs. When you encounter a demonic:

1. Don't do it alone (do it in pairs).
2. Be ready (we are always in a battle).
3. Speak with authority with the power of the resurrected Christ within you.
4. Be patient in the process. It might not happen right away.
5. Don't make it complicated. Nothing Jesus did was complicated.
6. Ask for the name of the demon.
7. Love that person in the process.

---

[5] I. Howard Marshall, *The Gospel of Luke*, New International Greek Testament Commentary series (Exeter, England: Paternoster Press, 1978), 341; quoted in Constable, 202.

Daily Word

The disciples literally cried out to Jesus, "We're going to die!" They had been sailing along on the lake, and they suddenly found themselves in a fierce windstorm. The water was swamping their boat, and they were in danger. They called out to the Lord. Jesus rebuked the wind and waves and the storm stopped. Peace came.

Do you ever feel as though you are going along your normal life when, suddenly, you find yourself in a windstorm? You think to yourself, "There is no way out, this is so hard, so bad, that surely I will die in this storm?" Here's the key to remember in the midst of your storm: Cry out to Jesus. Remember His power is within you. Jesus rebuked the wind and the waves. You can rebuke anything in the name of Jesus. Stand firm and know He is God. He will bring His peace when you call upon His name.

They came and woke Him up, saying, "Master, Master, we're going to die!" Then He got up and rebuked the wind and the raging waves. So they ceased, and there was a calm. He said to them, "Where is your faith?" —Luke 8:24–25

Further Reading: Psalm 34:4; Psalm 138:3; Colossians 3:15

Questions

1. In Luke 8:10, what did Jesus mean by "Looking they may not see; and hearing, they may not understand" (Isaiah 6:9)? Do you think Jesus was deliberately keeping them from understanding?

2. "For whoever has, more will be given to him; and whoever does not have, even what he thinks he has will be taken away from him" (Luke 8:18). What did Jesus mean by this? (Matthew 13:12)

3. After Jesus healed the demon possessed man, why did the people of Gerasenes ask Jesus to leave (Luke 8:37)? What were they afraid of? Have you been in a situation where someone is afraid of God based on what they have seen or experienced?

4. Why did Jesus ask, "Who touched me?" (Luke 8:45). Do you think Jesus already knew who it was? Have you ever considered the thought that even His very clothing contained power? (Matthew 9:20, Acts 19:11–12)

5. In verse 51, Jesus did not allow anyone but Peter, John, and James, plus the parents, to go into the room of the dead child. Why? Why did Jesus say the girl was not dead but asleep? (Romans 4:17b)

6. What did the Holy Spirit highlight to you in Luke 8 through the reading or the teaching?

Lesson 53: Luke 9

Son of Man: Disciples, Apostles, Ambassadors

Teaching Notes

Intro

I love the painting for the Gospel of Luke. When I look at it, all I really see are the hands of the *Son of Man*. In a real sense in Luke 9, the ministry is being handed off to His followers, who in turn become the body of Christ and the hands and feet of Jesus. How do we as sons of men become the sons of God?

Teaching

Luke 9:1–5: Jesus called the disciples to Him, gave the power and authority over all demons and the power to heal diseases, and sent them to preach the kingdom of God and heal the sick (vv. 1–2). Then He told them to take *nothing* with them on the journey—no food, money, a walking stick, not even an extra coat (v. 3). If they entered a house, they were to stay there. If they were not welcomed, they were to leave the town, shaking off the dust of the town from their feet as they left as a testimony against the people there (vv. 4–5).

In Luke 8, not only did Jesus have an encounter with the man possessed by demons called Legion (vv. 26–39), He healed Jairus' 12-year-old daughter (vv. 40–42, 49–56), and He felt healing power leave Him when a woman touched the tassel of His robe (vv. 42b–48). These encounters or interactions are the backdrop for chapter 9. The disciples had to have looked on these events, witnessed the power Jesus had to heal and cast out demons, and wondered how it all worked.

Jesus called His disciples (from the Greek word *mathetes* or students) together and He gave them power, possibly by explaining to them what had happened the day before so that they would understand the power and *authority* they were receiving from Him. The Greek word Jesus used for power is *dynamis*, which means "ability" or to have the ability to do something beyond yourself, and the Greek word Jesus used for authority is *exousia*, which means "the right to exercise power" and was something the disciples had to believe they had.[1] Jesus told them not to take anything with them so that they would have to depend upon Jesus'

---

[1] Thomas L. Constable, *Expository Notes of Dr. Thomas Constable: Luke*, 209, https://planobiblechapel.org/tcon/notes/pdf/luke.pdf.

hands to do what they were told to do. Jesus had been showing them the kingdom so they would know how it operated, and they could see how it all worked. That allowed them to see amazing miracles and events (like Peter at the transfiguration), as well as the times when people criticized Jesus, laughed at Him, and even mocked Him.

Disciples (followers) of Jesus have *citizenship* in the kingdom that has yet to be seen but is hoped for. The disciple has to understand who he is. Many people in the church today have been so far outside discipleship that they don't even know what it means. Yet, Jesus was doing it in Luke 9. A disciple recognizes that he/she doesn't know or understand something so he/she must take it in.

Jesus was saying the disciples already operate in a way that is natural to them, but He wanted to give them something that was *supernatural* and was of another kingdom. Jesus is the *Son of Man* and the Son of God. Therefore, Jesus, the Son of God, had to invade the kingdom of man so He could be the *Son of Man* and show them the *kingdom of God*. Jesus wanted the disciples to see the unseen kingdom and the unseen face, because what really matters is the touch. When these two kingdoms come into conflict, so to speak, even the angel coming down to the atmosphere of the earth caused an earthquake in the earth. I believe there is a cataclysm when the kingdom of God invades the kingdom of earth. There is such a movement between the supernatural power of God and the natural power of man that there are things that happen on the earth because of that.

In Luke 8, Jesus just walked into the scene and Legion spoke, asking why the Son of God had come. The intimidation that always works in the enemy happens when it encounters the true power and authority of God. Jesus told His disciples to go out in this authority and to preach what they had seen—the kingdom of God (Thy will be done, Thy kingdom come, on earth as it is in heaven.) And He told them not to take any crutches along . . . anything that would take their minds off what they had been sent to do. He wanted them to take nothing from their own lives with them so they could depend on the supernatural power and authority of God.

You've been in reviveSCHOOL now for a while. You've been reading and studying, and many of you have had revelations. Some of you have walked into places and recognized immediately the presence of God in that place or known there is an absence of God there. What you are doing is learning to walk in the Spirit at a deeper level, and you're not having to walk in the natural understanding of where you're living.

In Scripture, there are disciples and then apostles; there is the citizenship and then there is the *ambassadorship* (*ambassador* is a delegate who is sent); there is teachability and then there is responsibility. For example, when Moses delivered the Israelites out of the wilderness, they were promised a land of milk and honey. But the spies returned and told the people how big the enemy was in the

Promised Land. Because they didn't have enough faith, but instead had a captive mentality, the people said they couldn't do what they had been given to do. Instead, they spent another 40 years of discipleship in the wilderness. They didn't learn discipleship on the short journey, so they had to go through the long-term school. The people who could have gone in, died in the wilderness having never personally experienced God's promise.

Sadly, part of the church is dying today. We haven't walked in the power and authority of the Lord, but have made it a long-term discipleship program. We haven't entered into the ambassadorship or learned to walk in a more responsible manner instead of a teachable manner, and we deny the power of God to work in us. We want to see Jesus' face in the picture, so we are the ones always ministered to. Jesus never came to do that. He came as the Son of God in the clothes of the *Son of Man* so He could teach us how to be sons of God as we are sons of man. That is the concept of kingdom understanding. He came to give us authority—the idea of taking citizens of a kingdom and making them ambassadors of that kingdom in another kingdom. Therefore, when we become the children of light, we now are ambassadors of the kingdom of God into the kingdom of darkness. That means we can set up embassies, safe havens in the world, and that's what the church has been ordained to be—places of refuge and refreshment, not places where we live. We live in the kingdom, not the embassies. We are able to operate in another nation but still be under the authority of our country.

Jesus sent the disciples out with the power and authority over all the demons and to cure diseases. Does that mean they got it? In Matthew 17:14–21 (Mark 9:17–27), a man asked the disciples to heal his son who had seizures, but they couldn't. The man told Jesus, who rebuked the disciples for their lack of understanding, and then cast the demon out of the boy, and the boy was healed. Afterwards, the disciples asked Jesus why they couldn't drive out the demon themselves, and Jesus responded that they had little faith. Verse 21 concludes, "However this kind does not come out except by prayer and fasting." If we are disciples of the kingdom, we will be ambassadors who want to bring in, to a place of freedom and safety, those looking for asylum from the conflict of the kingdom they're living in.

There is a key principle here—there is an authority given and an authority understood in this kingdom experience that comes from prayer and fasting. If Jesus gave them authority over all demons, but they were unsuccessful, other keys were needed. When Jesus asked the disciples who people said that He was and who they believed that He was, Peter said, "You are the Christ, the Son of the Living God." Jesus responded that Peter was divinely given that understanding and said he would give him the keys of the kingdom. I believe those keys include what Jesus told the disciples when they returned—that the power to cast out demons only happened through prayer and fasting (two keys of the kingdom).

Closing

Matthew 13:58 states Jesus was in His home country and He did not do many works there because of their unbelief. There was no cooperation with who Jesus was as the Son of God, who had come as the *Son of Man*, to operate in that area. He didn't minister to them, because they couldn't be ministered to.

In Luke 9:10, Jesus called the disciples (notice that He did not use the title "apostles" as He did in Luke 9:1) together as their Teacher. He showed them they had the authority and experience to walk in the Spirit. We, too, have the responsibility, the power, and the authority to be the hands of Jesus.

Daily Word

The disciples helped Jesus pass out baskets of bread and fish the Lord had miraculously provided for five thousand men (plus women and children) from five loaves and two fish. Jesus continued to teach and instruct the disciples. He said to them, "If you want to come with Me, you have to deny yourself, take up your cross daily, and follow Me." Essentially He was saying that to be a true disciple of His, you have to deny yourself. Yes, it will be painful, because carrying a cross was a painful and humiliating execution.

Daily means *every day*. Every day, Jesus asks you to deny yourself, even through the pain and suffering, and follow Him. What does denying yourself look like for you today? Jesus promises by following Him and giving up your own pleasures and desires, you will find your true self. You will find joy. You will find peace. You will find freedom. Regardless of what the world may say, press on daily, and trust Him. He is faithful.

Then He said to them all, "If anyone wants to come with Me, he must deny himself, take up his cross daily, and follow Me." —Luke 9:23

Further Reading: Daniel 1:8; Romans 8:12–13; 1 Peter 2:11

Questions

1. In verse 3, why did Jesus instruct the disciples to take nothing with them when they left to preach?
2. What was the significance of mentioning the 12 baskets full of leftover food?
3. Ponder verses 23–25 of Luke 9. What does take up His cross and follow Jesus mean? What does this look like to you? What about hanging onto life but losing it? And to gain the whole world but lose yourself? In this context, how would you define "life"?

4. What are the differences between Exodus 34:29–30 and Luke 9:29? What are the similarities?

5. What do you think the meaning is behind verse 62 (2 Timothy 4:10)? What would this look like in your own life?

6. What did the Holy Spirit highlight to you in Luke 9 through the reading or the teaching?

Lesson 54: Luke 10
Son of Man: A Place at the Table

Teaching Notes

Intro

Mindi's painting for Luke may have become my favorite. It's all about coming to the table and how everyone is invited. I love sharing the gospel, so as I prayed through Luke 10, I naturally leaned toward the account of sending out the 70 (vv. 1–12) and sharing with the unrepentant towns (vv. 13–16). But when I consider the Parable of the Good Samaritan, I think about who is drawn to the table. That's our study for today.

Teaching

Luke 10:25–29: A lawyer wanted to test Jesus. The lawyer was an expert in the Mosaic Law. He knew the Pentateuch and the Torah. He knew Jesus' background and couldn't believe Jesus actually knew the law. The lawyer presented a common question (Matthew 19:16; Mark 10:17; Luke 18:18). King Solomon said that everybody searches for the answer to this question in their hearts. The lawyer asked Jesus, "What must I do to inherit eternal life?" (v. 25).

As a good teacher, Jesus asked the lawyer, "What is written in the law? How do you read it?" (v. 26). Jesus was making the lawyer go back to his own readings and explain his understanding of it to Him. Jesus was setting the lawyer up (Galatians 2:16) because there was no way the lawyer could answer Jesus' question from his understanding of the law (Galatians 3:21). The expert responded, "Love the Lord your God with all your heart, with all your soul, with all your strength, and with all your mind; and your neighbor as yourself" (Leviticus 19:18; Deuteronomy 6:5—the Shema). He quoted Scripture, but it wasn't on topic. Jesus told the lawyer that if he could do all this 100 percent correctly, he would live (Leviticus 18:5; Ezekiel 20:11). Jesus quoted Scripture in return. The lawyer had to know what he had shared was impossible to do, so he asked another question to justify himself: "And who is my neighbor?" (v. 29; Galatians 3:10–13). The reality is the lawyer wanted to know who his select group would be—those who look the same, smell the same, believe the same. It can be easy for us in the church to play this game about who our neighbors are. Psalm 139:21–22 explains this position,

"LORD, don't I hate those who hate You, and detest those who rebel against You? I hate them with extreme hatred; I consider them my enemies."

Luke 10:30–35: In response, Jesus began to tell a story that could have been true or a parable. Jesus doesn't identify it as either. Jesus told of a man who was traveling from Jerusalem to Jericho, descending down about 3,300 feet and 17 miles. The man came across robbers who took his clothes, beat him up, and ran, leaving him half dead (v. 30). The man was naked and injured. A priest just happened down the road, saw the half-dead man, and moved to the other side of the road to remain ceremonially clean (Leviticus 21:1). The priest would never have been able or willing to invite the half-dead man to the table.

Then a Levite arrived at the place, saw the man, and passed by on the other side of the road (v. 32). The Levite's role was to collect the sacrifices to give to the priests. He should have been able to help this man. *Nelson's Commentary* says, "How easy is it for those who handle the rituals of religion to become calloused and treat the opportunities to minister as trivial and commonplace."[2] I think the reason the Lord brought me to this passage today is that, if the church is not careful, we'll continue become more and more like this priest and this Levite.

Then a Samaritan, coming along on his journey, saw the half-dead man and had compassion. He went out of his way (came over to him), soothed the wounds with oil and bandaged them, and took the man, naked and covered with blood, on his own animal to a nearby inn. He took care of the man (vv. 33–34). Bible. org (https://bible.org/) says the Samaritan showed: (1) compassion, (2) care, and (3) paid the cost of the man's care (v. 35). 2 Corinthians 9:7 says, "Each person should do as he has decided in his own heart—not reluctantly or out of necessity for God loves a cheerful giver." The two denarii the Samaritan left for the man's care would have covered his stay for 24 days, and he told the innkeeper he'd come back to pay any additional expenses.[3] (James 2:15–16.) The Samaritan gave as much as he could to take care of a person he didn't even know. Jesus could have played the card as the High Priest in Heaven and not come down as the *Son of Man* to interact with people. When He saw we were half-dead, Jesus came down with compassion and took care of us. Jesus literally gave up His life to do this. We tend to want to live like the priest and the Levite, all to ourselves, but Jesus reminds us He came for everybody to have the opportunity to sit at the table.

Luke 10:36–37: Jesus asked the lawyer to decide which of these three (the priest, the Levite, or the Samaritan) was a neighbor to the injured man. Jesus asked the

---

[2] Earl D. Radmacher, Ronald B. Allen, and H. Wayne House, eds., *Nelson's New Illustrated Bible Commentary* (Nashville: Thomas Nelson, 1999), 1273.

[3] Radmacher et al., 1273.

expert who knew everything about the Law but wasn't ready to act upon it. We in the church may know everything, but that's utterly pointless if we refuse to go to people on the side of the road. It's almost like we've become so callous to the lost and the hurting that we never invite them to the table.

In verse 37, the lawyer, the religious guy, responded, "the one who showed mercy to him." The lawyer was so caught up in his hatred of the Samaritan that he couldn't even acknowledge what the Samaritan had done. And Jesus told him to go do the same. Go show compassion for the ones that appall you; go live like the Samaritan.

Closing

According to Bible.org, the robbers would say, "What's yours is mine, and I'm going to take it." A religious people would say, "What's mine is mine, and I'm going to keep it." But what I see with the Good Samaritan and with Jesus is, "What's mine is yours, and I'm going to share it. I'm not going to take it or keep it but share it."

When I think of the *Son of Man*, that's what He did—He gave it all up for those who needed His compassion, His care, and a place at His table.

Daily Word

While Jesus was traveling, he came to Bethany, and Lazarus's sisters, Mary and Martha, welcomed Him inside their home. As Jesus sat in their home and talked, Martha was distracted by many things while Mary sat at His feet and listened to what He said. Martha was bothered by Mary's act of sitting and listening to Jesus as His disciple. Martha wanted Mary to give her a hand. However, Jesus confirmed Mary's choice to sit and listen by telling Martha that Mary had made the right choice.

You live in a busy world. Like Martha, there are many, many tasks at hand. Your day could be filled for 24 hours doing tasks and staying busy. And, if it's not your tasks you need to do, it's friends and family and coworkers in need of your help. And yet the right choice in all the busyness is sitting at the feet of Jesus and listening to what He says. No matter what your day holds, take time to sit and listen to Jesus. This may look like opening the Bible and reading Scripture. This may mean sitting still and praying and pausing long enough for the busyness of the world to calm down around you. So today, stop doing so much. Even if your checklist is not checked off. Sit, even before you begin the checklist. Listen to Jesus and all He has to speak to your heart. He says, "That is the right choice." Make the right choice today.

> The Lord answered her, "Martha, Martha, you are worried and upset about many things, but one thing is necessary. Mary has made the right choice, and it will not be taken away from her." —Luke 10:41–42
>
> Further Reading: Luke 10:39; John 15:4; James 4:8a

Questions

1. In verse 2, we are told to pray for laborers. Do you see yourself as a laborer? Why or why not?

2. In verse 19, put your name in the place of the word "you." Does that change the meaning and power of this verse for you? Why or why not?

3. In verse 25b, what does it mean to "inherit" eternal life? Is this earned? Why or why not?

4. In verse 27, an expert of law quoted Deuteronomy 6:5 and Leviticus 19:18. Did this have the same meaning in Jesus' time? Why do you think that?

5. Verses 38–42 tell of two sisters who loved the Lord but came from different angles. What was the difference between them? Who do you think you most resemble: Mary or Martha? Why?

6. What did the Holy Spirit highlight to you in Luke 10 through the reading or the teaching?

Lesson 55: Luke 11
Son of Man: How to Pray Like Jesus

Teaching Notes

Intro

We started with Matthew who wrote to the Jews that Jesus is *King*. Mark focused on the Roman audience, and we saw Jesus as the *Servant* with so much action. Now, we're in Luke who focused on Jesus' humanity and His divinity, and we see Jesus as *Son of Man*. As a doctor, Luke was driven by Jesus' desire to heal, but there was so much more.

Teaching

Luke 11:1: In this verse, Jesus was showing His lifestyle of prayer, "praying in a certain place," and aligning Himself to the Father's will. "When He finished, one of His disciples said to Him, 'Lord, teach us to pray, just as John also taught his disciples.'" Jesus responded by retelling the Lord's Prayer. Luke placed it in a different place than Matthew did, and he condensed it. Jesus didn't teach the disciples this only once, but He kept coming back to it, energizing them with the teaching until they understood it.

Luke 11:2–4: Jesus began, "Whenever you pray . . ." The tense in the Greek indicates prayer is a habit, a lifestyle. The Lord's Prayer is not meant to be the prayer itself but the outline of the prayer. Mike Breen provides an outline of the elements Jesus included:[1] (1) The Father's Character (Matthew 6–9): "Our Father in heaven, hallowed be your name." (2) The Father's Kingdom (Matthew 6:10): "Your kingdom come, Your will be done, on earth as it is in heaven." (3) The Father's Provision (Matthew 6:11): "Give us today our daily bread." (4) The Father's Forgiveness (Matthew 6:12): "And forgive us our debts, as we also have forgiven our debtors." (5) The Father's Guidance (Matthew 6:13a): "And lead us not into temptation," (6) The Father's Protection/Deliverance (Matthew 6:13b): "But deliver us from the evil one." This one is not included in Luke's prayer.

---

[1] Mike Breen, *Building a Discipling Culture*, 3d ed. (Greenville, SC: 3DM Publishing, 2017), 133.

Luke 11:5–8: Luke knew Mark personally. He talked to Mark and got as much information as he could. Luke wanted to document the entirety of the ministry, the formation of the church, the call of the mission, and how that was to be lived out. Instead of including the Father's Protection/Deliverance, Luke included Jesus' teaching on lifestyle (v. 5). Jesus told the story of a man who goes to a neighbor's house in the middle of the night to find bread for a visitor who just showed up at his house. (vv. 5–6). The neighbor refused to get up (v. 7), but the man continued persistently (v. 8). The picture of persistence in prayer was the point. Do we continue persistently in prayer or is once enough, and we don't feel the need to keep repeating? Jesus presented this as the requirement to be in a persistent position of prayer.

Persistence (*anaideia*) literally means "shameless, importunity, or over-boldness." A type of brassiness. Hayford writes, "It isn't the brassiness of a smart aleck making demands, but the forwardness of a person who is so taken with an awareness of need that he abandons normal protocol. Jesus is saying, 'Your first barrier isn't God, it's your own hesitance to ask freely. You need to learn the kind of boldness that isn't afraid to ask—whatever the need or the circumstance."[2]

Luke 11:9–10: "So I say to you, keep asking, and it will be given to you. Keep searching, and you will find. Keep knocking, and the door will be opened to you" (v. 9). The Holman Bible translation does a nice job with the verb tense of this verse—keep on asking, keep on seeking, keep on knocking! Jesus followed the somewhat humorous parable with direct instruction on what was involved (vv. 9-10), as well as a reminder of the willing nature of the Father we are addressing (vv. 11–13). Notice that *ask*, *seek*, and *knock* are all persistent actions. It's constant positioning, getting ourselves in line with where God is going. All three verbs refer to the continuous, uninterrupted act. The practical implication is to begin . . . or keep at it . . . but do so in obedience and in relationship, not legalism.

> *Ask*: The word refers to the act of praying where the will is earnestly fixed on the answering of the prayer. The desire is not merely a vague or halfhearted request. Rather, we often don't have what we need because we haven't asked (James 4:2).
>
> *Seek*: The goal of seeking is to find someone. Our primary goal is to seek God. The word means to seek—as in to worship—after God with all one's heart.

---

[2] Jack Hayford, *Prayer Is Invading the Impossible* (New York: Ballantine, 1983), 49.

> *Knock*: The word refers to the urgent sincerity exercised in uninter-
> rupted knocking, praying, and seeking, expectantly waiting for an
> answer because we are so in tune with the Father.

Luke 11:11–13: If we who are evil know how to give good gifts to our children
(vv. 11–12), why would God, whose character is perfect, not want to give us what
is good (v. 13)?

Luke 11:14–19: Luke then moved to more demonic encounters. The disciples
had witnessed Jesus casting out the legion of demons in Luke 8, and then they
were sent out to do the same in Luke 10. Jesus taught again on how to do this.
Jesus drove out a demon that was mute. The terminology "demon possession" is
not a good handling of this. Literally it means "to have a demon," meaning the
demon has attached." Demons affect people in different ways, generally by how
they act. But, if you believe in angels, you have to believe in demons.

The crowds watched and were amazed (v. 14). But some suggested that Jesus'
power came from Beelzebul, the ruler of the demons (v. 15). Beelzebul seems to
be a translation of the Canaanite god Baal-zebub (2 Kings 1:2). This was another
name the Jews used for Satan, who at best is an archangel. Havilah Cunningham,
in *Stronger than the Struggle*, named Satan as "the angel with a god complex." The
Jews had made him the ruler. Jesus understood what they were thinking; as the
Son of God, He knew their hearts. Their logic was faulty. Satan would not have
created a family feud against himself—that would have brought ruin to his work
(v. 17–18).

Luke 11:20–23: God casting out demons on earth is proof that God's kingdom
is present (v. 20). In Jesus, God has shown Himself to be stronger than Satan (vv.
21–22). The presence of the kingdom of God overthrowing the power of Satan
does not call for an impartial audience who is enjoying the battle. Everyone must
take sides (v. 23).

Luke 11:24–26: Jesus told another parable to show that casting out demons was
not the point of life. We are to do more than just get rid of the bad. Demons do
not remain inactive, and the man who is not content—who did not fill in that
life with something to replace demons—will come under attack again (v. 26). As
a result, the man's condition will be worse than it was before.

Luke 11:27–28: In the middle of Jesus' teaching, a woman proclaimed that "the
womb that bore You and the one who nursed You are blessed!" (v. 27). In verse
28, Jesus responded to this well-meaning, nice sounding blessing, "Even more,
those who hear the word of God and keep it are blessed!" Jesus turned it around

on her. It wasn't about His mother or His teaching. Jesus turned the attention to those who inhabit God's kingdom, who hear His word and keep it. It's more than saying good things about Jesus. It means hearing and obeying. Hear and do it!

Luke 11:29–54: Jesus completed this section of teaching with a discussion on the Sign of Jonah (vv. 29–32), the importance of the eye being the lamp of the entire body (vv. 33–36), and pronouncing the woes on those who practice religious hypocrisy (vv. 37–52). Matthew 23:13–36 also lists the woes.

Closing

In this passage of teachable moments, Jesus has shown that lines have been drawn: lines between good and evil, between darkness and light. There are several takeaways from this passage:

1. Prayer is an essential part of the life of a Jesus follower.
2. We are in a battle—opposing demonic powers.
3. We have no need to fear Satan because a far Stronger One has come.
4. Let the light of Christ—His Word, His presence—fill you and help you help others.

Daily Word

After the disciples saw Jesus get away for a time to pray, they asked Him to teach them to pray. And Jesus said to them, "Whenever you pray, say: Father, Your name be honored as holy. Your kingdom come. Give us each day our daily bread. And forgive us our sins, for we also forgive everyone in debt to us. And do not bring us into temptation" (Luke 11:2–4).

Jesus later explained to His disciples to keep asking, keep searching, and keep knocking on the door. Because Jesus said the one who asks receives, the one who searches finds, and the one who knocks will find an open door. Start your day praying the prayer Jesus told His disciples to pray. And if you have a day when you feel hopeless and alone, remember Jesus is with you. Seek Him, and you will find Him. Keep asking—He promises He'll answer. His faithfulness stretches to the heavens. He is the God of the impossible, and He loves you today.

He said to them, "Whenever you pray, say: Father, Your name be honored as holy. Your kingdom come. Give us each day our daily bread." —Luke 11:2–3

Further Reading: Psalm 36:5; Psalm 86:15; Jeremiah 29:13

Questions

1. Jesus went straight from teaching the disciples how to pray to telling a story. Read Luke 11:5–8. In verse 8, Jesus said that because of the friends' persistence, the man would get up and give his friend what he needed. How does this tie into His teaching on prayer?

2. Luke 11:9–10 says to ask and it will be given; seek and you will find; knock and it will be opened to you. What are the things that will be given, found, and opened?

3. What does Luke 11:23 mean by "he who does not gather with Me scatters"?

4. The eye is described as the lamp of the body (Luke 11:34). What do you think it means—when your eye is bad, is your body also full of darkness?

5. In Luke 11:52, Jesus told the lawyers that they had taken away the key of knowledge. What does this mean?

6. What did the Holy Spirit highlight to you in Luke 11 through the reading or the teaching?

Lesson 56: Luke 12
Son of Man: Keep Watch; Be Ready

Teaching Notes

Intro

Luke used the picture of Jesus as the *Son of Man*. John 1:1 says, "In the beginning was the Word, and the Word was with God, and the Word was God." Then, John 1:14 adds, "The Word became flesh and took up residence among us. We observed His glory, the glory as the One and Only Son from the Father, full of grace and truth." Jesus became human flesh so He could connect to us and we can connect to Him. In verses 1–3, Jesus warned of the religious hypocrisy of the Pharisees. In verses 4–7, Jesus told His listeners to fear God, who has the authority to throw people into hell. In verses 8–12, Jesus told His listeners that if they acknowledge the Son of Man, He would acknowledge them before the angels of God. But those who deny Him will be denied before the angels. Verses 13–21 contains the Parable of the Rich Fool, and verses 22–34 consider the cure for anxiety. Verse 31 is the key verse for this passage.

Teaching

Luke 12:35–40: Today, we'll look at four different pictures of how we can be ready for Christ's return.

Gird your loins. The tunic worn in the first century wouldn't allow the wearer to do real labor, so the tunic would be pulled up through the legs and tied at the middle to allow for greater movement. The process took several steps and some time to do, so the man couldn't respond instantly. The church today is relaxed, maybe thinking about the battle to come, but definitely not ready. Jesus emphasized to be ready (vv. 35, 40).

Have your lamps lit. The lamp needs to be already lit. There won't be time to find matches or trim the wick (Matthew 25:1–13).

Servants waiting for the Master. Be ready to unlock and open the door when the Master arrives with His bride. Wiersbe wrote, "Jewish weddings were held at night, and a bridegroom's servants would have to wait by the door for their master to come home with his bride."[1] Those who are found ready when Jesus returns will be blessed for their faithful and obedient service (v. 37; Romans 14:10; 2 Corinthians 5:10). The servants were ready to serve the Master, and He will come to serve them. John 13:3–8 shares an example of Jesus' servant care of His disciples. This is a glimpse of how Jesus comes to serve us. Faithfulness will be rewarded.

Be ready for the thief in the night. Wiersbe explains, "In the Roman system the second and third watch would be 9 p.m. to 3 a.m. By the Jewish method, it would be 10 p.m. to 6 a.m."[2] The reality means Jesus could come at any time. If the homeowner had known when the thief was coming, he wouldn't have let the thief get in (v. 39).

> 1 Thessalonians 5:2 emphasizes: "For you yourselves know very well that the Day of the Lord will come just like a thief in the night."
>
> Peter 3:10: "But the Day of the Lord will come like a thief; on that day the heavens will pass away with a loud noise, the elements will burn and be dissolved, and the earth and the works on it will be disclosed."
>
> 1 John 2:28: "So now, little children, remain in Him, so that when He appears, we may have boldness and not be ashamed before Him at His coming."
>
> Romans 13:11: "Besides this, knowing the time, it is already the hour for you to wake up from sleep, for now our salvation is nearer than when we first believed."

In Matthew 26:40 and following, the disciples were sleeping, instead of keeping watch while Jesus prayed. It's time the church accepts the fact that Jesus is coming back sooner than we believe. We can't be the disciples who are sleeping.

Closing

In verse 41, Peter asked: "Lord, are You telling this parable for us or to everyone?" Jesus responded by talking about levels of faithfulness. If you're faithful, you will

---

[1] Warren W. Wiersbe, *The Bible Exposition Commentary: Matthew–Galatians* (Colorado Springs: David C. Cook, 1989), 222.

[2] Earl D. Radmacher, Ronald B. Allen, and H. Wayne House, eds., *Nelson's New Illustrated Bible Commentary* (Nashville: Thomas Nelson, 1999), 1279.

be rewarded. But if you're blatantly disobedient, even if you know Jesus is coming back, you'll be assigned to a place with the unbelievers. Seems to me, if you're placed with nonbelievers, then you are a nonbeliever. There are levels of reward, and I want you to experience the full reward that is available when Jesus returns. "Much will be required of everyone who has been given much. And even more will be expected of the one who has been entrusted with more" (v. 48).

So what do we do with all this information? Bible.org gives three suggestions: (1) He must be your Master. (2) You must be His servant. (3) You must be living in expectation of His return. Luke 12:40 says, "You must be ready, because the Son of Man is coming at an hour that you do not expect." *Be ready.*

Daily Word

Jesus told His disciples to be ready over and over. Have your lamps lit. Be alert because the Son of Man is coming. How about you? Are you living ready for Christ's return?

If you knew a guest was coming for dinner tonight, you'd get ready and prepare food. If you knew your car would be broken in to tomorrow, you would remove precious items or even open the windows so they wouldn't be damaged. But if you knew Christ was returning tomorrow, what would you do today? If you haven't surrendered your life to Christ and trusted Him as your Lord and Savior, then that is the best place to start. And if you are already a believer, ask the Holy Spirit to speak to your heart today about what it means for you to live ready for His return. Walk in faith and in obedience to what He's asking you to do. The Holy Spirit will give you the words and power to walk it out. Trust the Lord to empower you to remain ready for His return.

You also be ready, because the Son of Man is coming at an hour that you do not expect. —Luke 12:40

Further Scripture: Matthew 5:14–15; Romans 13:12; 1 John 2:5

Questions

1. In Luke 12:16–21, Jesus told a parable about a rich man. In verse 21, what does it mean to be rich toward God?

2. Luke 12:31 says to seek His kingdom. Do you think this is related to Luke 11:9–10 in regard to seeking and finding?

3. Chapter 12 speaks about value (vv. 7 and 24), riches (vv. 15 and 33), and treasure (vv. 21, 33, and 34). How would you explain verse 34? What reveals where our treasure is? (Luke 6:45)

4. What does "be dressed ready for service and keep your lamps burning" look like? (Luke 12:35)

5. In verse 37, who was the one serving, and who was the one reclining (Matthew 20:28; Luke 22:27)? Where in Scripture do we see this happen? (John 13:3–17)

6. What did the Holy Spirit highlight to you in Luke 12 through the reading or the teaching?

Lesson 57: Luke 13
Son of Man: Producing Fruit

Teaching Notes

Intro

In chapter 13, we'll look at cooperation within the kingdom of God.

Teaching

Luke 13:6–9: In all of Jesus' stories are kingdom principles. This one is no different. The fig tree is a fruit tree that has a maturing time when it puts all of its nutrients into growing the tree. Then the fruit should come. A fruit tree is supposed to bring benefit besides looking good. This passage suggests the tree should be producing fruit by the end of three years, or it may not have the nature of a fruit tree (v. 7). What is the significance of the three years? The three years possibly relate to Jesus' ministry on earth, while the fig tree represents the Jewish people. Yet the gardener wanted to make an allowance for the fig tree for another year, and then consider it as a bad tree if it still produced no fruit (vv. 8–9).

What is the purpose of contrasting the Son of God and the *Son of Man*? Jesus laid aside His deity, His right to be God, knowing He is God and knowing who He is would not change. Jesus came into the environment of the earth, subjected Himself to be born of a woman, to grow up as a child, and to become the *Son of Man*. This gives us the understanding that Jesus had to learn to cooperate with the laws of nature in a world He created. Look at the things He spoke into existence, that were in the mind of God first. Who else would know what the fig tree was meant to represent? Jesus, walking on the earth, knew what creation was supposed to be and do, and He could explain that to His listeners.

Mark 11:12–24 is another passage about a barren fig tree. The raising of Lazarus from the dead happened only a few weeks before Jesus was arrested. People were going back and forth between Bethany and Jerusalem because things were happening in Bethany, in addition to the fact that Lazarus died. That's why there were a lot of people present when Jesus arrived. When Jesus arrived, He raised Lazarus from the dead, announcing that He, Jesus, was the resurrection and the life. Then people began coming from Jerusalem, leaving the Passover feast, out to Bethany to see what Jesus had done. Jesus was also coming and going between Bethany and Jerusalem every day.

It was on one of those days He saw the fruit tree and was hungry. Jesus the Creator knew the natural order of what should happen—He knew He could expect fruit to be on the fig tree. In the natural order of nature in the kingdom, sin has destroyed it in the earth. God is eternal, spirit in man is eternal, life on earth is seasonal. The tree of life was created to constantly bear fruit in its season while in the spiritual kingdom, but the trees of earth have seasons of life and death. Jesus, who created all things, knew how He had created these things. So when the Spirit in Jesus saw the fallen nature of the tree, He cursed it, and it died from the root. He spoke that it was cut off from the nature of earth. Jesus was calling us into the conflict within the Scripture.

Luke 13:18–19: Jesus the Creator, the declarer of order, knows what He spoke into being and what it is capable of. I taught earlier this week about being a citizen and then an ambassador. If I'm truly looking at citizenship, I would look at this question, "What is the kingdom of God like, and what can I compare it to?" (v. 18). That includes, "What is it so that I can understand it?

Jesus said it was like a grain of mustard seed. *Everything* it needs to become what it will become is in its nature. The size of the mustard seed is very tiny, yet it grows into a considerable size. But the size of the seed is not the issue. The redwoods grow from seeds in pine cones. It's in the nature of the seed. Inside the pine cone is thousands of seeds. A million redwood seeds weigh around eight pounds and can grow more than 300 feet tall. God is not limited by the size of the seed as to what He can imprint on it that will determine its outcome. There is an order and imprint inside that seed, and when it cooperates with the soil and the elements around it, it follows its nature to what it becomes. The kingdom of heaven is to look like its nature that comes from the Creator.

What does a Christian life look like in the tree Jesus cursed? A tree that has wonderful leaves but no fruit. Fruitfulness comes from the cooperation with the declared order of God. Therefore, there is something inside the believer that sprouts and becomes more than anything the believer would have known. It doesn't matter how small or insignificant the believer is because God's imprint is already on that believer.

Luke 13:20–21: In making of bread, yeast is a very small part. You can't see it make any difference while it is in the mixing, but the natural result of it will be watching the bread rise. There is a nature to the unseen that will greatly affect the seen if we will bring out its understanding. The kingdom has a natural response when encountered in the natural world. It's about cooperation between the elements within the yeast and the environment it's placed in.

Have faith in God! Believe that He will do what He says for you and in you. We are designed to bear fruit. There is a maturing process of time, but there sure seems to be a testing period for fruitfulness.

Matthew 7:17–20: "In the same way, every good tree produces good fruit, but a bad tree produces bad fruit. A good tree can't produce bad fruit; neither can a bad tree produce good fruit. Every tree that doesn't produce good fruit is cut down and thrown into the fire. So you'll recognize them by their fruit."

Closing

How can I become fruitful in my pursuit of who God is and what God wants me to be? If God can grow a redwood seed into a mighty tree, then surely, He can use every one of us to be great fruit bearers in the kingdom of God. John 15:8 says, "My Father is glorified by this: that you produce much fruit and prove to be My disciples."

Daily Word

Jesus had compassion for people and the power to heal the sick. Much to the dismay of the synagogue leaders, Jesus showed compassion to the sick seven days a week. While He taught on the Sabbath, He healed a woman disabled by a spirit. She went on to glorify the Lord because of her healing. The synagogue leaders were upset that Jesus healed on the Sabbath. However, Jesus had such a heart for the lost and sick, He healed them—no matter what day it was.

As you go throughout your day, open your eyes and see people around you. Ask the Lord to give you compassion for others every day of the week. Allow the Holy Spirit to work within you for the kingdom of God, giving glory to His name. Rest in the Lord and draw strength from Him.

Then He laid His hands on her, and instantly she was restored and began to glorify God. —Luke 13:13

Further Scripture: Psalm 30:2; Psalm 34:3–4; Psalm 62:5–8

Questions

1. What was the point Jesus was trying to convey to the people when they asked Him about the correlation between sin and death?

2. What does God look for after our repentance (Luke 13:6–9)? What are some possible fruit that He could be looking for in us (Galatians 5:22–23)? What are some other possibilities?

3. Why were the Pharisees and leaders of the synagogue always so upset that Jesus healed on the Sabbath (Exodus 20:9–10; Deuteronomy 5:12–14; Luke 13:14)? How did Jesus respond? (Mark 2:27; Luke 6:5)

4. What's the difference in those entering the narrow gate (door) and those going down the broad road (Matthew 7:13–14)? Why is it difficult to enter through the narrow door? Who is the narrow door? (John 10:7, 9)

5. How do you see Jesus' love, compassion, and desire for protection for Jerusalem in Luke 13:34–35? (Isaiah 31:5)

6. What did the Holy Spirit highlight to you in Luke 13 through the reading or the teaching?

Lesson 58: Luke 14

Son of Man: Banquet Lessons and Cross Carrying

Teaching Notes

Intro

This week, we're jumping right into the banquet at the beginning of Luke 14. Luke 14:1–24 contains the scene of a formal banquet at the home of a Pharisee.

Teaching

Luke 14:1–6: On the Sabbath, Jesus went to eat at the house of one of the leading Pharisees. The other Pharisees were watching Jesus carefully. They brought out a man whose body was swollen with fluid, possibly from dropsy, which was a disease produced by the accumulation of water in various parts of the body. The disease was very distressing, painful, and commonly incurable. There is a chance this man was a relative of the leading Pharisee. The man just sat there. The people at the banquet kept looking back and forth between Jesus and the man.

Jesus asked the experts of the law and the Pharisees if it was lawful to heal on the Sabbath, but they didn't respond. So Jesus healed the man and sent him on his way. It was an awkward, bizarre, and wonderful moment. Jesus asked the Pharisees if their son or ox fell into a well on the Sabbath, would they pull their son or ox out of the well? Again, they had no answer. Can't you feel the uncomfortable tension permeating the room?

Luke 14:7–11: So much of the interaction in Luke happens around the table. Jesus took this awkward, uncomfortable moment and told another parable, this time giving them advice. He used a wedding banquet, which was used in both Old Testament and New Testament as a visualization of the expectation of the end times. He told them that when they entered the banquet, they should not take the best seats at the table because someone more distinguished might come later and they would have to move down the table and be humiliated. Instead, it was far better to adopt a position of modesty and wait to be invited to a better seat. The underlying message was that God exalts the humble and shames the proud—those who try to gain honor for themselves will be left humbled and humiliated. "For everyone who exalts himself will be humbled, and the one who humbles himself will be exalted" (v. 11).

Luke 14:12–14: Then Jesus turned to the host—a leading Pharisee, the one who had invited Him—and told the host how to throw a party. Jesus told the host to invite everyone and then the host would be blessed and repaid at the "resurrection of the righteous" (v. 13–14). Jesus was not condemning holding a party with one's family or friends—He went to such parties Himself (John 2:1–11). Jesus was condemning the attitude of doing good for the sake of a tangible, earthly reward. We should do good to those who cannot give us anything in return and leave the question of a reward to God.

Luke 14:15–21: One of the other guests at the table said, "The one who will eat bread in the kingdom of God is blessed" (v. 15). Jesus responded with another parable to say, "Yes, you admire the ideal, but you are not prepared to act on it." Jesus told of the double invitation given to guests, something that was characteristic of ancient practice. The invitations were often R.S.V.P., and the invited guests had already confirmed they were coming. When they received the final invitation with the announcement that the banquet was ready, the invited guests began to give excuses as to why they couldn't come. These excuses for not coming would have sounded very lame to Jesus' audience. They might even have enjoyed the humor of the story—until they realized that, in Jesus' eyes, this was how they were treating God's invitation to them.

In the first excuse, the guest said he needed to look at a field he had already bought. In reality, he would have examined the land before and may even have been legally obligated to go to complete the purchase. But late notice would be heard as a weak excuse that would serve as a grievous insult to the dignity of the host. Another excuse was the guest needed to try out the five yoke of oxen he had bought. First, five yokes of oxen meant the man was a wealthy landowner. It would have been inconceivable the guest would have done the work himself, rather than one of his servants. A third excuse was the guest had just gotten married. This one is closer to being a legitimate reason. Deuteronomy 20:7; 24:5 says that a man during the first year of marriage was exempt from going to war but not for skipping the feast he had promised to attend. The statement, "I ask you to excuse me," is better understood as, "I am telling you that I am excused." The first excuse was about possessions, the second about having to work, and the third about personal affections (three things people still prioritize above the kingdom today). Jesus basically said, "Your excuses excuse you."

Then the host's servant was sent out to bring in everyone they could find off the streets—the seedy, the sleazy, and the beggars. This was unheard of, but the image is what makes Jesus' parable so powerful. Jesus' message was exposing that the people of the street—the shamed and the disreputable—were not invited to the kingdom's table.

Here are banquet realities I want you to hear today:

1. God offers His banquet to ALL, and He sends His servants out to invite and bring them (v. 23). People have a choice to come to the banquet or to turn it down. Have you looked at your excuses to the Master lately?
2. He calls us to love Him more than anyone else. Verse 27 uses the word "hate," but it's best understood as "love less" or "to renounce" in terms of primary allegiance (Luke 6:27). The love for Jesus must be greater.
3. We can't carry our own cross. His audience understood that reality because crucifixion was a common event. "Carry his cross," literally means to be ready for martyrdom. Those who heard understood the level of commitment. Jesus told two stories to help them grasp it (vv. 28, 31).

First, how foolish is the builder who couldn't finish a building project because he ran out of money? In AD 27, a poorly built amphitheater had collapsed, causing an estimated 50,000 casualties. His audience remembered that. Second, how foolish is an army commander who didn't calculate strength of his army before engaging a stronger foe in battle? Jesus' point was that one must recognize the cost to being a disciple of Jesus. Herod Antipas had recently lost a war with a neighboring Roman landholder, so Jesus' audience understood the image of a foolhardy war.

There is a cost to accepting His invitation, and it may cost dearly (v. 33). We are to be controlled by Jesus' ongoing call on our lives, not by things or circumstances. This is God's plan to mature His people and church, and it has eternal implications.

Closing

This is both a command and a process. It's a personal commitment to go beyond the conversion experience and to walk with Christ and others in order to fulfill the mission of the church. In a sense, Jesus was saying there are no guarantees except the promise of His presence in our lives. What cost must you pay to be a disciple of Jesus?

Daily Word

Jesus told a parable about guests arriving at a wedding banquet. Some guests walked in and chose the most favorable positions. Then the host told them to move and sit at the lowest place, bringing humiliation to those guests. However, the guests who chose the lowest place at the table were invited to move up higher.

As a follower of Christ, you are called to walk in humility and think of others before yourself. If there is an open parking spot and another car pulls up at the same time, humility lets that person go ahead of you and take the spot. If you are waiting for a favorite cupcake with friends and there is only one favorite flavor left, humility lets your friend have the last favorite cupcake, while you try something new. Today, think of others before you think of yourself. When you live in such a way, you walk out the love of Christ. The Lord will honor your heart as you walk in humility. Open your eyes to see the way He blesses you for your unselfish and humble attitude.

For everyone who exalts himself will be humbled, and the one who humbles himself will be exalted. —Luke 14:11

Further Scripture: Proverbs 11:2; Philippians 2:3–4; 1 Peter 5:6

Questions

1. How do you think Jesus felt being closely watched by the people (Luke 14:1)? Do you think this is like people watching us as Christians to see what we do and say? Why or why not?

2. According to Jesus, what should our attitude be when we are invited to feast at the King's table? What does verse 11 mean? (Proverbs 29:23; James 4:6; 1 Peter 5:5–6)

3. What were some of the excuses people gave for not coming to the banquet? What are some excuses people give now for not coming to Jesus?

4. Jesus sometimes spoke harsh things to the crowd. What was He saying to them in Luke 14:26? (Matthew 6:33)

5. What does it mean to count the cost of following Christ? How does Jesus' analogy on salt fit in with this? (Matthew 5:13; Luke 14:28–35)

6. What did the Holy Spirit highlight to you in Luke 14 through the reading or the teaching?

Lesson 59: Luke 15
Son of Man: Jesus Seeks the Lost

Teaching Notes

Intro

As a reminder, the phrase for the Gospel of Luke is *Son of Man*. Jesus interacted with the people as the *Son of Man*. Jesus clearly showed He would do anything it took to love on people. In Luke 15, Jesus connected with every single heart.

Teaching

Luke 15:1: All the tax collectors and sinners approached Jesus to listen to Him. Aren't all of us sinners? Romans 3:23 says, "For all have sinned and fall short of the glory of God." All of us have missed the mark and sinned against God.

Luke 15:2: The Pharisees and scribes complained that Jesus welcomed and even ate meals with sinners. Their complaints indicated they didn't consider themselves to be sinners. In their minds, they were righteous and perfect. They were the men of the Law who wouldn't come to the table if there were sinners there. They wouldn't associate with ungodly people. They were mad that Jesus indicated acceptance of the sinners because He ate with them at the table. If we're not careful, we'll fall into that camp pretty quickly.

Luke 15:3–4: Jesus told them a parable about sheep. "What man among you, who has 100 sheep and loses one of them, does not leave the 99 in the open field and go after the one until he finds it?" But this was not the attitude of the Pharisees and scribes. In Ezekiel 34:1–2, God spoke to Ezekiel: "Son of man, prophesy against the shepherds of Israel . . . Woe to the shepherds of Israel, who have been feeding themselves! Shouldn't the shepherds feed their flock?" Jesus accused the Pharisees and scribes of being more concerned about the 99 and themselves than about the ones who were lost. Ezekiel 34:4–5 continues, "You have not strengthened the weak, healed the sick, bandaged the injured, brought back the strays, or sought the lost." The religious leaders had nothing to do with going and finding the lost and everything to do with becoming spiritually fat. In Ezekiel 34:10, God said, "I am against the shepherds . . . The shepherds will no longer feed themselves, for I will rescue My flock from their mouths so that they will not be food for them." God said He would save the flock from the religious. In Ezekiel 34:11–12, God said He would search for the flock Himself. "As a shepherd looks for his sheep on the day he is among his scattered flock, so will I look for my flock. I will rescue them from all the places where they have been scattered." God said He would save the lost sheep from their despair. We think we have to get people to come into the temple, the tabernacle, the church. But people don't respond like that. We need the Lord to pursue us. In Ezekiel 34:23 God said, "I will appoint over them a single shepherd, my servant David."

Jesus was clearly doing what Ezekiel prophesied. He was pursuing the lost. But the Jewish religious leaders were complaining. They were staying fat on their own righteousness.

Luke 15:4: The shepherd left the 99 to go after the one lost sheep. In 2 Peter 3:9, we learn that God's heart is that nobody perishes. God is not willing to let that one sheep go. If we're not careful, the church plays that game when we say one person isn't worth it, so we choose not to pursue them, but that conflicts with what Jesus said in John 3:16. God doesn't want any person to perish. He doesn't want those who don't know Him to die and go to hell. That includes Muslims, Hindus, and Buddhists. God's reckless love doesn't hold back. In 1 Timothy 2:4, Paul emphasized that God "wants everyone to be saved and to come to the knowledge of the truth." If someone isn't saved, then we have to go after them. Isaiah 40:11 says God "protects his flock like a shepherd; He gathers the lambs in His arms and carries them in the fold of His garment." The reason to seek the lost is because we love them. We love them because He first loved us.

Liefeld pointed out, "It was also normal for a shepherd to count his sheep every night."[1] Why? Because every sheep mattered. In John 10:7, Jesus said, "I assure you: I am the door of the sheep." Jesus serves as the door, and He doesn't allow anyone to get lost. In John 10:11, Jesus continued: "I am the good shepherd. The good shepherd lays down his life for the sheep." In other words, once you have found the lost sheep, you will do everything you can to keep them in the fold. In John 10:16, Jesus said, "But I have other sheep that are not of this fold; I must bring them also, and they will listen to My voice."

All the little sheep listen to Jesus' voice. If one slips out, the shepherd takes it personally and goes in pursuit of it. In Genesis 31:38–39, Jacob paid for the loss of Laban's sheep with animals from his own flock. If you were a shepherd, you had to pay up. In Exodus 22:10–12, if a man's animal was stolen while under the

---

[1] Walter L. Liefeld, "Luke," in *Matthew–Luke*, vol. 8 of The Expositor's Bible Commentary, ed. Frank Gaebelein and J. D. Douglas (Grand Rapids: Zondervan, 1984), 981; quoted in Thomas L. Constable, *Expository Notes of Dr. Thomas Constable: Luke*, 346, https://planobiblechapel.org/tcon/notes/pdf/luke.pdf.

care of another shepherd, the shepherd had to make restitution; he was responsible if a sheep was stolen.

Jesus feels the burden, the passion, and the love for every one of the sheep. Do we even care if a sheep gets out and goes wandering around? Scripture says we should care for every single one of them. But the Pharisees were hanging out together, getting fat on their own righteousness, and they didn't care about seeking after the lost. In Amos 3:12, God said, "As the shepherd snatches two legs or a piece of the ear from the lion's mouth, so the Israelites who live in Samaria will be rescued." The shepherd snatches back his sheep no matter how hard the situation. The shepherd goes after the lost sheep constantly until they are found. But we have places we are not willing to go.

Luke 15:5–6: When the shepherd finds the lost sheep, he puts it on his shoulders and throws a massive party. He rejoices because he found his lost sheep. We should rejoice and celebrate over every person who has been found in the Lord because they have gone from death to life. The church in America is slowly dying because we're not having parties to celebrate people coming to know the Lord. We don't seek the lost and celebrate when they are found. We need to rejoice and gather everybody. We're not having a party because people aren't being found.

Wiersbe said, "There is a fourfold joy expressed when a lost sinner comes to the Savior."[2] (1) The person found experiences joy; (2) the person who looked rejoices because they found the lost person; (3) others get to rejoice (who doesn't love to hear the story of one who was found?); and (4) joy is found in heaven. Look at all of the joy in this process.

Luke 15:7: "There will be more joy in heaven over one sinner who repents than over 99 righteous people who don't need repentance." In this context, the Pharisees and scribes were complaining. They didn't think they needed to repent because they didn't even understand they were lost. They were struggling with their own identity. Every time we hit the streets, we get to find those who are lost, those who are out of place, those who should be in the flocks but are wandering around, those that are out of God's service, and those who think they don't have any value. We're part of bringing them back, reconciling them to God and back into the fold, and giving them purpose. God has a different identity, purpose, and plan for you. God searches for the lost. The religious get offended because the lost don't look or smell like us. When Adam and Eve messed up, God found them. God is a father who is always going to take care of His wayward children.

---

[2] Warren W. Wiersbe, *The Bible Exposition Commentary: Matthew–Galatians* (Colorado Springs: David C. Cook, 1989), 233.

Closing

John Wesley said, "The church has nothing to do but to save souls. Therefore, spend and be spent in this work."[3] All throughout Scripture, Jesus instructs us to go after the one. Our challenge, first and foremost, is to love them. When you love them, think about the person who can be found. Think about how that could affect anyone else around you. Then there's a party in heaven.

Daily Word

Jesus told a parable about a man with one hundred sheep, who lost one of them. This man left the ninety-nine and went after the one sheep, searching until he found it. After the one sheep was found, the man went to all his friends and family and asked them to rejoice with him in finding the one lost sheep.

In this story, Jesus illustrated His great love for you. Do you realize Jesus loves each person so deeply that He will go after even one person who has not come to Him and repented? He doesn't miss the one. He seeks the one.

You are called to love like Jesus. But before you can love like Jesus, you need to *receive His great love for you.* Start every day believing you are a child of God, holding on to the truth that He loves you just as you are. His love is long and wide and deep and high. Today, receive His great love for you so that out of His love for you, you are able to love others and seek after the one in your own life.

I tell you, in the same way, there will be more joy in heaven over one sinner who repents than over 99 righteous people who don't need repentance. — Luke 15:7

Further Scripture: Psalm 103:11; Ephesians 3:17–18; 1 John 4:19

Questions

1. Luke 15:2 says that Jesus welcomed sinners and ate with them. The Pharisees did not approve of this. What are the pros and cons of socializing with unbelievers?

2. What does Luke 15:4 say to you about the purpose of Jesus' mission? (Ezekiel 34:11–16)

3. In Luke 15:7, Jesus referred to "righteous persons who do not need to repent." Do you think there are people today who go to church and put on the appearance of righteousness but feel no need to repent?

---

[3] Wiersbe, 234.

4. Why did the father give the youngest son his portion of the inheritance? (Luke 15:12) How have you squandered any of the inheritance you have been given?

5. In Luke 15:28, the older brother became angry when the father had a feast for the returning son. Can you understand why? Did he have valid reasons to be angry?

6. In Luke 15:32, the father said, "This brother of yours was dead and is alive again." Why did he compare him to having been dead?

7. What did the Holy Spirit highlight to you in Luke 15 through the reading or the teaching?

Lesson 60: Luke 16

Son of Man: Heaven—And Hell—Are Real

Teaching Notes

Intro

Romans 6:23 tells us, "The wages of sin is death." Sin always leads to death. Today, as depressing as it is, we're going to camp out on death and hell as we study Luke 16. The reason we can have good news is because we first had bad news. Yet we shy away from talking about the eternal punishment that is coming for the lost sheep.

Teaching

Luke 16:19: In this parable, Jesus described a rich man who dressed in purple and fine linen—his clothing alone let you know he was wealthy. He feasted lavishly every single day.

Luke 16:20: Jesus next described a poor man named Lazarus. This is the only parable in Scripture where a person is named, but this Lazarus was not the brother of Mary and Martha. This poor man was covered with sores and left at his gate.

Luke 16:21: "He longed to be filled with what fell from the rich man's table." Jesus invited people to come to the table, but the rich man didn't. Lazarus longed for scraps of food from the rich man's table. Instead, the dogs came and licked his sores.

What is our role toward the poor? This rich man probably saw this poor man at the gate every day, and instead of helping him, he probably thought he was annoying and wondered when he would leave. Proverbs frequently called people to care for those in need: "The one who despises his neighbor sins, but whoever shows kindness to the poor will be happy" (Proverbs 14:21). "Kindness to the poor is a loan to the Lord, and He will give a reward to the lender" (Proverbs 19:17). When we show kindness to the poor by giving them food, necessities, or money, God says He will give us a reward. Proverbs 21:13 says, "The one who shuts his ears to the cry of the poor will himself also call out and not be answered." Proverbs 28:27 is similar, "The one who gives to the poor will not be in need, but one who turns his eyes away will receive many curses." When the rich man continued to turn away from Lazarus, he became more focused on himself. We need to be reminded that we can never out give God. We have no excuses for refusing to help the "Lazaruses" around us.

Luke 16:22–23a: "One day the poor man died and was carried away by the angels to Abraham's side. The rich man also died and was buried." After death, their lives continued on. The rich man, "being in torment," or constant agony, looked up and saw Abraham. We have no problem thinking someone is in heaven, but we don't accept being in torment in Hades. Instead, we claim that hell isn't real. This rich man's attitude demonstrated why Jesus said, "I assure you: It will be hard for a rich person to enter the kingdom of heaven" (Matthew 19:23). When the disciples wanted to know who could be saved, Jesus answered, "With men this is impossible, but with God all things are possible" (Matthew 19:26). Zacchaeus, the rich tax collector, later proved that it was possible for a rich man to get into heaven (Luke 19:1–10).

Luke 16:23–24: Their situations were now reversed. Now the rich man, from a long way off, longed for what Lazarus had. The rich man called out, "Father Abraham!" like he knew Abraham. Notice he said, "Send Lazarus." Even now, he still wanted the poor man to serve him. The rich man wanted relief from the agony of an eternal flame and fire. If hell doesn't exist, there was no point in Jesus dying on the cross. Why would Jesus go through the pain and anguish prophesied in Isaiah 53? He came to set us free from the fire, flame, and torment in hell. Many Scriptures say that hell is real:

- Matthew 25:41, 46: "Then He will also say to those on the left, 'Depart from Me, you who are cursed, into the eternal fire prepared for the Devil and his angels!' . . . And they will go away into eternal punishment, but the righteous to eternal life." If you believe in eternal life, then you have to believe in eternal punishment. You cannot pluck certain things out of Scripture and claim it doesn't apply anymore. The reason we have to seek and find the lost is because there is eternal punishment for those who don't know the Lord.
- Isaiah 66:24: "As they leave, they will see the dead bodies of the men who have rebelled against Me; for their worm will never die, their fire will never go out." Their spirit will constantly be in torment because they'll never be in the presence of God.

- Jude 7: "Sodom and Gomorrah and the cities around them committed sexual immorality and practiced perversions . . . and serve as an example by undergoing the punishment of eternal fire."

- Jude 13: "For whom the blackness of darkness is reserved forever!" Have you ever been in a pitch-dark room? Can you imagine living forever in complete darkness apart from the presence of God?

- 2 Thessalonians 1:9: "These will pay the penalty of eternal destruction from the Lord's presence." We need to understand the magnitude of what eternity apart from God looks like. Lazarus was in the Lord's presence, in His eternal strength.

- Matthew 13:50: "And throw them into the blazing furnace. In that place there will be weeping and gnashing of teeth." We have too many images that tell us hell is not good. We cannot let the one sheep go because, if they don't know the Lord, this is where they end up. How much do you not care about somebody to let him or her experience this?

Anyone who communicates that hell doesn't exist has to be a false teacher because then there would be no reason for Christ to do what He did.

Luke 16:25–26: Abraham told the rich man, "During your life you received your good things, just as Lazarus received bad things, but now he is comforted here, while you are in agony." Their roles were flipped. "A great chasm has been fixed" meant that no one could cross over in either direction. There is no purgatory. There are no second chances. We can't pray or send someone across to heaven.

Luke 16:27–31: The rich man begged Abraham to send someone to tell his family so they won't get to this place of torment. But Abraham told him, "They have Moses and the prophets; they should listen to them." At least 300 times in the Old Testament, Moses and the prophets pointed to the Messiah. Jesus said, "Don't assume that I came to destroy the Law or the Prophets. I did not come to destroy but to fulfill" (Matthew 5:17). The rich man protested that if someone from the dead went to them, then they would repent. But Abraham countered, "If they don't listen to Moses and the prophets, they will not be persuaded if someone rises from the dead."

Closing

As a summary of heaven and hell, Mark Bailey made five statements about death:[4]

---

[4] Mark Bailey and Tom Constable, *Nelson's New Testament Survey* (Nashville: Thomas Nelson, 1999), n.p.

- "There is immediate consciousness after death." The rich man's life continued on, and he didn't like where he ended up.
- "Post-death destinies are irreversible." There is no purgatory or second chance.
- "No one can lose or gain salvation after death."
- "The judgments that determine the eternal destinies of either torment or blessing are just." It's not God's fault that someone is in torment because He clearly showed us that we can come to the table. Through the love of Christ, He gave us an out.
- "Signs should never be sought as a substitute for the Word of God." The Word is proof that God is real, but people would rather have miracles than turn to the Word of God.

There is heaven and there is a hell, and it's not what we experience here on earth right now. This is nothing compared to what's coming. When C. S. Lewis learned of a tombstone with the epitaph: "Here lies an atheist all dressed up and nowhere to go," he replied, "I bet he wishes that were so."[5] So what's the big picture? Find the lost lamb before it's too late. We must have an eternal perspective every day. Colossian 3:1–4 says we can live our lives in one of two worlds—the earthly or the eternal. Our minds, thoughts, actions, and words are all based on the eternal. Let's introduce this perspective to as many lost sheep, as many rich men, as we can.

Daily Word

Luke shared the story of a rich man and a poor man. When the rich man, who had lived a life of luxury and lavishly feasted every day of his life, died, he was tormented in hell. In contrast, when the poor man, who had been covered with sores during his life, died, angels carried him away to heaven. While the rich man suffered in hell, he requested to cool his tongue for relief from the heat. He begged Abraham to go to his five brothers and warn them about hell so they wouldn't endure the same suffering.

Heaven and hell are real. Sometimes people like to think maybe hell isn't that bad. But yes, as described in this passage, hell is truly an awful place. Jesus came so you may have eternal life in heaven forever. If you receive His gift of salvation and follow Him, you do not have to suffer in hell for eternity. The choice is yours. Will you believe in Jesus during your days on earth? Or will you be your own god? The Lord longs for you to receive His love. He wants to spend eternity with

---

[5] C. S. Lewis, *Christian Reflections*, ed. Walter Hooper (Grand Rapids: Eerdmans, 1967), xii.

you forever. And for those choosing to believe in Jesus, don't hold back sharing with others. You could help save them from eternity in hell. Today, go and share Jesus and help save a life!

Besides all this, a great chasm has been fixed between us and you, so that those who want to pass over from here to you cannot; neither can those from there cross over to us. —Luke 16:26

Further Scripture: Matthew 16:26; Colossians 3:2–4; 1 John 5:11–12

Questions

1. What is the definition of a steward? How should we treat our possessions? (Psalm 24:1; Proverbs 3:9)

2. If you had to give an account of your stewardship of time, talents, or possessions, how would you do? (Luke 16:2)

3. In Luke 16:13, why did Jesus say you can't serve two masters? How do you know if you are serving money more than God?

4. How did Lazarus, and not the rich man, end up in Abraham's bosom? How do we know that death is not the end of it all? (2 Corinthians 5:6–8; Philippians 1:21; Hebrews 9:27)

5. The rich man did not treat Lazarus very kindly; he even ignored him. How does Scripture teach us to treat the poor? (Proverbs 14:21; 19:17; 21:13; 28:27; Matthew 25:37–40)

6. What did the Holy Spirit highlight to you in Luke 16 through the reading or the teaching?

Lesson 61: Luke 17
Son of Man: The Kingdom of God

Teaching Notes

Intro

Our goal with reviveSCHOOL is to take you one step closer to the Lord, one step deeper into the Word. Today's topic from Luke 17 is a discussion of the kingdom of God—the kingdom of heaven. Yes, they're the same thing. See what you can catch through our study of the Word of God today.

Teaching

Luke 17:20: The Pharisees asked Jesus, "When will we get to experience the kingdom of God?" Jesus answered, "The kingdom of God is not coming with something observable." John Piper explained that God's kingdom is "God's kingly rule." In other words, you will experience His reign, His action, His lordship, and His sovereign governance here and now.[1] The Pharisees wanted the political deal—Jesus as king. But the kingdom wouldn't come with an outward show, nor was it as pretty or as flashy as they wanted.

Luke 17:21: Jesus explained, "The kingdom of God is among you." The Pharisees wanted to know when it would take place. Jesus said it was already here. *Nelson's Commentary* said they didn't need to hunt for the kingdom because the kingdom came with Jesus.[2] Then Jesus continued: "The days are coming when you will long to see one of the days of the Son of Man, but you won't see it." Now, Jesus was talking about the future.

Luke 17:23–24: Jesus said they shouldn't chase after those who said, "Look there!" or "Look here!" He then began to describe a future scenario when the *Son of Man* would be visible "from horizon to horizon" (v. 24). His words brought to mind the prophecy of Daniel 7:13–14: "I saw One like a son of man with the

---

[1] John Piper, "What Is the Kingdom of God?," Desiring God, September 8, 2017, https://www.desiringgod.org/interviews/what-is-the-kingdom-of-god.

[2] Earl D. Radmacher, Ronald B. Allen, and H. Wayne House, eds., *Nelson's New Illustrated Bible Commentary* (Nashville: Thomas Nelson, 1999), 1287.

clouds of heaven. He approached the Ancient of Days." According to Luke 11, these signs won't precede the kingdom of God. However, in Matthew 24, Jesus told His disciples that the sign of the coming of the *Son of Man* would precede the end: "For as the lightning comes from the east and flashes as far as the west, so will be the coming of the Son of Man" (Matthew 24:27). Eventually Jesus will return on the clouds for all to see. People won't have to worry about missing Jesus' return. Everyone will know. "Then the sign of the Son of Man will appear in the sky . . . and they will see the Son of Man coming on the clouds of heaven with power and great glory" (Matthew 24:30). Matthew 25:13 assures us that Jesus is coming again; we just don't know when. In Luke 12:40, Jesus said to be ready, "because the Son of Man is coming at an hour that you do not expect." He went on to say, "That slave's master will come on a day he does not expect him . . . and assign him a place with unbelievers." We don't know when!

The church today seems to think the kingdom of God is in the future. We forget we're a part of the kingdom of God now. When we were born, we became a citizen of the country in which we were born. Citizenship was instantaneous. According to John 3, when we are born again, we become citizens of the kingdom of God instantly. Jesus literally gives us the Holy Spirit, which allows us to be a part of the kingdom of God here and now. We have been given the power to function as citizens of the kingdom of God, but we don't function that way. We think we have to wait. There's an aspect of the kingdom of God that was established through Jesus' death, burial, and resurrection. *Nelson's Commentary* implied that Jesus' leadership reigns in our lives. His current and active work is to redeem the world.[3] It happens through us when we go find the lost sheep. In the future, the kingdom will come when Jesus returns. We don't know the time. It will happen suddenly and unexpectedly. We are citizens of the kingdom of God now and in the future. In Matthew 10:8, Jesus' disciples healed the sick, raised the dead, cleansed those with skin diseases, and drove out demons. We have the resurrection power inside of us. The kingdom of God is among us, and it is coming in the future. Some people think the church is the kingdom of God. But the church is a part of the kingdom of God.[4] God has a bigger picture in mind here.

Luke 17:24–25: Daniel actually prophesied that the *Son of Man* would come on the clouds in power and glory. We have to get ready for this. He's coming back in human flesh to hang out with humanity. Before that future return, He said He must suffer many things. He was talking about His death, burial, and resurrection.

---

[3] Radmacher et al., 1287.

[4] Radmacher et al., 1287–1288.

Luke 17:26–27: "Just as it was in the days of Noah." While everybody did what was right in their own eyes, God sent the flood and wiped out everyone. What happened in Noah's time will happen before the *Son of Man* comes back again. People lived life as usual, going through everyday stuff. The people paid little attention to God. They were focused on the rich man's mentality, thinking about earthly things. People would rather focus on daily activities without thinking about the eternal things. If we don't think about the future, then the torment (Luke 16) becomes reality.

Luke 17:28–29: "It will be the same as it was in the days of Lot: People went on eating, drinking, buying, selling, planting, building." People today are also focused on daily life, not the eternal, not living in expectation of Jesus coming back. "But on the day Lot left Sodom, fire and sulfur rained and destroyed them all" (v. 29).

Luke 17:30–33: "It will be like that on the day the Son of Man is revealed." We're literally talking about the apocalypse, the end, when Christ shows up, when total judgment will come. Are we trying to get people ready for the *Son of Man's* return? Or are we focused on earthly things? When we have the perspective of citizens of the kingdom of God, then we'll want to get ready for the future. Otherwise, we might just blend in with the people focused on worldly things. "On that day" (v. 32) referred to Jesus' second coming. It won't matter what a person has (possessions); they won't go back to gather them up. Nelson emphasized that people won't pause, won't look back, but will move quickly because the wrath is coming.[5] Jesus urged His disciples, "Remember Lot's wife!" She looked back and became a pillar of salt (Genesis 19:26). Something in her spirit was still connected to the earthly things. As Jesus' disciples, our eyes can't be on the earthly things; we have to focus on the eternal things. When we can't see what God is doing, it's hard to keep our eyes on the eternal. We naturally gravitate to the things that make us feel good. "Whoever tries to make his life secure will lose it, and whoever loses his life will preserve it" (v. 33). This is Mark 8:34 all over again. When you follow Jesus, you have to deny yourself (the earthly things you really like), take up the cross (be willing to suffer, to be rejected and persecuted), and follow Jesus. We can't "look back" or "go back to those things." As citizens of God's kingdom, we have to look forward.

Luke 17:34–36: These verses probably aren't talking about the rapture but rather are talking about the judgment. *Nelson's Commentary* explained that one would be taken in judgment and one would be left to live and reign with Christ.[6]

---

[5] Radmacher et al., 1288.

[6] Radmacher et al., 1288.

This perspective works when you understand that you're a citizen of the kingdom of God now, and you just can't wait for Him to come back. If you're always looking forward, you don't have time to look back or to grab at the earthly things.

Luke 17:37: "Where the corpse is, there also the vultures will be gathered." When judgment comes, you will smell the stench of death. You won't have to look for it because the predatory birds will be everywhere.

Closing

One of the things we need to understand is how can we actively pursue and expand the kingdom of God now? By praying and living out Matthew 6:10: "Your kingdom come, your will be done, on earth as it is in heaven." Because we expect His future return and judgment, we should desire to help others get ready. Romans 13:11–12 reminds us that "our salvation is nearer than when we first believed," and encourages us to put on the armor of life now instead of waiting until He comes back.

Daily Word

While Jesus was traveling, ten men with serious skin diseases met him. They stood at a distance and asked Jesus to have mercy on them. Jesus sent them on their way, telling them to go and show themselves to the priests. While they were going, the ten men were healed. Just one of the ten returned to thank Jesus. To this one man who did something different, Jesus said, "Go on your way, your faith has made you well." This one man was not only a leper and an outcast from society, but he was also a Samaritan, a foreigner. Even still, the Lord healed him physically and spiritually. The Lord saw his faith.

The Lord sees you, and He loves you. You may feel different. You may stand apart from the crowd as you make choices to follow Christ. Jesus is with you and sees you as you follow Him rather than the crowd. Today, follow the voice of the Lord. Humble yourself and give thanks to the Lord, even if you stand out as the different one. Remember, the Lord created you; you are perfectly and wonderfully made. Walk in faith, believing His love is with you.

But one of them, seeing that he was healed, returned and, with a loud voice, gave glory to God. He fell facedown at His feet, thanking Him. And he was a Samaritan. . . . And He told him, "Get up and go on your way. Your faith has made you well." —Luke 17:15–16, 19

Further Scripture: Psalm 139:13–14; Colossians 3:17; Revelation 19:5

Questions

1. What does it mean to cause another believer to stumble? (Romans 14:13; 1 Corinthians 10:32; 1 John 2:10) What are some examples of this? How can you keep from making someone else stumble in their walk with the Lord?

2. Forgiveness was taught in the first four verses of Luke 17. Why do you think the apostles immediately responded by asking Jesus to increase their faith? (Mark 4:30–32; James 2:14–26) How do faith and forgiveness go together?

3. Why did the lepers stand far off and lift up their voices to Jesus instead of coming to Him? (Leviticus 13:46; Numbers 5:2) When were the lepers healed?

4. What does Jesus want to find us doing when He comes back? (Luke 12:37, 43; 17:10; Acts 1:6–11)

5. Why do you think Jesus said, "Remember Lot's wife?" (Genesis 19:17, 26; Matthew 10:39; John 12:25) Is there anything in your life BC (before Christ) that you continue to look back at or long for?

6. What did the Holy Spirit highlight to you in Luke 17 through the reading or the teaching?

Lesson 62: Luke 18

Son of Man: Be Persistent in Prayer

Teaching Notes

Intro

We're painting a picture of Jesus, who was known as the *Son of Man* in the Gospel of Luke. Jesus was willing to engage with people. He was not a distant god; He was not a god who didn't interact with people. He was God in human flesh. He invited everybody to the table. He took away the main issue we had, which was the fall of man. He redeemed us. Yet sometimes when we think about God, we don't think He's approachable. God wants to connect with us. He wants to have a relationship with us.

Teaching

Luke 18:1: Jesus told a parable that emphasized the need to pray, always, without becoming discouraged. It's important to pray always so we don't become discouraged, depressed, and overwhelmed by the woes of life. Scripture says to give thanks in all things. When we keep on praying, we can fight the enemy.

Luke 18:2–3: The judge in this parable didn't fear God or respect man, which meant he was not a believer. The widow in this town kept coming to him, asking for justice against her adversary. Luke mentions widows more than all the other Gospels combined. Psalm 68:5 says, "God in His holy dwelling is a father of the fatherless and a champion of widows." God looks out for those who don't have support, who have lost a best friend. James 1:27 reminds us that God expects us to do the same: "Pure and undefiled religion before our God and Father is this: to look after orphans and widows in their distress." These are people who need help. In Luke 7:11–17, Jesus raised a dead man because "he was his mother's only son, and she was a widow" (v. 12). In Luke 20:47, Jesus warned the disciples to beware of the scribes because "they devour widows' houses and say long prayers just for show." Their religious leaders sought the widows and devoured them because they wanted something from them. Instead, God commands His people to take care of widows. The widow in this parable appeared before the judge asking him to please give her justice. Wiersbe said she had at least three things working against her: (1) she was a woman and therefore unimportant in the culture of the day; (2) she was a widow who had no one to speak up for her; and (3) she was probably poor so she couldn't afford to pay a bribe to get the judge to rule in her favor.[1]

Luke 18:4–5: The judge was initially unwilling to help her. He didn't care about what God would think, and he didn't care what she needed. But eventually the judge decided to give her justice so she wouldn't wear him out with her persistent requests. *Nelson's Commentary* said, "If an insensitive judge will respond to the continual requests of a widow, God will certainly respond to the continual prayers of believers."[2] Wiersbe contrasted the widow's situation with the position of believers. The widow was a stranger to the judge who didn't care about her. She didn't have an advocate to give her access to the judge. In contrast, as children of God, we have open access to God. We also have an advocate, Jesus, who sits at God's right hand and pleads for us.[3]

Luke 18:6–8a: Jesus then said, "Listen to what the unjust judge says. Will not God grant justice to His elect who cry out to Him day and night?" Jesus emphasized that God would swiftly grant justice to His people. As citizens of the kingdom of God, we can use prayer to tap into the power of God, so we are ready when the *Son of Man* comes. How do we do this? Let's look at some obvious verses:

- 1 Thessalonians 5:16–18: "Rejoice always! Pray constantly. Give thanks in everything."
- 1 Peter 3:7: "Husbands, in the same way, live with your wives with an understanding of their weaker nature yet showing them honor as coheirs of the grace of life, so that your prayers will not be hindered." Husbands have to treat their wives well, as coheirs. Maybe we don't see a move of God in the local churches because of bad marriages. Can you imagine treating your wife poorly and then coming to church, to God, as if nothing happened?
- Matthew 7:7–12: "Keep asking, and it will be given to you. Keep searching, and you will find. Keep knocking, and the door will be opened to you" (v. 7). When we keep on asking, God will answer. As children of God, we have open access to God, an advocate before Him, and the knowledge that He wants to give us good things. Can you pray for

---

[1] Warren W. Wiersbe, *The Wiersbe Bible Commentary: New Testament* (Colorado Springs: David C Cook, 2007), 199.

[2] Earl D. Radmacher, Ronald B. Allen, and H. Wayne House, eds., *Nelson's New Illustrated Bible Commentary* (Nashville: Thomas Nelson, 1999), 1288.

[3] Wiersbe, 199.

something over and over and over? Yes, as long as it's not gibberish or babbling. Matthew 6:7–8 says we can't "babble like idolaters" or pray just to be heard.

The value of prayer has been emphasized by many Christians:

- E. M. Bounds said: "We are ever ready to excuse our lack of earnest and toilsome praying, by a fancied and delusive view of submission. We often end praying just when we ought to begin. We quit praying when God waits and is waiting for us to really pray. We are deterred by obstacles from praying, or we succumb to difficulties, and call it submission to God's will."[4] "Our praying, however, needs to be pressed and pursued with an energy that never tires, a persistency which will not be denied, and a courage which never fails."[5] Do you want to be known as a person of prayer?

- Charles Spurgeon said: "If you are sure it is a right thing for which you are asking, plead now! Plead at noon! Plead at night! Plead on—with cries and tears spread out your case!"[6]

- George Müller said: "It is not enough to begin to pray, nor to pray aright, nor is it enough to continue for a time to pray; but we must patiently, believingly, continue in prayer until we obtain an answer."[7] That answer may not be what we are praying for, but we know that God wants to show up in our lives.

Luke 18:8b: As Jesus concluded the parable, He asked, "When the Son of Man comes, will He find that faith on earth?" How do we, as people of prayer, get to the point where Jesus will find that kind of faith in our lives? When we pray, do we show that kind of faith? Having that kind of faith means functioning in the power of prayer.

Matthew 17:19–20 explains that when we become citizens of the kingdom of God, we have faith the size of a mustard seed. If we want to develop the faith that Jesus is looking for, then we start with faith as small as a mustard seed. Luke 17:5 encourages us to pray for the Lord to increase our faith. Luke 18:8 confirms

---

[4] Edward M. Bounds, *The Reality of Prayer* (San Francisco: Bottom of the Hill, 2010), 38.

[5] E. M. Bounds, "Great Quotes on Prayer," Eternal Perspective Ministries, March 28, 2009, https://www.epm.org/resources/2009/Mar/28/great-quotes-prayer/.

[6] Charles H. Spurgeon, "The Importunate Widow," Christian Classics Ethereal Library, https://www.ccel.org/ccel/spurgeon/sermons15.ix.html.

[7] George Müller, "Great Quotes on Prayer," Eternal Perspective Ministries, March 28, 2009, https://www.epm.org/resources/2009/Mar/28/great-quotes-prayer/.

that Jesus is looking for children of God who don't stop coming before Him in prayer. They have radical faith that if they keep praying, God will show up. Romans 10:17 says, "So faith comes from what is heard, and what is heard comes through the message about Christ." We can't grow in the Lord if we're not growing in the Word of God. We can increase our faith simply by being in the Word of God every day. James 1:22 says, "But be doers of the word and not hearers only, deceiving yourself."

As we hear the word of God, we want to increase our faith and be doers of the word of God. As citizens of the kingdom of God, we have to act on our faith. But as we become doers of the word, we cannot forget to test the word. Malachi 3:10 says, "test Me in this way." See, by faith, God will show up. Hebrews 11:6 emphasizes that "without faith it is impossible to please God." Hebrews 11:1 says: "Now faith is the reality of what is hoped for, the proof of what is not seen." When we walk by faith, we actually have proof of God showing up. Hebrews 4:15–16 assures us that because the *Son of Man* existed here on earth, we can "approach the throne of grace with boldness, so that we may receive mercy and find grace to help us at the proper time." Jesus, the *Son of Man*, sympathizes with our weaknesses and invites us to come to Him, knowing He will give us mercy and grace.

Closing

Luke 18:1 tells us to pray so we won't become discouraged. To fight discouragement in everyday life, we have to keep on praying, knowing that God wants to bless us and give us the desires of our hearts. Psalm 116:2 says, "Because He has turned His ear to me, I will call out to him as long as I live." As long as we have breath, we should keep walking and praying by faith. We should be like the persistent widow who literally cried out in faith.

Daily Word

When Jesus was with His disciples, He shared a story about a persistent widow who went before a judge seeking justice against her adversary. The widow was so persistent and refused to give up to the point the judge called it pestering. The judge eventually gave her the justice she asked for because he was tired of her persistence. He just gave her what she wanted!

Jesus told this parable because He knew the disciples would need "to pray always and not become discouraged." Raise your hand if this is you! Have you sought the Lord for days, weeks, or even years for the same loved ones to receive Jesus as their Savior? Or for the prodigal son or daughter to come home? Or for your marriage to turn around for good? Or for wisdom and clarity on a decision?

The Lord knows. He knows the tendency to become discouraged in the midst of waiting. Jesus says pray always and don't be discouraged. Today, once again, come before Jesus with your requests. He hears you, and He will answer you. The answer may be no, it may be yes, or it may be to wait a bit longer. But He has promised—He will answer you when you seek Him with all your heart.

He then told them a parable on the need for them to pray always and not become discouraged. —Luke 18:1

Further Scripture: Isaiah 40:31; Matthew 7:7; 1 Thessalonians 5:16–18

Questions

1. In verses 1–8, a widowed woman repeatedly went before a judge asking for justice. Has there been a time when you repeated a request over and over until you received a response? Have you taken prayers to God like this? Why or why not?

2. Jesus told the Parable of the Pharisee and the tax collector. Have you ever found yourself in either of these positions at one time or another? What, if anything, did God reveal to you?

3. We are told in verse 17 to receive the kingdom of God as children. What does this look like to you?

4. Jesus said one would be repaid many times over in this life if he or she gave up possessions and/or family for the sake of the kingdom. Have you given up anything for the kingdom of God? If so, how have you seen restoration in these areas?

5. Are you as bold and precise in your prayer as the blind beggar was? (Hebrews 4:16)

6. What did the Holy Spirit highlight to you in Luke 18 through the reading or the teaching?

Lesson 63: Luke 19
Son of Man: True Faith

Teaching Notes

Intro

When one person wants to radically encounter Jesus in a new and refreshing way, it impacts a whole lot of people. In Luke 19, one "wee little man" was literally hungry for more. He wanted to experience more of Jesus, so he did whatever it took to encounter Jesus.

Teaching

Luke 19:1–2: As Jesus passed through Jericho, He encountered a rich tax collector named Zacchaeus. Since he was a chief tax collector, he was a hated man. At that time, there were three places in Israel where taxes were collected: Jerusalem, Jericho, and Capernaum. Zacchaeus was hated by everybody. "Zacchaeus probably oversaw a large tax district and had other tax collectors working for him."[1] Not only was he robbing those from whom he collected taxes, but he also probably robbed those who worked for him. He likely came from one of the three big cities. MacArthur contrasted this encounter with the account of the rich young ruler, when Jesus said, "How hard it is for those who have wealth to enter the kingdom of God!" (Luke 18:24). But Jesus also pointed out, "What is impossible with men is possible with God" (Luke 18:27). Even though Zacchaeus was rich, we have to allow God room to radically reach this guy.

Luke 19:3: Zacchaeus tried to see Jesus, but he was unable to because he was a short man and couldn't see over the crowd. Why would he want to see Jesus? He was a wealthy tax collector. He'd probably heard about Jesus from Matthew, Jesus' disciple who was once a tax collector.

Luke 19:4: Zacchaeus ran ahead and climbed a sycamore tree. A sycamore is a sturdy tree with low spreading branches so any small person could climb it. It has a short trunk with low hanging wide branches. Climbing a tree was childlike and

---

[1] John MacArthur, *The MacArthur Bible Commentary* (Nashville: Thomas Nelson, 2005), 1318.

undignified, not something a tax collector would normally do. John Calvin said: "Curiosity and simplicity are a sort of preparation for faith."[2] In Luke 18:13, Jesus described the prayers of a tax collector: "standing afar off . . . kept striking his chest . . . saying, 'God, turn Your wrath from me—a sinner.'" Jesus went on to say, "Let the little children come to Me, and don't stop them, because the kingdom of God belongs to such as these." The only people who play in trees today are kids. That's why they build tree forts. But in this case, the head money guy climbed a tree because his heart was softening, and childlike faith was beginning . . . maybe because he had heard of Matthew's faith.

Luke 19:5: Jesus looked up and invited Zacchaeus to come down so Jesus could stay with him. We don't know if Jesus had any interaction with Zacchaeus before this moment. But Jesus called him by name. When God calls us by name, it's an experience we never forget. Psalm 139:13–18 assures us that God knows every single little thing about us. Hebrews 1 says Jesus is the Creator. Since Jesus helped create Zacchaeus, He knew him by name. He knows way more than our names because He created us. Jesus told Zacchaeus, "Today, I must stay in your house." Zacchaeus was searching and hungering for more. Now that Jesus found him, He wanted to spend time with him. Zacchaeus humbled himself, became poor in spirit, and hungered and thirsted for Jesus (Matthew 5:3–6). We can't just tell people they need Jesus; they have to realize for themselves they need Jesus.

Luke 19:6: Zacchaeus came down quickly and welcomed Jesus joyfully. John 1:47–49 talks about a similar time when Jesus saw Nathanael under the fig tree and knew who he was. "Before Phillip called you . . . I saw you" (v. 48). Nathanael recognized Jesus as the Son of God. When someone is hungry for Jesus, Jesus will find him or her.

Luke 19:7: "All who saw it began to complain, 'He's gone to lodge with a sinful man!'" They complained that Jesus hung out with the sinners. Let's compare Zacchaeus with the Pharisees. On the outside, Zacchaeus was labeled a sinner. On the inside, based on him climbing a sycamore tree, he was hungry for the truth. On the outside, the Pharisees were religious and followed the letter of the law; they played that part really well. But on the inside, they were empty and had no hunger for Jesus; they rejected the truth. Zacchaeus welcomed Jesus, but the Pharisees criticized Jesus. Zacchaeus had been a mess for a while, but while the Pharisees looked good on the outside, they were empty inside. In Matthew 23, Jesus told the Pharisees they cleaned the outside of the cup and dish, but inside

---

[2] Warren W. Wiersbe, *The Wiersbe Bible Commentary: New Testament* (Colorado Springs: David C Cook, 2007), 202.

they were full of greed and self-indulgence. He told them, "Blind Pharisee! First clean the inside of the cup, so the outside of it may also be clean" (Matthew 23:25–26). Jesus condemned them for playing the game of religion. "Woe to you, scribes and Pharisees, hypocrites! You are like whitewashed tombs . . . you seem righteous to people, but inside you are full of hypocrisy and lawlessness" (Matthew 23:27–28). Jesus wants to spend time with those who seek Him.

Luke 19:8: Zacchaeus said to Jesus, "Look, I'll give half of my possessions to the poor . . . and pay back four times as much." Tannehill described Zacchaeus's reaction as "radical repentance."[3] "The law required a penalty of one-fifth as restitution for money acquired by fraud . . . The law required fourfold restitution only when an animal was stolen and killed."[4] Like the tax collector in Luke 16:13, Zacchaeus saw himself for who he was when he came into the presence of Christ—the almighty Creator who knew his name. Zacchaeus realized when he came down from the tree that he was letting go of the money because he couldn't be a slave to God and to the money. His response stands in stark contrast with the rich young ruler who, in Luke 18:18–23, refused to "sell all that you have and distribute it to the poor." Zacchaeus overcame the financial strings around him and gave it all up for Jesus.

Luke 19:9: Jesus said, "Today salvation has come to this house, because he too is a son of Abraham." Galatians 3:7 explains that "those who have faith are Abraham's sons." Because of Zacchaeus's faith in Christ, he was labeled as a man of faith who was Abraham's son. Romans 2:28 says, "For a person is not a Jew who is one outwardly, and true circumcision is not something visible in the flesh. On the contrary, a person is a Jew who is one inwardly, and circumcision is of the heart—by the Spirit, not the letter." This literally took place in Zacchaeus's life. His heart was circumcised.

Luke 19:10: "For the Son of Man has come to seek and to save the lost." Jesus came to earth to seek and save the lost—the sheep, the coin, the prodigal son, and Zacchaeus. Jesus came to fulfill the mission of the Messiah to bring freedom and save those who are lost, just as He announced in Luke 4:17–19.

Closing

Praise the Lord, Jesus is coming after us, and we can find hope in that.

---

[3] Robert C. Tannehill, *The Narrative Unity of Luke–Acts: A Literary Interpretation* (Philadelphia: Fortress, 1986), 124.

[4] MacArthur, 1318.

Daily Word

While Jesus was traveling through Jericho, the crowds followed Him. A rich tax collector named Zacchaeus climbed up a tree so he could see Jesus. As Jesus passed by, He saw Zacchaeus and told him to come down because Jesus must stay at his house. Zacchaeus hurried down and joyfully welcomed Jesus into his home. Zacchaeus's life was transformed as he made Jesus Lord of his life. Jesus, the Son of Man, came to seek and save the lost. Jesus saw Zacchaeus in a tree and wanted to spend time with him. In doing so, one life was changed forever as Zacchaeus received the love of Jesus.

Today, open your eyes to see the people who are watching you live your life for the Lord. And then, do the next thing. Invite them into your home for a meal or be willing to go into their home. Show them the love of Jesus by spending time with them. It may require you to get outside your comfort zone, but that's how Jesus lived His life. He was criticized for going to a tax collector's home, and yet He went and loved anyway. His mission is now your mission—to seek and save the lost. As you go on your way, open your eyes to see someone to love like Jesus!

"Today salvation has come to this house," Jesus told him, "because he too is a son of Abraham. For the Son of Man has come to seek and to save the lost." —Luke 19:9–10

Further Scripture: Romans 1:16; Romans 10:1; 1 Corinthians 9:22–23

Questions

1. In verse 9, Jesus said that salvation had come to Zacchaeus because he had shown himself to be a true son of Abraham. Why did Jesus say these things?

2. What did Jesus mean in verse 10, in your opinion?

3. In the parable of the ten servants, how many servants received money from the king? What were the results? Have you ever noticed verse 26 to be true in your own life? Why or why not?

4. What do you think verse 40 means? Where else might you find creation crying/singing out? (Psalms 19:1–4; 96:11–13)

5. What do you think Jesus meant by verse 42? How was peace hidden from their eyes? Why? (Exodus 7:3–14; Deuteronomy 2:30; Isaiah 6:10)

6. Could the anger Jesus showed in the Temple be considered righteous anger? Why or why not? What does Jesus say about anger? (Ephesians 4:26) What is the difference between righteous anger and anger?

7. What did the Holy Spirit highlight to you in Luke 19 through the reading or the teaching?

Lesson 64: Luke 20

Son of Man: Meeting the Sadducees' Challenge

Teaching Notes

Intro

Many of Jesus' interactions were with religious leaders. And in most of these interactions, there was some kind of loving tension. As He loved on the sinful and on the tax collectors, for some reason, people got upset. The religious guys were bothered by everything that didn't fit the norm or didn't fit into their 613 laws, rules, and regulations.

Teaching

Luke 20:1–8: The authority of Jesus was challenged by the chief priests and scribes in the temple complex.

Luke 20:9–19: Jesus told a parable about a vineyard owner who sent servants to check on his vineyard. The tenant farmers beat his slaves and killed his son. After telling the parable, Jesus asked, "Then what is the meaning of this Scripture: The stone that the builders rejected—this has become the cornerstone" (v. 17). The religious leaders set out to kill Jesus because they knew the parable was about them. The *Son of Man* knew God in human flesh needed to come to earth to connect with us to set us free. He even taught that people should not disrespect the local authorities. Jesus wasn't here to stir the pot and do illegal things. He came to set people free from the bondage that they were in.

Luke 20:27: The Sadducees had rejected the oral traditions the Pharisees obeyed. They based all of their teaching on the first five books of the Law—the Pentateuch. They did not believe in the resurrection, angels, and spirits (Acts 23:8). What did they have to live for? Wiersbe said, "Resurrection is not reconstruction; it is the miraculous granting of a new body that has continuity with the old body but not identity."[1] In Acts 4:1–2, they confronted the disciples for "proclaiming the resurrection from the dead, using Jesus as the example." Anytime the

---

[1] Warren W. Wiersbe, *The Wiersbe Bible Commentary: New Testament* (Colorado Springs: David C Cook, 2007), 207.

resurrection was taught, the Sadducees had an issue with it. In John 12:10–11, the chief priests decided to kill Lazarus because his resurrection was the reason people believed in Jesus. With this challenge to Jesus, they wanted to prove there was no resurrection from the dead.

Luke 20:28–33: The scenario the Sadducees presented to Jesus was based on the custom of levirate marriage. According to Deuteronomy 25:5–6, when a man died without a son, the widow married his brother to produce a son to carry on the name of the dead brother. *Nelson's Commentary* said, "the law was designed to perpetuate the name of the man who died childless."[2] In this scenario, the widow married seven brothers, and all seven died, leaving no children. Finally, the woman died. The Sadducees then asked, "In the resurrection, therefore, whose wife will the woman be?" They wanted to show that a resurrection would lead to weird results.[3]

Luke 20:34–36: Jesus answered, "The sons of this age marry and are given in marriage. But those who are counted worthy to take part in that age and in the resurrection from the dead neither marry nor are given in marriage. For they cannot die anymore." Even if all these people were counted worthy to be part of that age—the future kingdom of God—even if they participated in the resurrection, they would no longer marry. Jesus' answers revealed the future age would be different from this age. In heaven, we will be so focused on Christ that we won't need the helpmate mentality.

Luke 20:37–38: In the burning bush encounter, God called Himself the God of Abraham, Isaac, and Jacob (Exodus 3:6). Isaiah prophesied the resurrection: "Your dead will live; their bodies will rise . . . and the earth will bring out the departed spirits" (Isaiah 26:19). Daniel 12:2 said, "Many of those who sleep in the dust of the earth will awake, some to eternal life, some to shame and eternal contempt." The resurrection was also described in the New Testament. "For the Lord Himself will descend from heaven . . . the dead in Christ will rise first. Then we who are still alive will be caught up" (1 Thessalonians 4:16–17). The resurrection of the dead will take place in that day—in that age. When that takes place, there will be no marriage and no death. Matthew 24:31 says, "He will send out His angels . . . they will gather His elect from the four winds." In John 5:28, Jesus said, "Do not be amazed . . . all who are in the graves will hear His voice and come out . . . to the resurrection of life . . . [or] judgment." In John 11:25,

---

[2] Earl D. Radmacher, Ronald B. Allen, and H. Wayne House, eds., *Nelson's New Illustrated Bible Commentary* (Nashville: Thomas Nelson, 1999), 1293.

[3] Radmacher et al., 1293.

Jesus said, "I am the resurrection and the life. The one who believes in me, even if he dies, will live."

Luke 20:39–40: Why did the scribes respond, "Teacher, you have spoken well"? Jesus had just reiterated what the Law and Prophets said. They recognized that Jesus' answer was right according to their Scriptures, so "they no longer dared to ask Him anything." Through loving them and listening to them, Jesus discerned what they needed to hear. The Holy Spirit inside Jesus took over the situation and answered them exactly as they needed to be answered. In 1 Corinthians 9, Paul showed us how to interact with people. Paul made himself "a slave to everyone, to win more people. To the Jews I became like a Jew, to win Jews" (v. 19–20). What did Jesus do to interact with the scribes and win them to believe in Him? Jesus spoke their language, exactly what they needed to hear. He recited Exodus, Moses, and the burning bush story. Paul became like those "under the law" or "like one without the law" to win people to Christ (v. 20–21). To the weak, Paul became weak (not overbearing), using "every possible means, save some" (v. 22). Jesus and Paul went after the lost sheep. The American church often franchises everything from somewhere else. They may do what others do and implement into their community what worked in other churches instead of interacting in a way to meet the needs of the people in their area. Jesus engaged the religious people so well that they complimented Him on what He said. Even though they didn't agree, they came to the same page.

Luke 20:41–44: Jesus didn't stop there; instead, He asked them a question: "How can they say that the Messiah is the Son of David? For David himself says in the book of Psalms: The Lord declared to my Lord, 'Sit at My right hand . . . how then can the Messiah be his Son?" Jesus quoted David's words from Psalm 110:1.

Luke 20:44: "How can the Messiah be his Son?" If David recognized Him as Lord, the Messiah must be his God, the Messiah who is in control. Jesus was identified as the *Son of Man*. The first phrase identified Jesus as God and the second phrase identified Him as man. Jesus is the Son of God and the *Son of Man*. In Acts 2:32–36, Peter explained that they were witnesses to the fact that God had resurrected Jesus and exalted Him to the right hand of God. Peter concluded, "Let all the house of Israel know with certainty that God made this Jesus, whom you crucified, both Lord and Master" (v. 36). In Acts 13:22–23, Paul confirmed that God had promised to bring forth Jesus the Savior from David's descendants. This fulfilled God's promised to David in 2 Samuel 7:12–14 that His Son would come through David.

Closing

Romans 1:3–4 says, "Concerning His Son, Jesus Christ our Lord, who was a descendant of David according to the flesh, and who has been declared to be the powerful Son of God by the resurrection from the dead according to the Spirit of holiness." The reason the religious had a hard time comprehending the Lord as the *Son of Man* was because they didn't believe in the resurrection. Their hearts were hardened, and they were blinded to the truth. Jesus warned the disciples to beware of these religious leaders because they had this deliberate hypocrisy as a cover-up to fool people with their own truths and their own identities.[4] They didn't want to point people to the ultimate truth, and "they rejected their own Messiah and voted to crucify him."[5] Because they never bought into the truth that the Old Testament talked about the resurrection from the dead that would come through the Lord Jesus Christ Himself, they led a nation into ruin in their time. The religious leaders hardened their hearts. Hebrews 3:7–8 warns not to be like them. We must not harden our hearts to the truth—the resurrection and the life of Jesus Christ.

Daily Word

The scribes and the chief priests wanted to get rid of Jesus so they looked for a way to get their hands on Him. They asked Jesus many questions, trying to trap Him. Jesus discerned their craftiness in questioning Him and was slow to speak, using wisdom when answering them. He answered so well, they no longer dared to ask Him anything.

As you walk with Jesus, those around you may question you in an attempt to make you stumble in your faith. Remember, craftiness is a tool of the enemy. Just as the serpent was crafty with Eve in the garden, the enemy will send crafty people your way to try and shake your faith in Christ. But like Jesus, through the power of the Holy Spirit, you are filled with discernment and wisdom for all situations. When you respond, slow down as you speak, and don't take offense from others. Walk in the authority you have in Christ, and speak truth in love. Love never fails.

Some of the scribes answered, "Teacher, You have spoken well." And they no longer dared to ask Him anything. —Luke 20:39–40

Further Scripture: Genesis 3:1; Luke 12:12; Ephesians 4:14–15

---

[4] Wiersbe, 208.

[5] Wiersbe, 208.

Questions

1. Jesus taught in the temple and preached the gospel. What does "gospel" mean? Do you live as though you believe in the gospel? Do you share it with others? If not, what prevents you from doing so?

2. The chief priests, scribes, and elders confronted Jesus (Luke 20:1–2). What was their issue with Him? Have you ever had "religious" people confront you? Is this ever warranted? (Matthew 18:15–17; 1 Timothy 5:1–2; 2 Timothy 4:2)

3. In Luke 20:25 Jesus said, "Give back to Caesar the things that are Caesar's, and to God the things that are God's." What are those things that are God's?

4. What did the Holy Spirit highlight to you in Luke 20 through the reading or the teaching?

Lesson 65: Luke 21
Son of Man: The Coming of the Son of Man

Teaching Notes

Intro

Events in Luke's Gospel are building and moving to a climax. Luke 21:1–4 talked about the widow's gift, the two tiny coins that she gave to the temple treasury. Then Jesus predicted the destruction of the temple in Luke 21:5–6, the signs of the end of the age in Luke 21:7–19, and the destruction of Jerusalem in Luke 21:20–24. But in this lesson, I want to unpack the remaining verses in the chapter.

Teaching

Luke 21:25: Jesus described the events that would indicate His return was drawing near. The judgment God is going to send on the earth will happen in the last half of the time known as "Jacob's trouble."[1] Jeremiah 30:7 says, "How awful that day will be . . . but he will be delivered out of it." That means there is still hope for the Jewish people. The phrase "roaring seas and waves" appears in other verses. Psalm 46:1–6 says, "God is our refuge and strength . . . though the earth trembles and . . . its waters roar and foam . . . God will help her. Nations rage, kingdoms topple," but God will establish Himself in the midst of the chaos around the world. We should expect the nations to be bewildered by the roaring seas and waves.

Luke 21:26: "People will faint from fear and expectation of the things that are coming on the world, because the celestial powers will be shaken." Matthew recorded a similar statement in his Gospel (Matthew 24:29).

Revelation 15—19 describes the judgment God will send on earth during the second half of the seven years of tribulation. In the first three-and-a-half years, the world will see peace. In the second half of the seven-year agreement (Daniel 9), the antichrist will break the agreement and move to Jerusalem to set up his image in the temple. When this takes place, all the things we just described will begin to take place. God will begin sending down His wrath. Will believers

[1] Warren W. Wiersbe, *The Wiersbe Bible Commentary: New Testament* (Colorado Springs: David C Cook, 2007), 211.

be a part of this tribulation time? In a pre-tribulation view, believers won't be here on earth when this takes place. In a mid-tribulation view, believers will be here until the middle of this time; we'll be here during the years of peace but will be taken out before the wrath comes. In a post-tribulation view, believers will be here on earth during all seven years of this time of tribulation. No matter which position you take, you better be ready for the *Son of Man* to come. Believers have to be prepared because we might have to go through this.

Luke 21:27: "Then they will see the Son of Man coming in a cloud with power and great glory." Compare this to Matthew 24:30, "Then the sign of the Son of Man will appear in the sky." Luke didn't include that the sign of the *Son of Man* would appear first. No one knows what the sign of the *Son of Man* is, but as soon as it appears, everyone will see the *Son of Man* coming on the clouds. Something will catch the attention of all the peoples on the earth and cause them to mourn. According to Daniel 7:13–14, the sign will produce fear. "I saw one like a son of man coming with the clouds of heaven." Daniel prophesied the *Son of Man* would come. Revelation 1:7 says, "Look! He is coming with the clouds, and every eye will see Him." Whether you're in Russia, America, Australia, China, Mozambique, every eye will see Him. Maybe this will be accomplished through media. We have no way to know for sure how this will happen.

Luke 21:28: "Stand up and lift up your heads, because your redemption is near!" Psalm 24:7 says, "Lift up your heads . . . then the King of Glory will come in." The same mentality was demonstrated in the rich man and Lazarus. The rich man was head down, more concerned with material and temporal things. But when your head is up, you're looking for the Lord in everything. Psalm 111:9 says, "He has sent redemption to His people . . . His name is holy and awe-inspiring." Isaiah 63:4 says, "For I planned the day of vengeance, and the year of My redemption came." We can expect tribulation and redemption.

Luke 21:29–33: Jesus put all these things together by telling a parable. In verses 29–30, Jesus used the example of the tree that put out leaves to indicate summer is near. In Matthew 24:36, Jesus said that no one knows the time when the *Son of Man* will return. Even when Jesus was on earth as the *Son of Man*, He did not know. Mark 11 said the same thing. It might actually take place near summertime, based on verse 30.

In verse 31, Jesus said the kingdom of God would be near when they saw "these things." What things? The signs, *Son of Man* coming on the clouds, celestial powers shaking, people fainting from fear and expectation of things coming, anguish on earth among the nations. Jesus was clear: There is a *now* kingdom of God and a *future* kingdom of God. This is talking about the *future* kingdom of

God, when Jesus comes back to implement the kingdom of God. *Nelson's Commentary* said that when we see cosmic signs and earthly chaos, then we will see a spiritual change.[2] Isaiah 27:12–13 says, "On that day . . . you Israelites will be gathered one by one . . . and they will worship the Lord at Jerusalem on the holy mountain." We will see revival among the nation of Israel. Matthew 24:31 says, "He will send out His angels with a loud trumpet, and they will gather His elect." We will begin to see the gathering of His chosen people. Matthew 24:32 says, "I assure you: This generation will certainly not pass away until these things take place." One generation will see this unfold. What if we're that generation? What if we experience these seven years of crazy chaos, peace, turmoil, transition, the antichrist showing up, and the *Son of Man* coming back? What if we get to be a part of this ridiculous journey? We're supposed to live like we will. Our heartbeat should be, "Come, Lord Jesus!"

Luke 21:33: "Heaven and earth will pass away." The universe will literally be gone and then we'll see a new Israel, a new structure, a new earth, and a new heaven. "But my words will never pass away." Jesus confirmed what was written in Isaiah 40:8: "The grass withers, the flowers fade, but the word of our God remains forever." Luke 16:17 says, "It is easier for heaven and earth to pass away than for one stroke of a letter in the law to drop out." Everything in the Old Testament has to come to fruition and fulfillment in the New Testament, the New Covenant. God's Word always stays true to what He said in the beginning. Every one of the books of the Bible points to the Messiah. Jesus didn't come to destroy but to fulfill the Law and the Prophets (Matthew 5:17).

Because of all that is described in Scripture, what if we are part of seeing the *Son of Man* return on the clouds? What if we get to witness the coming of the Messiah? What if we get to see, as Wiersbe said, "the nations gather in the valley of Megiddo in Israel and fight the antichrist in Jerusalem, then see the sign of Christ, and then the *Son of Man* return to earth, defeat His enemies, be received by the Jews, and see the kingdom of God established here on earth"?[3] What if we got to see this reign on earth of 1,000 years take off?

Are we ready to see the church live out Luke 21:34–38? "Be on your guard so . . . that day doesn't come on you unexpectedly like a trap . . . Be alert at all times, praying that you may have strength to escape all these things." As the church, we should pray now that we will have the strength to endure the tribulation so that we can stand before the *Son of Man*. Likewise, 1 John 2:28 says, "So now, little children, remain in Him, so that when He appears, we may have boldness and

---

[2] Earl D. Radmacher, Ronald B. Allen, and H. Wayne House, eds., *Nelson's New Illustrated Bible Commentary* (Nashville: Thomas Nelson, 1999), 1296.

[3] Wiersbe, n.p.

not be ashamed before Him at His coming." Imagine if this was the challenge all of us took. This is a reality that will take place. Our calling is to get people ready for His return. What if the first step is to start praying for the strength to sustain the end times?

Closing

Jesus gave several instructions for preparing for the return of the *Son of Man*. We should be aware of what is happening because our redemption is near (Luke 21:28). When we see these things happening, we should recognize that the kingdom of God is near (Luke 21:31). We should be on guard (Luke 21:34) so we don't go back to the rich man's ways, the earthly things. We have to keep our minds on the eternal things. We should be alert at all times (Luke 21:36). One of the ways to remain alert is to pray for strength.[4] As the body of Christ, we have to strengthen our faith. To do that, we pray for faith. We have to be ready for the *Son of Man*'s return.

Daily Word

Jesus the Messiah is returning. Therefore Jesus repeatedly told His disciples to be ready, to be on guard, to look for the signs, and to not be surprised! He wanted their minds to be ready and not dulled from drunkenness and the worries of life. If their minds were dulled, the day would catch them off guard.

Notice how Jesus said to be on guard so your mind is not dulled from drunkenness *and* the worries of life. But *how* are you to be on guard? Jesus says by prayer, thanksgiving, and setting your mind on the hope in Him. Prayer will give you the strength to stand firm and not be ashamed of the gospel. As you embrace the anxieties of life, resist the temptation to worry or to seek out temporary pleasures. Rather, press into Jesus and remain steadfast. In doing so, you will be ready for Christ's return.

Be on your guard, so that your minds are not dulled from carousing, drunkenness, and worries of life, or that day will come on you unexpectedly like a trap. —Luke 21:34–35

Further Scripture: Luke 21:36; Colossians 4:2; 1 Peter 1:13

---

[4] Wiersbe, 211–12.

Questions

1. Jesus' followers were told, "They will lay their hands on you and will perse-cute you, delivering you to the synagogues and prisons, bringing you before kings and governors for my Name's sake" (Luke 21:12–13 NASB). What opportunity did Jesus say this would lead to? Have you ever viewed hard-ships through the lens of kingdom opportunities? If so, share the story with someone.

2. In Luke 21:16, Jesus warned His listeners that they would be betrayed, and some would be put to death; yet in verse 18, He told them not a hair of their head would perish. Explain this. (Luke 12:4–9)

3. Jesus often referred to Himself as the *Son of Man* (Luke 21:27, 36). What did this title mean to the Jews (Daniel 7:13–14)? Why do you think He used the third person point of view?

4. How is being on your guard in Luke 21:34 different from keeping on the alert in Luke 21:36?

5. What did the Holy Spirit highlight to you in Luke 21 through the reading or the teaching?

Lesson 66: Luke 22
Son of Man: The Lord's Supper

Teaching Notes

Intro

We are almost done with the Gospel of Luke! There are 24 chapters in Luke. We are wrapping up the synoptic Gospels. The book of Matthew describes Jesus as *King*, the book of Mark describes Him as *Servant*, and the book of Luke describes Him as *Son of Man*. We begin to see the humanity side of Jesus. We are going to walk through the Lord's Supper. It is an incredible picture! Christ invites every one of us to join Him at the table!

Teaching

Luke 22:1–6: The Festival of Unleavened Bread, also known as Passover, was approaching. We also see the fruition of the plot to kill Christ. Even in Mark, Jesus predicted His death three times.

Luke 22:7–13: How were they supposed to get ready for the Passover? Jesus asked His disciples to enter a city, find a guy carrying a jug, and stalk him! They were to ask this man where his guest room was where Jesus could celebrate the Passover with His disciples. The Lord goes before us to take care of the details (Exodus 12:13).

This Passover paints a picture of how Jesus remembered this time as a festival of the Lord and also honored the words of Moses. When we talk about the Lord's Table, everything is about remembrance! This Passover was also a prediction of the future. Wiersbe wrote, "Passover commemorated the Exodus of Israel from Egypt centuries before, but He would accomplish a greater 'exodus' on the cross"[1] (Luke 9:31).

Luke 22:14: When it came time for Jesus and the disciples to celebrate the Passover meal, they reclined at the table. Wiersbe wrote, "Jesus served as the host."[2]

---

[1] Warren Wiersbe. *The Bible Exposition Commentary: New Testament* (Colorado Springs: David C. Cook, 2008), 265.

[2] Wiersbe, 265.

Jesus always greeted His disciples with a traditional kiss of peace. John 13:23 shows us that John was on His right and Judas was on His left. He then kissed all the disciples. In Ephesians 2:20 it is written that the apostles were the 12 disciples. In John 13:1–20, we see that after the kiss and a greeting, Jesus picked up a towel and washed their feet. When Jesus washed their feet, He was modeling service and humility.

Luke 22:15: Jesus then revealed that this would be His last meal with them. He knew this was His last meal and that it was a fulfillment of what was to come. Jesus was pursuing the prophetic word (Matthew 5:17). In John 13:1, John wrote that Jesus loved His disciples and that He loved them until the end.

Luke 22:16: Jesus said, "This is my last meal!" Constable wrote, "Jesus announced that He would 'never again eat' another Passover meal until what the Passover anticipated, namely, His own sacrificial death, had transpired (cf. 9:31) . . . He would eat with them 'again' next in 'the kingdom,' specifically at the messianic banquet at the beginning of the kingdom."[3] He would eat with the disciples again at the messianic banquet in heaven. Revelation 19:9 is an incredible picture of the messianic banquet. This is what Jesus was talking about!

Luke 22:17: Jesus took a cup, gave thanks, and then shared it with His disciples. There is debate about which cup Jesus actually used during the Passover meal because we know four cups are used. Here are the four types of cups: (1) Used with preliminary course to bless the day; (2) after a liturgical explanation of the day with singing of the Hallel Psalms; (3) following the meal of the lamb, unleavened bread, and bitter herbs; and (4) following the concluding portion of the Hallel Psalms.[4] The cup shared would have been a common cup—only one.

Luke 22:18: Once again, Jesus implied that He would not drink again with His disciples until the messianic banquet. Jesus said, "This is my last one!"

Luke 22:19: Jesus took bread and gave thanks. The bread was a representation of His body. In Deuteronomy 16:3, the author shared that unleavened bread was a symbol of hardship and sin. Jesus gave the disciples bread, only one loaf of bread. I think it is important to note that it was one, representing one body of Christ. We forget that we are the body of Christ. We as Christians should not be so divided!

---

[3] Thomas L. Constable, *Expository Notes of Dr. Thomas Constable: Luke*, 465, https:// planobiblechapel.org/tcon/notes/pdf/luke.pdf.

[4] Darrell L. Bock, *Messiah in the Passover* (Grand Rapids: Kregel, 2017), 73.

Remember that Passover was a sacrifice offering. This was His last one because after His death there would be no need for a sacrifice offering. Jesus was the ultimate sacrifice offering. (Leviticus 6:25, 7:15; 1 Corinthians 10:16; 11:26; Hebrews 10:14.) In Jeremiah 31:31, we see a transition to the New Covenant.

Luke 22:20: In the same way He took a cup, probably the third, which was the cup of redemption. Jesus said, "My time is coming." Redemption only comes through the blood of Christ. Leviticus 17:11 says, "For the life of a creature is in the blood, and I have appointed it to you to make atonement on the altar for your lives, since it is the lifeblood that makes atonement."

Luke 22:21–22: Jesus then shared that he would be betrayed by one of His disciples. The disciples were puzzled, as if hearing it for the first time. This wasn't new news. Jesus previously predicted these betrayals in Matthew 17:22 and Matthew 20:18.

Closing

Why do we celebrate the Lord's Supper? We've been asked to do three things.

We have been asked to *remember*:
Luke 22:19: "And He took bread, gave thanks, broke it, gave it to them, and said, 'This is My body, which is given for you. Do this in remembrance of Me.'"

We have been asked to *participate* in how Christ lived His life:
1 Corinthians 10:16: "The cup of blessing that we give thanks for, is it not a sharing in the blood of Christ? The bread that we break, is it not a sharing in the body of Christ?"
John 6:53: "So Jesus said unto them, 'I assure you: Unless you eat the flesh of the Son of Man, and drink his blood, you do not have life in yourselves.'"
Mark 8:34b: "If anyone wants to be My follower, he must deny himself, take up his cross, and follow Me." This is how we participate in the bread and the cup.

We must look to *proclaim* His death into the world:
1 Corinthians 11:25–26: "In the same way, after supper He also took the cup and said, 'This cup is the new covenant established by My blood. Do this, as often as you drink it, in remembrance of Me.' For as often as you eat this bread and drink the cup, you proclaim the Lord's death until He comes."

Daily Word

While Jesus ate His final meal with the disciples, He shared with them His desire to eat this Passover meal with them before He suffered death on the Cross. He knew this time was near. Jesus served as a sin offering, dying for all the sins of the world so you could be saved. Years after Jesus' final meal with His disciples, we participate in the recreation of this meal. Communion, or the Lord's Supper, is a form of worship and remembrance of Jesus' sacrificial life for those who follow Him.

You may walk into church on any given Sunday and be given the opportunity to partake in communion. It may even be at your home with family and friends or at a wedding ceremony. As you partake in the Lord's Supper, you are asked to *remember* what Christ did for you on the Cross. You are asked to *participate* in how Christ lived His life. And finally, you are asked to *proclaim* His death until He returns again. Today, give thanks for Jesus and His life sacrificed to save the world.

And He took bread, gave thanks, broke it, gave it to them, and said, "This is My body, which is given for you. Do this in remembrance of Me." In the same way He also took the cup after supper and said, "This cup is the new covenant established by My blood; it is shed for you." —Luke 22:19–20

Further Reading: 1 Corinthians 11:24, 26; Hebrews 10:10, 14

Questions

1. Scripture prophesied that the Messiah would be betrayed by a friend. Do you think Judas or the chief priests and officers were familiar with this prophecy (Psalms 41:9; 55:12–14)?

2. Jesus stated in Luke 22:16 that He wouldn't eat the Passover again until it was fulfilled in the kingdom of God. What does this mean (1 Corinthians 5:7)?

3. While with the 12 disciples, Jesus told them (Luke 22:26) that the greatest among them must become like the youngest. Do you think this is related to what He said about becoming like a child to enter the kingdom of heaven (Matthew 18:3; Luke 18:17)?

4. Peter stated with certainty that he would be willing to face prison or death for Jesus. Have you ever been afraid, as Peter was, and chose to allow fear to keep you silent or in denial to avoid persecution or suffering (Luke 22:33–34, 55–62)?

5. In Luke 22:69, Jesus again referred to Himself as the *Son of Man*. The council of elders asked Him directly if He was the Son of God. Jesus responded, "you say that I am" (v. 70). What was significant and scandalous to them about His response (Exodus 3:14, John 8:58)?

6. What did the Holy Spirit highlight to you in Luke 22 through the reading or the teaching?

Lesson 67: Luke 23
Son of Man: The Son of Man Reality

Teaching Notes

Intro

There are strange happenings going on in Luke 23. We've been talking about Jesus as the *Son of Man* and what that looks like. Today we will be looking at the humanity of Jesus. Jesus referred to Himself most often as the *Son of Man*. Read Hebrews 4:14–16 and notice the relatability of Jesus: He got hungry (Mark 11:12) and thirsty (John 19:28); He slept (Mark 4:38) and wept (John 11:35); He rejoiced and had fun (Luke 7:34); He got angry (Matthew 21:12–13); and Jesus suffered, was rejected, and was a man of sorrows (Isaiah 53:3). Today we'll dive fully into this "Son of Man" reality.

Teaching

Luke 23:1: The whole assembly was the Council of Elders (or the Sanhedrin, which means "sitting together" or "assembly"). There was a Lesser Sanhedrin of 23 judges appointed locally in each city. The great Sanhedrin had 71 judges, who among other roles, acted as the Supreme Court. With a problem like Jesus, the great Sanhedrin would have been involved.

Luke 23:2: Right out of the gate in this chapter, Jesus was identified as *man*. That was the lens through which the Sanhedrin viewed Him. The word *man* is used eight times in relation to Jesus in this chapter. The accusative pretenses of the Sanhedrin were downright hilarious, really. The absurdity is astounding. In Luke 20:21, the Jewish leaders accused Jesus of "subverting the nation," but they were the ones deceiving and manipulating the system. They falsely accused Him of "opposing taxes," but Jesus was the One who hung out with tax collectors, loving people that were totally sold out to the cause of Roman taxation (Luke 20:24–26). They also accused Jesus of "claiming to be the Messiah," while they were the ones claiming it and trying to drag it out of Him (Luke 22:71).

Luke 23:3–6: Jesus didn't respond to Pilate's question, and Pilate said he found no fault with this *man* (vv. 3–4). The Jews said Jesus had been causing trouble by stirring up the people. Pilate asked if this *man* was a Galilean (vv. 5–6).

Luke 23:7: Pilate did not want to deal with this inconvenience. He was caught in the middle of an awkward situation. If Pilate didn't listen to the Sanhedrin, a riot could break out, but if he listened to them, then he feared a riot from Jesus' followers. Since the accusations were falling flat, Pilate passed Jesus over to Herod Antipas.

Luke 23:8–9: Herod was happy to see Jesus. Herod's dad was responsible for murdering hundreds of firstborn Jews because of major insecurity issues. Herod Antipas also had Jesus' cousin John the Baptist beheaded because John blew the whistle on Antipas's illegitimate divorce and remarriage to his half-brother's wife. The Antipas families had the trait of being dysfunctional. Herod wanted a show, to see a miracle from Jesus Christ "Superstar": "So, you are the Christ, the great Jesus Christ. Prove to me that you're no fool, walk across my swimming pool." Compare verse 9 to Isaiah 53:7—"He did not open His mouth."

Luke 23:10–14: In verse 10, "The chief priests and the scribes stood by, vehemently accusing Him." Satan means "accuser," and the word "vehemently" in the Greek, (*eutonos*) means "in a well-strung manner, vigorously, powerfully." The spirit of antichrist is full force, violently pressing the highest degree of opposition. Why did Herod and Pilate become friends? One idea is that, although Pilate didn't know or didn't care who Jesus was, and although Herod and his soldiers treated Jesus like a circus sideshow, both Herod Antipas and Pilate were mutually reluctant to execute Jesus. Throughout this account, Pilate is consistently the voice of reason. Although a pagan polytheist, Pilate must have had common sense (Proverbs 6:16–19).

Luke 23:15–21: Pilate had to release someone and planned to release Jesus, but the crowd wanted Barabbas, who was in prison because he had led a rebellion and committed murder. Jesus had agreed with the Sanhedrin that He was the Messiah. Isaiah 53:9 says, "He had done no violence, nor was there any deceit in His mouth." Mark said that Barabbas was "imprisoned with rioters." John called him a "bandit," and Matthew said he was a "notorious prisoner." It's interesting to note his name means son (Bar) of the father (Abba). The Son of the Father took the place for the son of the father. Pilate tried again to release Jesus, and the crowd kept shouting for Him to be crucified. This, of course, is the fulfillment of prophecy (Deuteronomy 21:23).

Luke 23:22–25: Pilate tried a third time, asking, "What has this man done wrong?" Note the persistency of Pilate. More prophecy was fulfilled here as the *Son of Man* was whipped (Isaiah 53:5). Pilate finally caved in and granted their demand but said, "I am innocent of this man's blood" (Matthew 27:24).

Closing

As we close this out, let's look at three Scripture passages, which point to Jesus as the *Son of Man*:

First, these prophecies were all fulfilled by Jesus:

> Psalm 22:14–19: "I am poured out like water, and all my bones are disjointed; my heart is like wax, melting within me. My strength is dried up like baked clay; my tongue sticks to the roof of my mouth. You put me into the dust of death. For dogs have surrounded me; a gang of evildoers has closed in on me; they pierced my hands and my feet. I can count all my bones; people look and stare at me. They divided my garments among themselves, and they cast lots for my clothing. But You, LORD, don't be far away. My strength, come quickly to help me."

Second, the *Son of Man* was bruised, He was hungry, and He thirsted on the cross.

> Isaiah 53:5–6: "But He was pierced because of our transgressions, crushed because of our iniquities; punishment for our peace was on Him, and we are healed by His wounds. We all went astray like sheep; we all have turned to our own way; and the LORD has punished Him for the iniquity of us all."

Third, even though He was God, He came as man.

> Philippians 2:6–8: "Who, existing in the form of God, did not consider equality with God as something to be used for His own advantage. Instead He emptied Himself by assuming the form of a slave, taking on the likeness of men. And when He had come as a man in His external form, He humbled Himself by becoming obedient to the point of death—even to death on a cross."

Daily Word

Jesus, the Son of Man, was fully God and fully human. The whole assembly wanted Jesus charged as a criminal. But Pilate found no grounds for charging him. Since Jesus was considered a Galilean, Pilate brought in Herod Antipas, the ruler of Galilee, to help make the decision. Still, Herod agreed with Pilate and found no reason to charge the Jesus with death. However, they agreed to whip Him, mock Him, and call Him insults. Eventually Pilate gave into the cries of the assembly and agreed to crucify Jesus, even if there was no substantial reasoning. Therefore Jesus endured humiliation and physical pain until He died on the Cross.

Your Savior, Jesus, the Son of Man, understands and can sympathize with you and your pain. The Word says you will suffer. You will face trials. You will be persecuted. Similarly, Jesus endured suffering, trials, and persecution. However, Jesus does not leave you alone. Even today, whatever you face, turn to the Lord. He understands the pain and suffering, and He promises to give you the strength you need to endure. Jesus promises He is at work in the middle of your pain and will restore, establish, strengthen, and support you. Ask Him for help. Turn to Him in your moment of weakness, and He will strengthen you. Remember today, you are not alone in your agony.

But they kept up the pressure, demanding with loud voices that He be crucified. And their voices won out. So Pilate decided to grant their demand and released the one they were asking for, who had been thrown into prison for rebellion and murder. But he handed Jesus over to their will. —Luke 23:23–24

Further Scripture: Hebrews 4:15; James 1:2–3; 1 Peter 5:10

Questions

1. Why do you think Luke mentioned in verse 12 that Herod and Pilate, who had been enemies with each other, became friends the day of Jesus' trial? (Psalm 2:1; Acts 4:27–28)

2. Do you see Luke 23:25 as another instance where the Israelites reject God (His Son) as King, in favor of their own will? (1 Samuel 8:6–7; Luke 23:2; John 19:15)

3. Most of us are familiar with Luke 23:34: "Father, forgive them, for they do not know what they are doing." What does He mean by this? Have you ever been treated unjustly and chosen to forgive those responsible? Are we, as His followers, called to forgiveness? (Matthew 18:21–22; Mark 11:25–26; Luke 17:3–4; Ephesians 4:32) Do you find this a difficult thing to do?

4. Neither Pilate nor Herod found any cause for death in Jesus (Luke 23:14–15). One of the thieves said He had done nothing wrong, and even the centurion deduced Jesus was innocent (Luke 23:41, 47). For whose crimes, then, was He punished? (Isaiah 53:5; Romans 4:25; 1 Corinthians 15:3)

5. Is it significant that in death, Jesus was wrapped in linen, the material priestly garments were made from? (Exodus 28:4–5; Luke 23:53)

6. What did the Holy Spirit highlight to you in Luke 23 through the reading or the teaching?

Lesson 68: Luke 24

Son of Man: How to Engage Others with the Risen Lord

Teaching Notes

Intro

This is the final lesson in the Gospel of Luke. Luke 24:1–2 gives the backdrop for this chapter. It's post-Resurrection day, and when the women arrived at the tomb, the stone was rolled away. Jesus predicted multiple times He would die and be resurrected three days later. The women were perplexed, but two men stood before them (v. 4) and pronounced Jesus' Resurrection (vv. 5–6) and reminded them that Jesus had told them the *Son of Man* would be betrayed, be crucified, and rise on the third day (v. 7). The women remembered Jesus' words and returned to tell the others (vv. 8–10). But the disciples didn't believe the women (v. 11). Peter ran to the tomb, looked in and saw the linen cloths, and went home amazed (v. 12). While the women and Peter were excited and amazed that Jesus had risen, two disciples left Jerusalem feeling discouraged, thinking Jesus was still dead. The church has to believe Jesus has overcome death as well, that He has risen from the dead, and that He conquered sin. Instead the church tends to act like Jesus is still dead, not victorious. Today we're going to consider four words that can equip us to be evangelists, to be able to share with those who are discouraged or defeated that Jesus is the Son of God who rose again.

Teaching

Luke 24:13–16: The same day the news of Jesus' resurrection was received, these two disciples were headed to Emmaus (the name means "warm bath"), a village about seven miles west of Jerusalem. They were discussing everything that had happened—crucifixion, death, resurrection, the empty tomb, and the women showing up. Their conversation became heated, possibly about whether or not the news was real, and Jesus appeared and walked with them. Jesus went out of His way to find them—love came near and walked with them. This is the opposite of the model of the church today. We expect people to come to us. Love comes from God (1 John 4:19). *Love* is the first step for us to begin engaging the community (1 Thessalonians 3:12). *Love* is the first word.

Luke 24:17–25: The second word is *listen*. Jesus asked them about their dispute. To listen we need to ask questions. Jesus didn't respond to their responses, but He continued to listen. Constable states that according to early Christian tradition, Cleopas was Jesus' uncle and Joseph's brother, and he became a leader of the Jerusalem church. He could have been the husband of "Mary, the wife of Clopas (a variant spelling of the same name), who was present at Jesus' crucifixion."[1] According to the early Byzantine church, Luke was the unnamed disciple on the road.[2] So Jesus talked to His uncle, who identified Him as a prophet. They talked about the crucifixion, but they didn't talk about the resurrection. As we listen to people, we need to listen to the heart issue.

The disciples told Jesus they had hoped the Christ was the One who was to redeem Israel, that women had discovered the empty tomb and seen a vision of angels who said Jesus was alive, and that some of the other disciples had gone to the tomb as well and found it empty. Their words poured out to Jesus (vv. 22–24).

Luke 24:25–27: Jesus told them they had been "unwise and slow" in believing what the prophets had spoken. In the Old Testament, a fool is defined as one who knows the Scriptures but doesn't adhere to what it says and doesn't allow the truth to influence his behavior. Jesus asked, "Didn't the Messiah have to suffer these things and enter into His glory?" Then Jesus led them through the Scriptures about the Messiah in the Old Testament (v. 27).

Luke 24:28–29: The third word is *discernment*, which means to perceive or recognize something from the Holy Spirit. Jesus gave the impression that He was going to continue on. *Discernment* comes from the Holy Spirit. Every person we meet is different, and *discernment* shows us how to relate and engage to each. They urged Him to stay with them. *Discernment* understands where the point of entry is.

Luke 24:30–35: The fourth word is *respond*. The Holy Spirit shows how to *respond*. Then Jesus broke the bread at the table and gave it to them, and they realized who He was. Their understanding may have come from the Lord's Supper or from the feeding of the 5,000 or the teaching about how Jesus was the bread of life. Jesus *responded* to them by showing them the bread. But as soon as they recognized Him, Jesus left them and disappeared from their sight. As soon as they realized Jesus had been with them, they got up and walked back to Jerusalem to tell the other disciples they had seen Him. They returned with victory because they had seen the risen Lord.

---

[1] Thomas L. Constable, *Expository Notes of Dr. Thomas Constable: Luke*, 518, https://planobiblechapel.org/tcon/notes/pdf/luke.pdf.

[2] Constable, 518.

Closing

The reality at the end of Luke is that Jesus is alive. Go *love* someone today. *Listen* to what he or she is saying. *Discern* from the Holy Spirit how to engage that person, and possibly *respond* by inviting that person to the table.

Daily Word

The disciples were startled and frightened when they first saw Jesus resurrected and physically with them again after His death on the Cross. However, Jesus spent time with them. They invited Him to stay with them for the evening. They shared bread together. Then He took the time to explain the Scriptures concerning His role as the Messiah and how the prophecies were fulfilled. He walked with them and blessed them to send them out as His witnesses. And then Jesus left them again and ascended to heaven. Because the disciples spent this time with Jesus, it helped ease their worries and fears. They sought truth and answers with Jesus. Then, after Jesus ascended into heaven, they had great joy and continually praised God.

In a similar way, you will find joy when you spend time in Jesus' in presence, seeking Him for answers to your questions. It is important for you to take time to spend with Jesus. Yes, life is busy, and there are many places to turn to with answers to your questions or solutions for your fears. But follow the example of the disciples. Today, take time to sit in Jesus' presence, study His word, and seek Him in prayer. As you seek Him, He will guide you along your path of life. You will be filled with joy and strength for the day.

After worshipping Him, they returned to Jerusalem with great joy. And they were continually in the temple complex praising God. —Luke 24:52–53

Further Scripture: Psalm 16:11; Psalm 28:7; Jeremiah 15:16

Questions

1. Why do you think the disciples responded the way they did to the women's report about Jesus (Luke 24:11)? Did they simply forget His word, not understand, or not believe what Jesus told them (Matthew 16:21; Luke 9:22)? How can you keep from forgetting or not understanding what the Lord says to you? (John 14:26)

2. What was the emotional state of the two travelers walking to Emmaus? Why were they feeling this way?

3. How do you see the compassion and patience of Jesus in speaking with the two travelers?

4. How do we know we can pour out our hearts to Him and He will listen and help us? (Psalm 62:8; Hebrews 4:16)

5. What were some evidences that should have led the two men to believe in the risen Christ? (Mark 16:6; 6:9, 12, 14; Luke 24:2–3, 6; 24:12; John 20:3–6)

6. Luke 24:37 (NKJV) says the disciples were terrified and frightened when Jesus appeared to them. How did Jesus use this time to calm their nerves (Luke 24:36; John 20:19–21)? How do you sense the peace of Christ during tough trials or circumstances? (Romans 5:1; Philippians 4:6–7)

7. What did the Holy Spirit highlight to you in Luke 24 through the reading or the teaching?

Lesson 69: John 1
Son of God: The Word Became Flesh

Teaching Notes

Intro

One of the things you need to know as we begin our study of John is that 98 percent of the material is unique to John. What we're going to see in our study is all new and fresh. Very rarely will you see material in John that you've already seen in Matthew, Mark, or Luke. Wiersbe says, "Whereas the first three Gospels major on described events in the life of Christ, John emphasized the meaning of these events."[1] John, the writer of this Gospel, described himself as "the disciple Jesus loved." John's older brother was James; together, they were known as the Sons of Thunder (Mark 3:17) and as the sons of Zebedee. John was also an apostle. Peter, James, and John were featured in Matthew as Jesus' inner circle.

John was a close associate of Peter and is often referred to as an eyewitness. He also wrote 1 John, 2 John, 3 John, and Revelation (1 John 1:1–4). John wrote five books of the Bible; his is a first-person account. The Gospel was written between AD 80–90, some "fifty years after John witnessed Jesus' earthly ministry."[2] Because of the large amount of unique material in the Gospel, John provided support for the other Gospels.[3] Of the four Gospels, John is the most theological and it emphasizes that *Jesus is God*.

The purpose of the book is found in John 20:30–31: "Jesus performed many other signs in the presence of His disciples that are not written in this book. But these are written so that you may believe Jesus is the Messiah, the *Son of God*, and by believing you may have life in His name." Signs and miracles are presented throughout the Gospel of John. MacArthur points out two themes for the book: evangelistic (100 times "believe" is mentioned in the book) and apologetic (to show the readers that Jesus' identity is the incarnate God). MacArthur outlines John 1:1–18 into six sections[4] that will be used below.

---

[1] Warren W. Wiersbe, *The Bible Exposition Commentary: John* (Colorado Springs: David C. Cook, 1989), 284.

[2] John MacArthur, *The MacArthur Bible Commentary* (Nashville: Thomas Nelson, 2005), 1339.

[3] MacArthur, 1339.

[4] MacArthur, 1343–46.

Teaching

John 1:1–3: The Eternal Christ. "In the beginning" (v. 1) relates back to Genesis 1:1. The Word was in the beginning and was with God and was God. "The Greek construction emphasized that the Word had all the essence or attributes of deity, i.e., Jesus the Messiah was fully God."[5] There's no genealogy in John, because He doesn't need one. Jesus was in the beginning, and everything was created through Him. By *eternal*, we mean that Jesus has been here since before the beginning.

> Colossians 2:9: "For the entire fullness of God's nature dwells bodily in Christ."
> John 17:5: "Now, Father, glorify Me in Your presence with that glory I had with You before the world existed."
> Ephesians 3:9: "And to shed light for all about the administration of the mystery hidden for ages in God who created all things."
> Hebrews 1:2: "In these last days, He has spoken to us by His Son. God has appointed Him heir of all things and made the universe through Him."

John 1:4–5: The Incarnate Christ. John 5:26: "For just as the Father has life in Himself, so also He has granted to the Son to have life in Himself." So there is life in God. The language that you hear with God is the same language that you will hear with Christ. John 10:28 says, "I give them eternal life, and they will never perish—ever! No one will snatch them out of My hand." Verses 4–5 provide a comparison of *light* and *darkness*. Light is biblical truth; darkness is false. Light is holiness and purity; darkness is sin and wrongdoing. This comparison leads to the truth: "The powers of darkness are overcome by the person and work of the Son through His death on the cross."[6]

John 1:6–8: The Forerunner of Christ. John the Baptist came after 400 years of silence to testify about the light that was coming into the world. This points to the evangelistic nature of Jesus' coming: "Who gives light to everyone" (v. 9). John was preparing the way for the light to come. Verse 8 points out that John was *not* the light but came to testify about it.

John 1:9–11: The Unrecognized Christ. John wrote that Jesus was coming into "the world." MacArthur explains that "John gives it several shades of meaning: (1) the physical created universe; (2) humanity in general; and (3) the invisible

---

[5] MacArthur, 1343.
[6] MacArthur, 1344.

spiritual system of evil dominated by Satan and all that it offers in opposition to God, His Word, and His people."[7] Jesus was coming into these environments in the world He created—He is the eternal Christ. But the world He created did not recognize Him. John stated that Jesus came to His own—the Jews—but they did not receive Him (v. 11). What Jesus received repeatedly from the Jewish people was rejection:

> John 10:25: "'I did tell you and you don't believe,' Jesus answered them. 'The works that I do in My Father's name testify about Me.'"

John 1:12–13: The Omnipotent Christ. John emphasized that though the Jewish people had rejected Christ, there was a remnant who believed.

John 1:14–18: The Glorious Christ. How do we know the Word was actually Christ? Because the Word became flesh (v. 14). Paul affirmed that fact to Timothy: "And most certainly, the mystery of godliness is great: He was manifested in the flesh, vindicated in the Spirit, seen by angels, preached among the nations, believed on in the world, taken up in glory" (1 Timothy 3:16). The statement, "The Word became flesh and took up residence," in the Greek means "to pitch a tabernacle." It means Jesus lived in the tabernacle. In the Old Testament, "God's Shekinah presence filled the entire structure. When the Word became flesh, the glorious presence of deity was embodied in Him."[8] The Jews who heard this would have automatically thought of Exodus 25:8, where God met Israel in a tent; Exodus 33:11, when God spoke to Moses face to face; and Exodus 40:34, when God's presence filled the tabernacle. Prophetically, these verses in Exodus point to John 1:14.

Closing

Eventually the glory of God departed from the disobedient Israel (Ezekiel 9:3; 10:4, 18; 11:22–23). Years later, the Word became flesh "and we observed His glory" (John 1:14)—the glory of the One come from the Father, full of grace and truth. All of that points out that Jesus is the answer.

Daily Word

John began his Gospel with the message that Jesus is life and this life is the light of men. Jesus as the light shines into the darkness. What if you said throughout your day these phrases of truth: "Jesus is my life. Jesus is my light"?

---

[7] MacArthur, 1345.

[8] MacArthur, 1346.h.

What are some things getting in the way of Jesus as your life? Is work your life? Is shopping your life? Are your loved ones your life? Today, make Jesus your life. Give Him all your affections and receive the abundant life found in Him alone. Jesus is also the light. The light shines in the darkness. There is absolutely no darkness in Jesus. If the light of Christ has grown dim in your life and darkness is growing around you, spend time with Jesus. Walk with Him and practice His truth. His light will grow within you and set you free.

Life was in Him, and that life was the light of men. The light shines in the darkness, yet the darkness did not overcome it. —John 1:4–5

Further Scripture: John 14:6; Romans 8:2; 1 John 1:5–7

Questions

1. How did John immediately portray Jesus in the first five verses of John 1?

2. What are the seven names and titles John gave in chapter 1 to identify Jesus as the eternal God? (John 1:1–3, 4–13, 14, 29–34, 35–42, 48–49, 50–51).

3. What was the essential work of John the Baptist? Did the Jews understand who he was and what he came to do according to the Scriptures?

4. How did John the Baptist present Jesus, who was coming toward him in John 1:29? What might have gone through the people's minds when he said this? (Genesis 22:7–8; Numbers 28:19).

5. Who was the one that witnessed to Nathanael? What convinced Nathanael to follow Jesus?

6. What did the Holy Spirit highlight to you in John 1 through the reading or the teaching?

Lesson 70: John 2
Son of God: The First Sign

Teaching Notes

Intro

We continue talking about Jesus as the *Son of God*. In Luke, we saw Jesus as the Son of Man. Now we identify with Jesus as the *Son of God*. Today, we are going to break down the Scripture into two parts: Jesus as the miracle worker and Jesus with all authority.

Teaching

John 2:1: The first half of this chapter concerns the wedding in Cana, a story that only appears in John's Gospel. The wedding was on the third day, which suggests that Jesus and His disciples had been traveling for two days.

John 2:2: Jesus and His disciples were attending the wedding. Jesus' mother, Mary, and probably more of His family, were attending the wedding as well. Was this the wedding of James, the brother of Jesus? We can't be sure, but we know Mary definitely had a role in the wedding. Whoever's wedding this was, they were connected not only to Jesus but also to the disciples.

John 2:3–4: Mary ran to Jesus and told Him they were out of wine. It is important to remember that Jesus had a mom, and they had a special relationship. You can choose to think that Jesus' response was really sassy or a gentle, playful banter. I think it was the latter, and I think they had a unique relationship. Mary knew exactly who Jesus was. Jesus claimed His time had not yet come, but He respectfully obliged His mother's request out of love.

John 2:5–7: I think this shows Jesus and Mary's playful relationship. Mary went to the servants and told them to listen to Jesus. It is clear that Mary had a key role in this wedding. She had some type of servant role in which people listened to her. The fact that people did what Jesus said showed a crazy level of faith.

At the wedding, they had purification jars. These jars would have been the only ceremonially clean jars, as they were made of stone. They were huge. Guests would wash their hands in the jars so they would be clean before they ate. This was not drinking water.

John 2:8–10: The crazy amount of faith Mary and the servants had was shown by them actually taking this water to the chief servant. He had no idea where it came from, and maybe that's a good thing. He called the groom and chastised him for saving the best wine for last. This was about Jesus coming right out of the gate; He is the wine of life. It was a prophetic act.

John 2:11–12: This was Jesus' first miracle. Then Jesus, the disciples, His mother, and other family members traveled to Capernaum. This is another detail pointing out that this wedding was probably a family affair.

John 2:13: Then Jesus went to Jerusalem for the Jewish Passover. At times, John's Gospel seems to be chronologically jumbled when lining up events next to the other three Gospels. Some theologians agree John's Gospel is out of sequence, as though it is an error. One theory is the manuscript got dropped and the pages were put back in the wrong order. Others have come up with far more complicated theories like each Gospel writer had different styles of writing, while other theologians have completely ignored the problem altogether. The bottom line is this: the story is in harmony with the other Gospels.

John 2:14–17: When Jesus arrived at the temple, He found livestock being sold and moneychangers everywhere. Jesus created a whip and drove the livestock and moneychangers out of the temple (Psalm 69:9).

Why was Jesus so angry? First, worshipers on pilgrimage to Jerusalem for Passover couldn't bring animals that long distance. Those selling livestock to these travelers were extorting worshipers with their prices. Second, these acts were happening in the temple, which was supposed to be a house of prayer. Third, for buyers, it was like cheap grace. It was little work for the people to make a sacrifice.

John 2:18: The Jews replied, "Who do you think you are? What gives you the right?"

John 2:19–21: In response, Jesus answered, "Destroy this sanctuary, and I will raise it up in three days" (v. 19). But the people did not understand what Jesus was saying! Jesus was talking about His own body. They were focused on the brick and mortar; they were ignorant and oblivious. The *Son of God* could be the only one to perform this sign. In John 11:25, Jesus said, "I am the resurrection and the life."

This temple the Jews were talking about was completed in 515 BC. It took 46 years to build (v. 20). (First Corinthians 6:19 talks about your body being a temple of the Holy Spirit). Jesus was saying, "I am aware that I am the temple of the Holy Spirit." He was showing us a glimpse of what the Christian life is supposed to look like.

John 2:22–23: Romans 10:9 says, "If you confess with your mouth, 'Jesus is Lord,' and believe in your heart that God raised Him from the dead, you will be saved." That's what this is all about. That is the Gospel, and the disciples changed the world with that simple belief.

John 2:24–25: There were few people to whom Jesus explained everything. Jesus revealed Himself to Peter, John, and James on the Mount of Transfiguration. There were others He could trust, but not as intimately, such as the other disciples. For these religious leaders, Jesus held His cards close, and reasonably so. Verse 25 describes another supernatural trait of Jesus' Sonship: "and because He did not need anyone to testify about man; for He Himself knew what was in man." The Father would reveal to Him the hearts of men—revealing the good, the bad, and the ugly.

Closing

So what about you and me? Are we a people God can trust? A people God can reveal Himself to? Do we follow Him to chase signs and wonders? Do we pursue Him for a free meal? For a miracle? For a healing?

Matthew 16:13–17: "When Jesus came to the region of Caesarea Philippi, He asked His disciples, 'Who do people say that the Son of Man is?' And they said, 'Some say John the Baptist; others, Elijah; still others, Jeremiah or one of the prophets.' 'But you,' He asked them, 'who do you say that I am?' Simon Peter answered, 'You are the Messiah, the Son of the living God!' And Jesus responded, 'Simon son of Jonah, you are blessed because flesh and blood did not reveal this to you, but My Father in heaven.'"

John 1:49: "'Rabbi,' Nathanael replied, 'You are the Son of God! You are the King of Israel!'"

John 6:66–69: "From that moment many of His disciples turned back and no longer accompanied Him. Therefore Jesus said to the Twelve, 'You don't want to go away too, do you?' Simon Peter answered, 'Lord, who will we go to? You have the words of eternal life. We have come to believe and know that You are the Holy One of God!'"

To whom will we go? Will we acknowledge Jesus truly is the *Son of God*? Where else can we go? After all, He does have the words of eternal life.

Daily Word

Jesus, His mother, and His disciples were guests at a wedding in Cana of Galilee. His mother turned to Jesus and told Him the hosts had run out of wine. Understanding her son's power, Jesus' mother turned to the servants and said to them, "Do whatever Jesus says to do." Jesus performed His first miracle, turning water to wine. Jesus told the servants what to do, and they did it. They didn't question Him. They didn't argue. They just did it. Because of their immediate obedience, the water turned into good wine. Jesus publicly displayed His glory, and His disciples believed Him.

What would happen if you listened to Jesus like the servants? Whatever He told you to do, you just did it. Whatever you read in the Word of God about His promises and truth, you believed immediately. You don't question it. You don't ask someone else what they think. Rather, you listen and obey immediately. In walking in immediate obedience, you begin to experience Jesus working in miraculous ways, like the servants seeing the water turn to wine. If they had waited, argued, rationalized, or asked someone else to do it, they would have missed the miracle. Today, listen to the voice of the Lord, and just do it.

"Do whatever He tells you," His mother said to the servants. . . . "Fill the jars with water," Jesus told them. So they filled them to the brim. Then He said to them, "Now draw some out and take it to the chief servant." And they did. —John 2:5, 7–8

Further Reading: Genesis 17:23; Isaiah 30:20b–21; John 2:11

Questions

1. At the marriage supper, Mary told the servants to do whatever Jesus said to do (John 2:5). This was after He told her it was not yet His time. What do you think led Mary to make that statement even after Jesus said no?

2. When Jesus was talking about rebuilding the Temple in verse 19, why didn't He say that He meant His body and not the actual building (Isaiah 6:9; Matthew 13:14; John 1:14)?

3. Meditate on verses 23–25 of John 2. What do these verses speak to you? What do you think they mean?

4. What did the Holy Spirit highlight to you in John 2 through the reading or the teaching?

Lesson 71: John 3

Son of God: The One from Heaven

Teaching Notes

Intro

Our phrase for the book of John is the *Son of God*. In the Gospel of John, Jesus continued to show who He is.

Teaching

John 3:1: There was a man named Nicodemus who was a ruler of the Jews and a high priest. Usually, this position was appointed because of family lineage or political affiliation because the Pharisees were considered the main ruling body of the Jews. The name "Pharisee" means "separated one." What we have here is a radical story! Christ was drawing man unto Himself. John 1:24–27: "Then some members of the religious sect known as the Pharisees questioned John, 'Why do you baptize the people since you admit you're not the Christ, Elijah, or the Prophet?' John answered them, 'I baptize in this river, but the One who will take my place is to be more honored than I, but even when he stands among you, you will not recognize or embrace him! I am not worthy enough to stoop down in front of him and untie his sandals!'" (TPT).

The Pharisees heard John say there was someone greater coming. Blackaby wrote, "Once you know where He is working you can adjust your life to join Him in His divine purposes."[1] That was what Nicodemus was doing.

John 3:2: Nicodemus came to Jesus at night. Why? He was of high profile and afraid. John 12:42 explains, "Nevertheless, many did believe in Him even among the rulers, but because of the Pharisees they did not confess Him, so they would not be banned from the synagogue." There was a good chance that if others found out Nicodemus met with Jesus, he would be done as a ruler.

Let's look at the end of Nicodemus's life. In John 7:50, Nicodemus stood among his peers and stood up for Christ. I think fear will eventually lead us to faith. Don't let fear dictate what you do! Be bold enough to talk to your

---

[1] Henry T. Blackaby, *Experiencing God: Knowing and Doing the Will of God* (Nashville: B&H, 2008), 70.

neighbors! In John 19:35, Nicodemus brought myrrh and aloe as preparation for Jesus' body. He broke free from the spirit of religion! We know how it ended for Nicodemus. How did he get there?

It would have been normal for people to hang out on the roof during the evening. Jesus and Nicodemus sat down to talk. First, Nicodemus complimented Jesus, and then he questioned Him.

John 3:3–5: Jesus told Nicodemus that unless he was born again, he could not see the kingdom of God. Nicodemus said, "What?!" Jesus again said one must be born again or they could not enter the kingdom of God. Jesus said, "You have to be born of water and the Spirit" (v. 5). This verse is challenging because it could mean so many things. It could mean physical birth and spiritual birth, or born of water could symbolize repentance and regeneration, while birth could refer to a spiritual birth.

John 3:6–7: Jesus said, "Do not be amazed that I say this." Born again means "born from above." Second Corinthians 5:17: "Therefore, if anyone is in Christ, he is a new creation; old things have passed away, and look, new things have come." You become a new person. Titus 3:5 says, "He saved us—not by works of righteousness that we had done, but according to His mercy, through the washing of regeneration and renewal by the Holy Spirit." Why was Nicodemus wrestling with this?

> 1 Corinthians 2:10: "Now God has revealed these things to us by the Spirit, for the Spirit searches everything, even the depths of God."
>
> 1 Corinthians 2:13–16: "We also speak these things, not in words taught by human wisdom, but in those taught by the Spirit, explaining spiritual things to spiritual people. But the unbeliever does not welcome what comes from God's Spirit, because it is foolishness to him; he is not able to understand it since it is evaluated spiritually. The spiritual person, however, can evaluate everything, yet he himself cannot be evaluated by anyone. For who has known the Lord's mind, that he may instruct Him? But we have the mind of Christ."

When you are born again from above, these things begin to make sense. In this moment, even though Nicodemus is hungry to learn more, he is not quite grasping what Jesus is telling him.

> Ezekiel 36:25–26: "I will also sprinkle clean water on you, and you will be clean. I will cleanse you from all your impurities and all your

> idols. I will give you a new heart and put a new spirit within you; I will remove your heart of stone and give you a heart of flesh."

There was enough language here that Nicodemus might have remembered the prophets and started to understand.

> Ezekiel 37:11–14: "Then He said to me, 'Son of man, these bones are the whole house of Israel. Look how they say, "Our bones are dried up, and our hope has perished; we are cut off." Therefore, prophesy and say to them: This is what the Lord GOD says: I am going to open your graves and bring you up from them, My people, and lead you into the land of Israel. You will know that I am Yahweh, My people, when I open your graves and bring you up from them. I will put My Spirit in you, and you will live, and I will settle you in your own land. Then you will know that I am Yahweh. I have spoken, and I will do it.' This is the declaration of the LORD."

Only things of the spirit can come from the Holy Spirit.

John 3:8–11: The Holy Spirit comes and goes just like the wind. The Holy Spirit never leaves you but moves in different ways in your life. Nicodemus once again said, "What?!" Jesus rebuked him, "Aren't you a teacher? We speak what We know and what We've seen but you do not accept Our testimony." Jesus was speaking as Father, Son, and Holy Spirit.

John 3:12: How can you fathom the things of heaven?

> Numbers 21:8–9: "Then the LORD said to Moses, 'Make a snake image and mount it on a pole. When anyone who is bitten looks at it, he will recover.' So Moses made a bronze snake and mounted it on a pole. Whenever someone was bitten, and he looked at the bronze snake, he recovered."

This was the beginning of Jesus referencing eternal life.

> *John 3:16*: "For God loved the world in this way: He gave His One and Only Son, so that everyone who believes in Him will not perish but have eternal life."

Jesus said, "Nicodemus I know you hear me. I am asking you to put one thing on your heart. Believe in me. Put your eyes on me as I am lifted up."

> John 19:39–40: "Nicodemus (who had previously come to Him at night) also came, bringing a mixture of about 75 pounds of myrrh and aloes. Then they took Jesus' body and wrapped it in linen cloths with the aromatic spices, according to the burial custom of the Jews."

Closing

Now is the time to overcome your fear. His love wipes away your sins. When you receive this gift, you will have eternal life. Be encouraged.

Daily Word

God loved the world so much He sent His only Son Jesus to earth. Jesus' purpose was to come to earth so that everyone who believed in Him would have eternal life. Jesus came not to judge the world but to save the world.

God gave up His Son out of a *great love*. Have you ever had to give something up? Maybe you sent a child overseas to work with orphans, and you gave up the dream of living near your grown child. Yet because you gave your child and dream up, hundreds of orphans' lives have been impacted. Maybe the Lord led you to give up a vehicle so the ministry family would have a working car. Because you gave up your car, this family impacted an entire city for the gospel. It's worth the sacrifice, right? God gave up His only Son, and now the entire world can be saved and have eternal life. But just like the family would have to receive the vehicle as a gift, you must receive the gift of God's Son as a gift, a free gift of salvation. As you receive this gift, you will be saved from death and your sins through Jesus' life. Today, receive the gift of salvation if you haven't made this decision. And if you have, ask the Lord if there is anything He wants you to give up so that His love, grace, and power can spread to others.

For God so loved the world in this way: He gave His one and only Son, so that everyone who believes in Him will not perish but have eternal life. For God did not send His Son into the world that he might condemn the world, but that the world might be saved through Him. —John 3:16–17

Further Reading: Romans 10:9–10; 1 John 4:8; Revelation 22:17

Questions

1. Put yourself in Nicodemus's shoes. How do you think the conversation would have been different with you? The same?

2. John 3:16, one of the most-quoted Scriptures, speaks of God giving up His only Son. When you think of this verse, can you imagine giving up your child for the world? One person? Why is that concept so hard to grasp?

3. Verses 19–21 speak of God's light and the darkness. Was this talking about actual light or something else? What do you think it is (Psalm 119:105; John 1:9)?

4. John the Baptist's disciples came to him and said everyone was going to Jesus instead of him. Do you think John's disciples really knew who Jesus was? Why or why not?

5. What did John the Baptist mean when he said Jesus must increase while he must decrease (v. 30)? What does verse 31 mean to you?

6. What did the Holy Spirit highlight to you in John 3 through the reading or the teaching?

Lesson 72: John 4
Son of God: Son of God

Teaching Notes

Intro

At the end of the Gospel of Luke, Jesus engaged people right where they were. John saw Jesus perform many miracles, but the ones he recorded, including the one in John 4, were written so that "you may believe Jesus is the Messiah" (John 20:31). Jesus modeled a four-word approach to evangelism in John 4: Love, Listen, Discern, and Respond.

Teaching

John 4:1–4: Religious Jews would never travel through Samaria. Even though it was easier to travel to Galilee from Judea through Samaria, Jews avoided the route because they looked down on Samaritans. Jews looked down on Samaritans because the Samaritans' worship practices were thought to be impure and imperfect. But Jesus said He had to travel through Samaria because He had a love for people (John 3:16).

John 4:5–6: Jesus was thirsty, but He set His needs aside to minister.

John 4:7–8: As the Samaritan woman approached the well, Jesus asked her for a drink of water. Here we see the humanity and dependence of Jesus. This was the hottest part of the day in Samaria. Jesus was exhausted and He was thirsty. He had no way to draw water, so He asked the Samaritan woman for a drink. It may have seemed to the Samaritan woman that Jesus was being forward, first because they were alone, and second because He was a Jew. But neither culture, nor tradition, or anything else, will stop Jesus from ministering to the people He loves.

John 4:9–15: As the Samaritan woman responded to Jesus with questions, He listened intently to her. Stephen Covey said, "most people do not listen with the intent to understand; they listen with the intent to reply."1 But Jesus listened to the Samaritan woman to understand her. If you love someone, you will listen to them. Jesus spoke about living water, but the Samaritan woman heard Him with a natural understanding (1 Corinthians 2:14). Her response in verse 15 was probably still natural. The Samaritan woman still didn't understand about the living water that Jesus was offering. Living water was a theme of Jesus' teaching. In John 7, Jesus stood up in the synagogue and proclaimed, "If anyone is thirsty, he should come to Me and drink! The one who believes in Me, as the Scripture has said, will have streams of living water flow from deep within him" (John 7:37–38).

John 4:16–20: As you listen to a person's question, you have to listen to their story. The woman recognized Jesus as a prophet, so she asked Him about one of the biggest differences between Jews and Samaritans.

John 4:21–22: After Jesus began to show love to the Samaritan woman by listening to her, He then stated the obvious. We can also learn to let the Holy Spirit lead us to do the same thing. This isn't someone else's responsibility. It's ours!

John 4:23–24: When we come to the table to worship Jesus, we have to come based on the Word of God (truth). At the same time, we have to come to the table in dependence of the Holy Spirit. We can't come just with knowledge and ignore the Spirit, nor can we come by the Spirit and ignore the truth.

John 4:25–26: Jesus loved the Samaritan woman, He listened to her, He discerned what she was saying, then He responded. The Samaritan woman was just avoiding life, and if we're not careful, we can fall into that same trap like others in the Bible:

- Exodus 14:13: As the Israelites left Egypt, Pharaoh decided to come after Israel. The Israelites were trapped between Pharaoh's army and the Red Sea. God showed up.
- Genesis 41:14–15: Joseph had been sitting in prison for years when he was brought to interpret Pharaoh's dream. God showed up.
- If you are like the Samaritan woman and just need Jesus to get you out of a situation, do this:
- Hold on to the promises (Isaiah 40:8; Matthew 5:17–18).
- Keep your eyes on Jesus (Psalm 25:15; Hebrews 12:2).

---

1 Stephen R. Covey, *The 7 Habits of Highly Effective People: Powerful Lessons in Personal Change* (New York: Free Press, 2004), 239.

Closing

It doesn't matter if you're following Jesus or if you are the Samaritan woman. Don't be like the disciples in John 4:27 who were amazed that Jesus was interacting with the Samaritan. We all need to be interacting with the Samaritans. The end of the story is that everyone in the town came to know about Jesus through the Samaritan woman's interaction with Jesus.

Daily Word

Jesus traveled through Samaria on His way to Galilee. But Jesus chose the path less traveled by other Jews and stopped at Jacob's well for a drink. He was worn out from His journey. He was without His disciples and alone, which was rare for Him. And then a Samaritan woman came near Him to draw water. Although tired and thirsty Himself, Jesus set His needs aside and took the time to love, listen, discern, and respond to this woman at the well. That day, as Jesus took time to love her, her life was changed forever as she came to believe in Him as the *Son of God*. And even the town was impacted and began to believe in Jesus.

Are you worn out from the journey? Do you feel as though you need time to sit and be served a drink of water? Jesus felt the same way. And yet, in the middle of that worn-out moment, someone came along for Jesus to love. As you rest and sit by a pool or read a book at a coffee shop, remember to keep your eyes open to whoever the Lord brings your way to love like Jesus. You may even be in your home and you just want to put your feet up and chill, but your child comes by and needs you. In those moments of weariness, call upon the Lord for strength to love and show grace. In these moments of weakness, Jesus' love shines through in a mighty way. Continue to rely on His love in and through you to impact the lives of others at unexpected and inconvenient times. You never know what a difference Jesus' love can make in one person's life.

Jacob's well was there; so Jesus, wearied as he was from his journey, was sitting beside the well. It was about the sixth hour. A woman from Samaria came to draw water. Jesus said to her, "Give me a drink." (For his disciples had gone away into the city to buy food.) —John 4:6–8 ESV

Further Reading: Isaiah 40:8, 31; 2 Corinthians 2:14

Questions

1. What is the fountain of "living water" in verse 10 (Isaiah 55:1; Jeremiah 2:13; 17:13)? How do you get it (Romans 10:9–10)?

2. In your opinion, what does it mean to worship the Father in Spirit and in Truth (1 Samuel 16:7; Luke 18:9–14; Romans 12:1)? What do you think that looks like?

3. In John 4:26, Jesus plainly told the Samaritan woman that He was the Messiah. Why do you think He told her flat out when He did not tell Nicodemus in John 3?

4. Jesus spoke on sowing and reaping in John 4:35–38. What are the differences between the two? Have you sown or reaped? Have you reaped where you didn't sow? Have you sown and not reaped?

5. When the official asked Jesus to heal his son in John 4:47, Jesus referenced not believing unless signs and wonders are seen (John 4:48). His son was healed and his whole family believed that very hour. Did it take signs and wonders for you to believe? Why or why not?

6. What did the Holy Spirit highlight to you in John 4 through the reading or the teaching?

Lesson 73: John 5
Son of God: Witnesses for the Son of God

Teaching Notes

Intro

We are jumping into John chapter 5. What I like about the Gospel of John is that it feels new and fresh. Yesterday we talked about Jesus and the Samaritan woman at the well. We saw Jesus break all the norms. He went out of His way to minister, love, listen, and respond to a woman who should not have been interacting with a Jewish rabbi at all. Jesus continued to model how He loves people. John 5:1–15 are all about signs. Jesus had performed the third sign. Remember, there are seven signs. Here Jesus was performing a miracle by healing a sick person. John 5:16–23 are all about honoring the Father and the Son. These verses serve as a transition from Father and Son to life and judgment. Remember, the phrase for the book of John is *Son of God*.

Teaching

John 5:30: This is a transitional verse. Dr. Tom Constable wrote, "Jesus' point was that He could not do anything independently of the Father ('on My own initiative'), because of His submission to Him ('I do not seek My own will'). His 'judgment' is the result of listening to His Father. His judgment 'is just' because the desire for self-glory does not taint it. The Son's 'will' is totally to advance ('seek' only) the Father's 'will.'"[1] Here you have the Father's testimony about the Son. God said, "This is my Son! This is Whom I am proud of!" The Father is one of the three witnesses to validate Christ's identity. (Deuteronomy 19:15.) For any claim to be considered true, two or three witnesses were required to validate it.

John 5:31–32: Jesus said, "If I testify about Myself, My testimony is not valid" (v. 31). Does this contradict John 8:14? I don't think so. In John 8:14, Jesus was talking about His personal knowledge, here Jesus was discussing the things

---

[1] Thomas L. Constable, *Expository Notes of Dr. Thomas Constable: John*, 163, https://planobiblechapel.org/tcon/notes/pdf/john.pdf.

His Father knew. When Jesus said, there was "Another" who would testify about Him, He was talking about the Father.

John 5:33–35: The first witness was John the Baptist. Keep in mind that Jesus was talking to the Jewish religious leaders. Jesus referred to the conversation that the religious leaders had with John the Baptist (John 1:7, 19). John spoke the truth about the identity of Christ. Jesus was the living Lord.

When John witnessed Jesus approaching him, he instantly recognized that Jesus was the *Son of God*:

> John 1:29: "The next day John saw Jesus coming toward him and said, "Here is the Lamb of God, who takes away the sin of the world!"
> John 1:33: "I didn't know Him, but He who sent me to baptize with water told me, 'The One you see the Spirit descending and resting on—He is the One who baptizes with the Holy Spirit.'"
> John 1:34: "I have seen and testified that He is the Son of God!"

Jesus pointed out that for a season these religious leaders were willing to enjoy John's light (Psalm 132:17; 2 Corinthians 4:7).

John 5:36: The second witness was Jesus' works. He said, "John's was good but I have a better witness! Look at My works!" (Isaiah 35:5–6; Isaiah 61; Luke 4; John 10:25; John 14:11). Jesus' works literally pointed to the Father working through Him. Jesus was using common language.

Dr. Constable wrote, "These works included all of Jesus' activities: His miracles, His life of perfect obedience, and His work of redemption on the cross. Miracles alone did not prove Jesus' deity, since Moses, Elijah, and Elisha had done miracles, too. Everything that Jesus did was simply an extension of the Father's work (vv. 19–30)."[2] John 17:4 said, "I have glorified You on the earth by completing the work You gave Me to do." Everything we do should point to or testify of Christ!

John 5:37–38: The third witness was the Father Himself. Dr. Constable wrote, "Probably Jesus meant the Father's total witness to Jesus, including: Old Testament prophecies, prophetic events, and Israel's institutions—including His witness at Jesus' baptism."[3] I believe there is a distinction between the Father and Scripture. Constable wrote, "He [Jesus] probably meant all of God's anticipatory

---

[2] Constable, 165.

[3] Constable, 166.

revelation about Jesus."[4] Hebrews 1:1 explains, "Long ago God spoke to the fathers by the prophets at different times and in different ways" (Genesis 32:30–31; Exodus 33).

John 5:39–47: The final testimony is the Scriptures.

> John 3:34: "For God sent Him, and He speaks God's words, since He gives the Spirit without measure."
>
> John 17:7–8: "Now they know that all things You have given to Me are from You, because the words that You gave Me, I have given them. They have received them and have known for certain that I came from You. They have believed that You sent Me."

You can see that the third and fourth witnesses definitely go together. These religious leaders believed that there was more hope in the Scripture than in Christ.

The Jewish leaders poured into the Scriptures (1 Corinthians 8:1). Your knowledge is pointless if you don't see the love of Christ. *Nelson's Commentary* states, "There are also those today who master the Scriptures but do not allow the Scriptures to master them."[5] Jesus wants more than Scripture reading; He wants Bible heeding (James 1:22–25). Why read Scripture if you have no love for God?

Jesus said, "Your accuser is Moses." Moses was always pointing to the *Son of God*. These religious leaders were not listening to Moses. If they had believed Moses, they would have believed Jesus (Luke 24:25–27). Jesus pointed out that if these men were really in the Word of God, they would see He was the *Son of God*.

Closing

Warren Wiersbe asked, "Does our knowledge of the Bible give us a 'big head' or a 'burning heart'?"[6] Paul emphasized, "We know that 'we all have knowledge.' Knowledge inflates with pride, but love builds up" (1 Corinthians 8:1).

Do you have a big head or a burning heart? If it's about knowledge, you've missed it. It is all about the heart change. We have only had time to literally just scratch the surface of these Scriptures. I encourage you to go back and dig into these verses.

---

[4] Constable, 166.

[5] Earl D. Radmacher, Ronald B. Allen, and H. Wayne House, eds., *Nelson's New Illustrated Bible Commentary* (Nashville: Thomas Nelson, 1999), 1326.

[6] Warren Wiersbe, *The Wiersbe Bible Commentary: New Testament* (Colorado Springs: David C. Cook, 2007), 224.

Daily Word

John wrote as though he was in a courtroom and Jesus was on trial, having to prove His equality to God the Father as He is God the Son. Jesus had four witnesses give their accounts to the unbelieving: John the Baptist, Jesus' works, His Father's witness, and Scripture. The people had the choice to make between believing Jesus was who the witnesses said He was and have eternal life or reject Him, choosing to disbelieve. Far too often the people, even those around Jesus, chose to disbelieve.

We are all witnesses to the *truth* of Jesus. When you experience Jesus display His power, mercy, or grace in your life, share it with those around you. Did you ask the Lord to provide funds for a graduating senior and He provided a scholarship in a crazy miraculous way? Tell someone! Did you ask the Lord for wisdom in buying a new home and He provided? Tell your coworkers! Did someone pray for healing for you and you were healed? Go and share that on social media! Were you lost in darkness, bound to sin and the ways of this world, and then received the love and light of Jesus in your life and are now walking in freedom? Share it! In doing so you will give the *glory* to God! You will allow someone else to see Jesus and His power and His glory! If we hide it and keep it to ourselves, we are not being good stewards of the gift of God's power inside us. Today, go and proclaim what Jesus has done for you to anyone who will listen! Testify just how He has impacted your life!

But I have a greater testimony than John's because of the works that the Father has given Me to accomplish. These very works I am doing testify about Me that the Father has sent Me. —John 5:36

Further Reading: Psalm 71:15–16; Mark 5:19; 1 John 5:11

Questions

1. Why do you think Jesus asked the man if he wished to get well (Matthew 7:7)?

2. Why did Jesus say, "Go and sin no more lest something worse comes upon you" (Leviticus 26:23–24; Matthew 12:45)?

3. Why has the Father given all judgment to the Son (Philippians 2:5–10)?

4. Why did Jesus say, "If I bear witness to myself, my witness is not true" (Deuteronomy 19:15; 2 Corinthians 13:1)?

5. Why did Jesus say that Moses would be their accuser before the Father (John 5:45)?

6. What did the Holy Spirit highlight to you in John 5 through the reading or the teaching?

Lesson 74: John 6
Son of God: Jesus Fed the 5,000

Teaching Notes

Intro

I'm excited because today we are studying the first "I am" statement. There are seven "I am" statements in the Gospels. In John 6:35, we are going to unpack what Jesus meant when He said, "I am the bread of life." The text we are studying today contains some hard truths that left people scratching their heads and questioning if they could really be followers of Christ. John 6:1–21 sets the background for the conversation Jesus was to have with the crowd and His disciples.

Teaching

John 6: 22–24: Warren Wiersbe wrote, "We see four responses of the crowd to the Lord Jesus in John 6: seeking (vv. 22–40), murmuring (vv. 41–51), striving (vv.52–59), and departing (vv. 60–70)."[1] After a big football game, like the Super Bowl or, in this case, after a big miracle, people tend to get hyped up. When the crowd couldn't find Jesus, they took to their boats to track Him down. Hebrews 11:6 has this theme of seeking. As a follower, we must all be seeking Jesus (Jeremiah 29:13). This approach of the crowd seeking Jesus is biblical (Proverbs 8:17; Matthew 6:33).

John 6:25–26: The crowds eventually found Jesus. When they found Him, they began to ask questions. With Jesus' first responses, He went straight for the jugular, "You are looking for me because you think I can provide food for you." Wiersbe wrote, "Jesus pointed out that there are two kinds of food: food for the body, which is necessary but not the most important, and food for the inner man, the spirit, which is essential."[2]

John 6:27: Jesus said, "Don't work for the food that perishes but for the food that gives eternal life." In our study, we are beginning to see more and more how the

---

[1] Warren Wiersbe. *The Bible Exposition Commentary: New Testament* (Colorado Springs: David C. Cook, 2008), 249.

[2] Wiersbe, 249.

Father was testifying of the Son. We need to have this eternal mindset (Matthew 6:20; 2 Corinthians 4:18). This situation was a classic—the crowd seeking Jesus for wrong motives.

John 6:28–29: The crowd's mindset was this: show us what we need to do to experience this eternal food. Wiersbe wrote, "The people picked up the word "labor" and misinterpreted it to mean they had to work for salvation"[3] (Ephesians 2:8–9). Jesus replied, "This is the work of God, not your work." These works were done so they would believe in Jesus as the *Son of God* (John 14:1: Acts 16:31).

John 6:30: The crowd responded, "So what are you going to do?" The crowd was seeking signs (1 Corinthians 1:22). This was a common mindset of the Jewish people who were constantly looking for signs. They had just witnessed the feeding of the 5,000, and now they wanted another sign.

John 6:31–32: The people questioned, "If God provided manna for our fathers, why can't you?" They were implying that Jesus needed to show up and provide manna as well (Psalm 78:24). They were reciting the Psalmist because they obviously hadn't experienced this and were implying that the manna was from Moses instead of the Father.

John 6:33: The phrase "who comes down from heaven" is seen multiple times in the Gospel of John. Jesus was conveying to the crowd that what they were going to see was truly a shadow of what was to come (Colossians 2:17). Jesus was saying that the substance is the Messiah.

John 6:34–36: The crowd replied, "Give us this bread always." In John 4:15, this same mentality is seen. It is like the crowd was thinking, "This would be great! We don't have to go to Walmart anymore." Jesus dropped the first "I am" in Scripture when He said, "I am the bread of life" (John 6:35). This is one of the seven "I am" statements. Jesus was saying, "No one who believes in me will ever be hungry or thirsty." The crowds needed to come to Jesus and to believe in Him. Wiersbe wrote, "Believing is not merely an intellectual thing, giving mental assent to some doctrine. It means to come to Christ and yield yourself to Him."[4] Jesus was again equating Himself to God (Exodus 3:14). Jesus said, "You've seen me, but you do not believe." Isn't that the craziest thing? They were seeking Him, but they didn't get it.

---

[3] Wiersbe, 249.

[4] Wiersbe, 250.

John 6:37–40: These verses are the process of personal salvation. The Father gives Jesus to everybody, and the ones who come to Christ are never cast out. There is a balanced approach of divine sovereignty and personal responsibility. We could unpack this for 16 weeks, but we are not going to! My emphasis is that as people seek Christ, He wants them to understand He is the bread of life.

John 6:41–45: The crowd began to complain. Now *this* sounds like the Old Testament Jews! The crowd exclaimed, "This is just the son of Mary and Joseph from Nazareth. He is not the bread of life. He's my neighbor!" Because their hearts were hardened, they could not see who He was. Jesus told them to stop complaining. Then, He reiterated that no one could come to Him unless they went through the Father. He was paraphrasing Isaiah 54:13, using Old Testament Scripture to point back to what the prophets were saying.

John 6:46–50: Anyone who believes has eternal life. Jesus pointed out that while their fathers ate manna, they also died. Jesus proclaimed, "I am more than the manna your fathers had. Yet you have the audacity to complain! My work is greater than that."

John 6:51–56: Again, Jesus proclaimed that He is the living bread that comes from heaven. Wiersbe wrote, "The manna came at night from heaven, and Jesus came to this earth when sinners were in moral and spiritual darkness. The manna was small (His humility), round (His eternity), and white (His purity)."[5] Jesus was saying, over and over again, "I am a sacrifice; I am atonement. I am giving everything up for your life." In John 3:16, Jesus died for the world; in John 15:13, Jesus died for His friends; in Galatians 2:20, Jesus gave up His flesh so that we could have life. This language about the flesh can be difficult to understand. The Jews were constantly taking Jesus literally, which kept them from understanding the true meaning of His words (John 2:19–21).

John 6:57–62: Jesus was stating the hardest truth and not backing down from it. He was constantly emphasizing the tie between the Father and Son. Jesus is the answer. He said it repeatedly, hoping they would hear Him. Because the truth was so hard, the people departed, including many of His disciples.

John 6:63–65: Wiersbe wrote, "Jesus explained that His language was figurative and spiritual, not literal. There is not salvation in 'flesh.' In fact, the New Testament had nothing good to say about 'the flesh'" (Romans 7:18; Philippians 3:3). You cannot find confidence in flesh; it has everything to do with the Spirit of

---

5 Wiersbe, 251.

God. There are some who don't believe, and people who don't want to participate. Once again Jesus talked about God's sovereignty and the human response.

Closing

Jesus needed the people to turn toward Him. Living a life dedicated to Christ is a lifestyle that is uncomfortable. We are to deny ourselves and pick up the cross. Our prayer is that none of us will depart.

Daily Word

After Jesus fed the five thousand with loaves and fish, He went away. The next day, the crowds went looking for Jesus and found Him on the other side of the sea. They saw Jesus performing a miracle and were hungry to see more works from God. Jesus said to them, "I am the bread of life." Jesus' will is for everyone who believes in the Son of God to have eternal life and be satisfied in Him.

If Jesus is the bread of life, what does that mean for you today? Bread is a physical essential. You can live on just bread and water a long time. Like bread, Jesus is essential for daily living. Every day, you need to fill up with Jesus. If you don't fill up with Jesus, you won't be satisfied in life. You will be hungry and want to fill your life with other things. So today, fill up with Jesus. Turn to Him, find your satisfaction in Him alone, and meditate on His Word. Give thanks to Him for His goodness, His beauty, and His provisions. Let Him fill you up as you go through your day so you have energy from the Lord to face whatever lies ahead. He *is* your daily bread.

"I am the bread of life," Jesus told them. "No one who comes to Me will ever be hungry, and no one who believes in Me will ever be thirsty again."
—John 6:35

Further Scripture: Psalm 107:9; John 6:40; Revelation 7:16–17

Questions

1. In John 6:16–21, the disciples left for Capernaum by boat, but a wind came up and they struggled to get anywhere. Jesus walked on the water toward them and calmed the winds. Have you had instances in your life where you were struggling, and Jesus showed up and things changed? Can you give an example?

2. In John 6:25, when the people found Jesus on the shore, they asked how He had gotten there. In John 6:26, Jesus said that others sought Him out because they were fed and not because of the signs. Do you know people who seek Him for what He can do for them and not what they can do for Him?

3. Meditate on John 6:51–58. How is Jesus the living bread, and how can we live for eternity on it (Deuteronomy 8:3; Matthew 4:4)?

4. Why did many of the disciples, not including the 12, turn their backs on Jesus and no longer follow Him (John 6:66)? Has there been a time that you walked away from following Jesus? Why or why not?

5. What did the Holy Spirit highlight to you in John 6 through the reading or the teaching?

Lesson 75: John 7

Son of God: The Coming of
the Holy Spirit to Dwell in Us

Teaching Notes

Intro

Yesterday we began to dig into the seven "I am" statements. The first was, "I am the bread of life" (throughout the world, bread is the staple), so Jesus was pointing out that He is the staple we need. In John 7, we'll take a little bit of a left turn to concentrate on the Holy Spirit. John 7:1–9 presents the family dynamics as His brothers tried to tell Jesus what He needed to do. In John 7:10–24, Jesus secretly left, and in John 7:25–36, people began to question Jesus' identity as the Messiah. For the Festival of the Tabernacles, every Jewish family within 20 miles of Jerusalem was required to attend. *Nelson's Commentary* states that the festival lasted seven days, and the people would make shelters from branches and leaves. "The feast commemorated the days when the Israelites wandered in the wilderness and lived in tents" (Leviticus 23:40–43).[1] This was to remind the Jews of when God took care of the Israelites in the wilderness and that God would continue to take care of them.

Teaching

John 7:37: In the context of verse 37, "on the last and most important day of the festival," scholars disagree if that meant it was on day seven or day eight.[2] Jesus stood up (which was unusual for when He was going to teach) and proclaimed, "If anyone is thirsty, he should come to Me and drink!" Every day of the festival, the high priest and the people would come with palm branches and march around the altar and recognize what God had done. Another priest would fill a golden pitcher with water that came from the Pool of Siloam and poured it on top of the altar as an offering. It is probably at that moment that Jesus stood up to

---

[1] Earl D. Radmacher, Ronald B. Allen, and H. Wayne House, eds., *Nelson's New Illustrated Bible Commentary* (Nashville: Thomas Nelson, 1999), 1330.

[2] Thomas L. Constable, *Expository Notes of Dr. Thomas Constable: John*, 218, https://planobiblechapel.org/tcon/notes/pdf/john.pdf.

speak.[3] Constable states the pitcher of water was carried through the Water Gate. While the priest was pouring the water, another priest would pour an offering of wine on the altar as well. The water was symbolic of the water that God provided in the wilderness, and the wine reminded the people that God would send His Spirit in the last days.[4] The crowd chanted praises using Psalms 18:1 and 118:5.

In Exodus 17:1–7, God poured water out of the rock. At the Red Sea, God split the water with His presence. *Nelson's Commentary* explains that on the last day of the feast, the people marched around the altar seven times to memorialize the Israelites' march around Jericho.[5] A lot was going on . . . people chanting and waving branches, the priests pouring the water and the wine and walking at the same time. Maybe while the priest poured the water, Jesus called the thirsty to Him.

John 7:38: Jesus explained that the one who believed in Him, just as the Scripture has said, would have streams of living water flow from deep within him. Where does it say this in Scripture?

- Isaiah 55:1a: "Come, everyone who is thirsty, come to the waters."
- Isaiah 12:3: "You will joyfully draw water from the springs of salvation."
- Numbers 24:7: "Water will flow from his buckets, and his seed will be by abundant water."
- Isaiah 58:11: "The LORD will always lead you, satisfy you in a parched land, and strengthen your bones. You will be like a watered garden and like a spring whose waters never run dry."

Jesus understood this image in Scripture—the water of the Lord will never run out.

- Zechariah 14:8: "On that day living water will flow out from Jerusalem, half of it toward the eastern sea and the other half toward the western sea, in summer and winter alike."

This is the beginning of the fulfillment of all the feast anticipated. John 4:14 describes the water from Jesus as "a well of water," water that will never run out.

John 7:39: In verse 39, John said the water is the Holy Spirit. God would be inside of them. But not yet, "because Jesus had not yet been glorified," meaning Jesus had not yet been crucified or resurrected. Up to this point, the Holy Spirit came upon people for certain times and certain roles, but not to dwell within

---

[3] Radmacher et al., 1331–1332.

[4] Constable, 219.

[5] Radmacher et al., 1332.

them. It was only for a season (Numbers 37:15; Ezekiel 2:2). However, once you believe in Jesus, the Holy Spirit never leaves you! That's a huge distinction. The pictures of the well that doesn't go dry or the river of water always moving signifies that the Holy Spirit never leaves once He dwells within us. The Spirit of God doesn't leave believers. In 1 Corinthians 12:13, we are asked to drink of one Spirit. Ephesians 1:13–14 explains that believers are "sealed with the Holy Spirit" and the Spirit is at work within us.

This water image is so important. There is nothing more satisfying on a really hot day than a glass of water. Tapping into water is not only important but necessary. And that's a good picture for us spiritually.

Closing

Kent Hughes explains how we should tap into this living water:

1. We must realize our thirstiness and our emptiness.
2. We need to admit that nothing we have within us will commit us to Christ.
3. We need to admit we are sinners.
4. We need to ask to be filled daily.[6]

Jesus said in John 7:37 that if anyone is thirsty, they should come to Him to drink. This verse is the pivotal verse in the book of John that turns the table away from us and totally onto Christ. The Word of God should radically change your life!

Daily Word

As the people gathered on the final day of the Feast of Tabernacles, Jesus said to them, "If anyone is thirsty, he should come to Me and drink! And if you believe in Me, you will have streams of living water coming from deep within."

Jesus is the answer to your thirstiness. What happens when plants need water but don't get any? They dry up and eventually die. The same is spiritually true for believers. You will dry up if you don't tap into Jesus, the source of living water. How do you know you are drying up? You become numb to the voice of the Lord. Perhaps your flesh tendencies are quicker to surface or you find yourself turning to things of this world for satisfaction rather than setting your eyes on Jesus. You may feel down and not filled with joy. Remember, in the presence of the Lord there is the fullness of joy. Turn to Him and ask a friend to pray for you to be filled up with Jesus. Right now, say out loud, "Jesus, fill me afresh with Your living water! Amen!"

---

[6] R. Kent Hughes, *John: That We May Believe* (Wheaton, IL: Crossway, 1999), n. p.

"If anyone is thirsty, he should come to Me and drink! The one who believes in Me, as the Scripture has said, will have streams of living water flow from deep within him." He said this about the Spirit. Those who believed in Jesus were going to receive the Spirit. —John 7:37–39

Further Scripture: Numbers 24:7; Isaiah 58:11; 1 Corinthians 12:13

Questions

1. Why did the brothers of Jesus tell Him to go into Judea so His works could be seen (John 7:3)?

2. What are the differences between John 7:34 and Deuteronomy 4:29? In what ways are they different?

3. What does it mean when it says, "Out of his belly shall flow rivers of Living Water"? How do you get this Living Water (John 7:38a)?

4. What did the Holy Spirit highlight to you in John 7 through the reading or the teaching?

Lesson 76: John 8
Son of God: I Am the Light of the World

Teaching Notes

Intro

Within John are seven "I am" statements. So far, we've only covered one: "I am the bread of life" (John 6:35). Today's passage presents the second "I am" statement. Before we get there, however, we'll look at a story in John 8:1–11 to build a case for why Jesus said, "I am."

Teaching

John 8:1–3: Jesus went across the Kidron Valley from Jerusalem to the Mount of Olives and spent the night there (v. 1). At dawn, Jesus returned to the temple complex, and "all the people were coming to Him" (v. 2). *All the people*. Jesus sat down to teach them. "Then," in response to what was happening, "the scribes and the Pharisees" came to Jesus (v. 3a). This is one of the few times John recorded the scribes and the Pharisees together. They brought an adulteress woman before Jesus (v. 3b). *Nelson's Commentary* states that they were trying to interrupt Jesus' teaching.[1] The scribes and Pharisees were looking for Jesus; they were looking for trouble (John 7:45). They brought the woman before Jesus and made her stand in the center.

John 8:4–5: The scribes and Pharisees explained about the woman's sin and reminded Jesus that the law of Moses required she be stoned (vv. 4–5a). Then they asked Jesus what He thought should be done to the woman (v. 5b). John wrote that the whole incident was a trap (v. 6). The trap actually had multiple layers: Deuteronomy 22:23–24 explains that if a young and engaged virgin has sex with a man, both of them should be taken to the city gate and stoned—her because she didn't cry out and him because he took his neighbor's fiancé. Leviticus 20:10 says if a man committed adultery with a married woman, both he and the woman were to be stoned. The act of adultery takes two people.

---

[1] Earl D. Radmacher, Ronald B. Allen, and H. Wayne House, eds., *Nelson's New Illustrated Bible Commentary* (Nashville: Thomas Nelson, 1999), 1333.

The scribes and the Pharisees brought a woman caught in the act of adultery to Jesus, but they ignored the male who was involved. They asked Jesus what to do only with the woman. If Jesus had said not to stone her, He would have contradicted the law, but if He had said to stone her, He would have gone against Roman law, which said Jews were not allowed to carry out executions.[2] Jesus was in a no-win situation.

John 8:6: They asked Jesus this question to trap Him and get evidence against Him (v. 6a). In response, "Jesus stooped down and started writing on the ground with His finger" (v. 6b). We don't know what Jesus wrote in the dirt, but one possibility is He was writing the Ten Commandments (Exodus 20:1–17). Exodus 31:18 says, "When He finished speaking with Moses on Mount Sinai, He gave him the two tablets of the testimony, stone tablets inscribed by the finger of God." *Nelson's Commentary* suggests that, "Maybe by writing the law Jesus is symbolically saying He is not a teacher of the law; He is the giver of the law."[3]

Jeremiah 17:13 provides another possible picture: "LORD, the hope of Israel, all who abandon You will be put to shame. All who turn away from Me will be written in the dirt, for they have abandoned the LORD, the fountain of living water." John 7 just recorded Jesus' teaching that the living water comes from God. What if Jesus had started writing their names in the dirt? Exodus 23:1 shows another possibility: "You must not spread a false report. Do not join the wicked to be a malicious witness."

John 8:7: They continued to question Jesus, so He stood up and told them: "The one without sin among you should be the first to throw a stone at her." Jesus knew the law and used it to turn it back at the scribes and the Pharisees. The accusers were to be the ones who stoned the guilty person (Leviticus 24:14; Deuteronomy 13:9; 17:7).

Nelson's Commentary states that Jesus "did not abolish Moses' law; rather, He applied that law to the lives of those who had accused the woman."[4] Jesus knows the word, because He is the Word.

John 8:8–10: Then Jesus continued to write on the ground (v. 8). While Jesus wrote, the scribes and the Pharisees began to leave one by one, "starting with the older men" (v. 9a). "Older" men tend to have the greater conscience—they've been down that road, experienced a lot, and learned from it. Finally, only Jesus was left with the woman still standing in the center (v. 9b). *Nelson's Commentary*

---

[2] Radmacher et al., 1333.

[3] Radmacher et al., 1333.

[4] Radmacher et al., 1333.

pointed out that this entire encounter "could have happened in a few minutes."[5] It was still early in the morning. Jesus stood up and asked the accused woman, "Has no one condemned you?" (v. 10). She replied, "No one, Lord." Jesus said, "Neither do I condemn you . . . Go, and from now on do not sin anymore" (v. 11). "Jesus forgave her. He did not condemn her, but neither did He condone her sin."[6] This means that when there is sin, we can forgive, but we cannot condone the sin.

John 8:12: Jesus said to those He had been teaching before the interruption, "I am the light of the world." The use of "I am" ties Jesus back to the Father when He said to Moses, "I AM WHO I AM" (Exodus 3:14). Those who follow Jesus will never be in darkness, but will have the "light of life." Verse 12 makes sense because of verse 11. "Go and sin no more," means to walk behind the light (Psalm 119:105). If we go back to the sin (such as the woman and adultery), we allow the darkness to take over, and we no longer walk behind the light. Remember that this took place right after dawn. *Nelson's Commentary* points out that "as the sun is the physical light of the world, so Jesus is the spiritual light of the world."[7] In John 8:1–11, Jesus exposed sin. In John 9:1–9, a blind man was healed because Jesus gave him sight. Jesus truly exposes sin and gives life.

We've seen two I am statements so far: "I am the bread of life," and "I am the light of the world." Constable explains that in the Old Testament, light was always associated with God's presence[8]:

- God created light (Genesis 1:3, 14–19).
- God showed Himself as flame to Moses (Exodus 3:2).
- God led the Israelites in the wilderness in a cloud of fire (Exodus 13:21–22).
- God appeared to the Israelites in fire on Mount Sinai (Exodus 19:11).

Isaiah 49:6 says, "It is not enough for you to be My Servant raising up the tribes of Jacob and restoring the protected ones of Israel. I will also make you a light for the nations, to be My salvation to the ends of the earth." Anyone in the temple complex who heard Jesus would have thought of Isaiah 49:6. During the Feast of the Tabernacles, the priests would light three huge candelabras in the women's court to symbolize God's presence.

---

[5] Radmacher et al., 1333.

[6] Radmacher et al., 1333.

[7] Radmacher et al., 1333.

[8] Thomas L. Constable, *Expository Notes of Dr. Thomas Constable: John*, 235 https://planobiblechapel.org/tcon/notes/pdf/john.pdf.

Closing

John recorded one claim the Pharisees continued to make against Jesus: He had not proven His claim to which Jesus said, "I am the light of the world" (v. 12), and that His testimony is valid because He knows where He came from and where He is going (v. 14). Then they asked a series of questions:

1. Where was Your Father? Jesus responded that if they actually knew the Father, they would also know Him (John 8:19–20).
2. Was Jesus going to kill Himself? Jesus said, "I am from above" and not from this world (John 8:21–24).
3. Who Jesus was? He responded that He was precisely who He had said He was and that He speaks only what the Father had told Him to speak (John 8:25–29).
4. How would He be made free? He responded that everyone could be made free in Him (John 8:30–37).

Each of these present Jesus as "I am"—I am the bread of life; I am the living water—I am God.

Daily Word

Jesus spoke to the scribes and the Pharisees in the Temple complex. After the Pharisees brought an adulteress woman to Him, Jesus told them not to condemn or judge others' sin. Jesus told this woman to go and sin no more. Soon after, Jesus proclaimed His second "I Am" statement: "I am the light of the world."

Jesus is the light of the world. His light is for every single person in the world—no one is left out. Jesus is not judging or condemning you. He came to be your light in life. If you walk with Jesus, you will never be in the darkness. What an incredible promise from the Lord!

Today, walk in step with Jesus, following Him and allowing Him to be your light. If you feel like darkness surrounds you, press into the light of Jesus. Remember, He loves you. So don't just sit there! Walk with Him. Then go into all the world and shine the light of Jesus!

I am the light of the world. Anyone who follows Me will never walk in the darkness but will have the light of life. —John 8:12

Further Scripture: Isaiah 49:6; John 8:58; 1 John 1:5–6

Questions

1. Jesus declares Himself to be the light of the world. Think back to the "wise men" following the light of the star to find the King and worship Him (Matthew 2:2, 9–11). What are attributes of light that can apply to Jesus (John 1:4–5, 9)?

2. Is following the light (John 8:12) the same as walking in the light (1 John 1:7)? What does walking in the darkness look like (Matthew 6:23; 8:12; John 3:19; Romans 13:12–13; Ephesians 5:11–12; 1 John 2:11)?

3. The Pharisees asked Jesus, "Who are you?" Jesus answered with a question: "What have I been saying from the beginning?" What are the things He has been saying about Himself (John 3:13–15; 4:26; 5:18, 39; 6:35; 8:12)?

4. The Jews who had believed Jesus claimed to have never been in bondage to anyone (John 8:33). Who were the Israelites in bondage to in Exodus (Exodus 2:23)? When this conversation took place, whose dominion were they under (Luke 2:1; 3:1)? Had they been in bondage to anyone else in the history of the Israelites (2 Kings 17:6; 2 Kings 25)? What did Jesus tell them they were slaves to (John 8:34)?

5. Even though John 8:30 says many came to believe Him, as the conversation continued, Jesus said their father was the devil (Matthew 13:38; John 8:44). Why did He say this if they believed Him (John 3:36; 8:31, 45; Romans 10:9; James 2:19)?

6. When Jesus stated in John 8:58, "Before Abraham was, I am," what was He actually claiming (Exodus 3:14)?

7. What did the Holy Spirit highlight to you in John 8 through the reading or the teaching?

Lesson 77: John 9
Son of God: Born Blind and Then Healed

Teaching Notes

Intro

We have now talked about two "I am" statements: "I am the bread of life" (John 6:35, 48) and "I am the light of the world (John 8:12). Jesus was emphasizing, based on Exodus 3:14, that God is "I AM WHO I AM." Jesus was saying, "I am, as well." In John 8:12, Jesus told the adulterous woman that she could no longer continue in sin and live in darkness. Because He is the light of the world, He could take her down the path of light. In John 9 are four different descriptions or themes of Jesus and a massive theme of healing.

Teaching

John 9:1–5: In verse 11, Wiersbe points out the use of the title "a man called Jesus."[1] Jesus saw a blind man as He walked by (v. 1). We pass by people every day, who need to be seen with compassion. Jesus had compassion for the man and we are called to do the same (Philippians 2:4). The disciples asked Jesus if the man or his parents had sinned to cause his blindness (v. 2). The disciples did not see the man as a suffering person but as a theological debate. One of the underlying themes is that both the disciples and Jesus saw the man, but Jesus' response to the blind man was totally different from His disciples (Job 4:7–8). In verse 3, Jesus responded that neither he nor his parents were guilty, but that his sufferings came about so God's works would be seen in him (John 5:36). Verse 4 talks about the idea of "night coming," and I'll get into that a little more in chapters 10—11. Jesus emphasizes again that He is "the light of the world" (v. 5).

John 9:6–7: Jesus spit on the ground to make mud and spread the mud on the man's eyes (v. 6). *Nelson's Commentary* explains that "mixing clay and saliva was a common practice used for eye infections."[2] What Jesus was doing would not

---

[1] Warren W. Wiersbe, *The Bible Exposition Commentary: Matthew–Galatians* (Colorado Springs: David C. Cook, 1989), 324.

[2] Earl D. Radmacher, Ronald B. Allen, and H. Wayne House, eds., *Nelson's New Illustrated Bible Commentary* (Nashville: Thomas Nelson, 1999), 1336.

have been seen as completely radical. Wiersbe suggests that the clay was used "as a picture of the *incarnation*. God made the first man out of the dust, and God sent His Son as a real Man."[3] Wiersbe suggests that the clay (our humanity) caused *irritation* (the sinfulness), which needed *irrigation* (the living water) to clean it out, leading to *identification*.[4] This makes sense to me, because in this process, I can see who I am as a child of God. In verse 7, Jesus tells the man, "Go, . . .wash in the pool of Siloam." Pool of Siloam means "sent." So the man obeyed, went to wash (irrigate) his eyes, and returned with the ability to see.

John 9:8–12: The people who had known the blind man as a beggar were astonished at what they saw. They kept asking if he was the same man, and he kept saying he was (vv. 8–9). They asked him how his eyes had been opened (v. 10), and he told them about "the man called Jesus" who restored his sight (v. 11). The people asked where Jesus was, and the man didn't know (v. 12).

John 9:13–23: In these verses, Jesus is going to be known as "a prophet."[5] Since Jesus had healed the man on the Sabbath (v. 14), the man's neighbors brought him to the Pharisees (v. 13). The Pharisees questioned what had happened (v. 15), especially since it was on the Sabbath. But they "did not realize that Jesus was offering the people something greater than the Sabbath—the true spiritual rest that comes from God (Matthew 11:28–30)."[6] The man told them what Jesus had done, but some of the Pharisees said Jesus couldn't be from God since He didn't keep the Sabbath, while others questioned how a sinful man could do such signs or miracles (v. 16). This created a division between the religious leaders. The Pharisees asked the man what he thought about Jesus, and he responded that Jesus was "a prophet" (v. 17).

The Jews still didn't believe the man, so they asked the man's parents if their son had been born blind and how he had been healed (v. 19). His parents identified the man as their son but had no knowledge of how he had been healed. They told the Pharisees the man would speak for himself because they were afraid the Pharisees might ban them from the synagogue if they identified Jesus as the Messiah (vv. 20–23). I've witnessed in the Amish community that if anyone starts to read the Bible and/or study it in a group, confessing Jesus as Savior, he or she is banned from the community. The parents of this healed man were so afraid they could be banned that they wouldn't respond. *Nelson's Commentary* outlines three levels of excommunication in the first century: a 30-day excommunication

---

[3] Wiersbe, 324–325.

[4] Wiersbe, 325.

[5] Wiersbe, 325.

[6] Wiersbe, 325.

when the excommunicated had to stay six feet away from everyone; an indefinite period of excommunication when the excommunicated could not attend worship or fellowship; or "absolute expulsion forever" during which no one can even do business with them.[7]

John 9:24–34: In these verses, Jesus is referred to as *"a Man of God."*[8] The Pharisees asked the man again about what happened and claimed that Jesus was a sinner (v. 24). The man responded, "I was blind, and now I can see!" (v. 25). They asked for details, and the man responded that they hadn't listened to him (v. 26). He asked them if they wanted to become Jesus' disciples too (v. 27). They ridiculed the man as one of Jesus' disciples, but they claimed to be Moses's disciples and they didn't know where Jesus had come from (vv. 28–29). The man responded that they didn't know where Jesus had come from, yet Jesus had healed his eyes (v. 30). The man explained that no one had ever been able to see before who had been born blind, so Jesus had to have come from God (vv. 31–33). The Pharisees became so angry with his response that they threw him out (v. 34).

John 9:35–41: Wiersbe points out the final title in John 9 is *"the Son of God."*[9] When Jesus heard what happened to the man, "He found him and asked, 'Do you believe in the Son of Man?'" (v. 35). The man asked who the Son of Man was. Jesus responded, "You have seen Him; in fact, He is the One speaking with you" (vv. 36–37). Think about this—this was the first time the man could see Jesus. Salvation took place in the man's life, and it began with physical healing (v. 36). Jesus said that He had come into the world for judgment—which was aimed at the religious (v. 37)—to let the blind see and those who do see to become blind. When some of the Pharisees heard this, they asked if they were blind (v. 40). Jesus said, "If you were blind, you wouldn't have sin. But now that you say, 'We see'— your sin remains." That means that their eyes were not on Jesus but could only see the religious. Their hearts had been hardened and their eyes closed.

Closing

To close, I want to talk about healing. The religious community had never seen anything like Jesus giving sight to the man born blind. Therefore, they pushed back against it. That's the same thing we do in the church today—we push back against the things that make us uncomfortable. *Nelson's Commentary* shares these characteristics of Jesus' healing miracles:

---

[7] Radmacher et al., 1337.

[8] Wiersbe, 325.

[9] Wiersbe, 326.

- Jesus' healing miracles revealed His divine power.
- He healed people from all walks of life—the rich, the poor, and the untouchables.
- He didn't heal everyone.
- He dealt with the emotional symptoms as well as the spiritual.
- He showed patience, compassion, and courage with those who were ill.
- He healed using the power of God, and nothing else.
- Sometimes there was a parallel between the sickness and the spiritual need.
- Sometimes He linked healing with faith and forgiveness.
- He knew that not all sickness was a sign of God's judgment but was to bring God glory.
- He didn't allow religious traditions to get in the way.
- He had the power to heal in any situation.
- That power to heal was given to His followers.
- Jesus' followers are not exempt from sickness.
- Eventually, there will be no sickness and no death (Revelation 21:4).

Daily Word

Jesus was walking with His disciples when He passed by a blind man. Jesus saw the man both physically and spiritually. Jesus stopped, talked with the man, and healed him. Now the blind man could physically see for the first time since birth. This physical healing also allowed the man to see the power and compassion of Jesus. The man testified about Jesus, calling Him "Jesus, a prophet, Lord and Son of Man." The blind man was given the spiritual eyes to see Jesus as His Lord, and he worshipped Him.

Jesus saw the blind man and took action. Ask yourself: *Do I look at people or do I see people?* Looking can take just a moment. Seeing people like Jesus requires you to discern the situation, sympathize, and take action. This world is busy and fast-paced. Who has time to see people like Jesus? You have things to do and places to go! Today, ask the Holy Spirit to open your eyes to see people and help you discern the action to take. By taking action, you may not just help them physically but also spiritually as you open their eyes to Jesus' love for them. Embrace the faith to believe Jesus will give you the grace and strength to see people.

As He was passing by, He saw a man blind from birth. —John 9:1

Further Scripture: Psalm 119:18; Psalm 146:8; Matthew 13:13–15a

Questions

1. The blind man was healed so that the works of God might be displayed in him (John 9:3). What was the purpose of displaying God's works (John 6:29; 10:25, 37–38)? Did anyone believe in Jesus because of these "works" (John 6:14; 9:16, 31–33; 10:41–42)?

2. In John 9:4, what did Jesus mean by "night is coming when no one can work"?

3. The man who was formerly blind stated that God does not hear sinners (John 9:31). What might he be basing this on (Psalm 66:18)? The Pharisees claimed to know that Jesus was a sinner in John 9:24. What sin did they believe He had committed (John 10:33)?

4. John 9 begins with a blind man whom Jesus healed and ends with Pharisees who claim to "see." How would you explain Jesus' statement in John 9:39 "That those who see may become blind"?

5. What did the Holy Spirit highlight to you in John 9 through the reading or the teaching?

Lesson 78: John 10

Son of God: The Door of the
Sheep—The Good Shepherd

Teaching Notes

Intro

In John 7, Jesus began to talk about the Spirit of God. This teaching really began to stir the pot. Jesus said, "If anybody is thirsty, he should come to Me and drink . . . streams of living water flow from deep within him" (John 7:37–38). At this point, Jesus began to emphasize the relationship, not the religion. The Pharisees and Sadducees didn't like it when Jesus said all the things they studied pointed to Him. Jesus called people not to be led astray by the religious leaders, but to follow Him. Jesus then made two more "I am" statements.

Teaching

John 10:1: "Anyone who doesn't enter the sheep pen by the door . . . is a thief and a robber." Let's talk about this image of sheep and shepherd. Isaiah 56:9–12 condemned Israel's leaders: "Israel's watchmen are blind . . . and love to sleep. [They] have fierce appetites . . . no discernment; all of them turn to their own way . . . for his own gain." If you're a shepherd who isn't concerned about the sheep, then you don't care who gets into the pen. You're only concerned for yourself. Ezekiel 34 serves as a backdrop for all of John 10. God condemned the shepherds who cared for themselves instead of their flock: "You eat the fat, wear the wool, and butcher the fattened animals, but you do not tend the flock. You have not strengthened the weak, healed the sick, bandaged the injured, brought back the strays, or sought the lost. Instead, you have ruled them with violence and cruelty. They were scattered for lack of a shepherd . . . My flock went astray on all the mountains . . . and there was no one searching or seeking for them" (Ezekiel 34:3–6). A shepherd who doesn't care does not defend the sheep against the thief or the robber. In contrast, Psalm 23 describes how God shepherds His people. "The LORD is my shepherd; there is nothing I lack" (Psalm 23:1). Isaiah 40:11 says, "He protects His flock like a shepherd; He gathers the lambs in His arms and carries them in the fold of His garment. He gently leads those that are nursing." These verses describe a relationship with God, not a religion. In Jeremiah 3:15, God said: "I will give you shepherds who are loyal to me and they will shepherd you." Which type of shepherd do you want to care for you? *Nelson's Commentary* indicated that a thief is quiet and sneaky, while a robber tends to be more vocal and violent.[1] Either way, the Shepherd has your back.

John 10:2–3: The shepherd enters the pen by the door, which the doorkeeper opens for him. He calls his own sheep by name and leads them out. The calling is personal. The shepherd will always call his sheep by name. Psalm 147:4 says, "He counts the number of the stars; He gives names to all of them." Isaiah 40:26 also says that God calls every star by name. This Shepherd calls every sheep by name.

John 10:4–5: "He goes ahead of the sheep." In Western culture, the shepherd walks behind the sheep and often uses dogs to guide the sheep. In Eastern culture, the shepherd walks in front and leads the sheep.[2] John the Baptist and Jesus did this—they prepared the way for us to follow. "The sheep follow because they recognize his voice." The sheep never follow strangers. Instead, they run away because they don't recognize the voice. How do you know His voice spiritually? You have to be in the Word of God. The Spirit of God inside you responds to Him as you read the Bible.

John 10:6: Jesus gave them this illustration of sheep and shepherd, but they didn't understand Him. How do you learn to hear from the Holy Spirit? You always have good models to follow—mentors who model for you how to hear from God, who allow you to watch as they listen and follow God.

John 10:7–8: Jesus said, "I am the door of the sheep" (v. 7). This was Jesus' third "I am" statement (and the first in John 10). "All who came before Me are thieves and robbers, but the sheep didn't listen to them" (v. 8). At night, the shepherds would lay their bodies in the open gap before the door of the sheep pen to protect the sheep.[3] Nothing could get to the sheep because the shepherd was between them and danger.

John 10:9: Jesus repeated His statement: "I am the door." He saves the sheep. Jesus is the only way to be saved. Jesus repeated this in John 14:6 "I am the way, the truth, and the life." Jesus is the only option.

---

[1] Earl D. Radmacher, Ronald B. Allen, and H. Wayne House, eds., *Nelson's New Illustrated Bible Commentary* (Nashville: Thomas Nelson, 1999), 1338.

[2] John MacArthur, *The MacArthur Bible Commentary* (Nashville: Thomas Nelson, 2005), 1391.

[3] Radmacher et al., 1338.

John 10:10: "A thief comes only to steal and to kill and to destroy." The thief is the enemy: Satan and anyone who wants to harm the sheep. The enemy wants to constantly steal, kill, and destroy. But Jesus gives sheep abundant life. He wants us to experience the abundance that He promises.

John 10:11: "I am the good shepherd." This is Jesus' fourth "I am" statement (and the second in John 10). "The good shepherd lays down his life for the sheep." Jesus came to give up Himself so we can have life. Let's dig deeper into this. In 1 John 3:16, John explained: "This is how we have come to know love: He laid down His life for us." We must give up our lives for somebody else.

John 10:12–13: Here's the religious picture: "The hired man . . . leaves them and runs away when he sees a wolf coming." The religious leaders were chickens who were afraid to engage the world and love people unless it benefited them. They didn't care about the sheep.

John 10:14–15: Again, Jesus repeated His statement: "I am the good shepherd." Twice, Jesus made both statements in the same chapter: I am the door and I am the good shepherd. "I know my own sheep and they know Me, as the Father knows Me." Jesus makes Himself known to us. Wiersbe pointed out: Jesus knows our names. He knows our nature, just as He knew Peter was impulsive, Thomas doubted, and Judas would betray Him. He knows our needs because He knows everything about His sheep. He makes Himself known to us so that we learn to love Him and trust His voice.[4]

John 10:16: "I have other sheep that are not of this fold." He welcomes all sheep and brings them together. This referred to the Gentiles, who had the chance to respond to the gospel and His voice. In Romans 1:16, Paul wrote: "For I am not ashamed of the gospel, because it is God's power for salvation to everyone who believes, first to the Jew, and also to the Greek." They will become one flock with one shepherd, according to Ephesians 2:16: "He did so that He might reconcile both to God in one body." Christ did this so we would be one. Galatians 3:28 says, "There is no Jew or Greek, slave or free, male or female; for you are all one in Christ Jesus." Jesus died for all. This fold is meant for both Jew and Gentile. First Corinthians 12:13: "For we were all baptized by one Spirit into one body." Those who believe in Jesus are part of the body of Christ.

---

[4] Warren W. Wiersbe, *The Wiersbe Bible Commentary: New Testament* (Colorado Springs: David C Cook, 2007), 265.

John 10:17–18: "This is why the Father loves me, because I am laying down My life so I may take it up again. No one takes it from Me, but I lay it down on My own." See the repetition again? Jesus chose to lay down His life so that He might give us abundant life.

Closing

Jesus is the good shepherd who was willing to give up His life to be the door for the sheep so we could have life; that's how this works. After Jesus revealed this to the religious leaders, a division took place among the Jews. The tension increased between the religious and those who wanted a relationship with Him.

Daily Word

In this passage, Jesus declared the third and fourth of the seven "I am" statements found in the Book of John: "I am the door of the sheep" and "I am the good shepherd."

Jesus came to give eternal life to those who believe and walk through the door of salvation through Him. You don't need to look anywhere else. Come through the door of Jesus. Inside the door, He will protect you as you come and go.

Jesus is the good shepherd, and like a shepherd, He laid down His life for you. Just as a shepherd knows every sheep and brings them into the protective sheepfold, Jesus loves and cares for you. As a shepherd goes after a missing sheep, Jesus will go after you. Open your heart, release any feelings of rejection or inadequacy, and receive His love today. He loves you just as you are. He created you, knows you, and calls you by name. Allow Jesus to be your shepherd and rest in His love and protection today. You will lack nothing.

Jesus said again, "I assure you: I am the door of the sheep. . . . I am the good shepherd. I know My own sheep, and they know Me, as the Father knows Me, and I know the Father. I lay down My life for the sheep." —John 10:7, 14–15

Further Reading: Psalm 23:1; Isaiah 43:1; Acts 4:12

Questions

1. What three declarations did Jesus make about Himself?
2. What did Jesus say a shepherd must do to be considered a true shepherd? What did He say someone was like if they didn't enter the sheepfold through the door?

3. Who was of the "fold" that Jesus spoke about in John 10:16? Who were the other sheep (Isaiah 42:6; 56:8; Ephesians 2:11–18)?

4. What were several things Jesus emphasized about being the Good Shepherd (John 10:11, 14–16, 17–18, 27–28)?

5. Why did the Jews take up stones again to stone Jesus in John 10:31 (Leviticus 24:16)?

6. What did the Holy Spirit highlight to you in John 10 through the reading or the teaching?

Lesson 79: John 11

Son of God: I Am the Resurrection
and the Life

Teaching Notes

Intro

We've talked about people coming back to life: in Luke 7, the widow's son; and in Luke 8, Jairus's daughter. Both came back to life right away. But in John 11, there was a little more time between Lazarus's death and when he came back to life. In John, there were seven miracles where Jesus radically showed up in someone's life. Jesus raising Lazarus back to life was the seventh of these miracles.

Teaching

MacArthur said the resurrection of Lazarus pointed to Jesus' deity. Jesus showed He was God by doing this. It strengthened the faith of the disciples. It led directly to the Cross because some of the religious didn't believe in the Resurrection.[1]

John 11:1–16: The Disciples
John 11:1–3: Lazarus of Bethany was sick. (This was not Lazarus, the poor man sitting at Abraham's bosom in Luke 16.) His sister Mary had anointed Jesus' feet with oil and wiped His feet with her hair. This was a prominent family in Bethany. Mary and Martha sent word to Jesus that Lazarus was sick. Note: Lazarus was not yet dead.

John 11:4–7: Jesus responded: "This sickness will not end in death but is for the glory of God." This pointed to Jesus' deity. These events would take place to glorify God. This is the key verse in chapter 11, if not the whole book of John. "Jesus loved Martha, her sister, and Lazarus" (v. 5). This showed Jesus' compassion and love. He wasn't blowing them off. Jesus was setting the stage for what was to come. "He stayed two more days in the place where He was" (v. 6). It was all about God's timing. Day 1: The messenger came to Jesus with the news of Lazarus's illness. Day 2: The messenger returned to Bethany. Day 3: Jesus waited.

---

[1] John MacArthur, *The MacArthur Bible Commentary* (Nashville: Thomas Nelson, 2005), 1394.

Day 4: Jesus arrived in Bethany.[2] Then Jesus led the disciples back to Judea, back into danger because He was hated in Judea.

John 11:8: The disciples protested this return to Judea because the Jews had tried to stone Jesus there. Look back at John 8:59: "At that, they picked up stones to throw at Him." Look back at John 10:31: "Again the Jews picked up rocks to stone Him." Over and over again, because Jesus pushed the envelope with the religious people, they wanted to kill Him.

John 11:9–10: These verses are all about timing. Wiersbe said: "Jesus lived on a divine timetable."[3] In John 2:4, Jesus said, "My hour has not yet come." In John 7:6–8, Jesus said, "My time has not yet arrived . . . My time has not yet fully come." He knew when His time would come. John 8:20 says, "But no one seized Him, because His hour had not come." Later in John 17:1, Jesus said, "Father, the hour has come. Glorify Your Son." Was there any significance to Jesus' statement about stumbling in the night (John 11:10)? In Matthew 26:47–49, Judas betrayed Jesus in the darkness of night. In Matthew 26:57, Jesus was led before the high priest, scribes, and elders during the night. How do you know all this took place at night? In Matthew 26:74–75, Peter denied Jesus three times and then a rooster crowed. Roosters usually crow at sunrise. Finally, Matthew 27:1 explains, "When daybreak came, all the chief priests and the elders of the people plotted against Jesus to put Him to death."

John 11:11–13: "Our friend Lazarus has fallen asleep, but I'm on My way to wake him up." The disciples thought Jesus was talking about natural sleep. They were clueless that Jesus was talking about Lazarus's actual death. As the New Testament unfolded, death was increasingly compared to sleep. In Acts 7:60, when Stephen was stoned to death, Luke said that "he fell asleep." In 1 Corinthians 15:51, Paul wrote, "We will not all fall asleep, but we will all be changed." In 1 Thessalonians 4:13–17, Paul said "those who are asleep . . . will rise first . . . to meet the Lord in the air." Whether asleep or dead, we will be raised to life to be with the Lord.

John 11:14–16: Jesus told them: "Lazarus has died. I'm glad . . . so that you may believe." Jesus had a specific purpose to fulfill when He allowed Lazarus to die. "Then Thomas said, 'Let's go so that we may die with Him.'" Wiersbe said we don't know the name of Thomas's twin, but we are all probably his twin. Sometimes Thomas demanded proof before believing Christ, but at other times he was

---

[2] Warren W. Wiersbe, *The Wiersbe Bible Commentary: New Testament* (Colorado Springs: David C. Cook, 2007), 267.

[3] Wiersbe, 268.

quick to follow Jesus into danger.[4] The disciples were just trying to figure out how to follow Christ.

John 11:17–40: The Sisters
John 11:17–23: When Jesus arrived in Bethany (near Jerusalem), Lazarus had been in the tomb for four days. Many had come to comfort Martha and Mary. Luke 10:38–42 revealed Martha was the busy sister while Mary was the one who sat at Jesus' feet. Martha rushed out to meet Jesus. "Lord, if You had been here, my brother wouldn't have died" (v. 21). Do you wonder what her tone was like? Was she accusing Him? Perhaps realizing only Jesus could help her, she went on, "Yet even now I know that whatever You ask from God, God will give You" (v. 22). Jesus told Martha, "Your brother will rise again." This exchange shows it's healthy to grieve and safe to express all our emotions to Jesus. We can say, "I don't understand, but I know you're in control." We can give everything to Jesus realizing that He knows what He's doing.

John 11:24–27: Martha clearly thought Jesus was talking about the end times. Daniel 12:2 said, "Man of those who sleep in the dust . . . will awake, some to eternal life." Jesus then made His fifth "I am" statement: "I am the resurrection and the life. The one who believes in Me, even if he dies, will live." When asked if she believed this, Martha said, "I believe you are the Messiah, the Son of God, who comes into the world." This statement supports the purpose of the book of John: "so that you may believe Jesus is the Messiah, the Son of God" (John 20:31).

John 11:28–34: Martha went back to tell Mary, "The Teacher is here." When Mary left the village, the Jews went with her assuming she was going to the tomb to cry. Like Martha, Mary said, "Lord, if You had been here . . ." At every funeral, according to oral tradition, families hired a minimum of two flute players and one professional wailing woman to mourn the dead. As Mary and Martha approached, these people followed. When Jesus saw this, He was angry because of their unbelief. He asked them, "Where have you put him?"

John 11:35–42: Jesus wept. The term indicated silent weeping rather than the wailing of the professional mourners.[5] Jesus was "a man of sorrows and acquainted with grief" (Isaiah 53:3 ESV). Even as the Jews commented on Jesus' love for Lazarus, they mocked Him for not preventing him from dying in the first place. Undeterred, Jesus told them to remove the stone, saying, "Didn't I tell you that if

---

[4] Wiersbe, 268.

[5] Wiersbe, 269.

you believed you would see the glory of God?" Jesus prayed aloud so the crowd would believe God sent Him.

John 11:43–45: Jesus shouted, "Lazarus come out!" Go back to John 10:1–5, where Jesus taught that His sheep hear His voice and follow Him. When Lazarus came out, Jesus told the people to "Loose him and let him go!" Many of the Jews believed in Him at that moment.

Closing

Jesus clearly said, "I am the resurrection and the life." Jesus is the only One who can give life! Regardless of where you're at in life, whether you're grieving or finding joy: trust the heart of God, trust that He wants what is best for you, trust His timing, trust He's always working for you (Romans 8:28). When the circumstances still don't make sense, trust that God's timing is bigger than yours. Don't try to force the hand of God—hold back and wait. Jeremiah 17:7 says, "The man who trusts in the LORD, whose confidence indeed is the Lord, is blessed. He will be like a tree planted by water: it sends its roots out toward a stream, it doesn't fear when heat comes . . . or cease producing fruit." Regardless of your situation, trust in the Lord's timing.

Daily Word

Jesus is in the business of bringing the dead to life. He told Martha, whose brother Lazarus had just died, "I am the resurrection and the life." Jesus' statement foreshadowed His own resurrection, but it's also the story of the gospel.

Seemingly dead things become alive through Jesus' power, grace, and love. Jesus miraculously brought Lazarus, who was dead for four days, back to life. Jesus can also bring life to hopeless situations. When you die to yourself and the sin in your life, surrendering everything you have to the Lord, His love and grace give you a new life in Christ. Jesus says to surrender it all: your life, your marriage, your kids, your finances, and pray, "Lord, my [fill in the blank] feels dead right now. I don't know how it will ever turn around and have life, but I trust in You." Jesus calls you to live this way every day. He promises you will live if you truly die to yourself. Do you believe this enough to walk this truth out in faith? Start today!

Jesus said to her, "I am the resurrection and the life. The one who believes in Me, even if he dies, will live. Everyone who lives and believes in Me will never die—ever. Do you believe this?" —John 11:25–26

Further Reading: Luke 9:24–25; Romans 6:8; 1 Corinthians 15:31

Questions

1. What was Jesus' first response to the messengers who brought word of Lazarus' sickness (John 11:4)? What was His next response? Why do you think Jesus waited two days to head to Bethany?

2. Why was it dangerous for Jesus to go back to Bethany? Why was He willing to go anyway (John 15:13)?

3. How did Jesus reveal Himself while speaking to Martha? How did this statement give hope to her and to you (John 5:21; 1 Corinthians 15:22)?

4. How did John 11:33, 35, and 38 speak to Jesus' humanity? How did they speak to His deity? How does this bring comfort to you (Isaiah 53:3; Hebrews 2:14–18)?

5. How does Lazarus's death and resurrection provide a good illustration for sinners who repent and trust Jesus (John 5:24; Ephesians 2:1–10)?

6. What did the Holy Spirit highlight to you in John 11 through the reading or the teaching?

Lesson 80: John 12
Son of God: Belief and Unbelief

Teaching Notes

Intro

John 12:1–8 describes the anointing at Bethany when Mary literally gave up everything to anoint Jesus' head and feet. John 12:9–11 said the religious leaders decided to kill Lazarus because his resurrection was the reason many Jews believed in Jesus. John 12:12–19 describes Jesus' triumphal entry into Jerusalem, which we covered in our study of the other Gospels. John 12:20–36 recounted one of the times when Jesus predicted His death.

Today, let's look at how the New Testament looks back to the Old Testament. Now that Christ was talking about who He was, He pointed back to the Old Testament prophecies that were going to be fulfilled.

Teaching

John 12:37–40: Constable said John described two crises of faith in the Jewish community.[1] The first crisis occurred in John 6:66, "From that moment, many of His disciples turned back and no longer accompanied Him." After hearing some of Jesus' hard teachings (John 6:60), many of His disciples didn't want to follow Him any longer. The second crisis occurred in John 12:37: "Even though He had performed so many signs in their presence, they did not believe in Him." Not only did the religious leaders not believe in Him, but they were trying to kill Him. Wiersbe described three aspects of the Jews' response to Jesus.[2] First, the Jews *would not* believe (v. 37). Second, they *could not* believe because their unbelief fulfilled the word of Isaiah the prophet (v. 38). Compare verse 38 with Isaiah 53:1, "Who has believed what we have heard? And who has the arm of the Lord been revealed to?" Third, they *should not* believe because God had blinded their eyes and hardened their hearts (vv. 39–40). MacArthur said these responses stressed the

---

[1] Thomas L. Constable, *Expository Notes of Dr. Thomas Constable: John*, 344, https://planobiblechapel.org/tcon/notes/pdf/john.pdf.

[2] Warren W. Wiersbe, *The Wiersbe Bible Commentary: New Testament* (Colorado Springs: David C. Cook, 2007), 274–75.

"sovereign plan of God in His judicial hardening of Israel."[3] However this hardening was "not apart from human responsibility and culpability."[4] Because they first chose not to believe, God hardened their hearts so they should not believe.

John 12:40–41: In verse 40, John quoted Isaiah 6:9–10. Isaiah had clearly seen God's glory (v. 41). Now John pointed out the Jews had seen Jesus' glory, but they didn't believe. MacArthur said their lack of belief made Jesus "the author of the judicial hardening of Israel."[5] In other words, Jesus served in the role of Judge. John alluded to this truth in other places. John 5:22–23 says God has given all judgment to the Son. John 5:27 says God has given Jesus the right to pass judgment. In John 5:30, Jesus said, "I can do nothing on My own, I judge only as I hear, and My judgment is righteous." Jesus was the Judge of His people, as described in Isaiah. God hardened the Jews' hearts for their unbelief and set them apart from God into hell so the Gentiles could walk into salvation. In John 5:42, Jesus recognized that the Jews had no love for God.

John 12:42: Many Jews, even rulers, believed in Jesus but wouldn't confess Him because they feared the Pharisees would ban them from the synagogue. Even though there was a hardening among the Jews, there was still hope because many did believe in Jesus. Did they harden their hearts, or did God harden their hearts? The answer is yes to both questions. It's 100 percent God and 100 percent man. John didn't just pick and choose these two passages. John interwove truths from the Old Testament and New Testament throughout his Gospel. These disciples knew the Word of God, so when Jesus began to release the Old Testament, they recognized it. See these examples:

- John 1:23: "He [John the Baptist] said, "I am a voice of one crying out in the wilderness: Make straight the way of the Lord—just as Isaiah the prophet said." John described John the Baptist as a voice in the wilderness "just as Isaiah the prophet said" (Isaiah 40:3). John established trust in the Word of God based on the Old Testament. He built his case throughout his Gospel. He was saying that John the Baptist communicated the truth.
- John 2:17: "And His disciples remembered that it is written: Zeal for Your house will consume Me." This was a quote drawn from Psalm 69:9.

---

[3] John MacArthur, *NASB MacArthur Study Bible*, updated edition (Nashville: Thomas Nelson, 2006), 1576.

[4] MacArthur, 1576.

[5] MacArthur, 1576.

- John 6:31: Jesus reminded them that God gave their fathers "bread from heaven to eat" before saying, "I am the bread of life" (John 6:35). Jesus was quoting from Psalm 78:24.

- John 6:45: "It is written in the Prophets: And they will all be taught by God." This was quoted from Isaiah 54:13. If you interacted with a Jewish person about the New Testament, they would recognize the writings from the Law and the Prophets.

- In John 10:34, Jesus asked, "Isn't it written in your Scripture, I said, you are gods?" (Psalm 82:6).

- When we get to the text of John 12, we see more connections. John 12:13 referred to Psalm 118:26. John 12:15 referred to Zechariah 9:9. John 12:38 was drawn from Isaiah. Why did John do this? Look at Matthew 5:17. Jesus did not come to destroy, but to fulfill the Law and the Prophets. Jesus walked out the fulfillment of these prophecies.

What purpose did God have for hardening of the hearts for the Jewish people?

First, it was a partial hardening (John 12:42). Some Jewish people, even rulers, believed in Jesus, but wouldn't publicly confess Him because they feared the Pharisees would ban them from the synagogues.

John 12:43: Even though they believed in Jesus, they were still afraid of man. (At some future point, Nicodemus and Joseph of Arimathea finally began to speak out.) MacArthur said the faith of the leaders "was so weak that they refused to take any position that would threaten their position in the synagogue."[6] Their desire for the praise of man took priority over the praise of God, so they refused to publicly announce their faith in Christ. First John 2:28, "So now little children, remain in Him so that when He appears we may have boldness and not be ashamed before Him at His coming." Even among those believers, their faith was weak. MacArthur stressed these rulers "demonstrated inadequate, irresolute, and spurious faith."[7] In other words, they were saying, "I'm in, but I'm kind of in." The Greek word for "believe" in John 12:42 typically indicates, without a shadow of doubt, saving faith. John 8:30 used the same language: "Many believed in Him." Yes, they believed, but they were afraid to admit it.

Second, because of the hardening of the hearts of the Jews, the gospel was released to the Gentile nations (Romans 11:11–12). "By their stumbling, salvation came to the Gentiles" (v. 11). This was God's game plan and purpose for hardening

---

[6] MacArthur, 1576.

[7] MacArthur, 1576.

the hearts of the Jews. The stumbling of the Jews brought riches to the world, to the Gentiles, but "how much more will their full number bring!" (v. 12). Paul went on to say, "So that you will not be conceited, brother . . . a partial hardening has come to Israel until the full number of the Gentiles has come in" (Romans 11:25).

John remembered that Isaiah said there would be a hardening of the hearts of the Jews. We can be OK with that because it released salvation to the Gentiles "until their full number" believes. How do we know when that is? We don't, so our responsibility has to be to share the gospel because we have no idea when this number will be fulfilled. "In this way, all Israel will be saved" (Romans 11:27).

Third, because of the fullness of the Gentiles, all Israel will be saved. What we read in John 12 about the hardening of the Jews should encourage us to go to Romans 11, because eventually all of Israel will be saved.

Closing

If we go and share the gospel with the Gentiles, the Jews should be encouraged. Why? Salvation is coming to them through their coming Messiah because of the fullness of the Gentiles.

Daily Word

Jesus used an agricultural example to teach His disciples: "Unless a grain of wheat falls to the ground and dies, it remains by itself. But if it dies, it produces a large crop." Jesus prepared His disciples for His upcoming Crucifixion and death. The hour had come for Jesus, the Son of Man, to be glorified. But from Jesus' death would come a great harvest of salvations!

In a similar way, Jesus instructed believers to make it a daily practice to die to themselves. When you die to yourself, you make room for more of the Lord to be glorified in your life, just as when wheat falls to the ground and produces a large crop. Today, say to the Lord, "Show me how to die to myself today, so that You, Jesus, may be glorified in me!" The Lord will give grace upon grace as you let go of the things He brings to mind, and new life will grow beyond what you can imagine. You may think you need to hang on to control or an area in your life, but Jesus says when you lose your life, you will gain even more. Follow Him. His love never fails.

I assure you: Unless a grain of wheat falls to the ground and dies, it remains by itself. But if it dies, it produces a large crop. The one who loves his life will lose it, and the one who hates his life in this world will keep it for eternal life. If anyone serves Me, he must follow Me. —John 12:24–26

Further Scriptures: Luke 9:23–24; Romans 8:12–13; Galatians 2:20

Questions

1. How did Mary show love to Jesus (Matthew 26:6–13; Mark 14:3–9)? Why did she do these things? Do you think she knew and understood what was about to happen to Jesus?

2. How was Mary a lot like King David in her costly giving (2 Samuel 24:24)?

3. Why were the chief priests plotting to put not just Jesus to death, but Lazarus as well?

4. In verse 28, God spoke audibly in the Gospels for the third time. Can you name the other two times He spoke audibly (Matthew 3:17; Luke 9:35)?

5. Why did some of the rulers believe in Jesus but refuse to confess Him out loud? Would you consider their belief to be a saving belief? Why or why not (Matthew 10:32–33; Romans 10:9–10)?

6. What did the Holy Spirit highlight to you in John 12 through the reading or the teaching?

Lesson 81: John 13

Son of God: Jesus Washes the Disciples' Feet

Teaching Notes

Intro

In a society in which everything changes, we need something to hang onto that doesn't change—and that's the Word of God. At the end of John 12, Jesus stated that He said and did only what He heard and saw His Father do. John 13 was the beginning of His farewell address to His disciples. He began to prepare them for what was coming.

Teaching

John 13:3: Jesus knew the time had come. He knew His identity, who He was, where He came from, what He had come to do, and where He was going. In Matthew 3:17, the Father spoke identity into His Son. God audibly declared Jesus as His beloved Son with whom He was well pleased. This statement was repeated after Jesus' transfiguration, with God's additional command to "listen to Him" (Matthew 17:5). How many times do we think that following Christ is only about having our sins forgiven, so we live the rest of our lives still seeking our significance in so many other things? But He has given us everything we need—our identity is found in Christ.

Peter reminded believers that God has given them "everything required for life and godliness" (2 Peter 1:2–4). We are no longer who we used to be; now we walk as one of His children. When we truly understand this, we will walk differently. We will walk with authority. In 1 Thessalonians 4:16–18, Paul said, "For the Lord Himself will descend from heaven with a shout . . . the dead in Christ will rise first. Then we who are still alive will . . . meet the Lord in the air . . . Therefore comfort one another with these words." Through Christ, we know where we came from, who we are, and where we're going. Romans 8:14 emphasized that, as children of God, we are led by the Spirit of God. If you're living under fear and bondage, that's from your old life. Since our identity is found in Christ, we don't have to seek it in other places. Ephesians 3:20 states that God can "do above and beyond all that we ask or think according to the power that works in us." We have to learn how to walk in His power.

John 13:4–5: Jesus washed His disciples' feet. Normally, a servant would perform this duty for the guests. Jesus performed this task to begin to prepare His disciples for the next part of their lives—to take leadership for what was coming. In Luke 22:24, as they approached Jerusalem, the disciples had argued among themselves about which one of them was the greatest. Now Jesus calmly rose from the table and began to model what greatness looked like in His kingdom. In Matthew 20:25–28, Jesus explained how greatness was found in His kingdom. In this act, Jesus demonstrated His understanding of His identity and Sonship. He also communicated the importance of humility. Through His actions, Jesus showed His disciples how to conduct themselves and how to show they valued another person. Because Jesus knew who He was, He could serve others and show them that they were valued. Peter challenged believers to "grow in the grace and knowledge of our Lord and Savior Jesus Christ" (2 Peter 3:18). Wiersbe said, "We are growing in knowledge, but not in grace."[1] In support, Wiersbe also quoted Andrew Murray, who wrote: "Humility is the only soil in which the graces root."[2] First Peter 5:5–6 states, "God resists the proud but gives grace to the humble. Humble yourselves, therefore, under the mighty hand of God so that He may exalt you at the proper time." God's grace flows in and through our humility. Although Jesus had everything, He humbled Himself and took the place of a servant.

John 13:6–10: Peter recognized Jesus' greatness, and because he knew "great" people shouldn't perform this task, he protested Jesus washing his feet (v. 8). When Jesus said, "If I don't wash you, you have no part with Me," Peter responded by asking Jesus to wash "not only my feet, but also my hands and my head" (v. 9). Peter wanted everything Jesus had to offer him. Jesus' response in verse 10 confirmed that when we come to Christ, our sins are forgiven, and we become the righteousness of God in Christ. That cleansing washes away all of our sins. In 1 Corinthians 6:9–11, Paul explained that all sinners are washed, sanctified, and justified in the name of Christ and by the Spirit of God. Titus 3:3–5 points out, "We too were once foolish . . . but when the kindness of God our Savior . . . appeared, He saved us . . . according to His mercy, through the washing of regeneration and renewal by the Holy Spirit." This explains why Jesus told Peter he didn't need to be washed again completely, but only his feet. Jesus' statement indicated that as we walk through life, we need to continually confess our sins as they happen, it's not that we lose our salvation.

---

[1] Warren W. Wiersbe, *The Wiersbe Bible Commentary: New Testament* (Colorado Springs: David C. Cook, 2007), 276.

[2] Andrew Murray, quoted in Wiersbe, 276.

This truth was first illustrated in the initial consecration of Aaron and his sons as priests. In Exodus 29:4, Aaron and his sons were washed with water when they were consecrated for service, but that was the only time they underwent that particular cleansing. In Exodus 30:17–18, God commanded Moses to make a bronze basin to place between the tent of meeting and the altar. "Aaron and his sons must wash their hands and feet from the basin" whenever they entered the tent of meeting to minister (Exodus 30:19–21). When we have unconfessed sin in our lives, we don't hear from the Lord. By confessing our sins, our relationship with Him remains strong.

John 13:12–16: Jesus gave His disciples an example of serving others that they were to follow. Jesus wanted them to have a heart of humility to serve others. Jesus wasn't after outward expression without heart transformation. That's why He called out the Pharisees in Matthew 23. Jesus calls us to take on humility as the very foundation of everything we do. If we want to be everything Christ has called us to be, we have to know who we are and walk in humility.

John 13:17: "If you know these things, you are blessed if you do them." The blessing comes when we do these things. Donald Carson said: "There is a form of religious piety that utters a hearty 'Amen!' to the most stringent demands of discipleship, but which rarely does anything about them."[3] James 1:22 emphasizes that believers should "be doers of the word and not hearers only." Jesus said the one who does the Word would be blessed.

Closing

Jesus wants you to know you're a child of God, and He wants you to walk with humility as one of His children.

Daily Word

Jesus knew the time had come for Him to depart from this world and go back to His Father. Jesus loved those around Him, and He poured into them until His final breath. He also understood His identity as God's Son. It was from this place of walking confidently in His identity that Jesus served and loved others. During dinner before the Passover Festival, Jesus served His disciples by humbly washing their feet. He even washed the feet of Judas Iscariot, who Jesus knew would soon betray Him.

---

[3] D. A. Carson, *The Gospel According to John* (Leicester, England: Inter-Varsity Press; Grand Rapids: Eerdmans, 1991), 496; quoted in Thomas L. Constable, *Expository Notes of Dr. Thomas Constable: John*, 356, https://planobiblechapel.org/tcon/notes/pdf/john.pdf.

When you love and serve others in humility, do it from the place of your identity in Christ as a child of God. Accept the truth that you are fearfully and wonderfully made for a purpose and fully loved by Jesus. When you walk in this identity, loving, serving, and humility becomes natural, just as it was with Jesus. It's not about *what* you do, it's about *who* you are in Christ. Jesus modeled this for you as He washed His disciples' feet. You may be the lead pastor, a schoolteacher, the CEO, the principal, or a mom or dad raising kids, but you are still called to serve and love others. Pause for a minute and ask the Lord, *Who can I serve a glass of water to today in love? Who can I carry trash for? Whose dirty feet can I wash in love and humility?* Look around you. Jesus loved you so you can love others.

Jesus knew that the Father had given everything into His hands, that He had come from God, and that He was going back to God. So He got up from supper, laid aside His robe, took a towel, and tied it around Himself. Next, He poured water into a basin and began to wash His disciples' feet and to dry them with the towel tied around Him. —John 13:3–5

Further Scripture: John 1:12; Philippians 2:3–5; 1 Peter 5:5b–6

Questions

1. Why did Jesus tell Peter, "If I don't wash you, you have no part with me"?

2. In John 13:14–15, do you think Jesus is commanding us to wash other people's feet or simply to humble ourselves and serve others?

3. In John 13:27, why do you think Jesus said to Judas, "What you're doing, do quickly"?

4. In John 13:34, Jesus said, "I give you a new command: Love one another. Just as I have loved you, you must also love one another." Why do you think He commanded this (Leviticus 19:18)?

5. What did the Holy Spirit highlight to you in John 13 through the reading or the teaching?

Lesson 82: John 14
Son of God: Let Not Your Hearts Be Troubled

Teaching Notes

Intro

At the end of John 13, Jesus told His disciples that someone would betray them. On top of that, Jesus predicted Peter's denial. But that wasn't all! Jesus also told the disciples that He would be leaving soon. All that bad news troubled their hearts.

Teaching

John 14:1: By believing in Jesus, we can help prevent our hearts from being troubled. Believing in Jesus means we have salvation and we are going to Heaven. This helps our hearts to not be troubled.

John 14:2: Wiersbe says, "Heaven is not a product of religious imagination."[1] Heaven is where our Father dwells. Heaven is where Jesus lives and intercedes on our behalf. That fact alone should take care of your heart trouble. Not everyone goes to heaven. Only those who believe Christ is the Messiah will get into heaven (Acts 4:12). When we have this salvation in Christ, we have a place in heaven. Heaven is also:

- A kingdom—"For in this way, entry into the eternal kingdom of our Lord and Savior Jesus Christ will be richly supplied to you." (2 Peter 1:11)
- An inheritance—"and into an inheritance that is imperishable, uncorrupted, and unfading, kept in heaven for you." (1 Peter 1:4)
- A country and a city—"But they now desire a better place—a heavenly one. Therefore God is not ashamed to be called their God, for He has prepared a city for them." (Hebrews 11:16)

---

[1] Warren W. Wiersbe, *Wiersbe Bible Exposition Commentary: New Testament* (Colorado Springs: David C. Cook, 2007), 272.

- Heaven is a home—"In My Father's house are many dwelling places; if not, I would have told you. I am going away to prepare a place for you." (John 14:2)

Robert Frost said, "Home is the place where, when you have to go there, they have to take you in."[2] For your heart to get you through times that are troubling, focus on the eternal.

John 14:3: Our job with reviveSCHOOL is to prepare you for the return of Christ. Acts 1:11 tells us that just as Jesus left, He will be coming back. Daniel 7:13 says that Jesus will come back with the clouds of heaven. Jesus is coming back!

John 14:4–5: The disciples didn't know where Jesus was going, so Thomas's question was reasonable. They didn't know if He was going to Bethany or Jerusalem, much less to heaven.

John 14:6: Jesus spoke another "I am" statement in response to Thomas's question, "I am the way, the truth, and the life" (v. 6). Thomas didn't know the way to where Jesus was going. He didn't know how to keep his heart from being troubled. Jesus told Thomas and the disciples the way: the way was Jesus!

The American church sometimes picks apart verse 6 and then we pick what we like best. We like Jesus being the truth. We like Jesus being the resurrection and the life. But we dislike following the narrow path. We dislike when Jesus asks us to take the little dirt path of faith. But no one comes to the Father except through Jesus. We can become so concerned with being politically correct that we never tell lost people about Jesus, who is the only way to heaven. The earliest followers of Christ were known as followers of "the way."

John 14:7–11: Knowing the Father right now helps our hearts to not be troubled. If you know Jesus, you know the Father. You can experience the Father right now. You don't have to wait to experience Him in an eternal state.

John 14:12–15: You can keep your heart from being troubled because you have the privilege of prayer. We have the privilege of coming before the Almighty God because of what Christ has done for us.

John 14:16–17: You can keep your heart from being troubled because you have the Holy Spirit. Think of the Holy Spirit as the one who comforts us to bravely

---

[2] Robert Frost, *The Robert Frost Reader: Poetry and Prose*, ed. Edward Connery Lathem and Lawrance Thompson (New York: Henry Holt and Co., 1972), 24.

face life. He is the Spirit of Truth. He will never remind us of anything that is untrue, and he will strengthen us.

John 14:18–24: You can keep your heart from being troubled by enjoying the Father's love.

John 14:25–31: You can keep your heart from being troubled by having God's gift of peace. If you are in Christ, you have this peace.

Closing

To recap, Warren Wiersbe gave us five ways we can keep our hearts from being troubled:

1. You are going to Heaven (John 13:36—14:6).
2. You know the Father right now (John 14:7–11).
3. You have the privilege of prayer (John 14:12–15).
4. You have the Holy Spirit (John 14:16–18).
5. You enjoy the Father's love (John 14:19–24).[3]

Daily Word

Jesus spoke directly to His disciples: "Your heart must not be troubled. Believe in God and in Me." Then, after discussing all the rooms in heaven where Jesus would go away to prepare, Jesus made another "I am" statement: "I am the way, the truth, and the life." Jesus understood His time here on earth was coming to a close, so He didn't use many words but went right to the point.

Wouldn't you say the same is true for today? People's hearts are troubled. They look in every direction for the way, the truth, and the life. They seek success. They try to remain in control of every situation. They research countless religions and philosophies. But the Word of God says, "Jesus is the way, the truth, and the life." Believe in Jesus and you will be saved. Do you know someone whose heart is troubled and searching for the way? Pray for him or her. As the Lord leads, share the message of salvation through Christ and share how you found what you were looking for in the love and grace of Jesus Christ. May the Lord lead many to His saving grace. May their hearts no longer be troubled because they have found the Way. Yes, Lord, please save the lost who need to be found by You. Amen!

---

[3] Warren W. Wiersbe, *Be Transformed: Christ's Triumph Means Your Transformation* (Colorado Springs: David C. Cook, 1986), 34–46.

Your heart must not be troubled. Believe in God; believe also in Me. . . . Jesus told him, "I am the way, the truth, and the life. No one comes to the Father except through Me." —John 14:1, 6

Further Reading: Acts 4:12; Romans 10:9; 1 Timothy 2:5

Questions

1. In John 14:5, Thomas asked Jesus how they would know the way to where He was going. Why did Jesus respond, "I am the way, the truth and the life; no one comes to the Father but through Me" (v. 6)?

2. In John 14:14, Jesus said, "If you ask anything in My name, I will do it." Could there ever be a time when God chooses not to answer your prayer, even though you ask in Jesus' name and, if so, why (Romans 14:23b, James 4:3)?

3. How does keeping God's commandments show that you love Him (Amos 3:3; Hebrews 11:5)?

4. In John 14:8–9, how was it possible that Phillip, after three and a half years, didn't comprehend that Jesus is in the Father and the Father is in Him?

5. What did the Holy Spirit highlight to you in John 14 through the reading or the teaching?

Lesson 83: John 15
Son of God: The True Vine

Teaching Notes

Intro

John 14—17 contains the Farewell Discourses, the last words of Jesus to the disciples right before He went to the cross. John was intentional about showing the divinity of Jesus. One of the ways John did this was through the seven "I am" statements in his Gospel. So far, we've looked at six of the seven "I am" statements: (1) I am the bread of life; (2) I am the light of the world; (3) I am the door of the sheep; (4) I am the good shepherd; (5) I am the resurrection and the life; and (6) I am the way, the truth, and the life. Today, we look at the final "I am" statement: "I am the true vine."

Teaching

John 15:1: Some translations have the Father as the gardener or the vine dresser. Jesus insisted that He is the true vine. He was trying to say something about who He is. It's an exclusive claim that makes Him distinct from other vines. In the Old Testament, Israel was referred to as the vine planted by God:

- Israel as the vine: "You uprooted a vine from Egypt; you drove out the nations and planted it. You cleared a place for it; it took root and filled the land. The mountains were covered by its shade, and the mighty cedars with its branches. It sent out sprouts toward the Sea and shoots toward the River. Why have you broken down its walls so that all who pass by pick its fruit? The boar from the forest tears it and creatures of the field feed on it" (Psalm 80:8–13).
- Israel as a choice vine: "I planted you as a choice vine from the very best seed. How then could you turn into a degenerate, foreign vine?" (Jeremiah 2:21).

In the Old Testament, God planted Israel as His vine, but Israel grew into something God had not intended. Israel strayed from the pure seed. Jesus' claim was that He was the true outgrowth of the pure seed that God the Father had planted in Israel. Jesus is the fulfillment of the true vine God intended, not the wild vine that strayed. Jesus and Israel both had the same Gardener, the Father. Jesus' vine is the same vine from the pure seed God planted in Abraham. He is the picture of what God's plan looked like when it grew in full health.

John 15:2: "Every branch in Me that does not produce fruit He removes, and He prunes every branch that produces fruit so that it will produce more fruit." In verse 2, "He" is God; God takes away the branches that do not bear fruit. Jesus didn't sugarcoat this truth. God prunes those who do produce fruit. Jesus addressed everyone with both categories of people who were to be pruned. Those who don't produce fruit are unbelievers. They are not connected to the vine, so they are unable to produce fruit. They will wither and die because they are not connected to the vine. This picture is made even more clear in verse 6 when Jesus said, "If anyone does not remain in Me, he is thrown aside like a branch and he withers. They gather them, throw them into the fire, and they are burned." It sounds harsh, but if Jesus is the true source of life and you choose to not be connected to the source of life, you are choosing death. Your choice has cut you off from the only source that can give you life. If a branch is cut off from the source, it will die. Its connection with the vine is what keeps it alive. Without that connection, the branch cannot survive.

The second group Jesus addressed were the people who produced fruit. If branches are connected to the vine, then they produce fruit because they are connected to the source. Fruit is the evidence that the sap from the vine is flowing. But pruning occurs even for those who produce fruit. Being pruned doesn't sound like fun. But Jesus said that when we are connected to Him, we will bear fruit, and God will prune us so that we can be even more fruitful. If you are connected to Christ, just expect pruning; God wants you to be more fruitful and good gardeners have to prune. Pruning involves cutting away what is dead in order to make room for something new to grow. It is a process of increasing health and shaping to a certain form. This is exactly what God does in our lives. He prunes the stuff in us that is not fully alive to make room for the newness and fullness He has in store for us. Pruning still hurts, but it's worth it. Pruning isn't something God does to punish us. God prunes us to enhance us and bless us.

John 15:3–6: There's an interesting word play in verse 3. The word translated "pruning" in verse 2 can also be translated "clean" as in verse 3. Jesus referenced how the disciples know true life already. They were connected to the vine because of the truth Jesus taught them.

In verse 4, Jesus introduced the concept of "remaining in Me," which He used seven times in verses 1–17. The very basic thing Jesus told His disciples was that they needed to remain in Him if they wanted to bear fruit. Apart from Jesus, they could do nothing. We have the tendency to read the verse as "apart from Me you can do some things." But Jesus said that apart from Him we could do nothing. So, we have to ask ourselves: "What is the fruit we are supposed to produce?" and "How do we abide in Him to do that?"

John 15:7–17: What is the fruit Jesus talked about? The easiest way to sum it up is to say we are to be like Jesus. Bearing fruit proves who are His disciples. Jesus said, "By this all people will know that you are My disciples, if you have love for one another" (John 13:35), and "As the Father has loved Me, I have also loved you. Remain in My love. If you keep My commands you will remain in My love, just as I have kept My Father's commands and remain in His love" (John 15:9–10). The Father loved Jesus. Jesus obeyed the Father. Jesus loved the disciples, and now they were to obey Jesus by remaining in Him. As they remained in Him, they would know His love that would lead to total obedience to God. Jesus said, "I assure you: The Son is not able to do anything on His own, but only what He sees the Father doing. For whatever the Father does, the Son also does these things in the same way" (John 5:19). We bear fruit when we do what we see Jesus doing. The fruit that we will bear is a description of Jesus—the fruit is Christlikeness: "But the fruit of the Spirit is love, joy, peace, patience, kindness, goodness, faith, gentleness, self-control. Against such things there is no law" (Galatians 5:22–23). When the sap of God's Spirit is flowing into you, you start bearing a resemblance to the life source—Jesus.

Abiding in Jesus leads to loving Jesus. Loving Jesus leads to obedience. Obedience leads to fruit. Fruit is the likeness of Christ. This process is cyclical. It repeats over and over again. It's the life cycle of following Jesus. Acting like Jesus includes sharing the good news with everyone you meet, just like Jesus did.

How do you stay connected to the vine?

1. Stay in the Word. This is what you are doing with reviveSCHOOL. You are staying in the Word because you meet Jesus here.
2. Pray. How do you stay connected to any friend or family member? You spend time talking to them. Prayer is your connection to God. It's your time spent talking to Him.

If you remain in Jesus and He remains in you, you ought to expect your prayers to be answered because you will be asking from His heart. Fruit isn't the end goal. God's glory is the end goal. Fruit points people to who God really is.

Closing

If you love Jesus, you will obey Him. You will start bearing more and more fruit that will point more and more people to the Father who will receive the glory.

Daily Word

Jesus introduced the seventh and final "I am" statement: "I am the true vine." In ancient Israel, grapes were a major agricultural product. So it was fitting for Jesus to use the illustration of Himself as the vine, God the Father as the vineyard keeper, and believers of Christ as the branches. The vineyard keeper knows what he wants his plant to look like and will prune it, cutting away branches, to allow it to grow in the way he knows is best. In the same way, God will cut away any branches in your life not producing fruit so that more fruit will grow.

Jesus clearly stated that if you do not abide in Him, you can do nothing. No fruit will be produced. Nothing. Period. You must remain on the true vine in Christ to produce life-giving fruit. Remaining or abiding in Christ means to read the Word and pray. Just like getting to know a friend, you must continue to spend time on your relationship with Jesus. When you abide in Christ, your fruit will resemble Christ's: love, joy, peace, patience, kindness, goodness, faithfulness, gentleness, and self-control. Those around you will want to know what is producing this fruit in you. Then you can point them to Jesus and glorify the Father.

I am the true vine, and My Father is the vineyard keeper. Every branch in Me that does not produce fruit He removes, and He prunes every branch that produces fruit so that it will produce more fruit. —John 15:1–2

Further Scripture: John 15:5; John 15:8; Galatians 5:22–25

Questions

1. What does it mean for branches to be "pruned" in John 15:2? Can you think of a time when God has pruned you? In what ways?

2. In John 15:5, Jesus said that He is the vine and we are the branches. Have you seen the fruit in your life that Jesus is talking about? In what ways? Why does He say that apart from Him, we can do nothing?

3. How does John 15:13 speak to you? Do you take this literally? Why or why not?

4. Jesus was persecuted, and He told us that we would be persecuted too. Do you feel you have been persecuted for Jesus' sake? In what ways?

5. What did the Holy Spirit highlight to you in John 15 through the reading or teaching?

Lesson 84: John 16

Son of God: The Spirit of Truth

Teaching Notes

Intro

John 15:26–27 says, "When the Counselor comes, the One I will send to you from the Father—the Spirit of truth who proceeds from the Father—He will testify about Me. You also will testify, because you have been with Me from the beginning." Jesus is truth. He comes from the Father and will send the "Spirit of truth" to us. And we will bear witness of this. We have the Holy Spirit getting us ready for something.

Teaching

John 16:1–3: "I have told you these things" (v. 1), refers to all Jesus taught the disciples about the coming of the Holy Spirit. "To keep from stumbling" implies that things will continue to come at us and to pull us away from God. God promises that when we walk into His presence, nothing can happen to us (Psalm 91:3–12). In John 16:2a, Jesus explained that "they," the religious, will ban those who follow Christ (John 9:22).

We live in a spiritual battle, and the church today doesn't even recognize the enemy. Time to Revive has found that it is the religious who don't like us, who try to stop what we're doing, because they can't control what the Holy Spirit is doing in our lives. As we walk forward with the gospel of Christ, we should expect people to be angry and threatened by us. If they're not, we have to ask if we're really doing the will of God. The Holy Spirit will help us learn how to deal with those who don't like us. Jesus said, "They hated Me for no reason" (John 15:25). As the time nears for Jesus' return, the opposition will ramp up even more. We don't see the persecution in America, possibly because we're not going out to do what Christ called us to do. Psalm 35:19 says, "Do not let my deceitful enemies rejoice over me; do not let those who hate me without cause look at me maliciously." Psalm 69:4 says, "Those who hate me without cause are more numerous than the hairs of my head; my deceitful enemies, who would destroy me, are powerful. Though I did not steal, I must repay."

Verse 2 continues with, "Anyone who kills you will think he is offering service to God" because "they haven't known the Father or Me" (v. 3). Philippians 1:28–30 points out that we will "all suffer for Him, having the same struggle" that Jesus had. We can expect to suffer, even to the point of death. Think about it—when we go into a community, it's never the lost who have issues with us, but it's the religious! It's always in-house. What I've seen is that it's difficult to elevate truth when people want most to elevate tradition.

Why were the religious against Jesus and His gospel? Dan Stewart (blueletterbible.org) suggests six reasons:

1. *Jesus' claims outweighed the authority of the religious* (John 7:48–49). Jesus didn't care about the religious leaders' authority because He didn't allow traditions to outweigh the triumph of what He had come to do.

2. *Jesus' deeds outraged the religious leaders* (Matthew 12:23–29). His deeds testified that He was the *Son of God*, and that outraged the Jewish leaders.

3. *Jesus was a threat to the Jewish religious system.* John 2:13–15 describes Jesus clearing out the Temple. Truth will always threaten the system created by those who don't walk by faith.

4. *Jesus was a threat to the Jewish leaders' way of life.* I've never understood territorialism in the body of Christ. Imagine if we really did all come together as the body of Christ!

5. *The people with whom Jesus socialized outraged the religious leaders* (Matthew 11:19; Luke 7:39). The religious leaders didn't socialize with sinners because they were filled with false pride.

Many times, our churches don't reflect their communities but reflect who they hang out with. Christ hangs out with us (Romans 5:8). A church becoming more diverse will encounter growing pains and cultural issues that will take time to work out. Jesus introduces the possibility for overcoming these issues and stumbling blocks by hanging out with our community.

6. *Jesus had a lack of respect for their traditions.* Colossians 2:6–8 says, "Therefore, as you have received Christ Jesus the Lord, walk in Him, rooted and built up in Him and established in the faith, just as you were taught, overflowing with gratitude. Be careful that no one takes you captive through philosophy and empty deceit based on human tradition, based on the elemental forces of the world, and not based on Christ." When traditions don't breathe life into your walk with the Lord, it's time to let them go (Mark 3:4–6; Acts 5:29; Hebrews 5:11—6:3).

John 16:4: Jesus told His disciples that He had told them all these things so that when their times of suffering came, they would remember He had warned them and also promised them the indwelling of the Holy Spirit to help them.

Closing

We all have to answer this question: Do we want to put our trust in truth or our trust in traditions? Traditions are important. Family traditions are fun. But please don't ever elevate those traditions over Jesus Christ. If we're not careful, it's easy to let that happen.

Mark 3:26–27 says, "And if Satan rebels against himself and is divided, he cannot stand but is finished! On the other hand, no one can enter a strong man's house and rob his possessions unless he first ties up the strong man. Then he will rob his house."

If you're dealing with the spirit of religion, gather other believers together and pray that the Spirit of Christ will bind up the spirit of religion.

Daily Word

Jesus told the disciples many things to keep them from stumbling because He knew the religious or the nonbelievers would try to throw the disciples off and make their feet stumble. But Jesus equipped His people with the Spirit of truth to guide them into all the truth.

Do you ever feel like you are being questioned for walking in the truth of Jesus? Remember, as you abide in Christ, you are being rooted and built up in Him—and established in your faith. Walk in the Spirit of truth and allow Him to guide you into all truth, beyond a religious mindset or traditions. This truth will bring glory to the Lord because you are walking with what the Spirit of the truth declares to you. Today, bind up the spirit of religion and function in the Spirit of truth, allowing freedom to reign in your life.

When the Spirit of truth comes, He will guide you into all the truth. For He will not speak on His own, but He will speak whatever He hears. He will also declare to you what is to come. He will glorify Me, because He will take from what is Mine and declare it to you. —John 16:13–14

Further Scripture: Psalm 69:4; John 16:1; Colossians 2:6–8

Questions

1. In John 16:2, Jesus said that "a time is coming." Do you think we are in those times spoken of in John 16:1–3? Why or why not?

2. Why was it important for Jesus to go away and the Counselor to come (John 14:16; 15:26)?

3. In John 16:33, Jesus said to take heart ("be of good cheer," NKJV) because He has overcome the world. What does that mean? How does that make you feel?

4. What did the Holy Spirit highlight to you in John 16 through the reading or the teaching?

Lesson 85: John 17
Son of God: Jesus' Prayer for Our Unity

Teaching Notes

Intro

John 14—17 is referred to as the Farewell Discourse because it contains Jesus' final teaching for His disciples. There are lots of references in the Bible that state Jesus went off to pray, but not many in which Jesus' actual words are recorded. That's what we have here—the heartbeat of Jesus just before He would be arrested, tried, and crucified. This prayer is called the High Priestly Prayer of Jesus. Hebrews 4:14–15 describes Jesus as our "great high priest," the mediator between us and God, the one who stands in the gap for us. Since we have the actual prayers of Jesus in John 17, and Hebrews 7:23–25 says He lives forever to intercede for us, eternally going to the Father on our behalf, then the prayers of Jesus in John 17 were not prayed only one time for us. I believe this is still Jesus' prayer now! Jesus' prayer follows the outline of the high priest Aaron in Leviticus 16. He prayed about His life and mission (vv. 1–5); He prayed for the people (vv. 6–19); and He prayed for future believers (vv. 20–29).

Teaching

John 17:1–5: These verses contain the beginning of Jesus' prayer. While Jesus prayed for Himself, there was no self-seeking here. His heart was for His Father's glory. Jesus knew what He was about to face, and He prayed that He would be lifted up so His Father would be lifted up. In verses 2–3, Jesus described eternal life found through salvation through the One whom God has sent. Jesus said He had done what He was asked and was ready to complete His mission (vv. 4–5). These verses connect us back to John 1:1: "In the beginning was the Word, and the Word was with God, and the Word was God."

John 17:6–19: Jesus then prayed for His disciples. He prayed for their protection and for the continued mission.

John 17:20–23: This is an important passage for us to look at for three reasons: it contains the recorded prayer of Jesus; it records what happened just before Jesus' arrest; and His prayer is for us. Of all the things Jesus could have prayed for, He chose *unity* (v. 21). Jesus prayed for them to be one as He and the Father were one—serious unity. In the same way that the Father, Son, and Spirit are distinct persons yet one God, we are called to be distinct members yet one church (Ephesians 4:4–5). Our unity is supposed to be a window for the world to see what God Himself looks like. When we tear apart this body, we are literally maiming the image of Jesus that we present to the world. Think about an actual image of Jesus, and picture in your mind what happens when you literally tear that image apart. Kevin DeYoung tweeted: "You know that you *really* want revival in your city when you are happy to see it happen through other people and other churches."

Let's be clear on what unity is *not*:

Unity is *not* uniformity. It's *not* about watering everything down to some lowest common denominator so we all look the same. You don't need unity when everyone is the same. The very concept of unity only makes sense when there is a connection between differing parts. The goal is *not* to see everyone start worshipping the same way with the same style and having the same practices. That's uniformity.

Unity is based on the gospel and the Holy Spirit uniting us . . . in spite of our differences. Unity means we are one family, even when we disagree on secondary issues. Unity happens because of our differences, not in spite of them. We tend to take Paul's teaching about one body with many parts and apply it locally only in the context of one congregation. But those parts are just individual people. Unity is bigger than that. Whole congregations and historical streams of Christianity help add necessary parts to the body.

I grew up in a Methodist tradition, sort of Wesleyan/Arminian stream. But I have dear friends who are in the Calvinist/Reformed stream who have taught me a deep love for Scripture. I have dear friends in the Charismatic/Pentecostal stream who have taught me about the Holy Spirit. I could go on, but you get my point—we need each other! Here's my point: You don't have to worship just like your brothers in the church down the street, but you need to actually know your brother down the street, and for the love of God, act like you are on the same team!

Unity is *not* tolerance. Jesus didn't say, "They will know you are my disciples by the way you tolerate one another." It's not just as simple as not being critical of the other churches (John 13:35).

Psalm 133 provides a picture of unity. This is a psalm of ascent, which was sung in praise on the way up to the temple in Jerusalem. These words were sung as the tribes of Israel came together in unity at the Lord's altar. In verse 1, David (the writer) began with "Behold"—there was something beautiful and noteworthy about the tribes of Israel coming together in unity. That unity in God's people is both "good and pleasant." David gave several pictures of what unity is like.

First, he described oil running down the head and beard and onto the priestly robes (v. 2). The oil represented the presence of God. When God's people dwell in unity, the Spirit of God shows up. When we seek unity with our brothers, God commands His blessing in that place. Also, the oil anointing Aaron set him apart for the sake of others. Aaron was set aside to serve as high priest to be the intermediary to God. The people of Israel had access to God through Aaron. As Christians, we are part of the same priesthood and are to extend forgiveness and the presence of God to this world (1 Peter 2:9). How will the world recognize God in us, if the priests of the same temple are at war with one another?

In verse 3, David described unity "like the dew of Hermon." Mount Hermon is the highest peak in Israel and important because it gathers snow that provides water to Israel. The melting snow seeps into rock channels and pores, feeding springs at the base of the mount, which form streams and rivers and all merge into the Jordan River. The psalm describes this as a blessing from the Lord. The Jordan River was the place where Jesus was baptized. And Zion (the land of Israel) is used as a metaphor for the coming heaven. Therefore, when brothers dwell in unity it commands God's blessing and actually gives us a picture of the glory that awaits us forevermore in heaven.

Closing

We are literally practicing for heaven. I often say during outreach events, "If you don't like worshipping next to people who are different from you, you might want to avoid heaven." We become the answer to Jesus' prayer by collectively fixing our eyes on Jesus.

Paul often used the metaphor of the human body for the church (Ephesians 1:22–23; Colossians 1:18). A body can only be one body when it has the same head. Remove the head and there is no life. You can remove a limb and still live. But remove the head and the body is dead.

A. W. Tozer wrote, "Has it ever occurred to you that one hundred pianos all tuned to the same fork are automatically tuned to each other? They are of one accord by being tuned, not to each other, but to another standard to which each one must individually bow. So one hundred worshipers together, each one looking away to Christ, are in heart nearer to each other than they could possibly be, were they to become 'unity' conscious and turn their eyes away from God to strive for closer fellowship."[1]

By learning to love our brothers and sisters and walk in unity, we get to literally become an answer to the eternal prayers of Jesus, our great High Priest. When Jesus returns, He is coming for His Bride . . . not brides.

---

[1] A. W. Tozer, *The Pursuit of God* (Harrisburg, PA: Christian Publications, 2015), 79–80.

Daily Word

In the time before Jesus was arrested and before He died, He went to the Father in prayer on behalf of all believers. He prayed for unity. He prayed all believers would be one, just as Jesus and the Father are one. He prayed as believers live in harmony and in unity, the world would witness how much God the Father loves God the Son and all who believe. God loves everyone unconditionally, and He longs for the world to see this love in those who follow Him and believe in Him.

How does the world see the body of Christ? Do they see believers working together in unity or believers doing their own thing? Since Jesus prayed for unity in the hours He had left on earth, clearly unity is important to the heart of Jesus. So what do we do about this? Pray for unity in the body and for the Holy Spirit to supernaturally bring the body together. Fix your eyes on Jesus and not on all the minor details. And today, go and ask someone from a different church to get together and talk about Jesus. Or go a step further: go together as one body to share Jesus with the lost. Just see what happens when you get outside the walls of your church. It's from the heart of Jesus for the body to be one so the world will know the great love of the Father. Let's start today!

I pray not only for these, but also for those who believe in Me through their message. . . . I am in them and You are in Me. May they be made completely one, so the world may know You have sent Me and have loved them as You have loved Me. —John 17:20, 23

Further Reading: Psalm 133:1; Ephesians 4:3–5; Hebrews 12:2

Questions

1. How does Jesus define eternal life in John 17:3?

2. In Jesus' prayer in John 17:4, He said He had "accomplished the work which You have given Me to do." What was the work God gave Him to do (John 3:16–17; 4:34; 5:20–21, 36; 14:6)?

3. In John 17:17, what did Jesus say would sanctify us (John 1:1; 17:19; Ephesians 5:25–26)? What does it mean to be sanctified?

4. Who did Jesus pray for in John 17:20? Who are those who will believe in Him through the disciples' word? How does that make you feel?

5. According to John 17:21, what is the purpose or goal of believers being one (in unity), and also being one with the Father and Son (John 17:23)?

6. What did the Holy Spirit highlight to you in John 17 through the reading or the teaching?

Lesson 86: John 18
Son of God: Peter's Denials; Jesus' Trials

Teaching Notes

Intro

In John 18, we're coming to the end of a section in which Jesus was preparing His disciples for His death and His resurrection. Through the last few chapters, we've looked at Jesus' teachings about what was to come, what the disciples could expect, and how they were to lead. In today's study, we're putting that aside because now everything Jesus told them was beginning to happen. We'll look at chapter 18 through five symbols[1] that will take us through Jesus' trial.

Teaching

John 18:1: The Kidron Valley is outside the east gate of Jerusalem, between the city and the garden of Gethsemane. Some suggest that this garden was walled and private. David also crossed the Kidron Valley while he was fleeing from his own nation.

The first symbol is *the garden*, and it represents obedience (v. 1). Jesus went often to the garden. He wasn't running away but walking toward what He was to do. Human history started in the garden of Eden, but disobedience brought sin into the garden and to mankind (Genesis 2:8). Christ went obediently to the garden, ultimately bringing righteousness and life to all who trust Him. History will one day end in another garden in the heavenly city (Revelation 21–22). There will be no death, sorrow, or pain there (Revelation 22:1–3a). Wiersbe described the garden of Eden as the garden of disobedience and sin, Gethsemane as the garden of obedience and submission, and heaven as the eternal garden of delight and satisfaction to the glory of God.[2]

John 18:2–9: The second symbol is *the kiss*. This is a little bit of a stretch here because it's not in John, but we know that Judas betrayed Jesus with a kiss (Matthew 26:48–49). The kiss was a sign of affection and devotion. Family members

---

[1] Warren W. Wiersbe, *The Bible Exposition Commentary: Matthew–Galatians* (Colorado Springs: David C. Cook, 1989), 372–75.

[2] Wiersbe, 372.

kissed upon meeting and parting, and disciples greeted a rabbi with a kiss as a sign of devotion and obedience. But Judas' kiss, instead of being a symbol of obedience, was a sign of treachery (v. 2). Judas came to Jesus with a detachment of troops (or a cohort of a tenth of a Roman legion) of 500 soldiers (v. 3). They had no idea what to expect from Jesus.

Jesus did not shrink away from Judas when the troops went out to meet them (v. 4). Jesus knew His time had come, and He was in full control. Earlier, Jesus had withdrawn from the conflict with the Jewish officials because His hour had not yet come. The soldiers told Jesus whom they were there to arrest, and Jesus said, "I am He" (v. 5). We've been looking at the "I am" statements of Jesus. Possibly, in this moment, Jesus responded, "I am He," to bring all those statements into the sum of His identity. The guards could not stand before that divine authority and fell to the ground before Him (vv. 6–7). Jesus identified Himself again and asked that His disciples be allowed to go free (vv. 8–9).

John 18:10: The third symbol is *the sword*. Simon Peter drew a sword, possibly a dagger, and cut off the ear of the high priest's slave, Malchus. Only John's account gives the name of the servant. The sword symbolizes rebellion against the will of God. Wiersbe explains that Peter "fought the wrong enemy, used the wrong weapon, had the wrong motive and accomplished the wrong result!"[3] Remember Peter's response to Jesus when He told His disciples that He would be arrested, tried, and crucified (Matthew 16:21–23). Peter actually hindered the work Jesus came to accomplish. While we admire Peter's courage and sincerity, realize that zeal, without knowledge, is dangerous. Peter ultimately discovered the "sword of the Spirit" (Ephesians 6:17; Hebrews 4:12). Jesus redeemed Peter and used him mightily—more than 3,000 souls came to the Lord at Pentecost (Acts 2:38, 40–42).

John 18:11–14: The fourth symbol is *the cup*, which represents submission. Jesus talked about the cup of submission and accepting God's will (Matthew 26:39, 42). Biblically, the cup often illustrates suffering and sorrow. For example, after Babylon captured Jerusalem, Isaiah 51:17 said, "You have drunk at the hand of the Lord, the cup of His fury." Jeremiah pictured God's wrath against nations as the pouring out of a cup (Jeremiah 25:15–28). However, as followers of Christ, we don't need to fear the cup the Father hands us. Jesus had already drunk from the cup before us. We may suffer pain and heartbreak, but Christ will eventually turn that into glory.

---

[3] Wiersbe, 374.

John 18:15–27: The fifth symbol is *the fire*, which represents denial. Jesus told Peter he would deny Him three times before the cock crowed, but Peter denied he could possibly do that. All of Jesus' disciples, except Peter and probably John, fled the scene. Since Peter followed the crowd when he should have fled with the other disciples, he put himself right into temptation and denied Jesus three times: with the servant girl who recognized him (v. 17), later when approached by other servants and officers (v. 25), and with Malchus' relative (v. 26). Because Peter did not walk away, he did something he never thought he could do. Peter's actions parallel Psalm 1:1 in this: Peter walked in the "counsel of the ungodly" (the high priest's courtyard), he stood with the enemy by the fire, and he sat down with the enemy (Luke 22:55). When we consider temptation, 2 Timothy 2:22 says to flee.

How easy is it for us to deny Jesus because we're comfortable staying in the upper room? It's easy to stay with those we're comfortable with and neglect going out to tell others about Jesus.

John 18:12–14; 28–40: Let's go back now to look at the trial itself. The soldiers arrested and bound Jesus and took Him to Annas (vv. 12–13). Only John mentioned Annas, the unofficial high priest. There were two types of trials: the religious (Jewish) trial and the civic (Roman) trial. The Jewish trial had three stages:

1. Before Annas, where Jesus was interrogated in Annas' house (v. 13).
2. Before Caiaphas the High Priest and some members of the Sanhedrin (v. 24).
3. Before the Roman council the next morning where Jesus was condemned to death (v. 28).

Based on Jewish authority, the Jews alone could have only stoned Jesus to death. Because Jesus was prophesied to die by crucifixion, only the Romans had the authority to execute Jesus that way.

After these three steps, Jesus was taken to the Praetorium where Herod was. The Jews did not enter with Him or they would have become defiled and unable to partake in the Passover. Constable explains, "Ironically, these Jews were taking extreme precautions to avoid ritual defilement, while at the same time preparing to murder the Lamb of God who takes away the sins of the world."[4] Jesus came to set us free. He became a curse for us so that we could walk in freedom (Galatians 3:13). Jesus was taken before Pilate (John 18:28–38), sent to Herod (Luke 23:6–12), and then sent back to Pilate again (John 18:39—19:16). John focused mainly on the Roman trial. By the time John wrote this Gospel, the Jewish

---

[4] Thomas L. Constable, *Expository Notes of Dr. Thomas Constable: John*, 468, https://planobiblechapel.org/tcon/notes/pdf/john.pdf.

nation had been scattered by Rome, the city of Jerusalem had been destroyed, and Roman power was all that mattered.

Pilate asked Jesus if He was the King of the Jews. Jesus asked Pilate a question in response, basically asking if Pilate was a sincere seeker of the truth or trying to give the Jews what they wanted (v. 34). Pilate was looking to find a "loophole" that would please both sides—he was afraid of the crowd, but he grew more afraid of the prisoner. At least three times (Luke 23:13–15, 22, and John 19:4, 6), Pilate announced Jesus was not guilty of any crime, and yet he refused to release Him (v. 39, John 19:16). Pilate asked if Jesus was a king (v. 37) and Jesus responded that "everyone who is of the truth listens to My voice." Who knows how Pilate asked about truth? He was in the presence of the Truth ("I am the way, the truth and the life," John 14:6). Those who were in the presence of Jesus didn't realize the truth was right in their midst because they didn't "hear His voice."

Closing

This is the reason Jesus came to earth as the sinless, spotless Lamb of God, who walked this out. He knew what would happen—falsely accused, falsely convicted, beaten, humiliated, spit upon—yet He held all the power. He allowed all this to happen *because* He walked in obedience. He did that for me and for you. Jesus came to die for us, even for those who hated Him and turned against Him. Therefore, in response, we should step forward in boldness in the power of the Holy Spirit. Don't be lukewarm but be bold (Revelation 3:15–16). The truth of Christ sets us free.

Daily Word

Judas Iscariot, one of the twelve disciples, betrayed Jesus to the Jewish religious leaders, leading to Jesus' arrest. Meanwhile, Peter, another disciple, denied Jesus three times. Eventually, Caiaphas and Annas, the high priest and his father-in-law, passed the decision to send Jesus off to Pilate at the governor's headquarters, wanting Jesus to be sentenced to die. After all of this, Pilate had a hard time deciding what to do with Jesus. He asked Jesus the question: "What is truth?"

Like Pilate, many in the world try to figure out truth. They look to social media, government, food, sports, academics, or entertainment, trying to discover what truth is. As a follower of Christ, you know Jesus is the Truth. Jesus came so the world would be saved. Look no further. Jesus is truth. Today, pray for those searching for the truth. And when someone asks you, "What is truth?" make sure you are equipped to share the truth with them!

"You say that I'm a king," Jesus replied. "I was born for this, and I have come into the world for this: to testify to the truth. Everyone who is of the truth listens to My voice." "What is truth?" said Pilate. —John 18:37–38

Further Scripture: John 1:17; John 17:17; 1 John 4:6

Questions

1. Adam was created and placed in a garden (Genesis 2:8). Do you think it is significant that the beginning of humanity and the fall of mankind both took place in gardens (Genesis 3:1–8), and, additionally, a garden is where Jesus' betrayal and arrest occurs, thus opening the way for our "rebirth" (John 18:1–2)?

2. Why do you think the Jewish leaders sent a Roman cohort (probably 500 soldiers) to arrest Jesus? After Jesus revealed that He was the one they were looking for by His response, "I am He," what occurred next (John 18:6)?

3. Jesus confirmed to Pilate that He was a king but explained His kingdom was not of this world. What did Jesus say would happen if His kingdom were of this world (Matthew 26:53; John 18:36)?

4. Both when praying in the garden (Matthew 26:39) and at the time of betrayal and arrest, Jesus referred to the suffering He would face as a cup. What does His willingness to drink it reveal (John 10:11, 18; 18:11)? In other Scriptures, what does a cup represent (Isaiah 51:17; Jeremiah 25:15; Ezekiel 23:33; Revelation 14:10)? In Scripture, a cup does not always reference something negative.

5. What did the Holy Spirit highlight to you in John 18 through the reading or the teaching?

Lesson 87: John 19
Son of God: The Day of Jesus' Passion

Teaching Notes

Intro

John 19 is at the end of Jesus' physical life on earth. There's a lot in this chapter. The story had to get worse before it could get better, and that's what John 19 is. Today, we'll look at what Jesus went through—the beatings, the scourging, and the crucifixion.

Teaching

John 19:1: Jesus was flogged by long "thongs to which were attached sharp pieces of metal and pieces of bone."[1] Being beaten this way meant the flesh and even the organs could have been damaged or ripped from the body. D. A. Carson lists three types of floggings, from the least painful to the most: (1) *fustigation*—a light beating only hooligans experienced; (2) *flagellation*—a severe beating criminals who were guilty of more serious crimes received; and (3) *verberatio*—the most brutal beatings given to the worst criminals, including those who were going to be crucified.[2] Before His sentencing, Jesus would have received the first two beatings; after His sentencing, Jesus received the third beating.[3]

John 19:2–6: After the flogging, the soldiers then created a crown of thorns, possibly from the date palm tree, and slammed the crown onto Jesus' head in "a mockery of a kingly crown" and wrapped Him in a purple robe, making Him "a caricature of a royal conqueror."[4] The soldiers mocked Him and hit Him with their hands, attacking Him verbally and physically (v. 4). All these things were prophesied by the Old Testament writers:

---

[1] Earl D. Radmacher, Ronald B. Allen, and H. Wayne House, eds., *Nelson's New Illustrated Bible Commentary* (Nashville: Thomas Nelson, 1999), 1355.

[2] D. A. Carson, *The Gospel According to John* (Leicester, England: Inter-Varsity Press; Grand Rapids: Eerdmans, 1991), 595; quoted in Thomas L. Constable, *Expository Notes of Dr. Thomas Constable: John*, 478, https://planobiblechapel.org/tcon/notes/pdf/john.pdf.

[3] Constable, 478.

[4] Radmacher et al., 1355.

- Psalm 22:7: He was mocked (John 19:3).
- Isaiah 53:9: He was innocent (John 19:4). Lenski wrote, "Jesus was not scourged in order to be crucified but in order to escape crucifixion."[5]
- Isaiah 53:5: He was beaten and pathetic (John 19:5).
- Isaiah 53:9: He was proclaimed innocent (John 18:38; 19:4, 6).
- Isaiah 53:3: He was hated (John 19:6).
- Isaiah 53:7: He was oppressed and afflicted, but He did not speak (John 19:9).
- Isaiah 53:10: He had authority from God (John 19:11).

Jesus said He came not to do away with Scripture, but to fulfill it (Matthew 5:17).

John 19:7–10: The Jews accused Jesus of blasphemy for claiming to be the *Son of God* (Leviticus 24:16), and therefore He should be executed (John 5:18; 8:58–59; 10:33–36). Pilate didn't care that Jesus claimed to be the *Son of God*, but he became more afraid when he understood the significance of Jesus' claims to the Jews. In verses 9–10, Pilate asked Jesus where He was from, but Jesus didn't answer (Matthew 26:23; 27:14).

Many Jews today do not even recognize that Isaiah 53:1–12 exists because to accept it they have to deal with the fulfillment of these prophecies about Jesus.

John 19:11–16: In verse 11, Jesus said He had been delivered or given over to Pilate. By whom? Possibly by Caiaphas or Judas. Constable explains that at this point, the Jews were becoming a bigger threat to Israel than Jesus was. Pilate made every effort possible to release Jesus, but he finally had to decide if he was willing to side with the Jews or with Jesus. Pilate decided to side with the Jews, so he brought Jesus out on the stone pavement, a large area inside the Antonia Fortress (v. 14).[6] Pilate offered Jesus "their king" to the Jews, but they shouted that Jesus should be crucified. It was Friday, the preparation day for the Passover around six o'clock in the morning. The Jews claimed complete allegiance to Caesar as their only king (v. 15). They began to compromise their beliefs and who they were in order to get their fleshly needs met. So Pilate handed Jesus over to be crucified (v. 16).

---

[5] Richard C. H. Lenski, *The Interpretation of St. John's Gospel* (Minneapolis: Augsburg, 1961), 1243; quoted in Constable, 478.

[6] Radmacher et al., 1355.

John 19:17–22: In verse 17 there is the controversial phrase, "carrying His own cross," as He went to the place called Golgotha (Place of the Skull). Jesus said during His ministry that His followers were to take up their own crosses and follow Him (Matthew 16:24). Jesus did what He required of His followers. Jesus was then crucified between two others—three crosses (v. 18). Pilate had a sign hung on Jesus' cross that proclaimed Jesus as King of the Jews (v. 19). The crosses were set outside the city wall, but close by, so many Jews saw Jesus on the cross and read the sign above His head. The sign was written in Aramaic, Latin, and Greek. Today in Jerusalem, signs are in Hebrew, Aramaic, and English, because people from all over the world flock there. The Jews complained about how Pilate worded the sign because he didn't say that Jesus "claimed" to be the King of the Jews, but Pilate refused to change it (vv. 21–22).

John 19:23–24: Jesus was crucified, and the soldiers divided his clothes between them and cast lots for His tunic (v. 23). John described how Jesus fulfilled the prophecies in both Psalm 22:18 and Isaiah 53.

John 19:25–27: Jesus made provision for the care of His mother. From that moment, Jesus' disciple, John, took Mary into his home and treated her as his mother.

John 19:28–30: This is the finished work of Christ on earth as He gave up His spirit.

John 19:31–37: Jesus' side was pierced (Zechariah 12:10). Verse 36 states that Jesus' bones were not broken, which fulfilled the requirement of the Passover Lamb (Exodus 12:46).

John 19:38–42: Jesus' body was claimed by Joseph of Arimathea, who was a rich man and a secret follower of Jesus. Joseph and Nicodemus placed Jesus' body in a new tomb, wrapped His body in linen cloths, and prepared His body for burial with spices. The provision of the tomb was another fulfillment of Scripture.

Closing

All of this tells us that we will be hated by those in the world who refuse Him. We have to embrace Psalm 22 and Isaiah 53 as we pick up our crosses every day and follow Him.

Daily Word

Pilate ordered Jesus to be flogged. The soldiers also mocked Him by crowning His head with thorns and clothing Him with a purple robe. Then Pilate continued to question what to do with Jesus, as he couldn't find a sufficient reason to crucify Him. Even in the midst of Jesus' pain and suffering for the sins of the world, He continued to live as an example. Pilate asked Him the question: "Where are You from?" Jesus paused. When He finally responded, He did so calmly and confident of His calling.

Have you ever been questioned about your decision to follow Christ and live for Him? Sometimes the way people ask can make you want to respond with angst, like you have something to prove. But in that moment, when you feel the need to defend your faith, don't get angry, prideful or flustered. Remember Christ's example to us, even when He was in the midst of suffering. Pause, breathe, and be slow to answer. Let the Spirit guide you and help you discern your response. Let the Spirit speak to the person questioning you. And then when the time is right, speak forth in the love and authority of Jesus.

He went back into the headquarters and asked Jesus, "Where are You from?" But Jesus did not give him an answer. —John 19:9

Further Reading: Exodus 14:14; Ecclesiastes 5:1–2; James 1:19–20

Questions

1. In mockery, the Roman soldiers did what to signify Jesus was a "king" (John 19:2–3)? Why did they do this (Psalm 22:7; John 18:37)?

2. How many times did Pilate state he found no guilt in Jesus (John 18:38; 19:4, 6)? John 19:12 says Pilate made efforts to release Him. What kept it from happening (John 19:12, 15; Isaiah 53:9)?

3. Were the chief priests sincere when they stated, "We have no king but Caesar" (John 19:15)? They clearly and completely rejected Jesus as king. When in the past had the Israelites rejected God as king (1 Samuel 8:7)?

4. In Genesis 22:6, Isaac foreshadowed Christ in what ways (John 19:17)? Abraham called the place where he offered his son Isaac as a sacrifice "The LORD Will Provide." Do you think John 19 is the fulfillment of this prophetic name?

5. What did the Holy Spirit highlight to you in John 19 through the reading or the teaching?

Lesson 88: John 20

Son of God: "I Have Seen the Lord"

Teaching Notes

Intro

John 19 was a tough passage yesterday as we looked at all that Jesus had to go through, and we ended by considering what we might also have to go through. We didn't end on good news because John 19 didn't end with good news. John 20 begins with the transformation to life and hope.

Teaching

John 20:1–10: Mary Magdalene came to the tomb early, and when she found the stone had been rolled away from the entrance, she ran to find Peter and John (v. 1). Note that John never mentions himself by name but as "the one whom Jesus loved," which was a sign of humility on John's part. Mary told the disciples that Jesus' tomb was empty and that His body was missing (v. 2). Simon Peter and John ran to the tomb. John made it there first but didn't enter (vv. 3–5). Simon Peter entered the tomb and saw the linen cloths folded up (v. 6–7). John saw and believed, but they didn't understand the Scripture that Jesus would rise from the dead (vv. 8–9). Then, the two left and went back to their homes.

John 20:11–18: Mary Magdalene also returned to the tomb and was crying, but no information is given about how she got there or if she saw the disciples there. Proverbs 8:17 says, "I love those who love me, and those who search for me find me," which is a beautiful picture of Mary Magdalene coming back to the tomb (Psalm 30:5). When she looked into the tomb, she saw two angels (v. 12). Remember Luke 24:4 recorded two angels as well, and Mark 16:5 and Matthew 28:2–3 each recorded one angel at the tomb. The angels asked Mary why she was crying (but they knew why!). She turned around and saw Jesus, but she didn't recognize Him. MacArthur suggests several reasons Mary might not have recognized Jesus: (1) possibly she couldn't see Him through her tears; (2) possibly she still had the sight of Jesus' bruised and beaten body on her mind; (3) possibly Jesus' post-Resurrection appearance looked very different; and (4) possibly she was "supernaturally prevented from recognizing Him until He chose for her to do so."[1] Jesus' disciples on the road to Emmaus also didn't recognize Jesus after His resurrection (Luke 24:16–31), and John recognized Jesus on the shore of the Sea of Galilee when the other disciples didn't (John 21:7).

It's important to note that Jesus first appeared to a woman. Constable states, "No Jewish author in the ancient world would have invented a story with a woman as the first witness to this most important event."[2] Jesus asked Mary the same question the angels asked her: "Why are you crying?" And He asked her who she was looking for (v. 15). She thought He might have been the gardener who knew where Jesus' body had been taken. She obviously did not expect Jesus to be alive. In verse 16, Jesus said, "Mary," and she knew who He was. John 10:27 says, "My sheep hear My voice, and I know them, and they follow Me." Mary heard His voice and recognized the Lord.

Mary's recognition of Jesus takes us back to His seven great "I am" statements, which are:

1. I am the Bread of Life (John 6:35).
2. I am the Light of the world (John 8:12).
3. I am the Door of the sheep (John 10:7, 9).
4. I am the Good Shepherd (John 10:11, 14).
5. I am the Resurrection and the Life (John 11:25).
6. I am the Way, the Truth, and the Life (John 14:6).
7. I am the True Vine (John 15:1, 5).

Constable has identified all of the post-Resurrection appearances according to Jesus' post-Resurrection time line[3]:

- On Easter Morning, Jesus appeared to Mary Magdalene (Mark 16:9–11; John 20:10–18), the other women (Matthew 29:9–10), and to Peter (Luke 24:34; 1 Corinthians 15:5).
- On Easter Afternoon, Jesus appeared to two disciples on the Emmaus road (Luke 24:13–32).
- On Easter Evening, Jesus appeared to about 12 disciples excluding Thomas (Mark 16:14; John 20:19–23).

---

[1] John MacArthur, *The MacArthur Bible Commentary* (Nashville: Thomas Nelson, 2005), 1425.

[2] Edwin A. Blum, "John," in *Bible Knowledge Commentary: New Testament*, ed. John F. Walvoord and Roy B. Zuck, (Wheaton, IL: Scripture Press, 1983), 342; quoted in Thomas L. Constable, *Expository Notes of Dr. Thomas Constable: John*, 521, https://planobiblechapel.org/tcon/notes/pdf/john.pdf.

[3] Constable, 519.

- On the Following Sunday, Jesus appeared to the 11 disciples including Thomas (John 20:26–28).
- During the following 32 days, Jesus appeared to seven disciples by the Sea of Galilee (John 21:1–23), 500 people (including the 11 disciples) at a mountain at Galilee (Matthew 28:16–20; 1 Corinthians 15:6), His half-brother James (1 Corinthians 15:7), His disciples in Jerusalem (Luke 24:44–49; Acts 1:3–8; 1 Corinthians 15:7), and His disciples on Mount Olivet (Mark 16:19–20; Luke 24:50–53; Acts 1:9–12).

The Resurrection appearance in today's chapter was only the first one. There's historical value to understanding that Jesus showed up to multiple people, groups, and crowds, on multiple occasions.

Mary is usually described as falling at Jesus' feet when she saw Him. So when she encountered Jesus after the Resurrection, He told her not to cling to Him (John 20:17). *Nelson's Commentary* defines the idea of "clinging to" as "to fasten oneself to" or "to hold."[4] Possibly, Mary wanted to cling to Jesus because she didn't want to lose Him again. Jesus sent her to tell His disciples that she had seen Him. Mary, a woman, was given the assignment to announce His resurrection to His disciples. She went immediately and announced, "I have seen the Lord."

John 20:19–23: The disciples were gathered together behind a locked door because they were afraid of the Jews. The Jews had killed Jesus, and they were afraid they might be next. Even though the door was locked, Jesus miraculously appeared before them and said to them, "Peace to you"—His ministry on earth had been completed. He showed them the scars in His hands and said, "Peace be with you. As the Father has sent me, even so I am sending you" (v. 22). He commissioned them to do exactly what He had been sent to do—bring the gospel of peace (John 17:18). We are to be like Jesus in the world.

Then, "He breathed on them and said to them, 'Receive the Holy Spirit'" (v. 22). *Nelson's Commentary* explains that this was "a special preparation of the apostles who were to become the foundation of the church at Pentecost," and that Jesus "breathed the Spirit into the disciples" in a way to remind them of God's breath giving life to Adam in Genesis.[5] The question is whether the disciples received the Spirit here or at Pentecost. Although there's no way for us to know, I believe that the disciples received the Holy Spirit in this moment with Jesus to prepare them for Pentecost (John 14:25–29) and that they received the baptism of fire at Pentecost. The Holy Spirit only comes through Jesus.

---

[4] Earl D. Radmacher, Ronald B. Allen, and H. Wayne House, eds., *Nelson's New Illustrated Bible Commentary* (Nashville: Thomas Nelson, 1999), 1358.

[5] Radmacher et al., 1359.

Closing

Jesus was constantly showing up to His disciples, and He is constantly showing up to us as well. And when we encounter Jesus, we will always have His peace.

Daily Word

The tomb was empty when Mary Magdalene, Simon Peter, and the other disciple went to the tomb early in the morning. Jesus had been resurrected from the dead just as He foretold! After His resurrection, the disciples spent time with Jesus and were commissioned for ministry. However, Thomas had not been with Jesus and did not believe He had indeed come back to life. Finally, after eight days, Jesus appeared to Thomas and the other disciples to physically show Thomas His nail-pierced hands and feet. Only when Thomas physically saw Jesus and His resurrected body did he believe. Jesus said to Thomas, "Because you have seen Me, you have believed. Those who believe without seeing are blessed."

Friends, most likely you have never physically seen Jesus. When He returned to heaven, He said He'd be seated at the right hand of the Father. It is with faith you believe in the Bible. It is with faith you believe in Jesus as the Son of God— the same faith the disciples had when Jesus returned. However, your faith may be more like Thomas's; you may want to physically see Jesus. Today, ask Jesus to show up in your life, maybe not in physical form, but allow Him to open your eyes to see His love and His special touch around you. When you ask, have faith He will answer. He knows just what you need today.

Jesus said, "Because you have seen Me, you have believed. Those who believe without seeing are blessed. —John 20:29

Further Reading: Jeremiah 32:17; Hebrews 11:1; Romans 10:17

Questions

1. Peter and John ran to the tomb, but they found the tomb was empty, and only the linen that had wrapped His body was left behind. Do you think Peter and John understood what it meant that the linen was still there but Jesus wasn't? Why do you think the cloth that was around His head was lying separate?

2. Why do you think Mary didn't recognize Jesus (John 20:14–16)? Who did Mary think He was?

3. Why did Thomas say he wouldn't believe it was Jesus unless he touched His wounds? What transgression was he guilty of (Mark 9:24; Matthew 17:17)?

4. Meditate on John 20:29. Do you think it takes a higher degree of faith to believe when one hasn't seen? Why?

5. What did the Holy Spirit highlight to you in John 20 through the reading or the teaching?

Lesson 89: John 21
Son of God: "Do You Love Me?"

Teaching Notes

Intro

This is the final lesson (of 89 lessons) from the Gospels. We've looked at the themes of *King, Servant, Son of Man,* and *Son of God.* In the Gospel of John, Jesus made seven "I am" statements that Mindi conveyed in her painting: (1) I Am the Bread of Life; (2) I Am the Light of the world; (3) I Am the Door of the sheep; (4) I Am the Good Shepherd; (5) I Am the Resurrection and the Life; (6) I Am the Way, the Truth, and the Life; and (7) I Am the True Vine. Every time Jesus said, "I am," He was implying that He is God. In this Gospel of John, Jesus also showed seven signs or miracles. John 20:30–31 provides the reason for these signs: "that you may believe that Jesus is the Christ, the Son of God."

Teaching

John 21:1–3: "After this" refers to the empty tomb, the first post-resurrection appearances, the commissioning of the disciples, and Jesus' appearance to Thomas. Jesus appeared to the disciples again at the Sea of Tiberias, also known as the Sea of Galilee. People give the disciples a hard time about retreating to Galilee, but Jesus told them three times that He would go to Galilee after His resurrection: "But after I am raised up, I will go before you to Galilee" (Matthew 26:32; Matthew 28:7; Mark 16:7). The disciples listened to what Jesus had said and went to Galilee to wait on Him. Verse 3 lists all the disciples who were fishermen: Simon Peter, Thomas the Twin, Nathanael of Cana, James and John, and two others who are unnamed. They all went fishing but caught nothing all night. Some scholars suggest the disciples were disobedient and went back to their old way of life. I believe they went to Galilee to wait for Jesus and fished while they were waiting.

John 21:4–8: At daybreak, Jesus stood on the shore, but the disciples didn't recognize Him (v. 4), just like Mary Magdalene and the disciples on the road to Emmaus hadn't recognized Jesus at first. Then Jesus called to them and asked them if they had any fish (v. 5). In the Greek, the words suggest that Jesus asked as if He wanted to buy fish from them. Jesus told them to cast the net on the right side of the boat to find fish. They did as He told them and caught more fish than they could pull into the boat (v. 6). This had happened before in Luke 5:1–7. Jesus used the repetition of something that had happened before to reveal Himself to them. John again referred to himself as "the disciple whom Jesus loved" and stated he had recognized Jesus (v. 7a). (John referred to himself this way five times: John 13:23; 19:26; 20:2; 21:7; and 21:20.) Do we have that burning passion and love for Jesus? Simon Peter immediately jumped into the water and swam to Jesus (v. 7b). The other disciples brought the boat and the fish the 100 yards to shore (v. 8). We tend to think of Peter's actions as impulsive, but possibly his running to the empty tomb and his swimming to the shore to meet Jesus is more about his recognition that Jesus is the Lord. He wanted to get back to Jesus and fix his relationship with Him after he had denied Him. It seems like those who have struggled with addiction or deep sin understand the depth of redemption more clearly than most of us. Peter wanted to get close to Jesus because he knew he had really messed up.

John 21:9–14: Jesus made them breakfast on a charcoal fire (v. 9), possibly as a picture of feeding the multitude with fish and bread. The last time Peter was at a charcoal fire, he denied Jesus three times (John 18:18, 25–27). Jesus told the disciples to bring some of the fish they caught to Him, and Peter got up and hauled the heavy net in (v. 10). There were 153 fish in the net (v. 11). John knew that because he was there as an eyewitness (1 John 1:1–4). Jesus invited the disciples to breakfast; He was still meeting their needs (v. 12; Matthew 6:25–33; Philippians 4:19). Wiersbe points out three times that Jesus invited people to Him: "'Come and see' (John 1:39); 'Come and drink' (John 7:37); and 'Come and dine' (John 21:12)."[1] This was the third time in the Gospel of John that Jesus appeared to His disciples (John 20:19–23; 20:26–29; and 21:7–14).

John 21:15–19: Wiersbe states that "Peter and his Lord had already met *privately* and no doubt taken care of Peter's sins (Luke 24:31; 1 Corinthians 15:5), but since Peter had denied the Lord *publicly*, it was important there be a public restoration."[2] Verses 15–19 record this public restoration. Three times Jesus asked Peter if he loved Him (John 21:15–17). Two synonyms are used for the word "love" in these verses. MacArthur explains that "when two synonyms are placed in close proximity in context, a difference in meaning, however slight,

---

[1] Warren W. Wiersbe, *The Bible Exposition Commentary: Matthew–Galatians* (Colorado Springs: David C. Cook, 1989), 397.

[2] Wiersbe, 397–98.

is emphasized."[3] The first time that Jesus asked the question, He used the word *agape*, which "signified total commitment," while Peter responded with the word *phileo*, which meant brotherly love or emotional friendship.[4] These words are used interchangeably throughout the New Testament, so there's not a radical difference between them. However, Jesus wanted Peter's complete commitment as a fisher of men. He wanted to give Peter the chance to stop playing around with his commitment and to embrace it full on. Jesus responded, "Feed My lambs." Jesus had said, "I am the Good Shepherd," so Peter's call was to take care of Jesus' sheep. "The word *feed* conveys the idea of being devoted to the Lord's service as an under-shepherd who cares for His flock (1 Peter 5:1–4)."[5] MacArthur explains that the word feed conveys giving constant nourishment to the flock, because the "primary duty of the messenger of Jesus Christ is to teach the Word of God."[6]

The second time Jesus asked Peter, He told Peter to shepherd or "tend" His sheep (v. 16), and the third time Jesus asked, He told Peter to "feed" His sheep (v. 17). Jesus asked Peter three times because Peter had denied Him three times. Jesus restored Peter back completely and in front of His disciples. Peter's denial of Jesus as the Christ bothered him so much that he wept bitterly.

There are people in ministry today who have really messed up, and the church tends to push them out, rather than finding a way to restore them to ministry.

As a part of his restoration, Jesus prophesied about what would happen to Peter in the future—he would die because of his faith in Jesus (vv. 18–19). Peter was martyred by the emperor Nero in AD 67–68 when he was, according to tradition, crucified upside down on a cross because he didn't want to be crucified like his Messiah. Even though Peter messed up three times (and *all* of us have messed up at least once), he could be restored to ministry because of his love for Jesus.

Closing

What we've learned through Peter is that we can be restored to Christ to the point that we need to be prepared to die and suffer for Him. Any of us can have an impact for the gospel of Jesus Christ, regardless of what we've done in the past, because Jesus is the *Son of God* who has come to give us life abundantly. And that life doesn't end because we've messed up. Don't ever give up on Christ because He never gives up on us.

---

[3] John MacArthur, *The MacArthur Bible Commentary* (Nashville: Thomas Nelson, 2005), 1426.

[4] MacArthur, 1426.

[5] MacArthur, 1427.

[6] MacArthur, 1427.

Daily Word

In the final chapter of John, Jesus demonstrated His grace and love through Peter's life. Before Jesus died on the Cross, Peter denied Him three times. Now, after Jesus' resurrection, Jesus physically helped Peter by instructing him where to fish, providing even more fish than imagined, and feeding him breakfast. And then Jesus gave Peter a second chance. Even after Peter had denied Jesus, He publicly restored him to ministry.

Friends, like Peter, Jesus loves you so much. Yes, He sees your heart. Yes, He knows when you sin, when you turn away from Him, and what your weaknesses are. But Jesus is *for* you. He calls you His own. So, just like Peter, if you have fallen into sin, if you have given into temptation or what seems like the easy way out, your life with Jesus is not over. Jesus is never done with you. He loves you, and He came to earth for you. Jesus gave Peter a new role. Yes, even with all of Peter's mess-ups, Jesus restored Peter to ministry of the gospel and called him to pour into His people with love and care for them. Friends, Jesus will do the same for you. His mercies are new each morning, and His faithful love never ends. Your story isn't finished.

He asked him the third time, "Simon, son of John, do you love Me?" Peter was grieved that He asked him the third time, "Do you love Me?" He said, "Lord, You know everything! You know that I love You." "Feed My sheep," Jesus said. —John 21:17

Further Reading: Lamentations 3:21–23; John 18:27; 2 Peter 3:9

Questions

1. In the opening verses of chapter 21, the disciples were once again fishing with no success. Why do you think they were fishing instead of sharing the gospel of Jesus?

2. In John 21:9, when the disciples got to shore, Jesus already had fish and bread over a fire. Where did He get the fish and bread? Did Jesus "feed" them more than just food?

3. In John 21:15–17, why did Jesus ask Peter three times if he loved Him? What did Jesus mean by "feed my sheep"? Who are the sheep?

4. Why do you think Peter asked Jesus about what John was to do in John 21:21? How did Jesus respond to Peter?

5. What did the Holy Spirit highlight to you in John 21 through the reading or the teaching?

Contributing Authors

Dr. Kyle Lance Martin
Kyle Lance Martin is the founder of Time to Revive, a ministry based in Dallas, Texas, whose mission is to equip the saints for the return of Christ. His heart's desire, aside from loving his wife and four kids, is to engage people with the Word of God directly in their own environment. Kyle believes when people turn to the Messiah in humility and have a willingness to walk in the Holy Spirit, they can know and experience the calling of being a disciple of Jesus Christ. Kyle received his master of biblical studies from Dallas Theological Seminary and his doctor of ministry in outreach and discipleship from Gordon-Conwell Theological Seminary.

Laura Kim Martin
Laura Kim Martin lives in Dallas, Texas, with her husband, Kyle Lance Martin, and their four children. Together they founded the ministry Time to Revive to equip the saints for the return of Christ. Through years of trusting the Lord's faithfulness, she passionately encourages others to press on in their faith journeys.

Pastor Gordon Henke
Gordon Henke is a pastor from northern Indiana, serving the church for 25 years. His passion is the studying of the Word. With confidence in the truth of the Word, he passionately helps people boldly share their faith.

Pastor Tom Schiefer
Tom Schiefer is the senior pastor of Nappanee First Brethren Church in Nappanee, Indiana. Prior to accepting a call to pastoral ministry, he was a band and choir director in Ohio. In the context of these two careers, he loves to orchestrate the Word of God, and the message it contains, into harmony with people's lives.

Pastor Fred Stayton
Fred Stayton is the lead pastor of Sonrise Church in Fort Wayne, Indiana, and has a passion for turning the hearts of fathers back to their children. Fred and his wife, Cheryl, have six children and one grandchild.

Ryan Schrag
Ryan Schrag is the national director for Time to Revive and has a heart to "equip the saints for the return of Christ" in the United States. Prior to joining full-time ministry, he was formerly the owner/operator of a lawn care business.

Wesley Morris
Wesley Morris is the Georgia state chairman for Time to Revive. A former construction worker turned pastor, he now trains and equips people to encounter Jesus and boldly share their faith.

Josh Edwards
Josh Edwards is the Minnesota state chairman for Time to Revive and leads worship both nationally and internationally. For the past 20 years he has been leading worship and speaking to the body of Christ about his heart's desire to see the church united, revived, and equipped to do the work of the ministry.

Shawn Carlson
Shawn Carlson is the executive director for Time to Revive. He has a strong desire to see people grow closer to Jesus through the study of God's Word and the carrying out of His mission.

Matt Reynolds
Matt Reynolds is the president of Spirit & Truth, a ministry aimed at equipping believers and churches to be more empowered by the Spirit, rooted in the truth, and mobilized for the mission. After serving as a local pastor for 13 years, Matt responded to a missionary calling to pursue Spirit-filled renewal in the church.

Larry Hopkins
Larry Hopkins is a businessman and entrepreneur in Dallas, Texas, who loves studying and discussing God's Word. He has a heart for revival, which stems from his love and desire for the Bible.

Pastor Kyle Felke
Kyle Felke is a former pastor in northern Indiana. He grew up in a home where both parents were teachers, which instilled in him a passion for teaching. This, combined with a love for Jesus, led him to pursue a biblical education and pastor a church in northern Indiana.

Contributing Authors

The Pentateuch
Kyle Lance Martin
Laura Kim Martin

The Gospels
Kyle Lance Martin
Laura Kim Martin
Josh Edwards
Ryan Schrag
Matt Reynolds

The Historical Books
Kyle Lance Martin
Laura Kim Martin
Wesley Morris
Josh Edwards
Pastor Gordon Henke
Pastor Tom Schiefer
Pastor Kyle Felke
Larry Hopkins

Acts
Kyle Lance Martin
Laura Kim Martin
Pastor Gordon Henke
Pastor Tom Schiefer
Wesley Morris
Shawn Carlson

The Wisdom Books
Kyle Lance Martin
Laura Kim Martin
Pastor Gordon Henke
Pastor Tom Schiefer
Wesley Morris
Ryan Schrag
Pastor Fred Stayton
Shawn Carlson
Josh Edwards

Paul's Letters
Kyle Lance Martin
Laura Kim Martin
Pastor Gordon Henke
Pastor Tom Schiefer
Wesley Morris
Shawn Carlson
Josh Edwards
Ryan Schrag

The Major Prophets
Kyle Lance Martin
Laura Kim Martin
Pastor Gordon Henke
Pastor Tom Schiefer
Pastor Fred Stayton
Ryan Schrag
Josh Edwards

General Letters
Kyle Lance Martin
Laura Kim Martin
Pastor Fred Stayton
Shawn Carlson

The Minor Prophets
Kyle Lance Martin
Laura Kim Martin
Josh Edwards

Revelation
Kyle Lance Martin
Laura Kim Martin
Pastor Gordon Henke
Pastor Tom Schiefer

www.ingramcontent.com/pod-product-compliance
Lightning Source LLC
Chambersburg PA
CBHW070405100426
42812CB00005B/1637